AF793948

Assessing the Harms of Crime

CLARENDON STUDIES IN CRIMINOLOGY

Published under the auspices of the Institute of Criminology, University of Cambridge; the Mannheim Centre, London School of Economics; and the Centre for Criminology, University of Oxford.

General Editors:
Mary Bosworth and Carolyn Hoyle
(University of Oxford)

Editors:
Alison Liebling, Loraine Gelsthorpe, and Kyle Treiber
(University of Cambridge)
Tim Newburn, Jill Peay, Coretta Phillips, and Robert Reiner
(London School of Economics)
Ian Loader and Lucia Zedner
(University of Oxford)

RECENT TITLES IN THIS SERIES:

Policing Human Rights
Martin

Normalizing Extreme Imprisonment: The Case of Life Without Parole in California
Vannier

Respect and Criminal Justice
Watson

Neighbourhood Policing: The Rise and Fall of a Policing Model
Innes, Roberts, Lowe, Innes

Respectable Citizens – Shady Practices: The Economic Morality of the Middle Classes
Farrall and Karstedt

Advocates of Humanity: Human Rights NGOs in International Criminal Justice
Lohne

Intimate Crimes: Kidnapping, Trust, and Gangs in Mexico City
Ochoa

Police Community Support Officers: Cultures and Identities within Pluralized Policing
O'Neill

Last Chance for Life: Clemency in Southeast Asian Death Penalty Cases
Pascoe

Assessing the Harms of Crime

A New Framework for Criminal Policy

Victoria A. Greenfield and Letizia Paoli

OXFORD
UNIVERSITY PRESS

OXFORD
UNIVERSITY PRESS

Great Clarendon Street, Oxford, OX2 6DP,
United Kingdom

Oxford University Press is a department of the University of Oxford.
It furthers the University's objective of excellence in research, scholarship,
and education by publishing worldwide. Oxford is a registered trade mark of
Oxford University Press in the UK and in certain other countries

© Victoria A. Greenfield & Letizia Paoli 2022

The moral rights of the authors have been asserted

First Edition published in 2022

Impression: 2

All rights reserved. No part of this publication may be reproduced, stored in a retrieval system, or transmitted, in any form or by any means, without the prior permission in writing of Oxford University Press, or as expressly permitted by law, by licence or under terms agreed with the appropriate reprographics rights organization. Enquiries concerning reproduction outside the scope of the above should be sent to the Rights Department, Oxford University Press, at the address above

You must not circulate this work in any other form
and you must impose this same condition on any acquirer

Public sector information reproduced under Open Government Licence v3.0
(http://www.nationalarchives.gov.uk/doc/open-government-licence/open-government-licence.htm)

Published in the United States of America by Oxford University Press
198 Madison Avenue, New York, NY 10016, United States of America

British Library Cataloguing in Publication Data

Data available

Library of Congress Control Number: 2021946677

ISBN 978–0–19–875817–4

DOI: 10.1093/oso/9780198758174.001.0001

Printed and bound by
CPI Group (UK) Ltd, Croydon, CR0 4YY

Links to third party websites are provided by Oxford in good faith and for information only. Oxford disclaims any responsibility for the materials contained in any third party website referenced in this work.

General Editors' Introduction

The *Clarendon Studies in Criminology* series aims to provide a forum for outstanding theoretical and empirical work in all aspects of criminology and criminal justice, broadly understood. The Editors welcome submissions from established scholars, as well as manuscripts based on excellent PhD dissertations. The series was inaugurated in 1994, with Roger Hood as its first General Editor, following discussions between Oxford University Press and Oxford's then Centre for Criminological Research. It is edited under the auspices of three centers: The Centre for Criminology at the University of Oxford, the Institute of Criminology at the University of Cambridge, and the Mannheim Centre for Criminology at the London School of Economics. Each supplies members of the Editorial Board and, in turn, the Series General Editor or Editors.

Greenfield and Paoli's monograph provides an analytical foundation for making normative decisions about criminal policy by taking harm, and its reduction, as a conceptual starting point. It then provides tools for systematic, empirical analysis in a harm assessment framework. By considering the role of harm in crime, criminal policy, and governance, it fits within a wider framework of international and transnational policy, practice, and activism, particularly in the context of drug crime. In this regard, the book may be of interest beyond the academy, particularly to civil society organizations that have for some time advocated a harm reduction approach to drug crime.

Having considered why an understanding of "harm" should be the starting point for criminal policy, the book develops a method for ranking harms that draws on diverse approaches and quantitative and qualitative methods and analysis, to rate and compare harms across society. The authors develop a framework for policymakers to apply a harm assessment approach and explicate the various processes for applying it. Their harm assessment framework is then applied to cocaine trafficking in Belgium and tested against cocaine trafficking in the Netherlands and human trafficking in Belgium, before moving on to consider its application to coca cultivation and processing in Colombia.

The book developed from a previous project analyzing the world heroin market, which was published by Oxford University Press in 2009. Its conclusion, that drug policy and enforcement have little effect on the drug market, persuaded the authors to take a harm reduction approach to drug crime. While this book considers the harms of cocaine production and trafficking, it seems that the approach could apply equally to other drugs and maybe other organized crime. Furthermore, the authors are clear that the framework they present is not fixed in time. New empirical data, for example, could allow them or others to adapt and refine it.

In laying the foundations for a new systematic approach to assessing harms, the authors do not discard normative positions; rather, they provide analysis that allows policymakers to make informed decisions but also to challenge unjust responses to crime. Indeed, the application of different dimensions of harm is compelling in part because it allows for clear normative claims, such as their position that the costs of law enforcement should not be included in the harm metric.

The depth of engagement with harm in relation to drug crime and the challenges to more traditional "what works" approaches make this an original and exciting monograph. As General Editors, we are pleased to welcome *Assessing the Harms of Crime* to the *Clarendon Studies in Criminology* series.

Mary Bosworth and Carolyn Hoyle
General Editors
Centre for Criminology, University of Oxford
July 2021

Acknowledgments

This book is the result of a transatlantic collaboration spanning two decades that—despite rare face-to-face encounters—has become a close friendship.

In the process of developing and testing the harm assessment framework and writing this book, we have accumulated a long list of debts.

To start, we owe our gratitude to the colleagues who have worked with us, together or separately, on applications of the framework. In chronological order, we thank several junior researchers who assisted us with collecting and analyzing the data, during their time at the Leuven Institute of Criminology of the KU Leuven Faculty of Law and Criminology: Andries Zoutendijk, Loes Kersten, Evelyn van Dun, Elke van Hellemont, An Adriaenssen, Cedric Verstraete, Jonas Visschers, Furtuna Sheremeti, Sarah Spiessens, Bryan Peters, Silke Betrains, and Nathan Sterckx. We also acknowledge collaboration with Tom Decorte (University of Ghent) and Susanne Karstedt (University of Griffith) on assessments of the harms of cannabis production and state crime, respectively.

In addition, we thank those colleagues who were most influential at the outset of this endeavor and before. First, Peter Reuter (University of Maryland), who first steered us toward thinking about harm, during our co-authorship of *The World Heroin Market*, which we completed in 2009. Second, Tom Vander Beken (University of Ghent) and Henk van de Bunt and Nicholas Dorn (both of Erasmus University, Rotterdam), each of whom encouraged and commented on our approach to harm assessment in its earliest stages within a joint project, "Danger: Appraising the Dangerousness of Organised Crime" (2008–11).

Since then, numerous colleagues, including many of those already noted, have offered feedback on chapters of this book or on the presentations, informal drafts, and articles from which this book draws. Hoping not to forget anyone, we would like to thank alphabetically: Anthony Bottoms (University of Cambridge), Daniel Ciccarone (University of California, San Francisco), Frances Cullen (University of Cincinnati), Tom Daems (KU Leuven), Adam Edwards (University of Cardiff), Manuel Eisner (University of Cambridge), Ian Loader (University of Oxford), Jeroen Maesschalck (KU Leuven), Michael Levi (University of Cardiff), Bryce Pardo (RAND

Corporation), Lois Presser (University of Tennessee), Lode Walgrave (KU Leuven), David Weisburd (Hebrew University of Jerusalem and George Mason University), James Willis (George Mason University), and Lucia Zedner (University of Oxford). One individual whom we cannot thank alphabetically is our anonymous reviewer, who offered us both encouragement and immensely constructive suggestions for strengthening the book.

While we have already thanked many of our colleagues, we would like to acknowledge more explicitly our co-authors' contributions to our past research, along with those of the reviewers who made that research better and the publishers who disseminated it and have allowed us to draw from it, sometimes heavily. Recognizing the difficulty of recalling—over many years of collaboration—where we first introduced or developed an idea, we present a list of prior work to which we can readily assign intellectual indebtedness:

- Paoli, L. and Greenfield, V.A. (2018). Harm: A substitute for crime or central to it? In A. Boukli and J. Kotze (Eds.) (2017). *Zemiology: Reconnecting Crime and Social Harm* (pp. 57–84). Cham, UK: Palgrave.
- Greenfield, V.A., Paoli, L., and Zoutendijk, A. (2016). The harms of human trafficking: Demonstrating the applicability and value of a new framework for systematic, empirical analysis. *Global Crime*, 17(2), 152–80. Abingdon, UK: Taylor and Francis.
- Paoli, L. and Greenfield, V.A. (2015). Starting from the end: A plea for focusing on the consequences of crime. *The European Journal of Crime, Criminal Law and Criminal Justice*, 23(2), 87–100. Leiden, the Netherlands: Brill.
- Paoli, L., Kersten, L., and Greenfield V.A. (2015). The harms of cocaine trafficking in the Netherlands and Belgium: Policy insights from comparative assessment. Presentation prepared for the Ninth Annual Conference of the International Society for the Study of Drug Policy (ISSDP), May 20–22, 2015, Ghent, Belgium, unpublished.
- Paoli, L., Greenfield, V.A., and Zoutendijk, A. (2013). The harms of cocaine trafficking: Applying a new framework for assessment. *Journal of Drug Issues*, 43(4), 407–36. Thousand Oaks, Calif.: The SAGE Journals.
- Greenfield, V.A. and Paoli, L. (2013). A framework to assess the harms of crime. The *British Journal of Criminology*, 53(5), 864–85. Oxford, UK: Oxford University Press.
- Paoli, L. and Greenfield, V.A. (2013). Harm: A neglected concept in criminology, a necessary benchmark for crime-control policy. *The*

European Journal of Crime, Criminal Law and Criminal Justice, 21(3–4), 359–77. Leiden, the Netherlands: Brill.

- Greenfield, V.A. and Paoli, L. (2012). If supply-oriented drug policy is broken, can "harm reduction" help fix it? *International Journal of Drug Policy*, 23, 6–15. Amsterdam, the Netherlands: Elsevier.
- Paoli, L., Zoutendijk, A., and Greenfield, V.A. (2012). De schade van georganiseerde criminaliteit (The harm of organised crime). In T. Vander Beken, L. Paoli, A. Zoutendijk, and N. Klima (Eds.). *Het inschatten van de gevaarlijkheid van georganiseerde criminaliteit (Assessing the Danger of Organized Crime)* (pp. 19–84). Gent, Belgium: Academia Press.
- Greenfield, V.A. and Camm, F. (2005). *Risk Management and Performance in the Balkans Support Contract.* Santa Monica, CA: RAND Corporation.

This body of research was not just formative to our thinking about harm assessment, but also represents the backbone of this book, as evident in citations throughout the text. If we have left out any other such work, hence co-authors, reviewers, or publishers, the omission is strictly unintentional.

Although we have never met Amartya Sen (Harvard University and University of Cambridge), we would like to acknowledge our intellectual debt to his writings on economics and philosophy. As an economist and philosopher, Sen has inspired our approach to harm and, though his writings, lent us insight to harmonize the theoretical, methodological, and normative components of this book. He has been with us, unwittingly, from start to finish, providing us with guidance on the conceptualization of harm as a matter of "capabilities," giving us the "standard of living" as a point of departure for benchmarking harm, and helping us see connections to broader societal issues, especially justice.

At a practical level, we acknowledge the generous funding of several, primarily Belgian, institutions. Belspo, the Federal Science Policy of Belgium, provided one of us (Paoli) and her research assistants with financial support through the abovementioned Danger project as well as the projects "Cannabis Production in Belgium: Assessment of the Nature and Harms, Implications for Priority Setting" (2012–13) and "Measuring Cost and Impact of Cybercrime in Belgium" (2014–18). We also thank the Research Foundation Flanders (FWO) for funding the project "From Farm to Fork: Identifying and Assessing the Crimes and Harms Associated with the Meat Industry and Evaluating Their Control" (2015–20); the

European Commission for the project "New Methodological Tools for Policy Analysis and Evaluation" (2011–13); and the KU Leuven Interfaculty Council for Development Cooperation for funding Furtuna Sheremeti's Ph.D. project "Assessing, Addressing and Redressing the Harms of State Crime: Stakeholders and Processes in Kosovo" (2016–20).

Victoria Greenfield would like to thank the Department of Criminology, Law and Society at George Mason University for welcoming her as a Visiting Scholar for much of the duration of this long-lived endeavor and providing her with opportunities to obtain feedback on refinements and extensions of the framework. David Wilson, in particular, might have had no idea what he was agreeing to when he said he'd be delighted to host her while she was writing, but he went along good naturedly and unflinchingly as time passed. In addition, Mary Schifferli and Elli Ambros provided moral support throughout and Sharon Corradino made certain that Victoria's position never expired unintentionally.

Letizia Paoli would also like to thank the Research Foundation Flanders (FWO) for funding her year-long sabbatical during the academic year 2017–18, including a five-month-long stay at the University of Cambridge. She is also very grateful to the colleagues and staff of the Cambridge Institute of Criminology and Clare Hall for warmly hosting her and providing her with the ideal intellectual and practical setting for conducting an extensive literature review and intensive analysis of documents concerning the relationships between harm and crime and criminal policy. Lawrence Sherman deserves a special mention because he allowed her to use his office during his absences from Cambridge.

We dedicated our previous joint book (with Peter Reuter) to our children: Leila in Victoria's case and Maddalena, Isabella, and Leo in Letizia's, and would like to give our thanks in this volume to our fathers. Victoria's helped her to imagine what she could accomplish academically and professionally and taught her how to choose well among life's many enticing options. Letizia's gave her unconditional love and trust and shared his optimism and *joie de vivre* with her and all those who surrounded him. We hope that they knew—or know—how much we appreciate their support early in our lives and throughout.

Contents

List of Figures

List of Tables

List of Abbreviations

ACC	Australian Crime Commission
ASBO	anti-social behaviour orders
BKA	German Federal Police Office
CHI	crime harm index
DEA	US Drug Enforcement Administration
EMCDDA	European Monitoring Centre for Drugs and Drug Addiction
EU	European Union
FARC	Fuerzas Armadas Revolucionarias de Colombia/Revolutionary Armed Forces of Colombia
FATF	Financial Action Task Force
FGP-Airport	Federale Gerechtelijke Politie OA Airport Team Zware Criminaliteit
GDP	gross domestic product
HDI	Human Development Index
ICC	International Criminal Court
ICTY	International Criminal Tribunal for the Former Yugoslavia
ICVS	International Crime and Victimization Survey
LMPS	London Metropolitan Police Service
MoRiLE	Management of Risk in Law Enforcement
NGO	nongovernmental organization
NPIA	UK National Policing Improvement Authority
OCGs	organized crime groups
PwC	Pricewaterhouse Coopers
SOC	serious organized crime
SOCA	Serious Organised Crime Agency
SOCTA	Serious and Organised Crime Threat Assessment
TFEU	Treaty on the Functioning of the European Union
UK	United Kingdom
UN	United Nations
UNGA	United Nations General Assembly
UNODC	United Nations Office on Drugs and Crime
VSL	value of statistical life

1 Introduction

1.1 Our Intent

Over the past few decades, criminology has created an impressive body of evidence on "what works" and "what doesn't work" in crime control and prevention (e.g. Sherman et al. 1997; Weisburd et al. 2016), but criminology and allied disciplines have had less success providing policy-makers with a firm analytical foundation for establishing priorities and allocating resources among them.[1] With few robust tools to turn to for guidance, policy-makers have been left to face an abundance of normative decisions about criminal policy and the governance of security as it concerns crime, including whether particular activities should be deemed "criminal" in the first place.[2]

The central aim of this book is to provide policy-makers with a firm analytical foundation for making those decisions and promote its use.

Such a foundation requires both a conceptual starting point—with an agreed guiding principle—and a rigorous and practical means of applying it. We believe that "harm," treated as a setback to a rightful stakeholder's legitimate interests (Feinberg 1984, 31–6; Greenfield and Paoli 2013, 864), and its reduction, can satisfy the first requirement and we present a concrete specification of harm, embedded in a framework for conducting systematic, empirical assessments, to satisfy the second. As we demonstrate

[1] For simplicity's sake, we refer to criminology as a discipline, even if this label is contested (e.g., Garland 2009).

[2] We use the term "criminal policy" to cover various phases of policy-making and implementation, focusing on criminalization, crime control and policing, sentencing and punishment, victims' assistance and restorative justice, and crime prevention as well as international criminal justice. We treat "governance of security" as a term that encompasses but transcends criminal policy, both for its scope and range of actors. Regarding scope, it addresses crime-related security threats and security threats that are unrelated to, or broader than, crime, as in the case of national security. As for actors, it includes those in the public and private sectors and the numerous and multifaceted partnerships and networks that connect them. At times, we also use the phrase "criminal and related policy" to cover a set of concerns that could, for example, include policy on crime-related security threats. For our use of these and other technical terms, see Appendix A, "Glossary of Terms."

Assessing the Harms of Crime. Victoria A. Greenfield and Letizia Paoli, Oxford University Press. © Victoria A. Greenfield & Letizia Paoli 2022. DOI: 10.1093/oso/9780198758174.003.0001

through an extensive literature review and document analysis, "harm" is central to crime and societal responses to crime, and "harm reduction"—understood broadly as encompassing prevention, mitigation, and remediation—constitutes a core, common, goal of both criminal policy and the governance of security.[3] Consequently, we provide tools and a process for decision-making and build the case for focusing on harm and its reduction.

Our proposed approach, specifically, the "harm assessment framework," acknowledges the multidimensionality of the human experience, as one that encompasses and reaches beyond material well-being, and recognizes the institutions and environmental surroundings that either shape that experience or are intrinsically valuable. The framework, which includes a method for rating and ranking harms of wide-ranging activities, can enable a comprehensive assessment of harms across society and stakeholders as well as comparisons among them, without resorting to the reductionism and necessary generalizations of point estimates or indexes (e.g., Ratcliffe 2014; Sherman et al. 2016). It treats quantitative and qualitative evidence—numbers and words—with equal respect, as potentially valid and informative, and it uses the evidence to produce structured narratives and rankings of harms to individuals, private and public institutions, and the surrounding social and physical environment.

We recognize that decisions about criminal and related policy cannot rest solely on science and acknowledge the inherent normativity of the exercise, but we contend that our proposed approach has two main advantages over current practices. First, informing decision-makers with a systematic, empirical analysis can result in policy that employs resources more effectively and with greater accountability (see also Ashworth 2006). Second, we see harm assessment as a "diagnosis of injustice" (Sen 2009, vii) and, thus, as contributing not just to the advancement of criminal justice, but eventually to justice, over all.

Whereas we maintain that harm and its reduction are "a"—if not "the"—main reason why activities that societies call crime have been criminalized in the first place, we do not claim that criminal law is the exclusive, or even main, tool a society has to deal with harm. Indeed, we make a plea for a less mechanistic approach to criminal policy that would use evaluation to focus attention on reducing the harms of crime instead of crime, per se. In addition, we acknowledge that crime is not only about harm but, despite the

[3] For a detailed discussion of the origin of the term "harm reduction" and the controversy around its use in the drug-policy community and elsewhere, see Greenfield and Paoli 2012.

growing number of strict-liability offenses, also about wrongfulness and offenders' culpability. Criminal law is concerned primarily with a subset of activities that are committed intentionally or recklessly and directly or indirectly "cause" harms and have therefore been considered wrongful and criminalized (see, e.g., Feinberg 1984, 31). Given our emphasis on harm and the extensive discussions on culpability in legal theory, we do not discuss the relationship between culpability and crime in this book.

In the sections that follow we set the stage for a deeper discussion of the relevance of harm and harm reduction in crime, criminal policy, and the governance of security and the value of our framework that will continue in later chapters; we describe the genesis of our interest in and approach to harm; and we provide our readers with a roadmap and guide to reading. We consider the relevance of harm and its reduction in each setting to establish the need for our framework and the "why?" of our endeavor, we tell our story because we believe that context and intellectual influences matter to research, and we include a readers' guide because the chapters are long and not everyone will want or need to read all of them.

1.2 Why Harm and a Methodology for Harm Assessment?

Harm's association with crime is well recognized in legal history and theory, dating back at least to the Roman era (see, e.g., Mueller 1955; Weber 1960), but less so in criminology, leaving a policy community that has shown increasing interest in harm and harm reduction with few analytical tools.

The centrality of harm to crime and societal responses to crime—and, by extension, its merit as a conceptual basis for making decisions about criminal and related policy—was clear to the founders of modern legal theory. Cesare Beccaria ([1764, 1872] 1995, 22) stated, "The one true measure of criminality is the damage done to the nation," in *Dei delitti e delle pene* [On Crimes and Punishment], a booklet that represents the cornerstone of contemporary criminal law and policy, criminal-justice systems, and criminology. Beccaria argued that the harm of crimes should serve as a gauge for establishing priorities in punishment, which he viewed as the main route to preventing crime, and, implicitly, to controlling and policing crime:

> It is in the common interest not only that crimes not be committed, but that they be rarer in proportion to the harm they do to society. Hence the

> obstacles which repel men from committing crimes ought to be made stronger the more those crimes are against the public good and the more inducements there are for committing them. Hence, there must be a proportion between crimes and punishments. [Beccaria (1764, 1872) 1995, 19; see Fijnaut 2017, 34]

Along those lines, Beccaria also raised the possibility of a "scale of wrong actions" based on their harm:

> Given men's need to come together, and given the compacts which necessarily arise from the very opposition of private interests, we can make out a scale of wrong actions, of which the highest grade consists in those which spell the immediate destruction of society, and the lowest those which involve the smallest possible injustice to its private participants. [Beccaria (1764, 1872) 1995, 20]

Adam Smith ([1763] 1896, 7–8), also stressed the relevance of harm to crime, positing that "delinquency is founded upon damage done to any person, whether through malice or culpable negligence" in his *Lectures on Justice, Police, Revenue and Arms*. Smith, however, departed from Beccaria by emphasizing the relevance of culpability to delinquency and focusing on harms to individuals, rather than society. Nearly 100 years later, John Stuart Mill ([1859] 1978, 9) formulated the yet-more-categorical "Harm Principle" and presented the prevention of harm as the only possible justification for coercive state actions, including those of criminal policy. In his unqualified words, "The only purpose for which power can be rightfully exercised over any member of a civilised community, against his will, is to prevent harms to others."

Since then, the centrality of harm, along with its reduction, to crime and societal responses to crime has been reaffirmed in academic and policy discourses, legal or otherwise, but it has fallen from view intermittently and is missing from formal definitions of crime. These definitions treat crime legalistically, if not tautologically, as violations of criminal law. Moreover, even when academia and officialdom recognize the relevance of harm and its reduction, a considerable part of each tends to view crime as a "harm" in its own right and, thus, cannot assess, or act on, harm separately. The debate among the defenders and critics of Mill's Harm Principle has also lacked concreteness. As Harcourt (1999, 113, emphasis in original), author of an especially powerful critique, acknowledges, "the issue is no longer *whether* a moral offense causes harm, but rather what type and what amount of harms the challenged conduct causes, and how the harms compare."

Mainstream criminology (i.e., positivist and post-positivist)[4] has focused traditionally on the causes—rather than the consequences—of crime and has not had much to say about harm, but the discipline has not been altogether silent on the subject. In addition to harm-related work among mainstream criminologists on policing (e.g., Ratcliffe 2014) and among victimologists and restorative justice scholars (e.g., Walgrave 2013), some critical criminologists led by Hillyard and Tombs (2004) have called for a radical, harm-based paradigm shift. They have proposed replacing "crime" with "social harm," reorienting social policy toward harm reduction (see also Pemberton 2007, 2015), and creating a new discipline, known as "zemiology," to study social harm. Other criminologists have applied the concept of harm to state crimes, mass atrocities, and a variety of environmentally detrimental and inhumane activities, not all of which are criminal (e.g., Presser 2013; Rothe and Kauzlarich 2014; White 2013).

With or without criminology's involvement, interest in harm and its reduction has been growing in recent decades across "phases" of criminal policy—spanning criminalization, crime control and policing, sentencing and punishment, victims' assistance and restorative justice, and crime prevention—in international criminal justice, and in related scholarly debates, but it has been doing so without commensurate methodological gains. For example, the Council of the European Union (2009a) affirmed harm's relevance to policy in a model provision on criminal law, and others, such as the United Kingdom, have introduced preventative and strict-liability offenses that explicitly aim to prevent harm (e.g., Ashworth and Zedner 2014; Simester et al. 2016), but, to our knowledge, the policy community has not backed—or been able to back—these steps with a systematic or empirical assessment of targeted activities or related harms. Similarly, efforts to act on "serious crime," a related concept, have garnered attention, yet fallen short (e.g., Europol 2013; see Paoli 2014). Despite calls from scholars (e.g., Rubin 1999; Sherman 2007) and some government agencies (e.g., Serious Organised Crime Agency 2008) to treat harm as the main criterion for establishing priorities in crime control and policing, methodologies remain scarce and inadequate for most purposes (e.g., Europol 2013; Sherman et al. 2016; Statistics Canada 2009).

[4] See Bottoms (2008) for definitions.

Unsurprisingly, given mainstream criminology's focus on the causes of crime rather than its consequences, the discipline has not yet developed instruments for systematically and empirically assessing the harms of crime. Positivist criminologists have assessed the harms of crime indirectly and reductively, if at all, by operationalizing the concept of harm either in terms of public perceptions of the seriousness of crime (e.g., Sellin and Wolfgang 1964), the cost of crime (e.g., Cohen 2005), or the sentences attached to sentencing guidelines (e.g., Sherman et al. 2016). Even the critical criminologists—and zemiologists—who have homed in on harm lack analytical tools (e.g., Hillyard and Tombs 2017; Pemberton 2015).

Arguably, harm plays a more overt role in the governance of security, both in general and in relation to crime, but insomuch as criminologists have entered this arena, they have tended to miss the connection. One might say that harm is inherent to the very concept of security, defined broadly as per Bentham (1843, I, 302), Buzan (1983), Smith ([1763] 1896, 5), and that its reduction is the driving aim of the many techniques that governments and businesses have developed to manage risk—jointly and separately—in pursuit of security (e.g., Greenfield and Camm 2005; Johnston and Shearing 2003; European Commission 2015; National Academies of Sciences, Engineering, and Medicine 2018). However, even if harm reduction—encompassing prevention, mitigation, and remediation—constitutes the main *trait d'union* between "traditional" criminal policy and the governance of security as it pertains to crime, criminologists have been slow to acknowledge or explore harm's relevance to security or to build on the methods of those who deal with security.

Two centuries have passed, but criminologists have not yet responded to Beccaria's proposal to assess crime for "the damage done to the nation" as preliminary and necessary to establishing a rational criminal policy nor have others responded for them. Diverse literatures across disparate fields, which we address more fully in later chapters, provide insight to elements of an answer, but none provides a complete solution. As developments in other literatures have not filled the gap in criminology, we believe that providing a firm analytical foundation to support decision-making on criminal and related policy represents a substantial contribution to both the literature and an answer to Beccaria.

At the time of this writing, this book is the first such endeavor to address harm and its reduction in relation to criminal policy, as a matter of both theory and application, in a single thread, from the point of conceptualization to the point of use and refinement. Others (e.g., Hillyard and

Tombs 2004; Sparrow 2008) have explored the relevance of harm to policy and proposed harm and its reduction as a guiding principle for policy and some (e.g., Dorn and van de Bunt 2010; Maltz 1990; Serious Organised Crime Agency 2008; von Hirsch and Jareborg 1991) have embarked on implementation to varying degrees, but none has gone as deep and far in tandem.

In Chapters 2 and 3, we back our claims with evidence from the literatures, but here we state them as "truth" and point to the gap between the growing interest in harm and the tools and processes that are available to policy-makers as a justification for our endeavor. We developed the framework to fill that gap and, because we believe that a systematic, empirical approach to harm assessment has merit, as a means both to improve criminal and related policy and to consider broader social issues, including the pursuit of justice.

1.3 The Genesis of Our Approach

Our story—the story of this book—begins where our last joint book, *The World Heroin Market: Can Supply Be Cut?* (Paoli et al. 2009), left off. We and our co-author, Peter Reuter, asked whether the world's supply of heroin could be cut and in 392 pages answered "No." Policy and enforcement can be used to rattle the market and relocate production, for good and ill, but with little effect on the long-term availability of heroin. So, we considered next steps. We proposed that "the main rationale for long-term policy should be to minimize the adverse consequences associated with opiate production, trafficking, and consumption in terms of human health, welfare, violence, corruption, and conflict" (p. 257). To paraphrase, we thought, "If you can't stop something bad, maybe you can make it less bad." This was not an entirely novel idea—members of the drug-policy community had been applying it to drug use for decades—but it was our point of entry to harm and it led us to the harm reduction literature.

Upon delving into that literature, we found near-countless reminders of the importance of definitions (see Greenfield and Paoli 2012). Volumes have been written on the question "What is harm reduction?" and disagreements on the meaning of the term have fanned the flames of an already-heated debate on related policies. Wodak and Saunders (1995) summarized the problem aptly, with the title of their well-cited paper, "Harm Reduction Means What I Choose It to Mean."

For these reasons, we set out both a concrete specification of harm (see Chapter 4) and, with that specification in mind, a working definition of harm reduction that encompasses prevention, mitigation, and remediation.

The story continues with our parallel "discovery" and investigation of the not insubstantial literature on harm and related concepts in criminology, legal theory, economics, philosophy, and other disciplines, including, somewhat unexpectedly, national security. This literature, which we will return to in Chapters 2, 3, and 4, reinforced our conviction in the relevance of harm to drug trafficking—and many other unrelated crimes—and helped shape our thinking about harm.[5] The writings of victimologists, critical criminologists, green criminologists, legal theorists, economists, policy analysts, and philosophers expanded and, at the same time, brought our horizon into focus. For example, we found that a comprehensive assessment of harm would require consideration of the perspectives of individuals, institutions, and the surrounding environment and that the analysis could not be strictly quantitative or monetary. Not all human and nonhuman interests are amenable to quantification, let alone monetization. Unfortunately, we also found that no such methodology yet existed. To be fair, the literature directed us toward some of the essential elements of a comprehensive approach and it warned us of the challenges we would face in our efforts, even if it did not hand us a ready-made framework.

In summary, our struggle to come to terms with the near-imperviousness of the world heroin market led us to harm and the broader literature kept us there. But, our insistence on a systematic, empirical approach to harm assessment was not just an outgrowth of our intellectual interests or perception of the need for tools, it was also a response to a specific request for help from the policy community.

In 2008, just as we were finishing the heroin book, we were drawn into a new project, "Danger: Appraising the Dangerousness of Organised Crime" (Vander Beken et al. 2012), that was funded by the Belgian Federal Science Policy Office.[6] We believed that "harm" could supply the conceptual underpinning for an evaluation of "danger" and that establishing the potential

[5] Throughout this book, we define "drug trafficking" as all transportation and marketing activities that occur prior to retail and refer to retail-level activities separately as "drug dealing" (see Appendix A).

[6] Paoli was drawn into the project directly under grant number TA/00/20.

harmfulness of a criminal activity would provide insight to its dangerousness and evidence for setting priorities in crime control. Accordingly, we began developing our harm assessment framework to account for both the severity and incidence of harm, not unlike others who had contemplated threats or risks previously.[7] Although the project addressed organized crime, our work—the harm assessment framework—was not specific to organized crime. In the course of the project, we began testing the framework with applications to cocaine and human trafficking, two activities that were of particular interest to the Belgian authorities. We also considered harms associated with tax fraud and with tobacco smuggling and counterfeiting, but only peripherally. Four years later, we published an initial conceptualization of our framework and preliminary observations in Paoli et al. (2012).

The story has not ended. Our work on the framework is an ongoing and iterative process—we are applying and refining our approach continuously, as evident in the research that we cite throughout this book and the book, itself. Since 2012, we have revisited and finalized the application to cocaine trafficking, which we present in Chapter 5; undertaken new applications to other drugs and activities, including coca cultivation and processing in Colombia, which we present in Chapter 6; continued to explore work in related disciplines; and incorporated our colleagues' feedback, also across disciplines. At this stage, we have completed the architecture of our framework and have used it in these and several other assessments, but, with each new application, we explore different facets of use.

Ironically, perhaps, we have not yet applied the framework to heroin.

We offer one final observation on our story. One of us, Greenfield, is an agricultural and resource economist by training, who now works often in national security, and one of us, Paoli, is a criminologist with a background in sociology and political science. When economists read our work, they tend to say the criminologist won out and when criminologists read our work, they tend to say the economist won out. We choose to view these conflicting statements as a sign of good balance in an interdisciplinary endeavor; others might view them differently.

[7] See Chapters 2 and 4 for a discussion of these approaches in criminology and other disciplines.

1.4 Roadmap and Readers' Guide

As the foregoing narrative suggests, much of our work on the framework has involved cross-disciplinary synthesis, learning-by-doing, and incremental, iterative gains. Consequently, we sometimes draw ideas from unexpected quarters and not everything about the book is linear. For example, we refined the framework that we present in Chapter 4 because of our experience with the applications that we present in subsequent chapters, but we could not go back and regather the data for each application to support and reflect all the refinements.

Nevertheless, the book looks as if it is linear and proceeds as follows.

Chapter 2, which expands on Paoli and Greenfield (2018), demonstrates the centrality of harm, including its reduction, to crime and societal responses to crime, by exploring harm's place in legal history, legal theory, criminology, and related fields, and by considering the relevance of harm and harm reduction in criminal policy and the governance of security, largely as it relates to crime. In so doing, it explains our interest in harm and its reduction as a conceptual starting point for our harm assessment framework. Chapter 2 should be of particular interest to readers who wish to locate our approach in the relevant academic literatures—especially legal history and theory, criminology, and security studies—and policy domains.

Chapter 3, which builds on Paoli and Greenfield (2013), reviews prior attempts to work with "harm" as an analytical device, either through empirical assessments of particular criminal activities or by spelling out what harm means and for whom. Finding a small body of work on harm and crime, it also considers research on drug-related harm and on related concepts of public perceptions of the seriousness of crime, the impact of criminal victimization, and the cost of crime. Reflecting on these studies, the chapter discusses the conceptual and technical challenges of assessing harm. By pointing to the achievements and deficits of past efforts and the obstacles facing them, the review gave us fodder to develop our own methodology, the harm assessment framework, and calls attention to the need for our framework. Chapter 3 will be attractive to readers who are interested in exploring the challenges of working on harm assessment.

In Chapter 4, we present our approach to harm assessment, consisting of a set of analytical tools and a multistep process for applying them (Greenfield and Paoli 2013), and discuss the ways in which it responds to each of the aforementioned conceptual and technical challenges. This chapter also contains essential background on the methodological origins of the framework, what is inside it, and how it works, including its strengths and limitations. The framework is intended to fill the role of the missing "firm analytical foundation," but we do not view it as fixed in time, as it stands today; rather, we will continue to refine it with experience, new knowledge, and collegial engagement.

In Chapters 5 and 6, we present applications of the framework. Chapter 5 presents our seminal application of the harm assessment framework to cocaine trafficking in Belgium (Paoli et al. 2013) and, for insight to the framework's reliability and robustness, compares the results to those of two other single-country harm assessments, cocaine trafficking in the Netherlands (Paoli et al. 2015) and human trafficking in Belgium (Greenfield et al. 2016). Chapter 6 presents another single-country assessment, but in a vastly different analytical context, consisting of coca cultivation and processing in Colombia. This assessment, which is new to this book, also differs from the others in that it represents our first attempt to apply the framework rapidly, by focusing on a relatively small number of issues of particular concern, and to implement what we call "full accounting," by considering the losses and gains associated with an activity.

Chapter 7 presents our concluding thoughts and closing arguments in the case for taking on harm—and its reduction—and conducting systematic, empirical harm assessments to support deliberations in criminal and related policy. After recalling our central aim, main findings, and accomplishments, we consider methodological lessons from our applications of the framework, pertaining to its reliability and robustness, as well as its validity across challenges and its ultimate utility. Can the framework serve to identify, evaluate, rank, and, eventually, reduce the harms of crime? Then, we turn to broader themes, concerning the role of harm and harm assessment in both criminology and policy. First, we argue that criminology would benefit from expanding its mission to include—and embrace—harm and its reduction and, second, that a systematic, empirical harm-based approach to criminal and related policy analysis can contribute to decisions about criminal policy and the governance of security, ranging widely from criminalization to sentencing to prevention. We also explore possible contributions of our approach to other policy fields and to advancing justice.

A set of technical appendixes, including a glossary of terms, supports the text.

2
The Centrality of Harm and Its Reduction to Crime and Societal Responses to Crime

2.1 Introduction

The purpose of this chapter is to demonstrate the centrality of harm, including its reduction, to crime and societal responses to crime and, in so doing, substantiate our interest in it—and its reduction—and lay the groundwork for our empirical framework.

To start, we discuss the most immediate obstacle to this enterprise; namely, the ambiguity of "crime," which, like many other terms in research and policy environments, lacks clear meaning.[1] Demonstrating the centrality of something (i.e., "harm") to something else (i.e., "crime") that is ambiguous is not easy, but it is not impossible. We proceed pragmatically, with a workaround, by looking across domains that involve crime, to explore harm's role and, thereby, uncover evidence of harm's relevance. More specifically, we explore harm's place in legal history, legal theory, and criminology and related fields (i.e., victimology and social harm studies or zemiology), and consider the relevance of harm and its reduction in criminal policy and the governance of security, which encompasses but transcends criminal policy. The link between harm and crime might not leap from the pages of legal dictionaries or scholarly publications, but we find it to greater and lesser extents throughout these domains.

Concurrently, we also consider whether legal scholars, criminologists, policy-makers, or others have conceptualized "harm" as separate from

[1] By the end of this chapter, even the most patient readers might find themselves facing fatigue from ambiguity, having encountered a large number of words and phrases suffering similarly from imprecision. Indeed, as we discuss later in Chapter 3, the term "harm," itself, also presents challenges.

Assessing the Harms of Crime. Victoria A. Greenfield and Letizia Paoli, Oxford University Press. © Victoria A. Greenfield & Letizia Paoli 2022. DOI: 10.1093/oso/9780198758174.003.0002

"crime," and whether and how those with a role in implementation have taken harm and its reduction on board in principle or practice.

The chapter draws from material presented in Paoli and Greenfield (2018), "Harm: A substitute for crime or central to it?," but it also expands on it, by digging more deeply into material on legal history and criminology and venturing into the governance of security, including related matters of risk. The deeper dig into the literatures of legal history and criminology yields a broader spectrum of opinions and reflections on the link between crime and harm and the look at security provides a new perspective. Two interrelated considerations drove our foray into the literatures on the governance of security and risk. First, private and public actors have come increasingly to share the tasks of preventing and dealing with crime-related security threats through a growing array of partnerships, networks, and techniques, including risk management, that are often treated outside the strict realm of "traditional" criminal policy (e.g., Dupont 2004; Johnston and Shearing 2003). Second, although harm reduction, through prevention, mitigation, or remediation, is a core aim of the whole security apparatus, the relevance—and more so centrality—of harm emerges fully only if we venture beyond the criminological literature into the security- and risk-related literatures.

With this new material, we have added depth and range to our analysis and, we believe, built a stronger case for harm. Our literature review and document analysis show that harm reduction—in some form—constitutes a fundamental goal of domestic criminal policy, international criminal justice, and the governance of security as it concerns crime and possibly beyond. Even if that goal is often or mostly implicit, our research suggests that these realms aim to prevent acts that are either deemed to be harmful *in se* or assumed to generate harm as well as to reduce the harms of such acts. While we point to such aim with the encompassing term of "harm reduction," we also note diversity in the way this overarching goal is interpreted and pursued across criminal policy, international criminal justice, and the governance of security.

We proceed as follows. In Section 2.2, we examine how scholars and others characterize crime, consider the implications of those differences for our efforts, and then, in Sections 2.3–2.5, pin down direct and indirect links between crime and harm. In Section 2.3, we focus primarily on the legal and criminological literatures. In Section 2.4, we turn to criminal policy and consider the relevance of harm and its reduction to criminalization, crime control and policing, sentencing and punishment, victims' assistance and restorative justice, and crime prevention as well as to international criminal justice. In Section 2.5, we conduct a similar exercise for the governance of security, largely as it pertains to crime, by considering the relevance of harm and its reduction to the concepts of security and risk and to related business practices, policies, and management methods.

2.2 The Ambiguities of the Concept of Crime

Despite being the subject of both criminology and criminal law, scholars do not agree on what crime is or should be and might never do so. Moreover, whereas criminal lawyers have, since the turn of the current century, engaged in a lively debate about criminalization (e.g., Duff et al. 2010; Simester and von Hirsch 2011), criminologists have not. As some scholars note (e.g., Reiner 2016; Zedner 2011), criminologists have lost interest in the very concept of crime and familiarity with criminal law and theory over the past few decades, leading Zedner (2011, 271) to call for "putting crime back on the criminological agenda."

In one of the very few criminological books devoted to the concept of crime, Reiner (2016, 3) argues that crime is "essentially contested." Gallie (1956, 169) coined the phrase, to characterize concepts that are accepted notionally, yet disputed widely in terms of meaning and use, in large part, because they are normative and complex (see also Waldron 2002, 150). As for the first requirement, normativity, many mainstream criminological circles have long preferred to deny criminology's inherent entanglement with normative issues, but modern societies use "crime" as a term to express censure and disapproval (e.g., von Hirsch 1993), which suggests that criminologists cannot escape the entanglement. As Bottoms (2008, 92) states, "the concept of crime itself, and the kind of criminal justice system that a given society develops, must necessarily be the product of political and moral choices."[2] As for the complexity of crime, one can wade through legal, criminological, political, and other social conceptions of crime, moral perspectives on crime, and media portrayals of crime that do not fully overlap let alone agree (see Reiner 2016 for a good overview).

In the midst of this cacophony, standard legal definitions of crime—understood as an infraction of criminal law—might represent an "anchor"

[2] Along similar lines, Matza (1969, 143–4) quipped that positivist criminology had "achieved the seemingly impossible, divorcing crime from the state."

(Reiner 2016), but only mechanistically. The Online Oxford Dictionary defines crime as "an action or omission which constitutes an offence and is punishable by law," and is matched by Tappan's (1947, 100) classical formulation, "an intentional act or omission in violation of criminal law (statutory and case law), committed without defence or justification, and sanctioned by the state as a felony or misdemeanor." This legalistic approach does not speak to the nature or crime—it asserts that a crime is a crime because the law says it is a crime. It underpins Wikstrom's (2008, 120) situational action theory, perhaps the most influential etiological theory of crime in contemporary criminology, which defines crimes as "acts that breach moral rules of conduct stated in law" (Wikstrom et al. 2012, 12).[3]

Constructionist understandings of crime, starting from the 1970s, have, in some instances, taken the legalistic approach to the extreme. According to Hulsman (1986, 71), for example, "crime has no ontological reality. Crime is not the object, but the product of criminal policy." This position has been further expanded by the postmodernists among them, who emphasize the discursive creation of crime. For Foucault (1977), for example, it is the discourse of punishment as a symbolic expression of power relations that constructs some behaviors rather than others as crime. These postmodernist positions, however, have been criticized because of their nihilistic and relativistic tendencies (e.g., Cohen 1993) and rejected by criminologists, who, like us, are committed to ontological realism—that is, to the existence of a world that we can perceive and investigate, albeit imperfectly (Bottoms 2008).

Even in its more moderate forms, the legalistic approach provides insufficient guidance on meaning and use, for both citizens who might not know what is or is not "criminal" and experts who must administer or enforce the law. The rapid pace with which jurisdictions establish new offenses has contributed to the opacity: Chalmers and Leverick (2014) counted the new offenses introduced in England and Scotland over a recent 12-month period and found the astonishing figures of 634 and 1,233 new offenses in each location, respectively. As Stuntz (2001, 505) maintains, "criminal law is not one field but two. The first consists of a few core crimes ... The second consists of everything else. Criminal law courses, criminal law literature, and popular conversation about crime [to which we, the authors, would add criminological analyses] focus heavily on the first. The second dominates

[3] Wikstrom et al. (2012), however, do not distinguish criminal law from other branches of the law.

the criminal codes." (See also Husak 2013; 2008, 8–11). Adding further confusion, many of the new offenses are rarely or inconsistently enforced, so that "formal" criminalization "in the books" differs from "substantive" criminalization "in action" (Lacey 2009).

Given the vast, rapidly growing, and shifting corpus of criminal law, Ashworth (2000), Duff et al. (2010), Wells and Quick (2010, 1–15), and other contemporary legal scholars contend that it is impossible to define criminal law substantively. Ashworth (2000, 253), a leading jurist, concludes that "the criminal law is ... a lost cause, from the point of view of principle."[4]

It is no wonder the procedural, legalistic, and mechanistic definitions of crime have often been considered unsatisfying and even tautological (e.g., Henry and Milovanovic 1996, 115; Hillyard et al. 2004) and that criminologists of different epistemological and political orientations have put forward alternative definitions of crime, independent of legal norms (e.g., Hirschi and Gottfredson 1990; Schwendinger and Schwendinger [1970] 2014; Sellin 1938). Some of these and other scholars have even suggested getting rid of the term "crime" altogether. Most of the scholars proposing elimination belong to the broad realm of critical criminology, starting from Christie's (1977) influential recast of crime as a dispute owned by the parties to it, which ultimately spawned the restorative-justice movement (e.g., Braithwaite 2002; see Section 2.4). Drawing from the virtually opposite premises of positivism, Gottfredson (2011, 38) has also recently pled for a "crime-free (in the legal sense) criminology."

As we will see below, some of the nonlegalistic definitions of crime explicitly relate it to harm (see Section 2.3). For example, Henry and Milovanovic (1996, 3) define crime as "the harm resulting from any attempt to reduce or suppress another's position or potential standing through the use of power that limits the other's ability to make a difference."[5] More recently, Hillyard, Tombs, and others have chosen a more radical path and, building on the tradition of critical criminology, have proposed replacing the notion of "crime" with that of "social harm" (e.g., Hillyard et al. 2004; Pemberton 2007). To that end, some of them, including Hillyard et al. (2004) and

4 Even the European Court of Human Rights lacks a substantive theory of crime and delineates the border between criminal and civil law in fundamentally formal and procedural terms. The leading case is Engel v. Netherlands, 1976 1 EHRR 647.

5 We discuss this and other definitions from the criminological literature in Section 2.3, "Harm in Relation to Crime," under the subheading "Criminology and Related Fields."

Hillyard and Tombs (2017), have founded an alternative discipline, known as "zemiology," which is dedicated to the study of social harm.

Although, we acknowledge the ambiguities of the concept of crime, we need not wander the desert of those ambiguities; instead, we approach the term as it stands and uncover the role of harm through a combination of direct and indirect means. In so doing, we aim to demonstrate the centrality of harm to crime, at least as a matter of principle. Scholars might never reach agreement on the meaning or appropriate use of "crime," but, looking back over centuries and decades, we find that "harm" presents a common thread in statutes and jurisprudence, across literatures, in criminal policy, even if harm has been lacking in articulation and application.

2.3 Harm in Relation to Crime

In this section, we look for links between crime and harm in legal history, legal theory, criminology, and related fields, including victimology. To avoid overlap, we address scholarly contributions to criminal policy in the following section.

Legal History

A brief review of legal history connects harm to crime, even if undefined, in the early legal systems that constitute the foundation of western law.

There is no consensus in the literature on whether Roman law and other ancient legal systems distinguished between what would now be called tort and crime—that is, between private and public wrongs (e.g., Eser 1966, 349–50)—but still they addressed "wrongs." Some scholars claim differentiation in Roman law, starting from Mueller (1955), who distinguished between *delicta privata* and *crimina publica*. More recently, Riggsby (2016) has proposed a tripartite classification, consisting of "criminal" actions, which were adjudicated by public courts, *delicta*, and *actiones populares*.[6] Others experts argue against the possibility of a clear-cut distinction

[6] According to Riggsby (2016), in late republican times, "criminal" actions included electoral bribery, counterfeiting, homicide, and violence (i.e., riot and sedition). *Delicta* consisted of theft, property, and bodily damage, which were considered private wrongs, and *actiones populares*, such as damaging public roads.

between tort and crime in Roman law (e.g., Waelkens 2015; Weber 1960). Certainly, neither Anglo-Saxon, Frankish, nor Normal law distinguished between criminal and civil cases (Berman 1983, 449). Nonetheless, each body of law, through a combination of tort claims and public prosecutions, intended to restore or prevent injuries done to certain goods, interests or rights of individuals, the community, or the ruler. The main reason for these claims and prosecutions was not the breach of law, but the harm to a valuable interest, such life, body or property, religion or morality, or statehood (Eser 1966, 349–59).

The sanctions provided in early legal systems also indicate the relevance of harm. According to van Ness (1986, 64–8), ancient Mesopotamian, Hebrew, and Greek civilizations provided for restitution even for what we would now call property and violent offenses, including homicide in some cases (see also Berman 1983, 55). Similarly, Roman law required the compensation of victims of *delicta*, although it also foresaw harsh penalties; for example, when the victim might have entered into debt to repair the harm, risking enslavement and exclusion from the community (Bryen 2016, 324–5; Waelkens 2015). The earliest surviving collection of Germanic tribal law, the *Lex Salica*, which King Clovis promulgated in 496, also includes monetary sanctions for offenses ranging from homicides to thefts—as did other Frankish, Anglo-Saxon, and other Germanic legal compilations of that same period, sometimes setting extraordinarily detailed schedules of tariffs (Berman 1983, 53–5).

These examples, coupled with an analysis of legal practices in simple non-Western societies, have led Braithwaite (2002) to posit that restorative justice was the dominant model of justice in prestate societies, coexisting with banishment. Zehr (1990, 99–10) points to the irony that many of the words of contemporary retributive justice may have had more restorative origins concerning private wrongs: "The Greek *pune* refers to an exchange of money for the harm done and may be the origin of the word for *punishment*. Similarly, *guilt* may derive from the Anglo-Saxon *geldan*, which, like the German word, *Geld*, refers to payment." Berman (1983, 55) notes, though, that the early-modern monetary sanctions also had a retributive component to reestablish the honor of the victim and his kin and thus prevent interfamily vendettas. Whatever their goals, the monetary sanctions constituted in his view, "a very sensible system."

Starting from the Norman invasions, focus shifted from harms to individuals or communities to harms to the interests of ruling or governing authorities, the king, or the state, and to acts of insubordination. According to Eser (1966, 351), "the disobedience against the king or the state emerged as the substance of crime." Emblematic of that shift, by the thirteenth century, English law and jurisprudence had linked the seriousness of wrongs to the idea that they involved breach of the King's Peace, rather than injury to the victim (Hudson 2012, 386). Whoever jeopardized such peace was liable for prosecution and punishment by the king or his representatives. Along with the progressive separation between criminal and tort law, the victim was displaced from the criminal process and his or her restitution ended up engrossing the Crown's coffers (McAnany 1978, 17). In many civil-law countries there was also a progressive shift from the accusatorial system, in which offenses were largely considered private matters, to the inquisitorial system, in which the prosecution and adjudication of the crimes was centralized in the hands of selected representatives of the princely or nascent state authority (e.g., Fijnaut 2017, 9–13).

In both common and civil-law countries, "the rise of state-centered justice" (van Ness 1986, 59) led to the adoption of formal definitions of crime, according to which crime is an act or omission in violation of a law with an associated punishment, much as described previously. With the shift in focus from individuals to kings and states, "harm" lost some visibility, but modern scholarly debates on criminalization, which we consider in the next section, still afford it a central role.

Legal Theory

As discussed in Chapter 1, the link between harm and crime emerges plainly from the foundational texts of modern legal theory, going as far back as Beccaria's ([1764, 1872] 1995, 20, 22) and Smith's ([1763] 1896, 7, 8) understanding of crime as, on the one hand, "all the actions which are inimical to the public good" or "the damage done to the nation" and, on the other, as "damage done to any person," respectively. From the nineteenth century, numerous legal theorists have also presented harm reduction as important—sometimes even as the exclusive or at least the main purpose of criminal law. Taking an unconstrained consequentialist position, Mill's ([1859] 1978, 9) "Harm Principle" treats the prevention of harm to others as the only justification for criminalization and, more broadly, the exercise of state coercion on fellow citizens.

Mill's Harm Principle unequivocally—and famously—ties crime to harm, but his approach has not been adopted unanimously. Most contemporary scholars offer qualifications, advocating consideration of additional factors, and some stand in direct opposition. As an early representative of the latter, Lord Stephen ([1873] 1967) advanced a moralist conception of crime, which makes the wrongfulness of the conduct and the moral culpability of the offender the focal concerns of criminal law (see, e.g., Duff 2013). In its extreme formulation, legal moralism leaves no room for consideration of the consequences of crime. According to Moore (1997, 35), for example, the only function of criminal law is to achieve retributive justice by punishing "all and only those who are morally culpable in the doing of some morally wrongful action."

More typically, however, scholars propose combinations of harmfulness and wrongfulness as components of crime, and of harm reduction and retributivism as goals of criminal law (Duff 2013). According to Hart ([1968] 2008) and others (e.g., Braithwaite and Pettit 1990), requirements of justice constrain a consequentialist approach to criminal law and preclude some practices, such as the criminalization of faultless conduct, even if those practices would further a goal of harm prevention. While emphasizing harm prevention as a major purpose of criminal law, Feinberg (1984, 1985) and others (e.g., Simester and von Hirsch 2011) also accept offense (that is, immorality), as an exceptional reason for criminalization or reduce Mill's reach by restricting criminal law's focus to wrongful harm.

Duff and Marshall (2014) derive two harm principles from Mill's ([1859] 1978) seminal principle, namely, a less rigid or absolute "harm-prevention principle," which they associate with Feinberg (1984) and a "harmful-conduct principle," which they associate with Simester and von Hirsch (2011). Whereas Mill identifies harm prevention as "the only good reason for criminalisation," Feinberg places harm prevention as "one among other sources of good reason to criminalise" behavior (Duff and Marshall 2014, 206) and the related harmful-conduct principle calls for criminalizing acts that elicit harm. The two harm principles can coincide when, for example, criminalizing a conduct that is inherently harmful serves to prevent harm, but can diverge when prevention justifies criminalizing conduct that is not in itself harmful.

Duff argues (2013) that the harm-prevention principle is superior to the harmful-conduct principle, because it justifies the criminalization of the many *mala prohibita* offenses established in contemporary criminal codes. However, he joins Harcourt (1999), Farmer (2010), and others who note that the Harm Principle, per se, can no longer serve its original function of limiting state power, because too many claims of legal protection have come to rest on claims of harms, which have, in turn, been used to justify criminalization or repression.

From a consequentialist perspective, Braithwaite and Pettit (1990, vii) are more supportive of the Harm Principle, even if they propose the maximization of "dominion," which they describe as "freedom in the social sense of full citizenship," as the end goal of both criminal and public policy. Arguing that harm reduction "foreshadows" their approach (1990, 48), they aim to develop "a theory of criminal justice which allows us to respond in the best way to harmful conduct, where responding in that way sometimes will, and more often will not, entail punishment" (1990, 2).

The relevance of harm to crime also emerges from Duff's (2014) theory of "modest" legal moralism, despite its apparent opposition to consequentialism.[7] Duff understands crime as a "public wrong," that "properly concerns the public, i.e. the polity as a whole" (Duff 2007, 141), whether it encompasses injuries to collective goods or to individuals' interests. However, even from Duff's perspective (2013, n.p.), criminal law is meant primarily to protect citizens against various kinds of harm, and harmfulness to others features prominently in crime, because the moral wrongfulness of a conduct often derives from its harmfulness. As case in point, he considers the *mala in se* crimes, such as murder, assault, and burglary, that involve attacks on protected interests and necessarily entail wrongful harm. Harmfulness, according to Duff, also plays a part when criminal law prohibits conduct that is not actually dangerous, in itself, but violates a regulation, such as a speed limit, that serves public safety and is meant to prevent harm (the so-called *mala prohibita*). For Duff, however, there are also circumstances in which harm plays a less central role and wrongfulness comes to the fore without it or with less consideration of it. In line with Feinberg (1985) and Simester and von Hirsch (2006, 2011), he defends the criminalization of extreme cases of pornography and discriminatory insults on the basis of the offense principle.

As we show in Section 2.4, this statement also finds support in current criminalization practices. Along similar lines, but more prescriptively, Ashworth (2000, 253) suggests that "the criminal law should be used, and only used, to censure persons for substantial wrongdoing." He further argues (2000, 244) that harm and the offender's culpability constitute the two

[7] Duff's (2014) "modest," "negative" version of legal moralism differs from Moore's (1997) "positive" legal moralism, because it only considers wrongdoing a necessary condition of criminalization, not a positive reason to criminalize.

main dimensions of the seriousness of wrongdoing and the "harmfulness of conduct must be judged in terms of its effect on valued interests, which may be individual interests or some form of collective interests" (see also Husak 2008; Simester and von Hirsch 2011).

Ashworth's attention to "valued interests" dovetails nicely with the Germanic concept of *Rechtsgüter*, which translates approximately to "legal interests."[8] In this tradition, criminal law is meant to protect legitimate individual and, to a lesser extent, collective interests against conduct that seriously threatens them (Roxin 2006, 8–47). Several authors argue that this doctrine constitutes the functional equivalent of the Harm Principle (e.g., Hassemer 2004; von Hirsch 2003). Both, in fact, are meant to protect and preserve citizens' freedom from excessive state punishment and set clear limits on the legitimate use of state punishment. However, more so than harm, the idea of legal interests has been extended in both legal theory and concrete policies (see Section 2.4) to cover collective legal interests (e.g., Hefendehl 2003).

With this literature in mind, we have reason to conclude that most contemporary legal theorists would agree with Zedner (2011, 275) that "harm is, quite as much as fault, central to criminal liability" and that harm reduction is a central, if not the exclusive, aim of criminal law. As we show in Section 2.4, these statements also find support in current criminalization practices.

Reaching beyond legal theory and criminology to other disciplines in the social sciences, Gary Becker, a prominent economist, identified social harm as an inherent component of crime in his seminal but controversial article, "Crime and Punishment: An Economic Approach" (1968), and included it in a stylized, optimal penalty scheme. Becker (1968, 198) contends that the "the assessment [and compensation] of the 'harm' done by defendants" should become "the primary aim of all legal (i.e., criminal) proceedings," replacing punishment and deterrence. In his view, much of traditional criminal law should become a branch of tort law, "in which the public would collectively sue for 'public' harm" (Becker 1968, 198) and a criminal action would only be necessary when the culprit is unable to compensate for the harm that he or she causes. Becker's policy recommendations appear extreme by common legal standards. However, as noted in our overview of legal history, the distinction between crime and torts is not a

[8] For different scholarly opinions on the merits of this approach, see Hefendehl et al. (2003).

"given" and many harmful behaviors, such as assault, can still be dealt with in both criminal and civil procedures (e.g., Wells and Quick 2010, 1–15).

Given the many scholarly voices highlighting the centrality of harm to crime, it is surprising that so few scholars have tried to elaborate on—or flesh out—the concept of harm. As Walker (1997, 611) once observed in relation to Feinberg (1984, 1985), a broad question still remains unanswered: "What sort (or sorts) of harm, and what probability that it will be perpetrated, justify legislation which permits the imposition on the unwilling of restraints which are not otherwise justifiable?"

Without addressing Walker's question, one which our framework might be ideally suited to answering, English-speaking legal scholars (e.g., Feinberg 1984; Simester and von Hirsch 2011) merely align with Mill's original formulation and the liberal tradition, and largely focus on harms to individuals' interests, rather than on harms to the interests of collectives. The latter are, instead, more visible in Germanic scholarship, even if their relevance is contested (e.g., Hefendehl et al. 2003). Among the English-speaking legal scholars, Feinberg (1984, 63 and 221–5) mentions harms to two types of public interests, community and governmental interests, but spends just a few pages of his books discussing them. Duff (2007, 2014) emphasizes harm to public institutions as a reason for criminalizing conduct that does not generate harms to individuals, but does not mention harm to communities, because he resorts to the principle of offense to justify the criminalization of damage to civic amenities, such as excessive noise and littering. In a deviation from the traditional focus on individuals, a few contemporary legal theorists (e.g., Braithwaite and Pettit 1990, 70; Duff 2014, 124; Simester and von Hirsch 2011, 37) have only extended the applicability of the harm-based approach to nonhuman animals.

Even for individuals, there has been little discussion of which particular interests society ought to protect. Von Hirsch and Jareborg's (1991) framework, which specifies four "interest dimensions" and provides a scale for rating harms, represents the only exception that we have encountered, but they developed it to support deliberations on sentencing, not criminalization (see Chapter 3, Section 3.2 and Chapter 4).

Criminology and Related Fields

The criminological literature presents the weakest link between harm and crime, likely because "mainstream" (i.e., positivist and post-positivist) criminology has long focused on a small set of crimes (murder, theft, etc.), which it considers "natural crimes," without regard to normativity or contextual variability. Through such an "intellectual fudge" (Bottoms 2008, 86), positivist criminologists have tried to meet the analytical standards and adopt the methods of the natural sciences, largely to identify the causes of crime. Doing so has required exclusive consideration of "sense data," understood as facts that we can allegedly observe with our senses without reference to theory and that are sharply separated from values.[9] Admittedly, over the past few decades, post-positivist criminologists have abandoned the clearly unsustainable tenets of positivism, such as the idea of theory-neutral sense data and the denial of the social construction of crime, but they still focus mostly on a small set of violent and property crimes and maintain an etiological perspective (e.g., Wikstrom et al. 2012).

Nevertheless, even this literature might endorse the link between crime and harm: it equates crime and harm, albeit with varying degrees of open recognition. Arguably, the underlying and unstated assumption of much of mainstream criminology is that crime constitutes a "harm" in its own right. As Eser (1966, 347) notes, *mala in se* crimes—the natural crimes on which generations of mainstream criminologists have focused—are so obviously harmful that there is no need to explicitly emphasize their harm. By contrast, we also find a few criminologists, such as Henry and Milovanovic (1996, 3; see Section 2.2), who equate crime with harm explicitly. Understanding crimes as public wrongs, Walgrave (2013, 50) also reasons that the criterion for establishing the latter must be "the harm it causes to fellow citizens and to social life in general" (see also Zedner 2007, 262).

Whether stated or unstated, many other criminologists of different schools have taken up the idea that crime generates harms or, itself, constitutes something akin to harm, even if they do not use the term "harm."

In the 1930s, for example, Bonger ([1932] 1936, 5) defined crime as a "serious antisocial act to which the state reacts consciously by inflicting pain." In the same era, Sutherland (1945, 132) introduced the concept of white-collar crime and argued that crimes are "socially injurious acts," for which sanctions are provided in criminal statutes or other legislation. In a seminal article in 1970, Herman Schwendinger and Julia Schwendinger ([1970] 2014) who drew from Sutherland, proposed treating crimes as violations of human rights and called for acknowledging that such rights are

[9] This articulation is consistent with Bottoms' use of the term, but for a more complete and technical definition, see Huemer (2017).

violated routinely by many legal social constructs, including "imperialism, racism, sexism and poverty" (p. 108). Although Cohen (1993) labeled such call a "moral crusade," many critical criminologists have put forth that "crime" needs to include socially injurious activities of powerful groups against the powerless (e.g., Taylor et al. 1973).

Others besides reformist and critical criminologists have also acknowledged the connection between harm and crime. In a thoughtful definition, combining the tradition of mainstream criminology with some insights of the labeling—i.e., social constructionist—approach of the 1960s (e.g., Becker 1963; Matza 1969), Hagan (1985, 49) first defines crime "as a kind of deviance, which in turn consists of a variation from a social norm, that is proscribed by criminal law." He then adds that "the most serious acts of deviance, which are most likely to be called 'criminal,' are likely to involve 1) broad agreements about the wrongfulness of such acts, 2) a severe social response and 3) an evaluation of being very harmful" (Hagan 1985, 50).

Since the 1980s, harms to different categories of victims have become more prominent in criminological discourse with the consolidation of victimology as a semi-autonomous field (e.g., Fattah 1986, 2010; Walklate 2007a), paralleling the growing visibility and importance of victims in criminal policy and the rise of the restorative-justice movement (see Section 2.4). From a theoretical perspective, Boutellier (2000, 16) has emphasized the growing relevance of victimization, speaking of the "victimalization" of both morality and criminal policy. In our morally fragmented, postmodern societies, he argues (pp. 150 and 147, emphasis in original), "morality has come to be a matter of what we do *not* want" and "the victim is the only reason why we need a policy on crime." Clarifying the link to harm, he stresses (p. 147) that he does not refer to individual victims, but to "more generalized victimhood in terms of damage done to society." Drawing from Rorty (1989, 1990), a philosopher, he adds: "Everyone can have their own god and even be their own god as long as they do not legitimate or propagate any harm to others. John Stuart Mill's harm principle has become a sociological reality" (p. 150).

Since the turn of this century, the topic of harm has sparked new interest within criminology and other related fields. Presser (2013) has explored "why we harm" (that is, why people commit, tolerate, or legitimate harmful activities), with case studies of genocide, meat eating, intimate partner violence, and penal harm. Her work draws particular attention to harms to nonhuman animals. Other researchers have applied the lens of harm to crimes that remain "invisible" (Davies et al. 2014), activities that are "lawful but awful" (Passas and Goodwin 2004) and corporate crimes (e.g., Freudenberg 2014). Harm is also central to a new offshoot of (critical) criminology, "green criminology," which centers on harms to the physical environment, whether they derive from criminal, otherwise illegal, or legal activities (e.g., Beirne and South 2007; Brisman and South 2017; White 2010 and 2013).

Zemiologists (e.g., Hillyard and Tombs 2004 and 2017) and other proponents of the study of "social harm" (e.g., Pemberton 2007 and 2015; Yar 2012) claim its superiority to "crime." In their early texts, Hillyard and Tombs (2004) suggested four categories of harm, but left further specification to future empirical studies.[10] More recently, Pemberton (2015, 23 and 24) speaks of "socially mediated harm," which is harm resulting from the "relations, processes, flows, practices, discourse, actions and inactions that constitute the fabric of our societies." Yar (2012, 63) and Pemberton (2015, 24; 2007, 38) restrict their focus to preventable harm, but include both harms resulting from intention and from indifference. They exclude harms arising from natural events and from processes beyond the scope of human intervention. Others—and ultimately also Pemberton (2015)—zoom in on the "structural" harms that they see as inherent consequences of capitalism (e.g., Hillyard and Tombs 2017 and Lasslett 2010) and/or globalization (e.g., Cain and Howe 2008).

As Hillyard and Tombs (2017, 295) rightly note, harm is mentioned with increasing frequency, as either an addition to or component of crime. In evidence of this claim, a number of books and special issues of scholarly journals have been published recently that are devoted to harm and carry the word "harm" in their titles. In addition to those mentioned previously (Davies et al. 2014; Pemberton 2015; White 2013), we also refer here to *Crime, Law and Social Change's* special issue on social harm and to Corteen et al.'s (2016) and Boukli and Kutze's (2018) edited collections.

With few exceptions, however, there has been little theorizing on harm and its facets in this literature. None of the earlier scholars, for example, elaborated fully on the concept of harm or injury as it might relate to harm. Henry and Milovanovic (1996) distinguish between "harms of reduction" and "harms of repression,"[11] but only to reflect on the previous

[10] We discuss these categories in Chapter 3.

[11] Harms of reduction occur "when an offended party experiences a loss of some quality relative to their present standing" and harms of repression take place "when an offended party experiences a limit or restriction preventing them from achieving a desired position or standing" (Henry and Milovanovic 1996, 103).

literature and without substantiation. Moreover, neither victimologists nor critical criminologists have taken the opportunity to delineate the individuals, entities, or others that might bear harm or the nature of those harms.

According to Hughes (2006, 198), Loader and Sparks (2011, 24–2), and others, zemiologists have spent too much time criticizing criminology and not enough time describing what would replace it. Along similar lines, Yar (2012, 59) has faulted Hillyard and Tombs for failing "to define what makes something a 'harm' or 'harmful,' or what distinguishes the 'harmful' from the 'non-harmful.'" As discussed in Chapter 3, Pemberton (2007, 2015) only partially overcomes these deficiencies, by drawing on Doyal and Gough's (1991) theory of human needs.

A peculiar challenge facing green criminology is that, in accounting for harms to nonhumans as well as humans, it cannot conceptualize harms in terms of human needs, rights, or well-being (White 2013, 2). Whereas most green criminologists do not explicitly define harm, White (e.g., 2013) deals with this problem by linking harm to injustice and singling out three justice-based approaches to environmental harm, pertaining to humans ("environmental justice"), eco-systems ("ecological justice") and animals ("species justice"), but without much additional elaboration.

Reflecting a more general lack of attention to harm in mainstream criminology, Corteen et al.'s (2017) edited collection on harm and crime only touches on some harms of some crimes and crime-control interventions.

2.4 Harm in Relation to Criminal Policy

Harm, as a concept, and harm reduction, as a goal, each play a substantial part in deliberations and scholarly debate on different "phases" of domestic and regionally coordinated (e.g., across the European Union [EU]) criminal policy, consisting of criminalization, crime control and policing, sentencing and punishment, victims' assistance and restorative justice, and crime prevention, as well as in international criminal justice. Figure 2.1 depicts the phases of domestic criminal policy in which harm and its reduction are relevant. However, as much as in criminological theorizing, the relevance of harm and its reduction are acknowledged inconsistently and sometimes emerge only implicitly and the emphasis varies, depending on the scholars, the particular phase of policy, and the scholars' and policy-makers' political

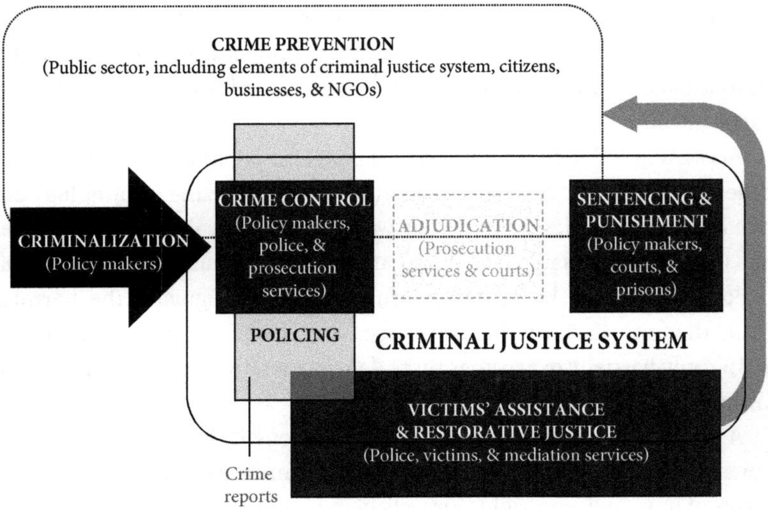

Figure 2.1 Phases of domestic criminal policy
Source: Authors' analysis.

and legal backgrounds. Moreover, even if concerns for harm and harm reduction are a unifying presence throughout, the overarching goal of harm reduction is interpreted and implemented differently in different phases of policy and international criminal justice. We highlight these differences in the concluding remarks of this chapter (Section 2.6).

In this section we briefly discuss the role of harm and its reduction in each phase of policy. In so doing, we also consider whether the policy community—or academia—has attempted to operationalize and empirically assess harm and, so, we build a bridge to Chapter 3, where we discuss prior attempts to assess harm.

Criminalization

Despite ambiguities in the doctrine, harm reduction, largely through prevention, has long served as a main goal of criminal law in the United States, Europe, and elsewhere. Until the surge of retributivism that began in the 1980s (see the discussion later in this section), "punishment theories, institutions, policies, and practices in the English-speaking countries were based largely on consequentialist ideas" (Tonry 2011, 6), with specific and general deterrence[12] and offenders' rehabilitation presented as the leading tools for achieving crime prevention and thus harm avoidance (see also Garland 2001a, 27–52). The American Model Penal Code, which was first published by the American Law Institute in 1962, was shaped by consequentialist ideas. It declares that the first general purpose of the provisions governing the definition of offenses is "to forbid and prevent conduct that unjustifiably and inexcusably inflicts or threatens substantial harms to individual or public interests" (s. 1.01(1), quoted in Duff 2013).

Harm is also a prominent criterion for justifying criminalization both in academic discourse and, at least in principle, as a matter of policy. Whether they were inspired by the Germanic concept of *Rechtsgut*, the substantive part of the penal codes of most Continental European countries are organized in sections defining crimes against specific individual and collective legal interests. For example, in France, the penal code is delineated by "the physical and psychological integrity of the individual" and "the nation, state and public peace" (Mayaud 2016; see also Grosso et al. 2017; Roxin 2006).

The legal-interests approach and attendant concerns for harm are also visible in deliberations on criminal law in the governing bodies of the EU. For example, in 2009, the Council of the European Union (2009a) adopted model provisions on criminal law, stressing the link between legal interest and harm: "The criminal provisions should focus on conduct causing actual harm or seriously threatening the right or essential interest which is the object of protection … " (p. 3). In addition, the Council called for consideration of "how serious and/or widespread and frequent the harmful conduct is, both regionally and locally within the EU" (p. 2) before adopting new criminal provisions.[13]

We have not considered how harm has been defined or the extent to which the principle of harm reduction has been implemented across jurisdictions in the EU or elsewhere, but we would not be surprised to learn that implementation has been patchy. The repeated scholarly criticisms of the inconsistencies and even aberrations of current systems of criminal law, including the tendency towards "overcriminalization" (Husak 2008; see also

[12] Specific deterrence focuses on the individual in question. The aim of criminalization and the subsequent phases of criminal policy is to discourage the criminal from future criminal acts by instilling an understanding of the consequences. Instead, general or indirect deterrence focuses on general prevention of crime and, thus, harm prevention, by labelling a specific act as criminal and by educating the general public through the stigmatization and punishment of specific offenders.

[13] This was the second of three factors for consideration (Council of the European Union (2009a), 2).

Ashworth 2000; Wells and Quick 2010), leave little doubt that any single principle, let alone the Harm Principle, has been applied consistently.

Nonetheless, recent trends have—more or less inadvertently—expanded the relevance of harm and its reduction in criminalization and criminal policy. Harm—with no regard for fault or culpability—underlies the strict-liability crimes that, according to Zedner (2011, 275–6), make up the majority of new criminal offenses in the United Kingdom (UK). Harm prevention is also stimulating the growing array of "preventative offenses" that seek to avert harms before they occur, such as crimes of weapon or drug possession and of membership in a criminal organization, and what Ashworth and Zedner (2014, 3–4) call "offences of risk creation." The last category involves conduct that might yield harm, such as speeding, drunk-driving, or breaching other health-and-safety regulations. The many preventative offenses that have been introduced to counter terrorism since the 2000s are regarded as especially controversial: in particular, they have been criticized for being remotely—not directly—related to the harms they seek to prevent and for failing to satisfy standard culpability requirements (e.g., Ashworth and Zedner 2014, 113–14; Galli and Weyembergh 2012; Roach 2011).

The will to prevent harm has also played a part in motivating the growing number of hybrid civil–criminal preventive orders that have been introduced since the 1990s in a number of jurisdictions, especially in the UK (e.g., Crawford 2009). The anti-social behaviour orders (ASBO), which the UK introduced under the Crime and Disorder Act of 1998, present a well-known example. They were established as "civil orders to protect the public from behaviour that causes or is likely to cause harassment, alarm or distress" (Parliament of the United Kingdom 2014.). Although ASBOs were repealed in England and Wales in 2014, they have been followed by more-specific orders concerning, among other things, sexual offenses and serious crime. Such orders blur the line between criminal and civil law. They can be imposed on a person who has never been found guilty of any offense and for behavior that is not, itself, criminal; however, breaching an order constitutes a criminal offense (see Ashworth and Zedner 2014, 74–94; Gledhill 2011; and von Hirsch and Simester 2006 for discussion and examples).

Despite the oftentimes explicit relevance of harm and its reduction to criminalization, we have not encountered any legal text that has elaborated on "harm" nor any decision to criminalize or decriminalize a certain activity that has been supported by an empirical assessment of the harms of that activity.

Crime Control and Policing

Although the terms "crime control" and "criminal policy" are sometimes used synonymously, we use the former to denote a distinct phase of criminal policy, occurring just after criminalization and consisting of the official or de facto identification of criminal policy priorities as well as of the investigation of specific crimes and their suspected perpetrators. In many environments, the police and prosecutors are, together, responsible for criminal investigations. Along with their prosecutorial colleagues, the police also play an important role in the official or de facto identification of criminal priorities, even if policy-makers in the Ministries or Departments of Justice, Interior, and Security and lower-level administrative or governing units, such as cities, are also often involved. Despite the essential role of police in crime control, we distinguish policing from crime control because the two are not congruent. While other institutions—as just discussed—are also involved in crime control, police functions are often broader than crime control. Police may undertake other forms of problem solving (e.g., Goldstein 1990), assist victims (e.g., Hoyle and Sanders 2000), and fill other regulatory roles (e.g., van Daele et al. 2017). In the United States, for example, police are part of a cadre of "first responders" that assist victims in the immediate aftermath of natural and other disasters, though their mandate and competencies have come under question and protest.

Both crime control and policing can contribute to the overarching harm-reduction goal of criminal policy, through harm prevention (as well as the establishment of culpability through investigation of specific crimes and offenders). However, police might also help to mitigate or remediate harm, if, through broader functions, they solve community problems that are not framed as crime and support victims.

Within crime control, harm is particularly important in the identification of criminal priorities, but there are considerable differences in how such priorities are established from one country to another country. In countries such as Germany and the Netherlands that subscribe to the "opportunity principle" (e.g., Tak 2005),[14] policy-makers in the competent agencies sometimes identify criminal-policy priorities in official

[14] The opportunity principle states that a crime will be punished only if its prosecution is considered opportune. This means that public prosecutors have the discretion to cancel the prosecution of a crime for a variety of reasons, including their or the Justice Ministry's or Department's decision to neglect petty crimes and focus scarce resources on the prosecution of serious crimes (see Tak 2005).

documents mostly in cooperation with police forces and prosecution services. Whether or not such documents exist, policy priorities are also established de facto by police and prosecutors—even in jurisdictions, such as Italy and Spain, that are officially bound by the legality principle and supposed to investigate and prosecute any suspected offense, unless there is an apparent lack of evidence to institute a proceeding (Illuminati 2005; Barona Vilar 2005). Corroboration of this selectivity emerges not only from case studies on specific topics (e.g., Paoli and Donati, 2014) but also from the large shares of criminal cases that European prosecutors dismiss because they do not deem it in the public interest to bring these cases to court (Wade 2005).[15]

In this scattershot picture, only Finland has—to our knowledge—emphasized harm reduction explicitly as the discriminating criterion for selecting crimes for prosecution. Since the 1970s, minimizing the costs and other harmful effects of crime and crime control have served as the main goal of its criminal policy (Lappi-Seppälä 2007). But, even this country, often regarded as a model for its humane criminal policy and low imprisonment rates, lacks a strong theoretical and empirical foundation for delineating or weighing harms (Lappi-Seppälä, personal communication).

Despite the leeway of the opportunity principle, we are not aware of many other jurisdictions that have established law-enforcement priorities on the basis of an explicit harm-based criterion. In most countries, the goals of criminal policy are less clear and consist of a mix of not-necessarily-congruous intentions (e.g., Garland 2001a). Usually, crime control and the enforcement of criminal law, particularly regarding ordinary crimes, are considered or presented as worthy policy objectives in themselves—even if only a small portion of such cases might reach a criminal court (Wade 2005). Even in the field of *mala prohibita*, such as drug trafficking, we know of few official assessments of whether law-enforcement interventions effectively minimize, or instead inadvertently promote harm (e.g., Corsaro et al. 2012). Indeed, the Scientific Committee of the European Monitoring Centre for Drugs and Drug Addiction (2017), the EU drug agency, has repeatedly pressed for an evaluation of supply-side drug control policies (see also Greenfield and Paoli 2012; Greenfield and Paoli 2017).

Only recently, have some policy-making and police agencies started to see harm reduction, rather than crime control, as a guiding principle

[15] The shares are large, but vary from country to country (see also Aebi et al. 2014, 118).

of police and prosecutorial action. In 2008, the UK stated that "the overarching aim of the [Organised Crime] Control Strategy is to achieve a tangible and lasting reduction in the harm caused to the UK by organised crime" (Serious Organised Crime Agency [SOCA] 2008, n.p.). Although the UK later abandoned the goal, some police and governmental agencies in the Anglo-Saxon world—including SOCA's successor, the National Crime Agency (Management of Risk in Law Enforcement [MoRiLE] 2017), the UK Metropolitan Police Service, and the Australian Crime Commission—have developed indicators of consequences to assess and rank the harm or seriousness of different crimes (Tusikov 2012 provides a review).[16]

Likewise, policing scholars traditionally have paid little explicit or systematic attention to harm, but interest, as manifest in research in the 1990s, might be growing. For example, Goldstein's (1990) appeal for "problem-oriented policing" called for a "systematic inquiry" (p. 36) to identify competing interests in the underlying concerns of society and answer three specific questions, consisting of, "Why is the community concerned?," What are the social costs?," and "Who is being harmed and to what degree?" (p. 40). Others have drawn the connection subsequently, for example, Rubin (1999), Sherman (2007), Sherman et al. (2016), Ratcliffe (2015), and some practitioners have called explicitly for a harm-based approach to crime control. Whereas Rubin (1999) provides no specification for "harm," some of these scholars (e.g., Sherman et al. 2016) and government agencies (e.g., Statistics Canada 2009) have suggested using harm-related indexes to monitor crime trends, to measure changes in the severity of crimes being committed, and to improve resource allocation and policy accountability. Although it is doubtful that these indexes can account fully for the harms of crime,[17] they indicate a collective, emerging realization that all crimes cannot be treated equally in policy-making or implementation and that the consequences of crime require more-systematic monitoring and consideration.

In the UK, Australia, and at the EU level, interest has turned to combatting "serious crime," implying the growing relevance of harm as a benchmark for crime control in policy and research. The UK adopted two Serious Crime Acts in 2007 and 2015,[18] while Australia allocates substantial resources to serious crime police units. Both Eurojust and Europol, which

[16] See additional discussion in Chapter 3.

[17] We discuss our concerns in Chapter 3.

[18] Available online at http://www.legislation.gov.uk/ukpga/2007/27/contents and http://www.legislation.gov.uk/ukpga/2015/9/introduction/enacted (both accessed September 2, 2021).

are the two main EU agencies in the field of crime control and internal security, claim the fight against serious crime as their mission (Council of the European Union 2009b, 2009c). Although serious crime is not defined consistently (Paoli et al. 2017, provide a review), EU policy documents, including treaties, highlight "the nature and impact . . . of the offences" (Treaty on the Functioning of the European Union [TFEU] 2008, Art. 83(1)), which can be interpreted as encompassing harm, as the main substantive criterion for identifying serious crime.[19] Scholars also emphasize the link between serious crime and harm. Dorn (2009, 284), for example, welcomes the policy community's growing attention to serious crime because "it opens up the possibility of Europol priorities being defined in terms of the seriousness of the harms impacting on individual collective or corporate victim" (see also Sheptycki et al. 2011; Paoli et al. 2017).

Moving in that direction, the European Council (2010) set up "an EU policy cycle for serious international and organised crime" in 2010. The establishment of the policy cycle constitutes—at least in principle—a major step toward developing a policy process that is more rational and leads to more consequentialist, effective, and accountable policy (Paoli 2014). Each cycle lasts four years, renewed at least through 2021, with steps for prioritizing criminal activities and developing, setting, implementing, monitoring, and evaluating policy. A "Serious and Organised Crime Threat Assessment" (SOCTA), entrusted largely to Europol, supports the first step, prioritization and policy development.[20]

While Sherman et al. (2016) and others operationalize harm in terms of sentencing guidelines or meted sentences, Europol and other public agencies have developed methods that attest both to the will of some governments and agencies to adopt a more consequentialist, effective, and accountable crime control policy and to the difficulties of conceptualizing and assessing harms empirically (see Section 3.2).

Sentencing and Punishment

Harm reduction might be said to motivate sentencing and punishment at the same time as harm, itself, also more specifically relates to each

19 The other criterion is the "special need to combat them on a common basis."
20 We discuss the SOCTA in more detail in Chapter 3.

of these two crucial and emblematic phases of criminal policy. Since the time of Beccaria ([1764, 1872] 1995), sentencing and punishment have been expected to contribute to crime prevention and—at least implicitly—harm prevention. Initially, they were thought to serve preventatively through deterrence and offenders' incapacitation and later also through rehabilitation. The link with harm, though, is not always explicit in the recent literature. Since the 1970s, there have also been growing doubts about the effectiveness of imprisonment, the sentence most frequently meted out to deal with serious offenses, in securing deterrence and offenders' incapacitation and rehabilitation beyond a small portion of the current prison population (e.g., Garland 2001a; Owen 2009; Nagin 2013).

In sentencing, harm plays its most visible role as a constraint or guiding principle, largely through the related concept of "seriousness." Today, "nearly every theorist" (Husak 2008, 83) holds that appropriate sanctions should be proportional to the seriousness of an offense, which, in turn, depends on a combination of the harm done or risked through the commission of a criminal act and the offender's culpability. The requirement for proportionality dates back to Beccaria ([1764, 1872] 1995, 20), who in his seminal work, *On Crimes and Punishment*, stressed the need to develop a "scale of wrong actions" for setting sanctions, and it has been reinforced by retributivism, which aims to impose a "just desert" on offenders for their deeds.

Since the 1980s, retributivism has become the dominant sentencing philosophy in the UK and United States (e.g., Tonry 2011), but, even without an explicit commitment to retributivism, many countries, attempt to uphold the link between sentencing and seriousness, and thus harm, at least implicitly. For example, penal codes might set maximum sentences for particular offenses that track to seriousness or appellate courts might regard sentences that are grossly excessive in relation to the gravity of the offense as unfair. Finland, Sweden, England and Wales, and several US states have adopted statutory guiding principles or sentencing guidelines that require proportionality between the severity of the penalty and the seriousness of the offense. In addition, Canada and New Zealand have enacted statements of desert-oriented sentencing aims (von Hirsch 2011). In England and Wales, sentencing guidelines provide the court with a step-by-step decision-making process for sentencing different offenses. In step one, they aim to determine the category of offense, consider "the actual or potential harm caused as a result of the offence" in addition to the offender's culpability, and identify different levels of harm (e.g., Sentencing Council 2017).[21]

Harm is also relevant to sentencing beyond questions of proportionality or retributivism. In opposition to the latter, Braithwaite (2002), Canton (2017), and others argue that sentencing ought to restore the harm and the wrongs suffered by the victim and call for sanctions that can achieve that goal better than imprisonment. As Walgrave (2003) observes, some existing criminal sanctions, such as compensation or community work, entail a restorative component and, in his view, other criminal sanctions, such as fines or even imprisonment, should be reformed to fulfill a restorative aim. In a " 'maximalist' agenda for restorative justice," Bazemore and Walgrave (1999, 7), alongside others (e.g., van Ness 1986), appeal for the development of a fully fledged justice system that is oriented towards doing justice through restoration, and which, with time, would replace the existing punitive and rehabilitative justice systems.

Nonetheless, Beccaria's ([1764, 1872] 1995, 20) interest in developing a "scale of wrong actions" for setting sanctions and his proposal to assess crime in terms of damages (p. 22; see related discussion in Chapter 1), remain unsatisfied for lack of an empirical and systematic assessment of the harms of different kinds of crime. Prior to our work in this area (e.g., Greenfield and Paoli 2013), von Hirsch and Jareborg (1991) offered one of the few fully fleshed conceptual frameworks for categorizing the harms of crime for sentencing, but neither their nor our framework has been put to this purpose in academia or practice. According to Lippke (2012, 464), the absence of "anchoring points" for a sentencing scheme remains "one of the unsolved, and seemingly insoluble, problems of sentencing theory."

Harm also features prominently in discussions of imprisonment, which has greatly expanded especially in the United States and other English-speaking countries since the 1970s (e.g., Lappi-Seppälä 2011). Whereas many legal scholars working in the retributivist tradition and elsewhere, see punishment under certain conditions as justified (e.g., von Hirsch 1993; Duff 2011), others—in particular several criminologists starting from Christie (1977)—have questioned the justification of state policies of inflicting pain on citizens via imprisonment and other sanctions. In one

[21] In the case of robbery, the Sentencing Council (2016, 4) sets three categories of harm: (1) serious physical and/or psychological harm caused to the victim or serious detrimental effect on the business; (2) other cases where characteristics for categories 1 or 3 are not present; and (3) no/minimal physical or psychological harm caused to the victim or no/minimal detrimental effect on the business.

such critique, Clear (1994, 5) coined the term "penal harm" to emphasize that "organized, intentional harm against a fellow-citizen" is the essence of the penal sanction and this harm sets this sanction apart from other governmental actions. A growing empirical literature (e.g., Clear 2007; Liebling and Maruna 2005; Travis et al. 2014; Wacquant 2001) documents the serious harms to offenders, to their families, and to entire communities, generated by the unprecedented expansion of prison systems, but often does not mention harm explicitly and has worked with implicit or partial criteria.

Victims' Assistance and Restorative Justice

In these phases of criminal policy, the overarching goal of harm reduction manifests not through harm prevention, as it does in other phases, but through harm remediation, which has gained global prominence in recent decades.

Since the 1970s, concern has risen on both sides of the Atlantic about individuals who are harmed by crime, as evidenced by the extensive media coverage of victims and their experiences, the great expansion of victimology, and the wide range of victim initiatives, programs, and legislation (e.g., Walklate 2007a). Whereas actual victims were barely visible in the criminal-justice process in prior eras, now they are well evident and have also become symbolic figures: in Garland's (2001a, 11) words, "the personalized, real-life, it-could-be-you metonym for a problem of security that has become a defining feature of contemporary culture."

The United Nations (UN) Declaration on the Basic Principles of Justice for Victims of Crime and Abuse of Power, which was adopted by the United Nations General Assembly (UNGA) (1985) in 1985, was a landmark for the global victim movement. This declaration recognizes the centrality of harm to the very concept of victim of crime: " 'Victims' means persons who, individually or collectively, have suffered harm, including physical or mental injury, emotional suffering, economic loss, or substantial impairment of their fundamental rights, through acts or omissions that are in violation of criminal laws operative within Member States." On the long-lived wave of the UN Declaration, many policies have been adopted in developed and, increasingly, developing countries to grant victims of ordinary crimes access to justice and fair treatment; restitution and compensation for the harm suffered; and material, medical, psychological and social assistance (e.g., Hall 2010). While most commentators welcome such policy developments, others—most prominently Garland (2001a)—are concerned that the prominence of victims in the criminal-justice process legitimizes punitive and preventive justice and trumps suspects' and offenders' rights.

The restorative-justice movement, as evident in both scholarly debate and policy initiatives and programs, also emphasizes matters of harm and repair.[22] Whether presented as an alternative or complement to conventional criminal justice measures, the main purpose of restorative justice is to repair harm through "conversations with those who have been hurt and with those who have inflicted the harm" (Braithwaite 2004, 28). For Zehr (1990) too, a defining principle of restorative justice is that an offense creates an obligation for offenders to repair harm (see also Walgrave 2008).

Restorative justice has spread rapidly since the late 1990s, leading to the establishment of victim–offender mediation and family conferencing for juvenile—and increasingly adult—offenders in most countries of the world (e.g., Thilagaraj and Liu 2017; Yuan 2017). According to Braithwaite (2002, 8), "the late modern revival of restorative justice," reflects a shift of focus in state regulation. Whereas the focus from the eighteenth to the late twentieth centuries was on individuals and their bodies, the focus in the present day is on organizations, as the central objects of state regulation that is handled restoratively. The worldwide growth of restorative-justice initiatives has been recognized by the UN Economic and Social Council (2002a), which adopted a resolution entailing Basic Principles on the Use of Restorative Justice Programmes in Criminal Matters.

Despite the obvious centrality of harm to victimization, related assistance programs, and restorative justice, "harm" remains oddly out of focus in both the scholarly and policy debates on these issues. Neither the victimological literature nor related policy documents elaborate on the link between "victim" and "harm" (see Section 3.3). In restorative justice "restoration" confusingly addresses both harms—or damages—and positive interests. Braithwaite's (2002, 14–15) list of restorative-justice values, for example, includes both restoration of property loss and injury, and restoration of human dignity, communities, the environment, and freedom. In numerous texts and practices (e.g., Marshall 1996), more attention is given to the process—the empowerment of victims, offenders, and the community—than to the restorative outcome, itself. Moreover, the assessment

[22] For an overview of initiatives and programs, see, e.g., Restorative Justice International at http://www.restorativejusticeinternational.com (accessed September 2, 2021) and Walgrave (2011).

of the harm is left entirely to the victims' perceptions and idiosyncrasies, raising concerns among some legal scholars and practitioners (e.g., Duff 2003; van Ness 1999) about whether agreed restorations are proportional, as per UN principles (United Nations Economic and Social Council 2002, Art. 7).

Crime Prevention

Since the 1980s, crime prevention has become so prominent in criminal policy in Western countries that some commentators speak of a "preventive turn" (e.g., Edwards and Hughes 2009) and many others support Zedner's (2007) idea of a broader shift from the "post-crime" logic of criminal law to the "pre-crime" logic of security and risk preemption (see Section 2.5). For some, this shift might constitute no more than a reappraisal of the mainly preventive goal of the criminal justice systems in the late eighteenth and early nineteenth centuries (e.g., Ashworth and Zedner 2014, 27–50; Garland 1996, 464), but preventive interventions come in myriad forms. While many different private actors have assumed responsibility for crime prevention (see Section 2.5), state agencies pursue prevention through wide-ranging approaches, including developmental and situational crime prevention, rehabilitation and treatment, and medical measures (e.g., Welsh and Farrington 2012; Tilley and Sidebottom 2017).

Although not always recognized, many public preventive measures also involve coercion, such as the preventive criminal offenses and civil preventative orders mentioned earlier in the context of criminalization. As noted, punishment, too, pursues preventive rationales (i.e., deterrence and offenders' incapacitation and rehabilitation), whether or not they are combined with retributivism (see Schauer 2013). Police agencies and prosecutors also hold extensive preventive powers, above all, the power to stop and search and to detain pretrial (e.g., Ashworth and Zedner 2014; Sullivan and Dennis 2012). Police officers can also prevent crime from happening by merely patrolling a neighborhood or other area—what Nagin (2013) terms the police's "sentinel function."

The link to harm is often not explicit in the practice or study of crime prevention, but it is not without mention or reference. The Economic and Social Council (2002b, [3]) of the UN adopted guidelines on crime prevention in 2002 that are among the few high-level policy documents that acknowledge a link between crime prevention and harm, as they include the reduction of the "potential harmful effects [of crime] on individuals and society" in their definition of crime prevention. Among scholars, Ashworth and Zedner (2014, 5) offer the most explicit—and emphatic—connection between crime prevention and harm, defining prevention as "the significant reduction of potentially harmful behaviour, or the reduction of (potentially) harmful behaviour to a tolerable level." Arguing less forcefully, Bjørgo (2016) considers reducing the harmful consequences of crime as one of the nine general mechanisms through which crime can be prevented, while others (e.g., Tilley and Sidebottom 2017) do not make the connection at all.

Despite the UN's recognition of the relevance of harm to crime prevention, we have not found any policy or academic text that delves into harm as a guiding principle for crime prevention, specifically. Ashworth and Zedner (2014, 5) note that, regardless of technique or application, "we are left with the problem of determining which degree of reduction of harms is required, which must depend on what are thought to be socially acceptable levels of risk." Although this problem might be especially pressing in the case of coercive preventive measures, we have not located any attempts to weigh the predicted level of harm against the curtailment of liberty.

International Criminal Justice

In addition to playing a part in domestic and regionally coordinated (e.g., EU-wide) criminal policies, harm also plays its part in international criminal justice. At the end of the Second World War, the Nuremberg and Tokyo trials signaled the birth of present-day international criminal justice; that is, the prosecution of individuals for international crimes before international tribunals. Since then, the UN has set up several other ad hoc international tribunals, starting with the International Criminal Tribunal for the Former Yugoslavia (ICTY) in 1993 (see Cassese et al. 2011 for a historical overview). In 1998, the Rome Statute established the first permanent tribunal, the International Criminal Court (ICC), and granted it jurisdictions over four core international crimes; namely, genocide, war crimes, crimes against humanity, and aggression (O'Keefe 2017).[23] Internationally, "harm reduction" might also constitute the overarching policy goal, but the

[23] These four crimes largely overlap with the criminological category of "state crime" (see e.g., Chambliss 1989; Chambliss et al. 2013).

restoration of harm, hence "harm remediation," features more prominently in the ICC than in domestic criminal courts (Arts. 75 and 79).

However, in the context of international criminal justice, harm restoration is not called "restorative justice"; rather, it is called "reparation." The Rome Statute (1998, Art. 75) calls on the ICC to "establish principles relating to reparations to, or in respect of, victims, including restitution, compensation and rehabilitation" and to "determine the scope and extent of any damage, loss and injury to, or in respect of, victims." It also allows the ICC to impose orders against a convicted person specifying appropriate reparations. The Trust Fund for Victims, established by the same statute (Art. 79), implements and supports these orders.

The relevance of harm and harm remediation to international criminal justice is also apparent in the UN Resolution (UNGA 2006) establishing *Basic Principles and Guidelines on the Right to a Remedy and Reparation for Victims of Gross Violations of International Human Rights Law and Serious Violations of International Humanitarian Law.* The Resolution (pp. 6–9, Art. VII-X) sets out three major rights for covered victims: "access to an effective judicial remedy," "adequate reparation," and "access to information," clearly distinguishing reparation from national or international criminal justice processes of trial, conviction, and punishment. Further, the Resolution (pp. 7–9, Art. IX) identifies five major forms of reparation: restitution, which would repair the victim to their original situation; compensation for economically assessable damage; rehabilitation; satisfaction; and guarantees of nonrepetition.

Notwithstanding the many analogies between domestic restorative justice and reparation, two important differences are noteworthy. Reparation primarily addresses serious human rights abuses occurring in conditions of virtual state failure, not ordinary crimes. Moreover, unlike domestic restorative justice, reparation is concerned with both individual victims and collective bearers of harm as well as with regime change and state building (Daly and Proietti-Scifoni 2011; Karstedt 2014).

Despite the ICC's and UN Resolution's reparative mandates, victim reparations have not reached the forefront of international criminal justice actions yet. The ICC can only start a reparation proceeding once the defendant is found guilty and the judgment is final and, as of mid-2021, it had awarded reparations in only three cases (ICC [2021]). From this meager record, Antkowiak (2011), Clarke (2015), Garbett (2013, 2017), and others contend that the ICC has largely implemented a retributive approach in its judgments. Moreover, they claim that international justice judges have no framework or expertise to assess harms or establish appropriate reparations. A 2015 petition called for establishing a specialist reparations bench within the ICC apparatus (Stahn 2015). Even according to Robinson (2011, quoted in Sheremeti 2017, August 30), the then-president of the ICTY, which has the strongest record of investigations and convictions among the tribunals, "the Tribunal cannot, through the rendering of its judgments alone, bring peace and reconciliation to the region." Robinson, according to Sheremeti (2017), then called for a truth and reconciliation commission and for a non-judicial assessment and restoration of the harms resulting from war crimes and other serious violations of human rights. Academia also appears to be lagging in its efforts to bring harm to bear in this arena. As Letschert and van Dijk (2011), Pemberton et al. (2007), and others admit, there have been few empirical studies (e.g., Parmentier et al. 2009) on victims' perceptions of harm, victims' needs and requests for reparation, or actual reparations.

2.5 Harm in Relation to Security and its Governance

In this section, we demonstrate that harm and its reduction are central not just to crime and criminal policy, but also to security, as it manifests across related literatures, in related policy arenas, and in common business practices, including those pertaining to crime. In our coverage of these policies and practices, we refer to the "governance of security," a term that encompasses and transcends criminal policy (see Appendix A), but we home in on issues that tend to fall through the cracks of deliberations and debates on "traditional" criminal policy, particularly governance that mixes or melds private and public arrangements to address crime-related security threats. As a related matter, we also consider the connection between harm and risk and the methods that private and public bodies use to manage risk through assessment and mitigation. Throughout, we argue that criminology does not fully appreciate the centrality of harm, with regard to either the governance of security or risk.

Security

The link between harm and security emerges vividly from Jeremy Bentham's and Adam Smith's foundational reflections on security. Bentham (1843, I,

302) memorably presented security as the enduring preservation of body and property against injury, which is an interpretation that places harm at the center of security. Bentham (p. 302) then specifies that security "relates to the person, to the honour, to property, to condition," and posits security as "the principal object" of the law, arguing that even liberty represents a branch of security. Although less well-known, Adam Smith ([1763] 1896, 5) proposed a similar but richer understanding of security eighty years earlier. While not seeing injury—and thus harm—as an exclusive product of crime, Smith (pp. 5–6) distinguishes different roles of individuals and dimensions that can be harmed, anticipating some of the categories of our framework:[24]

> A man may be injured in several respects: First, as a man. Secondly, as a member of a family. Thirdly, as a member of a state. As a man he may be injured in his body, reputation, or estate. As a member of a family he may be injured as a father, as a son, as a husband or wife, as a master or servant, as a guardian or pupil ... As a member of a state, a magistrate may be injured by disobedience, or a subject by oppression, &c.
>
> A man may be injured: First, in his body by wounding, maiming, murdering, or by infringing his liberty. Secondly, in his reputation, either by falsely representing him as a proper object of resentment or punishment, as by calling him a thief or robber, or by depreciating his real worth, and endeavouring to degrade him below the level of his profession ... Thirdly, a man may be injured in his estate. His rights to his estate are called acquired or iura adventitia, and are of two kinds, real and personal.

Smith went a step further than Bentham, by tying security to justice, when he asserted "the end of justice is to secure from injury." Bentham (1843, I, 302) was, instead, the first to emphasize the forward-looking nature of security: "Security," he argues, "necessarily embraces the future ... [and] implies extension in point of time, with respect to all the benefits to which it is applied."[25] This realization points to the close connection between security and risk, which we consider below.

[24] We admit that we developed the framework before reading Smith's lectures. Hence, we drew no inspiration from them.

[25] This understanding of security is in line with the Latin root of the word: security come from Latin *se-cura*, which means absence (*se*) of worry (*cura*).

Smith's and Bentham's understanding of security still resonates in as varied fields as national security (e.g., Greenfield and Camm 2005), international relations (e.g., Buzan 1983), and philosophy (e.g., Shue 1996). Buzan (pp. 19–20), in particular, distinguishes four types of "social threats" to individuals' security that, coincidently, closely match the categories of our framework: "physical threats (pain, injury, death), economic threats (seizure or destruction of property, denial of access to work or resources), threats to rights (imprisonment denial of normal civil liberties) and threats to position or status (demotion, public humiliation)."

Although some criminologists who write on security refer to Bentham (e.g., Brodeur and Shearing 2005), few, if any, emphasize the link between security and harm and most either omit harm entirely or just reference it in passing. Zedner's (2009) authoritative summary of the academic debate on security illustrates the latter stance (i.e., the passing reference). Writing from the perspective of a criminologist and criminal lawyer, Zedner (pp. 10, 15) advances the distinction between objective and subjective security and refers to Shue (1996, 21) and Buzan (1983) and other (noncriminological) authors who characterize objective security as protection from physical harm. However, Zedner (pp. 15, 16) does not expand on this view and, instead, speaks of the "real impossibility of objective security," contending that "objective security is arguably less readily distinguishable from the subjective state than at first appears."

We acknowledge this difficulty and recognize, per Zedner (2003) and others, that policy-makers often react to public perceptions of insecurity and private security companies might have an interest in sustaining those perceptions, which could affect the direction of private–public governance, a point that we take up later. Nonetheless, our work is premised on the possibility to distinguish between objective harm and perceptions and, by extension, between objective and subjective security.

Business Practices and Public Policy

Generally speaking, businesses govern their own security to avoid harm, even if they use different vocabulary to describe their actions. Understanding harm objectively and often measurably, they rely on more-or-less formal evaluations of benefits and costs, valuing the avoidance of harm as a benefit, to decide whether to prevent or control a crime or other threat. Along those lines, businesses tend to frame harm in terms of their functionality, material interests, or reputation and pursue security though "actuarial calculation rather than conventional moral proscription" (Johnston and Shearing 2003, 16). For Shearing and Stenning (1984) benefits and costs, alone, drive businesses' preventative interventions, without regard for a principled commitment to a moral or legal rule; for example, businesses pursue a case of theft to the extent that it is beneficial for them to do so, not necessarily because it is "wrong."

Harm prevention might also be said to inspire public institutions' understanding of security and related strategies for addressing security. In the twentieth century, the term "security" referred primarily to external or "national" security—with an emphasis on geopolitical boundaries—and to the collective interests of the state, but since 9/11 many countries also stress internal or "homeland" security, often conceptualized as protecting citizens from the harms of crime, especially organized crime and terrorism. With that shift, the ideas of external and internal security have progressively merged and the lines between them have blurred. The shift has, in turn, raised questions about the traditional division of labor between policing, including efforts of public law-enforcement agencies and private security firms, on the one hand, and intelligence and military services (which previously handled internal and external security, respectively), on the other (see, e.g., Loader and Percy 2014).

At the EU level and in numerous countries in Europe, North America, and elsewhere, cybersecurity, another arena that calls out harm explicitly, has also become a major policy goal. For example, the definition of cybersecurity that the EU adopted in its first dedicated strategy in 2013 explicitly acknowledges the relevance of harm for both civilian and military stakeholders. Accordingly, in that document, cybersecurity "refers to the safeguards and actions that can be used to protect the cyber domain, both in the civilian and military fields, from those threats that are associated with or that may harm its interdependent networks and information infrastructure" (European Commission and High Representative 2013, 3).

The UN has taken security even further into new domains. Starting with the Brundtland Commission's (1987) report, the United Nations Security Council and its specialized agencies, including the United Nations Development Program (1994) and the Commission on Human Security (2003), have promoted sustainable development, defined intergenerationally as development that "meets the needs of the present without compromising the ability of future generations to meet their own needs" (Brundtland Commission 1987, Chapter 2, para. 1), and the related ideas of human and environmental security, including, climate, water, and food security.

This expansion has cast attention on the security of people and the environment and on meeting people's basic needs. The UN Commission on Human Security (2003, 4) defined human security as "protecting fundamental freedoms (freedoms that are the essence of life)"; "protecting people from critical (severe) and pervasive (widespread) threats and situations"; "using processes that build on people's strengths and aspirations"; and "creating political, social, environmental, economic, military, and cultural systems that together give people the building blocks of survival, livelihood, and dignity." Currently, these issues are being addressed by political, social, environmental, economic, and cultural programs targeting poor, developing, and transitional countries under the aegis of the United Nations Millennium Development Goals (UNGA 2000) and the 2030 Agenda for Sustainable Development (UNGA 2015). In each case, the driver has been the will to protect human and environmental security from anthropogenic harm, further encouraged by the growing awareness of the negative impact of human action on the biosphere (e.g., Dalby 2014; Shearing 2015).

The provision of security, long considered a quintessentially "state" activity (e.g., Hobbes ([1668] 1994, is not only delegated to private actors—businesses and individuals—but is also being governed increasingly through private–public partnerships and networks of public, private, and hybrid institutions. These partnerships and networks form the core of the contemporary governance of security and operate under a variety of arrangements, ranging from government entities' dictates, to third-party participation in official delegations, to full abdication of government regulatory functions to third parties (Dupont et al. 2003). Under these various arrangements, a considerable share of crime prevention and control now occurs outside the strict realm of "traditional" criminal policy (e.g., Dupont and Wood 2006; Johnston and Shearing 2003; Schuilenburg 2015). Along such lines, large businesses maintain order on their premises, for both employees and customers (Shearing and Stenning 1984), and a vast private market for security has developed with private-security personnel outnumbering law-enforcement officials in Australia, Canada, China, the UK, the United States, and other jurisdictions (Provost 2017). At the same time, the general public has taken charge of its own protection with home alarm systems and weapons of varying lethality (e.g., Zedner 2003).

Moreover, the preemptive—and, thereby, harm-preventing—logic of the governance of security has driven the expansion of public and private surveillance methods and tools, such as use of closed-circuit television, use of smart cards, and data mining (Lyon 2001, 2015). The global market for private security services, which include private guarding, surveillance, and armed transport, was estimated at $180 billion in 2016 and is projected to grow to $240 billion by 2020 (Provost 2017, n.p.). According to estimates collated by *The Guardian* (Provost 2017, n.p.), the private security sector employs more people worldwide—about 20 million—than inhabit the Netherlands.

All told, these developments are affecting criminal policy, for example, by focusing attention on crime prevention, and some commentators (e.g., Bayley and Shearing 1996, 585–606; Loader and Sparks 2002) claim that they have transformed traditional criminal justice systems beyond recognition.

Faced with this changing environment, a substantial number of criminologists (see, e.g., Ericson and Haggerty 1997; Garland 2001a; Loader and Walker 2007; Lyon 2001, 2015; Wood and Dupont 2006; Zedner 2003, 2009) have focused on the public–private governance of security as it concerns crime and explored what they identify as its negative impact on criminal and public policy and the broader society. Although we appreciate that society can—and often does—gain from turning to private actors to deliver services in seemingly public contexts (see, e.g., Greenfield 2008 among many others), we add our own concerns: first, in broad terms, can society be certain that private actors will adequately account for the public good in their decisions about priorities and resource allocation, based on their perceptions of the need for security services and, second, can the security industry's interest in promoting its services affect—or sway—the public's perception of the need for those services?

We return to these issues in Chapter 7.

In their analyses, few of the aforementioned criminologists have hinted at harm: for example, Ericson (2007, 1) claims that the logic of security justifies "treating every imaginable source of harm as a crime," while for Schuilenburg and van Steden (2014, emphasis in original) it only entails "protection *against* something or somebody." With the partial exception of Edwards et al. (2013), no criminologist has—to our knowledge—expanded on the relationship between security and harm or used harm as an evaluative criterion to assess whether security has been improved.

Risk and Risk Management

Risk, as an object of concern and organizing principle, has also garnered much attention in contemporary society (see, e.g., Beck 1992; Giddens 1999) and, in some quarters, it also shares a close link with harm. Risk, in simple terms, can be framed as a statement of probability and outcomes, negative or positive; however, as reflected in many context-specific definitions, assessment methods, mitigation strategies, and other management techniques, including those of security, concerns about outcomes often tilt toward the negative, as downside risk, and are often "bound up with the aspiration to control and particularly with the idea of controlling the future" (Giddens 1999, 3).

Reframing the negative as "harm," the aspiration to anticipate and control harm is spelled out in the more-or-less stringent actuarial understandings of risk, which focus on the probabilities of harmful events or negative outcomes. Hence, for example, in their work on law and risk, Leiss and Hrudey (2005, 3) characterize risk as "the chance of harm," whereas Haines (2017, 183), writing on regulation and risk, defines actuarial risk as "the possibility of harm to an individual, collective or the environment arising out of an unwanted event" (for a review of this debate, see Mythen 2014).

The national security community, from which we have drawn to develop our framework, offers a clearer rendering, by looking at the possibility of the harm and its virulence (see, e.g., Greenfield and Camm 2005, 44–9; National Academies of Sciences, Engineering, and Medicine 2018; US Department of the Army 1998, 2006, 2014; US Department of the Army, Marine Corps, Navy, and Air Force 2001).[26] More specifically, it juxtaposes the probability of a negative outcome or bad consequence, such as an injury or death, property damage or destruction, and mission failure, and its severity. Risk, then, is an overall measure of the two attributes, probability and severity, in relation to a particular harm. It also speaks directly to Walker's (1997, 611) interest in addressing the "sort... of harm" and the "probability it will be perpetrated" in the "imposition on the unwilling of restraints."

That same community offers strategists and operators, alike, a five-step risk-management process for guiding risk assessment and mitigation (Figure 2.2) along with various tools to support it, including a matrix for

[26] For a more complete discussion of the national security community's approach to risk management and its relevance to this effort, see Greenfield and Paoli (2012, 10–11) and Chapter 4, Sections 4.2 and 4.4 of this book.

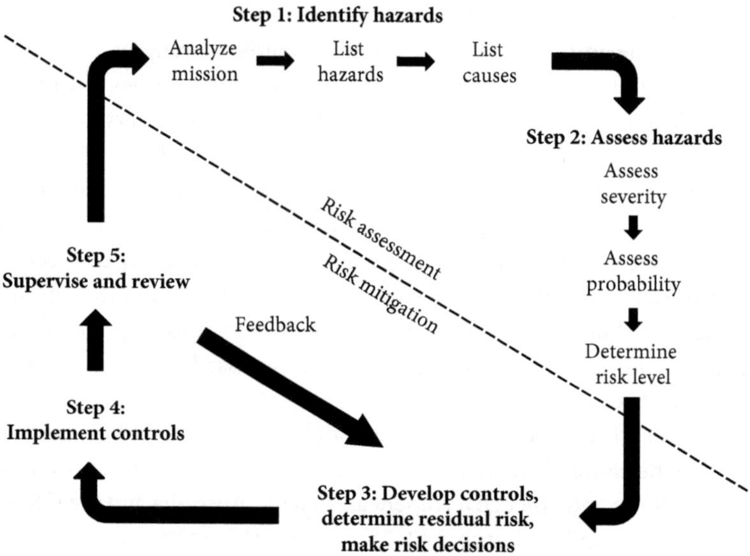

Figure 2.2 Five-step risk management process (Consisting of risk assessment and mitigation)

Source: Authors' adaptation of Greenfield and Camm (2005, 47), drawing from US Army (1998), US Army et al. (2001), and other US military doctrine.

ranking threats by severity and frequency that we present, discuss, and adapt for our purposes in Chapter 4.

But neither an actuarial perspective nor an "aspiration to control" is common to all scholars who concern themselves with risk. For example, Beck (1992, 23–4), who launched the term "risk society" with his influential book on the subject, conceptualizes risk as an obscure and incontrollable threat—closer to what some term uncertainty or danger (e.g., Douglas 1992, 44–5)—yet he connects risk with harm. In Beck's view, risk refers "above all" to threats like radioactivity, toxins, and pollutants that "induce systematic and often *irreversible* harms, generally remain *invisible*, are based on *causal interpretations*, and so initially only exist in terms of the (scientific or anti-scientific) *knowledge* about them (emphasis in original)." By contrast, Giddens (1999, 3), who is also closely associated with the term "risk society," stresses the distinction between risk and danger, defining risk as "the chance of avoiding an unwanted outcome," and characterizes the risk society by its ambition to manage risks.

Risk has also gained prominence in the criminological and public debate on crime and criminal policy, with similarly far-ranging definitions, but with little explicit reference to harm, especially among criminologists. Whereas the literature on risk assessment might understand risk as the chance of a particular harm and others, including Beck (1992), refer to harm, the debate on crime and criminal policy largely bypasses "harm" and either focuses on the risk of crime, primarily violent crime, or leaves the very idea of risk undefined. Few criminologists explicitly connect risk to harm (e.g., O'Malley 2008; Zedner 2009), but if they do, they do it in passing—O'Malley (2008, 458), for example, speaks at some point of "risk/harms"—and none has, to our knowledge, discussed the relationship or specified what they mean by harm.

Risk—or threat—assessment methodologies roughly akin to those found in the national security literature have been developed and employed by some police and other government agencies in Australia and the UK (see Tusikov 2012) and by Europol (2013) to set crime control priorities (see also United Nations Office on Drugs and Crime 2010a).[27] Like our framework, which also draws from the national security literature, these methodologies aim to assess the probability of criminal events or their harm on the aggregate for a country or region. (Because of their attention to harm, we consider them in Section 3.2.)

Within criminology and criminal policy, actuarial types of risk assessment methodologies have been developed and employed primarily to assess the likelihood of violent behavior and crime occurring: Singh et al. (2014) report more than 200 such tools. These tools have been deployed widely to inform initial decisions regarding sentencing, parole, and post-release monitoring and rehabilitation. In some jurisdictions, including Canada, New Zealand, and, until 2012, the UK, such tools for assessing the risk—or at least the probability—of violence have also been used to justify indeterminate post-sentence detention (Mythen 2014, 52–5; O'Malley 2006). Risk assessments are also used to screen youngsters and even children who, because of their own, their parents', or their environment's characteristics, are considered in danger of becoming criminals (e.g., Singh et al. 2014).

[27] These methodologies and their applications, like some of their national security counterparts, are mostly known as "threat assessments," not "risk assessments" (e.g., Europol 2017; see also United Nations Office on Drugs and Crime 2010a, Zoutendijk 2010).

Despite the growing popularity of these tools, many criminologists have voiced concerns about their reliance on deterministic assumptions (e.g., Sampson and Laub 2005), ineffectiveness, questionable ethical justification, and policy consequences. Speaking to their ineffectiveness and ethical implications, Fazel et al.'s (2012) meta-analysis shows that more than half of individuals judged by risk assessment tools as "high risk" are incorrectly classified and will not go on to offend. Some research also shows that these so-called "false positives" may be especially common in minority ethnic groups (e.g., Shepherd and Lewis-Fernandez 2016). The low predictive accuracy of these tools (see also Douglas et al. 2017) has fueled ethical concerns about the increasing reliance on actuarial techniques in criminal justice, specifically, the potential for racial and other demographic profiling (e.g., Shepherd and Lewis-Fernandez 2016) and the possibility that the tools, themselves, might cause harm.

Feeley and Simon (1992, 1994) use the terms "new penology" and "actuarial justice" to describe the increasing reliance of the policy community on risk assessments for decision about sentencing and crime prevention. In their view, the language of morality has given way to actuarial techniques used "to identify, classify and manage groupings sorted by dangerousness" (Feeley and Simon 1992, 452), and in so doing changing the character of criminal law and justice. For them and others (see also Garland 2001b), the focus of actuarial justice is on the safety of the public and the cost-effective management of offenders to the detriment of offenders' rehabilitation.

Nevertheless, these tools enjoy support ranging from staunch (e.g., Farrington 2000) to qualified. Some scholars (e.g., Douglas et al. 2017) endorse the tools in concept, by calling for improvements, not abandonment, and by arguing that they still represent an improvement over past practice. From a slightly different perspective, O'Malley (2006) contends that the impact of actuarial justice on the contemporary criminal justice systems has been smaller than Feeley and Simon (1992) once claimed.

Of particular importance to our work, O' Malley and others remind us that risk assessment is a generic technology that can be put to progressive or injurious use, depending on the method and application. Speaking to the progressive, Shearing and Johnston (2005) explore how aggregate risk—or threat—assessments can serve as means to reduce the excessive use of punishment. Likewise, O'Malley (2006, 2008) argues that some risk-minimization strategies, such as drug harm-reduction interventions, represent positive developments, because they offer promise for linking risk to a broader understanding of security and to social justice.

We believe that our efforts to draw insight from these approaches to develop our framework fall well within the bounds of "progressive" not "injurious" use, but we leave that to the reader to decide.

2.6 Concluding Remarks

The extensive literature review and document analysis in this chapter leave us with contradictory findings on the relevance of harm and harm reduction to crime and societal responses to crime, but a common thread runs through them. Harm and its reduction are central to both crime and societal responses, even if a considerable part of academia and officialdom views crime as a "harm" in its own right and, consequently, has failed to recognize or act on the link. Insomuch as it has taken up this equivalence, neither community has found need to address harm, per se, but rather has sought primarily to reduce crime.

We have observed contradictions in two related domains; one concerns crime, law, and policy and the other concerns the governance of security.

In the realm of crime, law, and policy, we find that the relevance of harm to crime emerges most compellingly in legal history and theory, can be teased out of criminal and related policy, and enjoys pockets of support in criminology, largely outside the mainstream, but it is all-but lost in formal definitions of crime. Harm and its reduction play a part—at least implicitly or in principle—in all the phases of criminal policy that we considered (Table 2.1); that is, in every phase that does not focus primarily on establishing culpability, such as the trial of specific offenders and the prosecutorial disposition of cases. The acknowledgment is strongest in criminalization, sentencing and punishment, and victims' assistance and restorative justice and weakest in crime control and policing and crime prevention, even if it is gaining traction there too. Harm and its reduction also surface plainly in deliberations on reparation in international criminal justice. Still, harm has not been conceptualized or implemented fully in any phase, even when it has been taken up in formal policy statements.

Similarly, in the realm of security, we find a tension between "what is" and "what is acknowledged." One could argue, as we have done, that harm and its reduction are inherent to the very concept of security, defined broadly, and to the many partnerships, arrangements, and techniques that governments and businesses have developed to manage risk in pursuit of security. Abandoning retributivist justifications, the whole multilayered edifice

Table 2.1 Harm and harm reduction in relation to criminal policy: Extent of acknowledgment and implementation

Policy phase or arena	Acknowledgment of relevance		Implementation	
	Scholarly debate on policy-related matters	**Policy documents**	**Harm-based approach to policy implementation in general or to specific interventions**	**Systematic/ empirical harm assessment**
Criminalization	Strong in legal theory, weak in criminology	Strong, but declining in UK and US	Yes, but not systematically	No
Crime control and policing	Generally weak or not explicit (e.g., Problem-Oriented Policing) in both criminology and legal theory, but growing in UK and US (e.g., Sherman et al. 2016)	Generally weak, but acknowledged in Finland since 1970s and growing in UK, EU, and Australia (e.g., SOCA 2008; Europol 2013; Tusikov 2012)	Usually no, but starting in UK, EU, Australia and in single interventions in US (e.g., High Point DMI)	Usually no, but starting (e.g., MoRiLE [2017] and High Point DMI)
Sentencing and punishment	Strong in both legal theory and criminology	Strong	Yes	No
Victims' assistance and restorative justice	Strong in criminology and related fields, but focus on individuals' harms and perceptions	Strong	Yes, but focus on individuals' harms and perceptions	No
Crime prevention	Generally weak in both legal theory and criminology, with few exceptions (e.g., Ashworth and Zedner 2014)	Generally weak, with few exceptions (e.g., 2002 UN guidelines on crime prevention)	Usually not explicit in crime prevention interventions, even if prevention of future harm might result from these and some policing interventions; explicit harm reduction policy in drug and other policy fields	No
International criminal justice	Strong	Strong	Yes, with added focus on reparations (e.g., in ICC's Luganga, Katanga and Al Mahdi cases and other reparative interventions at national/local level)	No

Source: Authors' analysis.
Note: "Hight Point DMI" refers to the drug market intervention in High Point, North Carolina that was piloted in 2004. For more information about this intervention and the evaluation, see https://www.crimesolutions.gov/ProgramDetails.aspx?ID=361 and https://nnscommunities.org/our-work/strategy/drug-market-intervention (both accessed September 2, 2021).

of the public–private governance of security is aimed to prevent harmful events from occurring or, in failing to prevent, mitigate their effects. However, such a goal is not yet fully acknowledged in the specific criminological literature on the governance of security, risks, and risk assessment.

On that basis, we conclude that harm, including its reduction, is a central element of crime and societal responses to crime, even if it is acknowledged inconsistently and a sizable portion of the criminological literature on crime, security, and risk has neglected it, by implicitly identifying harm with crime. In northeastern Italy, the native country of one of us, the sinking streams associated with karst formations, known as "carsismo," present an apt, physical analogy: like those streams, harm is sometimes manifest and sometimes buried, but it is nonetheless mostly there. Even a prominent legal moralist such as Duff (2013: n.p.) admits, "surely at least a central part of the purpose of a modern system of criminal law must be to protect citizens against various kinds of harm, by preventing kinds of conduct that cause such harm." Going further, we posit that harm reduction constitutes a shared—indeed the main—common ground between traditional domestic and international criminal policy and the public–private governance of security.

We also note, though, differences in how harm reduction is understood and pursued in the different phases of criminal policy, international criminal justice, and the governance of security as it pertains to crime (see Table 2.2).

Whereas criminalization centers on harm prevention, primarily through general and specific deterrence, crime control and policing also seek to establish culpability by investigating specific crimes and offenders. Moreover, in their daily work, police can contribute to harm mitigation and remediation through problem solving and first-line victims' assistance. In sentencing and punishment, deterrence, rehabilitation, and incapacitation are each meant to play a part in harm prevention, but in the debate on sentencing, harm primarily serves as an anchor for establishing proportionate sentences, while the infliction of harm is inherent to the act of punishment. In their turn, victims' assistance and restorative justice speak to harm remediation through support and restoration, but not without reference to harm prevention and mitigation. International criminal justice shares the same goal and objectives as lower-level criminal policies but, to a larger degree than its domestic counterparts, it emphasizes—at least in principle, if not in practice—harm restoration and thus remediation. Harm reduction through prevention and mitigation is also central to private–public

Table 2.2 Harm-related goals and objectives in criminal policy and the governance of security as it pertains to crime

Policy phase or arena	Harm-related goal or objective
Domestic or regionally coordinated criminal policy	Harm reduction through prevention, mitigation, and remediation
• Criminalization	• Harm prevention through deterrence
• Crime control and policing	• Primarily harm prevention (and establishment of culpability through investigation of specific crimes and offenders) but, in policing, also harm mitigation and remediation
• Sentencing and punishment	• Punishment proportional to harm (and culpability) and, through deterrence and offenders' rehabilitation and incapacitation, harm prevention
• Victims' assistance and restorative justice	• Harm remediation through victims' support and restoration
• Crime prevention	• Harm prevention and/or mitigation
International criminal justice	Harm reduction through prevention, mitigation, and remediation with emphasis on remediation through restoration or reparation
Governance of security as it pertains to crime	Harm reduction through prevention and mitigation

Source: Authors' analysis.

governance of security. Because of its preemptive logic, though, the latter grants less relevance to remediation.

Whereas the expression "unity in diversity" is often used to point to harmony and unity between dissimilar individuals or groups, we make no claims about the "good fit" of the different objectives of criminal policy and the related realms. On the contrary, as we will address more extensively in Chapter 7, we are convinced that an overall evaluation is due and perhaps overdue, to ensure that the different objectives do not conflict or leave gaps and undermine the overall goal of harm reduction.

As for the governance of security, the scholarly debate, policy documents and concrete practices give no clear answers as to which harms are—or ought to be—targeted in public and private reduction efforts. In this realm, we found that private and public actors might work together to reduce harm, but that they might also view harm differently, largely in accordance with the differences in their interests. Private actors might tend to focus on their functionality, material interests, and reputation, whereas policy-makers are tasked with protecting the whole polity from harm, at least in theory. However, the differences between private and public delineations of harm are not entirely clear-cut. Across generations, policy-makers have been criticized for serving the interests of specific groups, classes, or constituents, rather than all society, much as might be said of private actors, themselves. Insomuch as private actors lobby public officials to represent their interests, the lines further blur. Moreover, the interests that governments have deemed most worthy of protection have changed over time, as evident in the remarkable evolution in how they have come to understand security and related policy strategies since the Second World War (see Section 2.5).

Given the centrality of harm and harm reduction in both criminal policy and the governance of security as well as the attendant contradictions, complexities, and ambiguities, the next step in this analysis is to consider how the long-standing concern about harm that runs through these and other policy fields (Sparrow 2008) can be transformed into concrete, practicable research questions and agendas. As we show in Chapter 3, neither scholars nor the larger policy community has embraced the task fully, but, in our own research and as this book attests, we believe that a closer look at harm assessment is a necessary and feasible advancement. In particular, we have sought to develop a method for assessing and comparing the harms of different activities, crimes especially, thought to entail substantial adverse consequences and to give careful consideration to the role of policy in either reducing or adding to those harms.

3 Prior Attempts to Assess Harm and the Challenges They Have Encountered

3.1 Introduction

If harm—and its reduction—is to serve as a guiding principle for criminal and related policy as part of a "firm analytical foundation," it needs to be put into operation so that academic and policy communities can assess and compare the harms of crime and of other activities thought to entail substantial adverse consequences. In this chapter, we review previous attempts to work with the concept of harm as an analytical device but, finding few attempts in the domain of crime, we also consider analytical frameworks and empirical studies focusing on drug-related harm and on related concepts, such as public perceptions of the seriousness of crime, the impact of criminal victimization, and the cost of crime. This review enabled us to gather material to construct our methodology, the harm assessment framework, and to delve into the conceptual and technical challenges of assessing harm so that we could tackle them as effectively as possible with our framework in Chapter 4.

By pointing to the achievements and deficits of past efforts and the obstacles facing them, the review also helps demonstrate the value of our approach.

Despite the centrality of harm to crime, criminal policy, and the governance of security (see Chapter 2), our searches have indicated little systematic reflection on criminal harms or their empirical identification, evaluation, and comparison. In September 2012, near the start of our work in this field, a publication search in *Criminal Justice Abstracts*, using "harm" and "crime" as keywords, yielded only 11 "hits," of which 5 were not relevant because they concerned harm reduction in drug- and alcohol-control policy and

Assessing the Harms of Crime. Victoria A. Greenfield and Letizia Paoli, Oxford University Press. © Victoria A. Greenfield & Letizia Paoli 2022. DOI: 10.1093/oso/9780198758174.003.0003

two were of limited use because they only described the harm suffered by victims of violent crimes. Notwithstanding growing interest in harm in criminology (see Section 2.3), our more recent searches have yielded little new evidence of systematic and empirical research on the harms of crime, other than our own (e.g., Greenfield et al. 2016; Paoli et al. 2013, 2015; Paoli and Greenfield 2018).

To gain a full understanding of pertinent analytical developments, we examine, in Section 3.2, the core studies that we found in our searches; other attempts to measure the harms of crime, even if unsatisfying; the methodologies of police, government, and other agencies; and work on drug-related harm. In Section 3.3, we consider research on three concepts that both relate to harm and present significant literatures—public perceptions of the seriousness of crime, the impact of criminal victimization, and the cost of crime. In each arena, we found either a reason, by way of inadequacy, or a means, by way of insight, to advance a harm-based approach in the criminal domain.

Drawing on all these studies, we discuss in Section 3.4 the conceptual and technical challenges of assessing harm. We conclude the chapter by arguing that these challenges almost certainly have played a part in hindering progress toward assessing the harms of crime systematically and empirically and likely have reinforced policy-makers' hesitance to use harm as a guiding principle in their deliberations on criminal policy, but, as we demonstrate in Chapter 4, the challenges are not insurmountable.

The chapter builds on Paoli and Greenfield (2013), "Harm: A neglected concept in criminology, a necessary benchmark for crime-control policy."

3.2 The Conceptualization and Assessment of Harm

In this section, we consider prior attempts to use "harm" analytically in the domain of crime, specifically, and, finding only a small body of pertinent work, we turn to analytical efforts in the field of drug-related harms. Very few scholarly advocates of harm-based approaches to criminal policy have developed rigorous typologies or assessment tools (Chapter 2). Maltz (1990), von Hirsch and Jareborg (1991), Dorn and van de Bunt (2010), Pemberton (2007, 2015), and Pantazis and Pemberton (2009), which we review below, account for the small number of scholarly attempts to categorize criminal harms in detail. We also consider other efforts to measure the harms of crime, even if we believe they fall short of their aim (e.g., Kopp and Besson 2009; Sherman et al. 2016), and the methodologies that police and government agencies (primarily in the United Kingdom (UK) and Australia) and the European Union (EU) intelligence agency, Europol, use to assess the harms of organized and other crimes. Drug-related harms have received comparatively more scholarly attention, which leads us to consider the major taxonomies and empirical assessments in this overlapping field.

Previous Conceptualizations and Assessments of the Harms of Crime

In an early attempt to evaluate the efficiency and cost-effectiveness of the US federal government's efforts to combat organized crime, Maltz (1990) identifies five dimensions of harm: physical, economic, psychological, community, and societal. Distinguishing between *mala in se* and *mala prohibita* crimes and relying on his professional judgment, he qualitatively assesses the harms of several offenses, such as arson and extortion, which were then commonly associated with organized crime. His rankings of their harms range from "little or no" to "very significant."

Von Hirsch and Jareborg's (1991) "Gauging criminal harm: A living standard approach" offers a more structured attempt to categorize the harms of crime, one which Ashworth (2006, 37) describes as "path-breaking" and has had considerable impact on the subsequent legal debate (e.g., Bagaric 2000–1; Burton 2007; Walker 1997).[1] Von Hirsch and Jareborg focus on the damages associated with common interpersonal crimes, such as theft, burglary, and assault (pp. 3–4), and develop guidelines for assessing the "standard" impact (pp. 4–5) that a crime has on the immediate victim's "standard of living," drawing loosely from Sen (1987). On that basis, the authors posit four "generic-interest dimensions" (p. 19) upon which crime typically intrudes (i.e., physical integrity, material support and amenity, freedom from humiliation, and privacy or autonomy) and identify four living-standard levels for gauging the severity of intrusions upon each interest (p. 17). A "harm scale" with five broad bands of gravity, ranging from grave to lesser, completes the framework (pp. 28–9). To rate the harms of crime, von Hirsch and Jareborg would assess the impact of different

[1] Von Hirsch et al. (2005) offer a restatement with modest changes.

crimes on a hypothetical victim, assumed to have interests at each living-standard level (p. 21).

Other legal theorists have criticized elements of von Hirsch and Jareborg's approach. Among them, Bagaric (2000–1) points to a lack of underlying moral theory and Ryberg (2004, 62–8) highlights the absence of the probability or likelihood of occurrence. Another obvious limitation of von Hirsch and Jareborg's (1991, 34) approach, which we address in Chapter 4 along with probability, is that it concerns only "ordinary victimizing offences."

Loosely building on von Hirsch and Jareborg (1991), others have compared the seriousness of assaults and criminal justice outcomes, finding no linear relationship between them. In one paper, seriousness was judged by lawyers on the basis of nine heterogeneous factors (Clarkson et al. 1994); in another, it was judged according to medical injury severity (Shepherd 1997). Apart from our own work, we have identified no other empirical applications of von Hirsch and Jareborg (1991).

In a report for the Dutch Ministry of Justice and the Public Prosecutor's Office, Dorn and van de Bunt (2010) suggest articulating the harms of organized crime along three dimensions: "hurts to victims," "threats to public and private sector guardians," and "systemic damage." They provide examples of hurts to victims, focusing primarily on monetary indicators (pp. 8–13), but they gain little empirical traction.

Hillyard and Tombs' (2004) early texts on harm and zemiology also lacked a full conceptualization, let alone operationalization, of harm but they propose four categories of harm—physical, financial or economic, emotional or psychological, and cultural safety[2]—that closely resemble those proposed by von Hirsch and Jareborg (1991), and, by extension, ours (see Chapter 4).

Pemberton (2007, 2015)—and more recently, through Pemberton, also Hillyard and Tombs (2017)—rely on Doyal and Gough's (1991) theory of human needs to conceptualize social harm. This theory defines needs as "a particular category of goals which are believed to be universalisable." Their nonfulfillment generates "serious harm," which Doyal and Gough (1991, 50) define both as a "fundamental disablement in the pursuit of one's vision of the good" and as "an impediment to successful social *participation*." From this, they deduct two basic needs, health and autonomy, and eleven

[2] The last category encompasses autonomy, development, and growth and access to cultural, intellectual, and informational resources (Hillyard and Tombs 2007, 17).

"universal satisfiers," such as food, clean water, and appropriate education (Doyal and Gough 1991, 52–4, 155–9), which Pemberton (2015, 30–1), however, no longer mentions. To our knowledge, this conceptualization has only been applied once empirically in our field. Pantazis and Pemberton (2009), though, use it not to assess the harms of specific crimes but rather to compare the harms of the UK and US "neo-liberal" political and economic systems with those arising in "corporatist" and "social-democratic" countries, such as Germany, Japan, and Sweden.

Of these efforts, ours draws most directly from von Hirsch and Jareborg (1991), which we will revisit in Chapter 4, when we present our framework.

Other Studies Intended to Measure the Harms of Crime

In our exploration of the literature, we found a small number of studies that aim to measure the harms of crime explicitly, but in our view, they fall short of their aim. Some of the studies, for example, de facto equate the harms of crime with its social cost (e.g., Kopp and Besson 2009; Levi and Burrows 2008; Porteous 1998).[3] Following the cost-of-crime literature (e.g., Cohen 2005), most of them include the costs of societal reactions, which, as we discuss below and in later chapters, might serve to overemphasize or reinforce existing priorities.

Sherman (2007), Sherman et al. (2016), Ratcliffe (2014) and others follow a different path. Sherman (2007, 312) proposed the creation of a total-harm index, based on public perceptions of crime seriousness (see Section 3.3) and, to lesser or greater extents, Ratcliffe (2014) and Sherman et al. (2016) advance the ball. Sherman et al. (2016) present and implement a "Crime Harm Index" (CHI) that relates crimes to penalties, specifically the number of prison days that crimes of each type would incur, using the Sentencing Guidelines of England and Wales as a reference point.

The CHI has garnered attention as a low-cost, accessible step forward, but it has shortcomings that limit its utility as a true reflection, let alone full measure of harm.[4] Because the index works with sentencing guidelines, it does not measure the actual harms of crimes but unavoidably reflects and

[3] See the related discussion in Section 4.3.

[4] See e.g., *The Economist* (2016) and Sherman et al. (2016) for references to the adoption of the CHI among local police forces in the UK.

codifies prior policy decisions, which, in turn, involve a mix of public perceptions and political imperatives.[5] For that reason, it cannot be used to establish policy priorities, criminality, or related sentences because it already embodies decisions about each. Arguably, "the thing that is broken" cannot be used to fix "the thing that is broken." The same can be said of the indexes of government agencies in Canada, New Zealand, and the UK that take similar approaches and are more modestly called crime severity or seriousness scores (for Canada, see Statistics Canada 2009; for New Zealand, see Sullivan and Su-Wuen 2013; and for the UK, see Office for National Statistics 2016).

Moreover, the sentencing guidelines of England and Wales are not apt to measure "harm, independent of culpability" as Sherman et al. (2016, 172) intend, because they concurrently address harm and culpability with three levels of each, ranging from highest to lowest.[6] It is also unclear how Sherman et al. (2016) account for the different levels of harm. If, as it seems, they always adopt the lowest level, which they call the "starting point" (p. 177), this could imply a substantial underassessment of harms. Using the metric of prison days, the index also cannot be applied to lesser crimes for which the guidelines only provide a fine.

The exportability of the CHI to other locales is also questionable, because it implements sentencing guidelines specific to England and Wales and, perhaps more fundamentally, because the approach depends on the very existence of guidelines. However, even if indexes were possible everywhere, they would be noncomparable from one jurisdiction to the next insomuch as the underlying guidelines differ.

Practitioners' Harm Assessment Methodologies

Since the start of the century, several national or regional agencies and international organizations have set out to report on the harms of organized crime and to develop methodologies to assess the harms of organized and other crime, more generally, sometimes as part of larger risk-management strategies.

5 See e.g., Sentencing Council (2017), introducing draconian sentences for preventative terrorism offenses, such as the possession of terrorist information.

6 The guidelines set sentences for three levels of harm in conjunction with three alternative levels of culpability.

Tusikov (2012) reviews several assessment methods and describes most as quantitative. The Australian Crime Commission (ACC)'s macro-level harm analysis, the UK National Policing Improvement Authority (NPIA)'s "Organized Crime Group Mapping," and the London Metropolitan Police Service (LMPS)'s "Criminal Network Harm Assessment Matrix" all aim to assign a numerical score to harms associated with either broad criminal issues or single organized crime networks. Academics, policy-makers, industry representatives, and other experts inform the ACC assessment, whereas police analysts assign the NPIA scores. The LMPS, by contrast, uses maximum statutory penalties as indicators of the harm of each offense. Statutory penalties—like the sentencing guidelines in Sherman et al.'s (2016) CHI—might serve as a useful proxy for severity for establishing short-term operational priorities in these settings; however, they necessarily confirm the prior opinions and decisions of lawmakers, which would lead to circularity in strategic planning.

Moreover, the ACC's macro-level harm analysis and the NPIA's Organized Crime Group Mapping are conceptually problematic. Specifically, both methods assign scores to weigh concerns that are several steps removed from harm, if even related. The NPIA, for example, delineates six scoring categories, of which one addresses the network's criminal capability and another addresses the spread of network activities across agency responsibilities and boundaries.[7]

These exercises bear the inevitable limitations of quantitative reductionism, an issue that we take up later in this section, in relation to drug harms, and in Section 3.4, in relation to quantification and commensurability.

Key parts of Europol's "Serious and Organised Crime Threat Assessment" (SOCTA) methodology are not defined well, if at all, in publicly available documents. Both the Council of the European Unions's (2012) SOCTA methodology and Europol's (2013 and 2017) SOCTAs define serious crime only as a residual category for criminal activities that are deemed serious and worth reporting but are not committed by organized crime actors. Moreover, the two bodies fail to define the "tailored indicators" that Europol (2013, 43) claims to use to "describe and assess the intrinsic characteristics of OCGs [organized crime groups] and SOC [serious organized crime] areas and ... to assign their respective level of threat." Without

[7] The other four scoring categories are potential or actual injuries, community harm, economic effect in a specific context, and impact on police reputation (Tusikov 2012).

defining them, Europol specifically speaks of "effect indicators," which are said to "measure the effect that OCGs and crime areas have on EU society [and] ... are key to identifying priority threats and arriving at substantiated recommendations." Europol (2013, 43) further adds that "the effects of OCG activities can be assessed as high, medium or low on any or all of the dimensions including physical and psychological, political, financial and economic, social technological and environmental"—but does not explain its scoring method. Europol's analysis brings attention to new, emerging crimes, such as environmental crime and energy fraud, but it confirms previously recognized rankings of crimes uncritically.[8]

For its "Global Money Laundering and Terrorist Financing Threat Assessment," the Financial Action Task Force (FATF) (2010) also published a "harm framework," proposing a classification of the harms of crime and terrorism. It distinguishes between physical, social, environmental, economic, and structural harms, suggesting that these harms can occur "at three levels—individual and local, community and regional and national and international" (FATF 2010, 64). FATF, though, only provides examples of each type of harm and does not attempt to operationalize the categories or offer a method for measuring their incidence or severity (see also FATF 2013).

National and international police agencies' efforts in this area attest to the underlying challenges of assessing the harms of criminal activities, which we consider in detail in Section 3.4, but they might also speak to another major, if unstated, dilemma: their analyses must be systematic and rigorous without disrupting crime control priorities founded on a political and public consensus. A police agency that asserts that some forms of drug trafficking render few harms (Paoli et al. 2013) or that immigration policies are a source of harms associated with human trafficking (Greenfield et al. 2016) might fear pushback in a budget cut or worse. As the term "law enforcement" suggests, police agencies exist to enforce the law, not typically to challenge it.

The Management of Risk in Law Enforcement (MoRiLE 2007) program shows, though, that the UK police agencies are searching for tools to set their strategic and tactical priorities through a more transparent, informed, and consistent decision-making process that revolves around the concepts of harm and risk. The MoRiLE program starts with a "tactical area,"

[8] Paoli (2014) provides a critique of the methodology and analysis. See van Duyne and Vander Beken (2009) and Zoutendijk (2010) for earlier criticisms.

consisting of an activity or group regarded as willing and able to inflict harm, and shares its understanding of risk directly from the national security community, which considers risk as an overall measure of the probability and the severity of harm (see Section 2.5), much as we do in our framework. The MoRiLE program defines harm and impact prospectively as the "anticipated harm of the tactical area on individuals, communities, [and] the environment and geographical scope," even if the last dimension cannot suffer harm. It operationalizes the possibility of harm in a complex and heterogeneous way by mixing intent, capability, past frequency, and volume of the crime(s) and victims' vulnerability. The MoRiLE program aims to provide a single numerical score of risk, by multiplying the "total harm score by total likelihood score" and using a quantitative nonlinear scale for both.

Although quantitatively reductive, the MoRiLE program could render harm more fully than indexes based on statutory penalties or sentencing guidelines and, if adopted nationwide to set policing priorities, it could present a major step forward.

Taxonomies and Assessments of Drug-Related Harms

Several drug-policy scholars have developed taxonomies of drug-related harms and some have also attempted to assess them empirically.[9] Newcombe (1992, 2–5) offers one of the first such taxonomies; others have followed, largely, but not entirely, addressing the harms of use. MacCoun et al. (1996), representing an exception, present a three-dimensional taxonomy of drug-related harms. They distinguish categories of harm (health, social and economic functioning, safety and public order, and criminal justice); those who bear harm (users, dealers, intimates, employers, neighborhood, and society); and primary sources of harm (use, illegal status, and enforcement). They initially considered drug trafficking as a primary source of harm, but eventually excluded it, arguing that the harms associated with trafficking are mostly related to policy (i.e., illegality and enforcement). MacCoun (1998) also offers a conceptual framework that traces the paths through which policy can affect drug-related harms and, as we note

[9] For a more comprehensive discussion of the drug-related literature on harm reduction from which we draw here, see Greenfield and Paoli (2012).

in Chapter 4, suggests the analytical benefits of dividing harm into its constituent parts, however defined.

Some scholars and domestic and international agencies in the drug-policy community (e.g., MacDonald et al. 2005; McFadden 2006; Moore 2007; Nutt et al. 2007, 2010; Slack et al. 2008; United Nations Office on Drugs and Crime 2005) have sought to develop quantitative indexes of total drug-related harms.[10] Nutt et al. (2010), in particular, have attracted considerable scholarly and public attention and no less controversy. (See, e.g., Caulkins et al. 2011; Caulkins and Reuter 2011; Fischer 2011; Nutt 2011; Obot 2011; Room 2011; and Rossow 2011 for a lively debate.) They propose and test an index that combines the score of 20 psychoactive drugs on 16 criteria. Of the 16 criteria, 9 relate to the harms that a drug produces in individuals and 7 pertain to harms to others. Among the latter, 6 refer to social harm, covering such disparate issues as crime, environmental damage, family adversities, international damage, economic cost, and "community," defined as the decline in community cohesion and reputation.

Despite their seeming attractiveness, Caulkins et al. (2011, 1) view these indexing efforts as "fundamentally flawed, both conceptually and methodologically," largely because they mingle noncomparable dimensions and disregard social context, including the underlying policy regime. In broad terms, they argue that harm cannot be reduced to a single, policy-relevant measure and that efforts to do so are "quixotic" (see also Caulkins and Reuter 1997; Paoli and Greenfield 2013). Rather than tilting at windmills, they call for embracing harms' multidimensionality in matrix form. Others (cited above and Ritter 2009) view indexation more favorably, but recognize the challenges, some of which we revisit in Section 3.4 and, again, in Chapter 4, when we develop our own matrix-based methodology.

3.3 Frameworks and Methodologies for Related Concepts

Given the limited number of frameworks and methodologies focusing on harms of crime, we also review those concerning related concepts of perceived seriousness, the impact of criminal victimization, and the cost of crime.

[10] See Pacula et al. (2009) for a review of studies that estimate drug-abuse costs.

Perceived Seriousness of Crime

Starting with Sellin and Wolfgang (1964), a number of predominantly North American studies have addressed the perceived seriousness of crime. Warr (1989), who was the first to conceptualize "perceived crime seriousness" explicitly, identified two main components, namely "perceived wrongfulness" and "perceived harmfulness." Perceived wrongfulness results from "a normative evaluation" of the "moral gravity of committing the act," while perceived harmfulness is assessed through "a factual assessment of the consequences of the offence upon the victim" (p. 796). O'Connell and Whelan (1996) and Rosenmerkel (2001) confirmed Warr's conceptualization.

In a recent study, Adriaenssen et al. (2018) extend Warr's conceptualization, using core elements of our framework. Specifically, the authors incorporate the incidence of harm and model perceived seriousness in terms of: (1) perceived crime wrongfulness; (2) perceived harm severity of crime; (3) perceived incidence of crime, defined as the perceptions of the frequency with which crime actually happens; and (4) perceived incidence of crime harms in relation to crime. They ask whether respondents assess the seriousness of a standard event of a certain crime, which would not require consideration of incidence, or the seriousness of all occurrences of that crime, which would require consideration of incidence. The former, which they call "typical," is relevant for sentencing and the latter, which they call "total," is important for establishing crime control and prevention priorities. In empirical testing, wrongfulness and severity are statistically significant, but incidence is not, and the predictive power of wrongfulness is much greater than that of severity, suggesting that individuals place more weight on morality than on other factors. Similarly, O'Connell and Whelan (1996) and Alter et al. (2007) report that people emphasize the wrongfulness of crime over the harmfulness of crime in assessing crime seriousness.

These studies sow doubts about use of public perceptions of crime seriousness as indicators of the actual harmfulness and seriousness of crime for policy-making purposes, as Sherman (2007) and Tonry (2015) have proposed.

Other scholars (e.g., Roberts 2011; Ryberg 2004, 60; von Hirsch and Jareborg 1991) also stress the limitations and hazards of relying solely on public opinion for sentencing and criminal policy more generally, by raising the possibility of knowledge deficits, factual misjudgment, unprincipled attitudes, and volatility of perceptions. For example, according to Cohen (1988), US public-perception surveys tend to underestimate the harm associated with violent crimes relative to property crime. Moreover, several experiments in psychology have shown what Nordgren and McDonnell (2011) call "scope insensitivity," referring to people's insensitivity to the scope or magnitude of outcomes. In their experiment, respondents attributed greater severity to a fraud case that involved 3 victims rather than to the same case when it was reported to involve 30 (see also Kahneman 2011). Sunstein (2002, 2005) relates such findings to other policy domains and shows that policy measures often end up being ineffective and even harmful, when they are driven primarily by public perceptions and fears. Anthropologists (e.g., Douglas 1992) and social psychologists (e.g., Joffe 1999) also point to the role of emotions and culture in shaping the perception and assessment of crimes and risks. Bauman (2000), speaking to societal context, notes that the anxieties and fears driving perceptions of crime and the market for security do not derive solely or primarily from crime but, instead, reflect the unpredictability and uncontrollability of our "liquid" late-modern societies.

Impact of Criminal Victimization

Since the 1960s, victimization surveys have supplemented police and other official crime statistics to estimate the incidence of victimization of ordinary crimes; that is, the extent to which the general public has been the victim of certain crimes over a period of time. Examples include the US National Crime and Victimization Survey (e.g., Bureau of Justice Statistics 2017), which has been repeated yearly since 1973, and the International Crime and Victimization Survey (ICVS), which was repeated in numerous countries five times between 1989 and 2005 (e.g., van Dijk et al. 2008).

Usually addressing individuals and households, some of these surveys also entail questions about the impact of the crimes. The ICVS, for example, asks how serious the incident was for the victim or their household "taking everything into account." Using the victims' answers to a similar question in Crime Survey for England and Wales, Ignatans and Pease (2016) have developed an index of crime seriousness. Presenting victims' assessments in a summary score, this data is undeniably useful. However, based on a single question, it cannot give a full rendering of actual harm, perceptions, or experiences. Moreover, victimization surveys cannot capture harms of rare events (such as homicides), consensual crimes (such as drug exchanges), or crimes that have no immediately manifest harms (such as many corporate crimes).

In addition to criminal victimization surveys, several victimologists have explored the consequences of a broad range of crimes on individuals. In reviewing these studies, Spalek (2017, 85–93) distinguishes the psychological, emotional, behavioral, physical, and financial impact of different types of crime on the victim, but this body of research has been largely descriptive, with most studies focusing on a specific experience of victimization (e.g., Resick 1990; Stanko and Hobdell 1993) or specific impacts (e.g., the household's moving decision in Dugan 1999). With very limited interest in aggregation and generalization, researchers working in the qualitative victimological tradition have tended to focus on factors that influence the severity of the experience of victimization, differentiating between the victims' demographic and psychological characteristics (which Walklate 2007, 75, calls the victims' "personal or structural vulnerability"); factors relating to the victimization event (e.g., the type of event and victim–perpetrator relations); and "post-victimization factors" (i.e., the time elapsed since the event and systems of support) (see also Spalek 2017, 97–101).

This literature has been criticized for focusing almost exclusively on traditional crimes and their individual victims (e.g., Fattah 2010, 54–7), unwittingly "perpetuat[ing] the false dichotomy between offenders and victims and the popular stereotypes of both" (p. 57). As much as victimization surveys, qualitative victimological studies have given little attention to corporate crimes and other offenses lacking immediate individual victims. Moreover, despite the recent development of surveys focusing on businesses' victimization experiences (e.g., PwC 2016; Williams 2016), both quantitative and qualitative methodologies have granted little attention to victims other than individuals (Fattah 2010, 54–7; Whyte 2007).

Serving to complement the victimological studies, a more recent and rapidly growing public-health literature on the impact of victimization on physical and mental health (see, e.g., Spalek 2017) can—and has—shed light on particular harms to individuals. Much of the research in this field uses standard measurement units (such as birth weight, e.g., in Brown's (2018) assessment of the violent crime on birth outcomes during Mexico drug war) or validated measurement instruments (such as those for identifying mental-health-related concerns, e.g., Abas et al. 2013; Oram et al. 2012, citing others; Zimmerman et al. 2008), that allow comparisons across crimes and between crimes and other causes of harm.[11] While some public health research has ventured on to newer forms of crime (e.g., cybercrime, Kaakinen et al. 2018), most of it—almost per definition—focuses on the impact of crimes on individuals' health and cannot capture other effects on individuals or their environment.

Cost of Crime

Following Becker (1968), a large economic literature has developed that implicitly, if not explicitly, equates the costs with the harms of crime.[12] This literature has traditionally distinguished among costs caused by criminal behavior; those incurred by society in response to crime either to deter or prevent future incidents or to exact retribution; and, in some instances, those incurred by the offender (Miller et al. 1996, 11; Cohen 2005, 9). The first category of costs relates most closely to harm and includes direct, indirect, and intangible costs. Direct costs typically entail a monetary exchange, as in the case of a property damage or loss, repair costs, and medical and mental health care; indirect costs include productivity losses as well as the cost of "avoidance behavior"; and intangible costs are much harder to estimate as they include pain and suffering, loss of quality of life, and loss of affection or enjoyment (Cohen 2005, 10–11). (See Czabański (2008, 10–17) for a different categorization.)

Early studies focused largely on out-of-pocket tangible costs to victims and used ground-up or accounting-based methods, but the literature has expanded, both through its use of those methods and by borrowing methods, such as "hedonic valuation" and "contingent valuation," from other disciplines (see Table 3.1).[13] Hedonic and contingent valuation can be used to establish an individual's "willingness to pay" to avoid an undesirable outcome, as might be associated with a crime, but they take different tacks. Whereas hedonic valuation involves "revealed preferences," contingent valuation involves "stated preferences." In the case of hedonic

[11] We drew from this literature in our assessment of the harms of human trafficking in Belgium (Greenfield et al. 2016).

[12] Cost of crime estimation dates back to the 1931 Wickersham Commission. In this discussion, we do not attempt a comprehensive review of the literature and the methodologies that have emerged from it, but refer the reader to more complete discussions in Heaton (2010) and Roman (2011).

[13] Heaton (2010) provides an accessible overview of these approaches, as do Dominguez and Raphael (2015).

Table 3.1 Comparison of cost-of-crime methods

Method	Features					Comments
	WTA	WTP	Uses Market Data	Yields Omnibus Figure	Direction of Bias	
Contingent valuation (Stated preference)	No	Yes	No (surveys)	Yes	+[1]	• Requires respondent's knowledge of consequences and likelihood • Depends on income
Hedonic valuation (Revealed preference)						
Real estate	No	Yes	Yes (Prices)	Yes	+[2]	• Requires consumer's knowledge of consequences and likelihood • Cannot parse crime(s)
Value of statistical life (VSL)	No	Yes	Yes (Wages)	No	+[2]	• Requires worker's knowledge of consequences and likelihood • Does not value life, per se
Accounting (Actual costs, mostly)	Yes	Maybe	Yes (various)	No	+/–	• Incorporates VSL, jury-award data, and/or other proxies to cover intangibles

Source: Authors' analysis based on Dominguez and Raphael (2015), Heaton (2010), and others.
Notes:

WTA = willingness to accept; WTP = willingness to pay; + = positive; – = negative.

[1] Hypothetical bias and plausible overestimation bias.

[2] Omitted variable bias.

valuation, individuals reveal their preferences (e.g., through purchase, job, and other market decisions); in the case of contingent valuation, individuals state their preferences directly (e.g., through a survey). Contingent valuation consists of asking individuals directly how much they would pay to avoid certain crimes, the so-called "willingness to pay." Accounting-based methods may also incorporate an individual's "willingness to accept" an undesirable outcome, as manifest in the payment they would require—or have received—as compensation for the consequences.

Attempts to include intangible costs began with Thaler (1978), who used hedonic valuation to estimate willingness to pay for crime avoidance, by comparing property values in high- and low-crime areas. Although rendering an omnibus figure—one that should encompass all dimensions of cost—this approach cannot reach beyond place-specific crime (e.g., robbery) or readily distinguish among the effects of different types of crimes (e.g., robbery versus assault) (Heaton 2010, 4). Moreover, effective "revelation" requires that homeowners know something about relative crime rates.[14] Phillips and Votey (1981) were the first to incorporate value-of-life estimates, using estimates of foregone income in an accounting framework, and Cohen (1988), also appealing to accountancy, followed with monetary estimates of pain, suffering, and lost quality of life for nonfatal injuries, using jury-award data. However, estimates of intangible costs based on jury-award data reflect the "extreme difficulty of translating pain and suffering into monetary equivalents" (Sunstein 2008, 157). Roman (2011) used jury awards and newly compiled criminal event data to estimate the prices of victimization in different types of serious crimes against persons, less serious crimes against property, and least serious crimes against property. In so doing, he edges closer to addressing the fullness of "harm," as we envision it.

In later work, Cohen et al. (2004) used contingent valuation to establish the value of crime reduction, by asking individuals how much they would pay to avoid certain crimes. This method, like hedonic valuation, can also capture the total cost of crime, including intangibles (Cohen and Piquero 2009, 35), but depending on how the question is framed (e.g., whether it is general or specific), it may not provide a means of identifying particular components of that cost, whether it is harm to individuals' autonomy or the environment's functional integrity. Survey responses can also rest on

[14] It is also hard to separate the effect of crime rates on housing prices from other neighborhood characteristics that tend to occur along with crime (see Heaton 2010, 4).

the wealth of the would-be payer and can suffer from "hypothetical bias," as individuals tend to overstate their willingness to pay as long as they do not need to pay (Heaton 2010, 3–4). Both survey-elicited willingness-to-pay and jury-award estimates are also affected by the so-called "hedonic forecasting error" (e.g., Sunstein 2008): people greatly exaggerate most of the pain, suffering, and the forgone gains[15] associated with a loss from the status quo (Sunstein 2008, 159–60) as they underassess human beings' resilience and capability to adapt (see Kermer et al. 2006).

The "value of statistical life" (VSL), which is a mainstay of US regulatory analysis, eventually supplanted foregone income as a proxy for human worth, as a stand-alone measure and in the context of accounting-based estimates of overall costs, but the VSL does not measure the value of life, as such. The VSL identifies and measures—through monetization—society's willingness-to-pay for a small reduction in the risk of premature death.[16] Although one could ask individuals what they would pay to avoid the risk, VSL estimates typically derive from market-based evidence, such as wage differentials across employment activities and, so, they also involve "revealed preferences." In this case, though, effective revelation requires workers' knowledge of the likelihood of death under different occupational circumstances.

Zimring and Hawkins (1995) voiced concerns about initial efforts to evaluate the cost of crime, but this literature has grown and matured considerably (e.g., Brand and Price 2000; Cohen et al. 2004; Cohen and Piquero 2009; Dubourg and Prichard 2007; Heaton 2010; Mayhew 2003; Roman 2011; and many others since then). Nevertheless, the literature is not without its contemporary detractors. Whereas Heaton (2010) and Dominguez and Raphael (2015) point to consistency among findings[17] (e.g., murder and rape are most costly and nonviolent crimes are least costly), others, such as Wickramasekera et al. (2015), who find similar rankings, raise concerns about the quality and usefulness of results. The latter point to wide variances in the estimates, if not the rankings, and the lack of standardization across studies. One might also ask whether the rankings are consistent by design, perhaps by virtue of a dependency on intangibles and the VSL in crimes that

15 Forgone "gains" refer to foregone quality or enjoyment of life, also known as "hedonic damages."

16 For more on the VSL, see Viscusi (2008) and Viscusi and Aldy (2003). For an approach to estimating nonfatal health-related losses, see the discussions of "quality adjusted life years" or "QALYs" in Roman (2011).

17 See also McCollister et al. (2010).

involve loss of life and what might be seen as a high degree of self-referencing and reuse of numbers. Lastly, some question whether the results are meaningful or plausible.[18] Regarding plausibility, Dominguez and Raphael (2015), point to a $1.6 trillion estimate of the cost of crime in the United States.

Although none of the forgoing cost-of-crime methods can render harms fully and without shortcomings, Dominguez and Raphael (2015) suggest approaches to judicious use and we would caution against discarding the baby with the bathwater. These methods can, within appropriate bounds, still provide insight to certain elements of harm that are amenable to monetization. Moreover, as we have argued previously (e.g., Greenfield and Paoli 2012, etc.) and will argue again in this book, the idea of "notional" benefit–cost analysis holds promise for policymaking and evaluation.

3.4 The Challenges of Assessing the Harms of Crimes

In our review of prior efforts to assess harms, we observed substantial conceptual and technical challenges.[19] None of the challenges is wholly "conceptual" or "technical," but some of the challenges, such as those of morality and quantification, are more one than the other. Although we have bundled the challenges into three groups, neither the challenges nor groupings are cleanly separable and readers will notice overlaps among them. In no small part, all of these challenges might be termed challenges of "counting," either figuratively or literally; that is, what harms really "count" and how should we "count" them, if we can?

Throughout the literatures, one message is clear: harm cannot be addressed through scientific means alone. As we note in Chapter 1, the assessment of harm—as much as the study of crime—cannot be divorced fully from social norms, environmental circumstances, and subjectivity (see also Pemberton 2015, 32).

[18] Although not a recent commentary, see Ackerman and Heinzerling (2002) for a criticism of the approach's validity and, perhaps, legitimacy.

[19] This section draws extensively from Paoli and Greenfield (2013), which, in turn, builds on our earlier explorations (e.g., Greenfield and Paoli 2012).

Morality, Cultural and Socioeconomic Variability, and Legitimacy

If harm is, as we understand it, a setback to a rightful stakeholder's legitimate interests (Feinberg 1984, 31–6; Greenfield and Paoli 2013, 864), then the idea of harm unavoidably entails value judgments—on rightfulness and legitimacy—that could depend on moral, cultural, and socioeconomic factors that can differ across settings. As MacCormick (1982, 30) maintains, "criminal law in so far as it is concerned with fending off harmful behaviour is *necessarily* geared to protection of what are legitimate interests *according to a certain dominant political morality*" (emphasis in original).[20] In turn, this "political morality" depends on a society's cultural and socioeconomic arrangements, so much so that different settings might present different crimes or attribute different harms to the same crime. As von Hirsch et al. (2005, 190) suggest, the impact of a burglary on our homes would be less if we slept in tents and relied on communal assets.

In some instances, however, one might question the validity of appealing to the "dominant political morality" as a determinant of interests and, thus, harm. If, for example, a country is under foreign authoritarian rule, should the proclivities of that rule—which could diverge from those of the populace—be taken as indicative of the "true" interests of the country's populace?[21] As harm is not, unlike crime, a legal construct, one might decide, instead, to look beyond the jurisdiction for guidance. Following Gert and Gert's (2017, n.p.) distinction between "normative" and "descriptive" definitions of morality,[22] we note that the definition of harm could be based respectively either on universal ethical claims, as Gert and Gert (2017) understand normative morality, or, more pragmatically, on international codes of conduct or laws, such as those concerning human rights.

In any case, questions of morality, underlying cultural and socioeconomic circumstances, and legitimacy (e.g., Duff 2013) pertain to the

[20] Similarly, risk assessment might also be said to depend on moral standards. As Douglas (1990, 10) observes, "risk is not only the probability of an event, but also the probable magnitude of its outcome, and everything depends on the value that is set on the outcome [that is, in our case, the harm]. The evaluation is a political, aesthetic and moral matter." (See Ericson and Doyle 2003.)

[21] One might ask a similar question about subjugation to domestically rooted tyranny.

[22] Gert and Gert (2017, n.p.) refer to "normative morality," defined as universal ethical claims that all rational persons under certain conditions would endorse, and "descriptive morality," defined as codes of conduct developed by actual groups and societies.

analytical treatment of interests and to claimants and their sometimes competing perspectives on the consequences of criminal activities. Here, we highlight two related questions for harm assessment, both of which involve matters of "standing," defined as a rightful stake in a particular matter (see Appendix A).[23]

First, should all claimants be treated as legitimate or equally so, implying that harms to all individuals, entities, etc. would count with the same weight or importance, regardless of their status and the circumstances of rendering? A body-packing drug courier might overdose en route to a delivery and a wholesaler might beat a retailer during a transaction, but should harms to the courier or retailer, having been sustained in the commission of a criminal act, be included or discounted in a harm assessment? One might argue against inclusion (e.g., on the basis of free will in the decision to traffic or deal), but the line between perpetrator and victim is not always clear. Moreover, many crime- and drug-control policies aim to minimize harms to the physical integrity of all parties to a criminal activity, regardless of their role (e.g., European Council 2005, 2). Even if one were to exclude harms to criminals from an assessment, one might still include related costs borne by taxpayers and others in the larger community, such as those of treating overdoses and injuries.

Second, how should we address outcomes that might look like harms from one claimant's perspective and benefits from another, even within the same value system? Consider, for example, the characterization of criminal revenues.[24] On the one hand, a crime might generate revenues that benefit both perpetrators and the larger economy; for example, by fueling consumption and generating sales for legitimate businesses. In extreme cases, such as opium production in Afghanistan (e.g., Greenfield et al. 2015a), the revenues might provide additional income that represents a means of survival for many rural households and—quite possibly—a considerable fraction of the rural population. On the other hand, the revenues might also drive inflation that places consumer products and real estate out of reach for many households and businesses. Analytics aside, policy-makers and police agencies typically consider illegal revenues a serious adverse consequence of criminal activities.

[23] See Trumbull (1990) and Whittington and MacCrae (1986, 1990) for a discussion of criminality and standing in benefit–cost analysis.

[24] We address these issues in detail in Chapter 6.

Some of these issues, which we face in our harm assessment in Chapter 6, in the context of coca cultivation and processing in Colombia, might be new to the field of criminology, but work on drug policy has been grappling with them for decades (e.g., Newcombe 1992; Caulkins and Reuter 1997; and Riley et al. 1999).

Infinitude and Causality

The problems of infinitude and causality, like those of morality, cultural and socioeconomic variability, and legitimacy entail matters of "counting," but more directly involve matters of limitations and boundaries.

Practically speaking, a list of harms, however broad and inclusive, cannot be exhaustive. First, we, as mere mortals, lack the foresight and imagination to identify, let alone assess, all harms a priori and, second, a list that includes ancillary—second, third, and nth order—effects could go on forever. For example, an injury that removes a parent from his or her children might yield additional harms to the children through loss of parental involvement, some of which might eventually affect their children. And, as we consider again, below, as a matter of measurement, one might ask how "far," either temporally or geographically, to go in counting harms.

This leaves us with a question of scope: How broad and inclusive should we be in establishing a list of harms? With a hint of wry humor, Levi and Burrows (2008, 294) ask whether the production of their own paper on fraud "and the whole of the criminological estate" should be defined as a cost of crime.

In legal theory, the issue of causality is known as a problem of "remote harms" because of the temporal, spatial, or behavioral "distance" between conduct and outcomes (Ryberg 2004, 64–6; Simester and von Hirsch 2011, 70–88).[25] Remote harms are not only distant from a conduct, but, because they are distant, they are also not clearly attributable to that conduct. For example, drug trafficking triggers events that are harmful, in part, because of the intervening choices of other actors (e.g., dealers, users, law-enforcement officers, and healthcare professionals). Doubtlessly, drug use can—and does—hurt users (e.g., through deteriorating health) and the rest of

[25] Many offenses entail remote, rather than, direct harm, such as the "inchoate" offenses, which prohibit actors from inciting, conspiring, or attempting to commit a (substantive) crime, and the numerous offenses of risk creation mentioned in Chapter 2.

society; however, drug use and its harms result from a series of choices over which wholesale traffickers have no control.[26] Legal scholars have expressed concerns about such extensive interpretations of harms (e.g., Harcourt 1999; Husak 2008; Wallerstein 2007) and suggested criteria to limit these interpretations (e.g., Simester and von Hirsch's fair imputation, 2011).

The potential for "accumulative harm" adds another complication that bears on attribution. Some harm follows from an act only when the act is combined with similar acts of other or of the same harming agents (Feinberg 1984, 225–7). It is hard to claim, for instance, that any single case of tax fraud represents a significant fiscal harm or triggers a significant loss of social services, but the combined impact of widespread and repeated fraud could be substantial. In the cost-of-crime literature, accumulative harms, once monetized, are sometimes treated as "indirect costs" and cannot be attributed to any particular offender separately (see Cohen 2005, 26).

Standardization, Measurement, and Commensurability

These challenges might seem more technical than the others—and more obviously related to counting, literally—but appearances can be deceiving and each has conceptual implications. Standardization is not just about units of measure (e.g., numbers of individuals, businesses, etc.), but also about how we value those individuals, businesses, etc., and the harms that befall them; similarly, matters of measurement and commensurability speak to bigger societal issues.

Standardization

Individuals, institutions, and the environment, all of which can bear harms from criminal or other activities, come in heterogeneous circumstances or forms that suggest differences in how constituents of each group—or "class"— of bearer might accrue harm, but a harm assessment would be analytically intractable without some standardization for each group. Speaking to individuals, victimologists (e.g., Spalek 2017) stress that the hurtfulness

[26] Moreover, as von Hirsch and Jareborg (1991, 33–4) and others (e.g., Husak 2008) note, drug use and its harms may occur with the consent of the users and the victim's consent ordinarily eliminates criminal liability.

of a crime, hence the realization of harm in our lexicon, depends on the specific situation of the victim, which might differ greatly from one victim to another. For example, a person who is physically, psychologically, or socially vulnerable might suffer more harm—or harm of greater intensity or longer duration—from the same crime than someone who is not. However, a broad-based empirical study cannot assess the harms to each and every victim fully and separately. The exercise might not stretch to "infinity," but it would require tracing, interviewing, or monitoring victims over a number of years and controlling for individuals' differences. Along similar lines, neither businesses, nongovernment organizations, public agencies, nor the social and physical environment come in strictly homogeneous units. Businesses, for example, vary by size, scope, resources, and management practices. Thus, some amount of standardization, at least for individuals and likely for others, seems unavoidable.

Measurement

Under the banner of measurement, we focus on two related areas of concern, first, the difference between gross and net harms and, second, quantification.

Gross v. Net harms

Some criminal activities might yield direct or indirect gains that could offset losses associated with harms, but should they be tallied in the assessment? Recalling the foregoing discussion of standing and perspective, the immediate and reverberating effects of Afghanistan's drug-related revenues provide a good example of potential gains at the start of a supply chain, but gains might accrue elsewhere, too. For example, at the finish, drug users might experience both ill-effects of drug use and some benefits (e.g., appetite stimulation and relaxation). Some scholars who assess the costs of drug use subtract those benefits (see Pacula et al. 2009, 81, for a discussion of approaches). If one were to assess harms along a supply chain, from start to finish, should they subtract the gains from the losses? This question could be framed as one of "gross" versus "net" harms or, equivalently, as one of "partial accounting" versus "full accounting." In Greenfield and Paoli (2012) and other work we have argued that full accounting is necessary for a truly comprehensive analyses of the consequences of criminal activities and the policies intended to address them, preliminary to what we call a "notional" benefit–cost analysis, and in later chapters, especially Chapter 7, we return to this issue.

Quantification

As many scholars have noted (e.g., MacCoun et al. 1996; Caulkins and Reuter 1997, 1147; Brand and Price 2000, x; Kopp and Besson 2009; Sparrow 2008, 181–90), data on the harms of crime and related concepts are often scarce and problems of measurement all too apparent. We might be able to conceptualize a basis for quantifying a harm and even an estimation method, but still lack the data or other technical means to quantify the harm. Consider the relatively simple case of the harm to a business's reputation resulting from its employees' involvement in a drug-trafficking operation. One might try to assess the reputational effect of a trafficking incident on the value of the business, but how much of a change in value, be it measured in profits, returns, stock prices, or some other unit, should one attribute to the criminal entanglement? A variety of statistical methods might be brought to bear to isolate the effect, but it might be hard to find the effect among all the other factors at play.

Insomuch as harms can be quantified, we might also ask for how long or across what geography. For example, should we measure harms for a year, a decade, or a lifetime? Von Hirsch and Jareborg (1991) propose a year, but, as we address in later chapters, this might be too short to accommodate recurring or lasting harms, such as those associated with human health or environmental degradation. This question ties back to concerns for infinitude, standardization, and causality, even in the absence of quantification, but it becomes all the more pressing when we try to put numbers to harm and must consider related computational issues.[27]

Speaking to the conceptual dimensions of quantification, one might make the case that any insistence on quantification is, itself, normative because it suggests that only harms that are quantifiable should "count." In excluding harms that are nonquantifiable, the policy community risks inadvertently judging their importance—or unimportance—by implicitly assigning them a weight of zero in the policy calculus. In prior work, we have referred to this as a "quantification bias." As a famous sentiment often attributed to Einstein, but perhaps better attributed to Cameron (1963, 13), reminds us, "not everything that can be counted counts, and not everything that counts can be counted."

[27] Among economists, for example, the question of intertemporal "discount rates," which capture the relative value of money received at different points in time, prompts debate and can alter the outcomes of policy analyses.

Commensurability

Caulkins and Reuter (1997, 1148) ask rhetorically, "With what common unit can one denominate both battered children and burglaries?" and allude to a principle challenge of assessing harm. Many types of harm are not commensurable; that is, they cannot be measured or compared by a common standard, whether quantitative or otherwise (see Caulkins and Reuter 1997, 1148; Caulkins et al. 2011; Sen 2009, 395–6), at least not fully and, perhaps, not usefully. A single measure, be it an index or monetary estimate, might capture some facets of the loss or degradation of life, institutional integrity, and environmental quality, but certainly not all. Comparisons of harms across different classes of bearers—individuals, institutions, and environments—pose special challenges insomuch as it might be possible to develop an internally consistent measure of harm within each class—such as von Hirsch and Jareborg's (1991) "standard of living" for individual victims of crime—that circumvents many of the challenges noted already, but that measure might not apply to other classes.

Acknowledging incommensurability—and working within its strictures—requires a level of analytical comfort with complexity, normativity, and the necessity of underlying judgment. As Sen (2009, 395) argues, "those who are insistent that human beings cannot cope with determining what to do unless all values are somehow reduced to no more than one, are evidently comfortable with counting ('is it more or is it less?') but not with judgement ('is this more important than the other?')."

Any effort to reduce harms to a single, simple measure, such as a crime- or drug-harm index (Section 3.2) or cost-of-crime estimates (Section 3.3), must limit itself to harms that are amenable to that measure. Commensurability, albeit desirable for some purposes, comes at a price, specifically a loss of information and, as addressed previously, vis-à-vis quantification, the possibility of analytical bias.[28]

3.5 Concluding Remarks

Notwithstanding the centrality of harm to crime, criminal policy, and the governance of security, the review of literatures in this chapter indicates that few methodologies have been proposed, let alone implemented, to

[28] For a fuller discussion of analytical biases, see Greenfield and Paoli (2012).

assess empirically the harms of crimes as distinct from the perceived seriousness or cost of crime.

It is always hard to know why people abstain from doing things, but the conceptual and technical challenges under review in this chapter have most likely dampened interest in harm as an alternative lens. Our review has identified problems of scope, scale, and commensurability and points to issues of data deficiencies. The challenges are all the more daunting if one addresses harm as a concern that spans a range of interests, not all of which are amenable to quantification or indexation. Only recently in the scheme of criminology's history have we developed a framework (Greenfield and Paoli 2013; see Chapter 4) to assess the harms of crime that, in reaching out across disciplines, addresses many of the challenges. We present the framework and spell out its limitations in the following chapter.

Along similar lines, we suspect that these analytical challenges have done little to aid in the recruitment of policy-makers to the "cause" of harm as a guiding principle and evaluative criterion, when other forces already act as beacons. A large literature (e.g., Garland 2001a; Tonry 2007) suggests that policy-makers prefer making decisions about criminal policy to satisfy what Durkheim ([1893] 1997) called the "collective conscience"—the dominant morality in a "descriptive sense" (Gert and Gert 2017, n.p.)—even if the decisions might clash with "universal ethical claims" or assessments of benefit–cost trade-offs. On other occasions, policy-makers might have felt bound to act upon the "moral panics" (Cohen 1972) developed by media and moral entrepreneurs around certain sets of "folk devils" and their deviant activities. In so doing, the policy-makers may have served to amplify those panics. Moreover, as Bauman (2000) and others (e.g., Young 2007) note, criminal policy has been misused increasingly to placate the growing anxieties of the middle classes at living in the ever more uncertain and insecure world of the late modernity.

In fairness to policy-makers, we realize that they must respond to immediate emergencies, such as terrorist attacks and mass shootings, and to other shocking or fearsome criminal events, and cannot simply bide their time, waiting around for the results of a multiyear academic study or long-term policy evaluation. And, insomuch as policy-makers have sought to use harm as a guiding principle for policy-making, the lack of a strong evidentiary base for making decisions about criminal policy, the underdevelopment of the concept of harm, and, as we have shown in this chapter, the challenges of assessing harms empirically, might have discouraged them.

One might have expected criminologists to approach "harm" with intellectual relish, befitting Beccaria's proposal to assess crime in terms of damages (Chapter 1) but they have not yet taken it up wholeheartedly, even if interest in the topic has grown in some quarters of the discipline, such as critical and green criminology, and in criminal and related policy. As the pages of Chapter 2 suggest, several other factors—in addition to the challenges—likely have contributed to the underdevelopment of harm assessment, including the long-standing focus of many mainstream criminologists on the causes of crime, rather than the consequences (Paoli and Greenfield 2015), their lack of familiarity with criminal law and theory (Zedner 2011), and their deep-seated aversion for purportedly "unscientific" normative theorizing (Bottoms 2008).

In the next chapter, we present our answer to Beccaria's call, namely our harm assessment framework. Cognizant of the challenges facing past—and any—attempts to assess harm systematically and empirically, we have sought to fill a gap in analytical capabilities and "add value" to decision-making on criminal policy and the governance of security as it relates to crime with a firm analytical foundation.

4

A Framework to Assess the Harms of Crime

4.1 Introduction

This chapter sets out our approach to harm assessment. It provides the methodological foundation for the analyses undertaken in Chapters 5 and 6 and the policy applications proposed in Chapter 7. The chapter draws from Greenfield and Paoli (2013), "A framework to assess the harms of crime," but it also advances that work by delving into the framework's methodological origins, strengths, and weaknesses, and by incorporating lessons from our empirical applications, more-recent findings of related literatures, and the expertise of our colleagues.

Much as we did in that article, we begin by recapitulating the conceptual and technical challenges of harm assessment. It is our intent to give readers a convenient reference to material that plays a prominent role in this chapter, but not to repeat all the content of the previous chapter, verbatim.[1] As our presentation of the framework unfolds, we explain how each component, be it a tool or step in the assessment process, responds in part or whole to each challenge. Having developed the framework as a means to respond pragmatically to those challenges, our ability to do so represents a measure of our success and speaks to the validity of our approach; that is, its ability to assess that which we intend it to assess.

Morality, Cultural and Socioeconomic Variability, and Legitimacy

These challenges result from the inherent normativity of calling an outcome "harmful" in the first place. The decision to apply this label depends

[1] We explore the challenges in greater depth in Chapter 3.

Assessing the Harms of Crime. Victoria A. Greenfield and Letizia Paoli, Oxford University Press. © Victoria A. Greenfield & Letizia Paoli 2022. DOI: 10.1093/oso/9780198758174.003.0004

on the identification of legitimate claimants and interests according to the "dominant political morality" (MacCormick 1982, 30), which, in turn, depends on a society's particular cultural and socioeconomic arrangements. Pertinent analytical questions involve "standing," defined as a rightful stake in a particular matter (see Appendix A); for example, does a potential claimant have standing, hence legitimacy, in a harm assessment and, if claimants' interests diverge or conflict how should they be weighted in the assessment?

Infinitude and Causality

Both of these challenges involve matters of limitations and boundaries. The challenge of infinitude arises from the infeasibility of creating an exhaustive list of harms, owing to both the limits of imagination and the possibility of harms begetting harms through secondary, tertiary, and nth-order effects. In Chapter 3, we note, for example, the potential for intergenerational ripple effects. The challenge of causality arises largely from the temporal, spatial, and behavioral distance—or "remoteness"—that can separate conduct from consequences and complicate attribution (Ryberg 2004, 64–6; Simester and von Hirsch 2011, 70–88), but "accumulative harms" (Feinberg 1984, 225–7) can pose similar challenges. An accumulative harm only arises if the act that triggers the harm is combined with other similar acts, making it difficult to attribute the harm to a particular act or actor.

Standardization, Measurement, and Commensurability

These challenges, albeit seemingly "just" technical, have conceptual implications. As a practical matter, some standardization (e.g., an average individual) is unavoidable in a broad-based empirical study, but the hurtfulness of a crime depends partly on the specific situation of the victim. The problems of measurement and commensurability can be stated simply: not everything that matters can be measured or compared usefully (Caulkins and Reuter 1997, 1148; Caulkins et al. 2011), by conventional methods. As a corollary, measuring something usefully might require considering the negative and positive consequences, if gains can accompany losses.

In reaching across disciplines and literatures, the framework provides means to overcome many but not all of those challenges. To start, we join Feinberg (1984, 31–6), and others who treat harm, broadly understood, as a setback to a rightful stakeholder's legitimate interests (Greenfield and Paoli 2013, 864) and accept some normativity as inevitable, but our approach and its transparency, including explicit criteria for the legitimacy of claimants and interests, allow us to circumscribe the normative and proceed analytically.[2]

4.2 Overview of Our Approach

The harm assessment framework consists of a set of analytical tools and a multistep process for applying them. The tools, in order of application, are a data template for articulating the "business model" or "script" of a criminal activity,[3] a taxonomy for identifying the types and bearers of harms associated with that activity, scales for evaluating the severity and incidence of those harms, and a matrix for ranking and prioritizing them. (We refer to potential claimants as "bearers" and we distinguish them by "class"—i.e., individuals, private-sector entities, government, and the social and physical environment.) The taxonomy specifies "types" of harms in relation to damages to the "interest dimensions" of each class of bearer. The first dimension is functional integrity, which can apply in some form to all classes of bearers. The other three dimensions—material support, reputation, and privacy and autonomy—can apply to individuals, private-sector entities, and government, but not to the environment.

When we use the word "harm" in our framework we refer to a multifaceted phenomenon, consisting of a negative outcome of a particular type, severity, and incidence that emerges from a particular activity or set of

[2] We discuss these criteria in Section 4.3.

[3] In our first articles (Greenfield and Paoli 2013; Paoli et al. 2013; Greenfield et al. 2016), we spoke only of the "business model," borrowing from economics, but here we have added "script." We have done so because the latter resonates with a broader range of crimes, not just economically oriented crimes, and because it has become a term of art in criminology (Cornish 1994; see also Haelterman 2016; Leclerc 2014). However, we have retained "business model," because the term is, in our view, a more immediate, if still imperfect, fit for economically oriented activities, such as drug trafficking and production. As we assess the harms of such activities in Chapters 5 and 6, we speak only of traffickers' and producers' business models in those chapters. In other contexts—e.g., an ongoing study with Sheremeti on the harms of state crimes in Kosovo—we consider "business model" inappropriate and use, instead, "script."

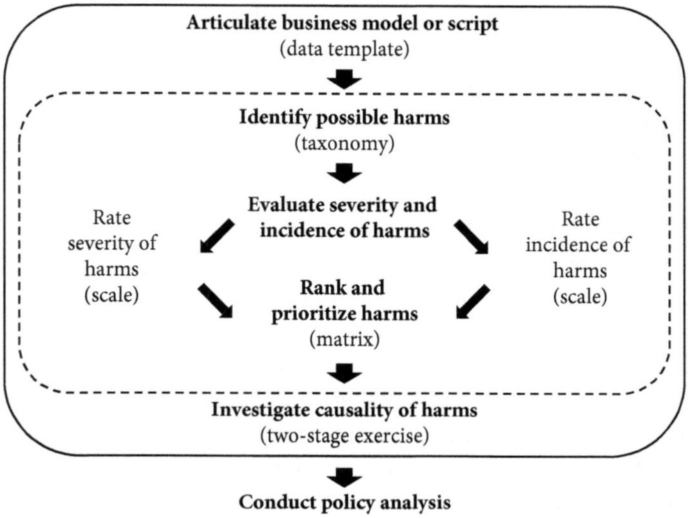

Figure 4.1 Harm assessment process
Source: Authors' adaptation of Greenfield and Paoli (2012) and Paoli et al. (2012, 2013).

activities and is borne by particular individuals, entities, or the environment. To be somewhat more formal, we can describe the unit of observation for a specific harm as a "bundle" of attributes; namely, (1) activity, including a harming event; (2) type, by interest dimension; (3) bearer; (4) severity; and (5) incidence that can be parsed more or less finely.[4] Any one of the five can serve as a point of reference or sorting mechanism; if, for example, we group harms by an activity, such as cocaine or human trafficking, it remains for us to identify particular events that can give rise to harm in that context and to specify the type, bearer, severity, and incidence. Regardless of the nomenclature, the framework, including the assessment process, should account for each attribute as comprehensively and consistently as possible.

As shown in Figure 4.1, the process of harm assessment begins with the characterization of the criminal activity and the articulation of the business model or script and ends with an investigation of the causality of harms. The final step addresses causality, first, by considering the distance between

[4] We discuss these attributes in Sections 4.3 and 4.4. Feinberg (1984, 24), who did not draw such distinctions, spoke of "wrongful harm" and restricted criminal law's focus to them. Instead, we are able to attribute—and confine—wrongfulness to the activity and consider all harms resulting from it.

harms and activities, and, second, by examining the extent to which harms are intrinsic to an activity or arise from policy and related law enforcement practices. This step supports comparisons of alternative policy scenarios, including the status quo. The assessment process does not produce point estimates or fuel an index; rather, it yields rankings of harms by class of bearer that can be used to establish priorities for criminal and related policy.

The components of the framework reach across disciplines, but they draw most heavily from the literatures on harm assessment, most notably in criminal-law theory, and on risk assessment, primarily—but not exclusively—in the national security community.

Von Hirsch and Jareborg (1991)[5] offer a well-structured attempt to categorize the harms of crime. Focusing on individuals and the damages associated with common interpersonal crimes, such as theft, burglary, and assault, they develop guidelines for assessing the typical impact that a crime has on the immediate victim's standard of living. In a loose adaptation of Sen's (1987) work, they define "standard of living" in terms of economic and noneconomic "means" and "capabilities" for achieving a certain quality of life (von Hirsch and Jareborg 1991, 7, 10–11).[6] Like Sen, they focus less on outcomes, such as "actual life quality or goal achievement," and more on life's opportunities and the ability to achieve, but differing from him, they consider means as on par with capabilities. Sen (1993, 33) does not assign means or commodities, such as income, wealth, or resources, any intrinsic value; instead, he treats them as instrumental to attaining capabilities: "These variables are not part of the evaluative space, though they can indirectly influence the evaluation through their effects on variables included in that space." Von Hirsch and Jareborg's version of "standard of living" serves as the benchmark for assessing the severity of harms in their framework. We take a similar approach in crafting our benchmarks, but we have tried to maintain closer alignment with Sen's theory.[7]

[5] Von Hirsch et al. (2005) restate the approach with modest revisions.

[6] Sen treats capabilities as a manifestation of the freedom to be or do (see the discussion in Section 4.3 of this chapter), and the standard of living as a subset of well-being, but his views on the distinction between the two have shifted over time. He first argues that the living standard concerns only material capabilities, and that well-being encompasses material and nonmaterial concerns, but he later reconsiders and asserts that the difference between the two constructs is not materialism, but perspective—both constructs encompass material and nonmaterial concerns, but the living standard is strictly "self-regarding" and well-being can derive from "sources other than the nature of one's life" (Sen 1984; 1987, 26–9). Thus, the standard of living constitutes a subset of well-being. He maintains the latter distinction in later writings (Sen 1993, 36–8) as do we in our framework.

[7] As Sen, himself, has noted (1993, 31), the "underlying theory" sometimes presents interpretive and operational challenges. We refer readers to Sen (1987, 1993, 2009), and Clark

The national security community faces similar concerns about negative outcomes or bad consequences in military operations (e.g., injury or death, property damage or destruction, and mission degradation or failure) and has long used a combination of risk-management processes and tools for risk assessment and mitigation that bears directly on our effort.[8] The related literature and military doctrine (e.g., Greenfield and Camm 2005; National Academies of Sciences, Engineering, and Medicine 2018; US Department of the Army 1998, 2006, 2014; US Department of the Army, Marine Corps, Navy, and Air Force 2001) offer a five-step risk-management process (see Section 2.5 and Figure 2.2) that calls on users to identify and assess hazards on the basis of the severity and probability of bad consequences. A complementary matrix—which we have adapted for our purposes in this chapter (see Section 4.4 and Table 4.3)—combines ratings of severity and probability to arrive at priorities for risk mitigation and controls. Some police and government agencies in Australia and the United Kingdom (UK) employ similar approaches (e.g., Tusikov 2012), usually known as "threat assessments," but, to our knowledge, they have not been in play as long and have had less opportunity to evolve.

Although a widely used and enduring tool, scholars warn of the limitations of risk matrixes, including insufficient scientific testing, and the dangers of their indiscriminate use (see National Academies of Sciences, Engineering, and Medicine 2018, 148–9, citing Cox 2008 and Rozell 2015). For example, if bad actors, such as terrorists, are more likely to attack high-impact targets, correlations between severity and probability can invert the results. Simplifying what are typically multidimensional concerns to just two parameters (i.e., severity and probability) has also raised red flags. In our work, we also employ a two-dimensional matrix, but we would argue that, in parsing harms carefully by attributes, breaking down probability into its constituent parts, and dealing in bandwidths, not point estimates (see Section 4.4), we factor-in substantial complexity.[9]

(2005, 2006) for an introduction to the capabilities-based approach and to Bruni et al. (2008, 5–7), Clark (2005, 2006), Nussbaum (2003), Sen (2005, 154), and Williams (1987) for critiques.

[8] For a more complete discussion of the national security community's approach to risk management and its relevance to this effort, see Greenfield and Paoli (2012, 10–11).

[9] Others, such as the MoRiLE program (see Chapter 3, Section 3.2), have also introduced substantial complexity to their efforts, albeit eventually reducing their analysis to a single point estimate. In Section 4.4, we discuss additional concerns about quantification, including with respect to our matrix.

The national security community also emphasizes the necessity of understanding the underlying or root causes of bad consequences, hence harms, in developing plans for mitigation and control and for considering trade-offs among options. It raises the possibility that it might not be feasible—or even desirable—to drive risk to zero and suggests the need for benefit–cost analysis, a theme that we return to in this and later chapters.

In addition, we appropriate insights from the long-standing debate on harm reduction in the drug-policy literature (e.g., Caulkins and Reuter 1997; Caulkins et al. 2011; MacCoun 1998; MacCoun and Reuter 2001; MacCoun et al. 1996; Newcombe 1992; Nutt et al. 2010; Wodak and Sanders 1995).[10] The literature offers cautionary tales on the use of vocabulary, the limits of measurement and commensurability, and the dangers of politicization, but it also lays down markers for methodological advances. For example, MacCoun (1998, 1202) models "total harm" by the average harm per use of a drug, such as heroin or cocaine, for users and nonusers, and "total use" by the number of users, the quantity of drugs each user consumes, and the distribution of consumption.[11] In effect, he treats harm as multifaceted, setting the stage for our attribute bundles.

We discuss each of the components of the framework in greater detail in Sections 4.3–4.5, dedicating separate sections to the discussions of the taxonomy and the scales and matrix, which we view as central to our approach.

4.3 The Taxonomy of Bearers and Types of Harms

The taxonomy, which represents the heart and soul of our approach, gives practical meaning to "harm" by calling out the "bearers" or potential claimants of harm and the "types" of harms they might experience in association with each criminal activity under consideration (Table 4.1). In so doing, the taxonomy confronts issues of legitimacy head on.

As Sen's writing on "Well-being, agency, and living standards" (1993, 36–8) implies, we cannot speak of harm in isolation, because harm can only exist in relation to someone or something, from a particular perspective.[12]

[10] Hunt et al. (2003) date the debate to the late 1980s. For a detailed discussion of this literature and its implications for our framework, see Greenfield and Paoli (2012) and the related commentary.

[11] For a looser conceptualization of "total harm," see Sherman (2007).

[12] See also Sen's discussion of "value-objects and evaluative spaces" (1993, 32–3).

Table 4.1 Taxonomy of types and bearers of harm

Type of harm by interest dimension	Bearer of harm by class			
	Individuals	Private sector	Government	Environment
Functional integrity	X[a]	X[b]	X[b]	X[c]
Material support	X	X	X	n/a
Reputation	X	X	X	n/a
Privacy and autonomy	X	X	X	n/a

Source: Authors' adaptation of Greenfield and Paoli (2013) and Paoli et al. (2012, 2013).

Notes:

X = applicable; n/a = not applicable.

[a] Functional integrity refers to physical, psychological, and intellectual integrity.

[b] Functional integrity refers to operational integrity.

[c] Functional integrity refers to physical, operational, and aesthetic integrity.

Thus, we cannot proceed without naming a "who" or "what" and, as a consequence, we cannot avoid weighing-in on the legitimacy of particular bearers—that is, their standing—and interests.

Our taxonomy distinguishes among four classes of bearers, consisting of individuals; private-sector entities, including businesses and nongovernmental organizations (NGOs); government; and the social and physical environment (Table 4.1). So far, we have implicitly equated "individuals" and "humans" and conceptualized nonhuman animals as either property of humans or part of the physical environment. If we were to undertake an assessment in which nonhuman animals featured prominently (see, e.g., Presser 2013), we could identify them separately as autonomous bearers. We define "government" broadly as consisting of all state entities (executive, legislative, or judicial), including local, regional, and national bodies. If relevant to a particular assessment, we could extend the definition to include supranational entities and other publicly funded and publicly managed bodies, such as those of the European Union (EU) and United Nations (UN), or allocate them to their own class of bearers. In framing the environment, we delineate the "social environment," which concerns the interactive regions (i.e., relationships) between and among individuals and institutions and the "physical environment."

By implication, the constituents of these classes, subject to just a few exclusions, have standing in our assessments. By giving them standing, we go beyond the liberal tradition that has focused largely on individuals or at most on nonhuman animals (see e.g., Braithwaite and Pettit 1990, 70 and our discussion in Section 2.3) and we recognize private- and public-sector institutions as well the social and physical environment as bearers of harm. In our view, this extension might ease the frequent counterposing in criminal law theory of the harm and offense principles (e.g., Feinberg 1985; Simester and von Hirsch 2006, 2011; see Section 2.3). The latter, in fact, has been introduced to justify criminalizing extreme cases of pornography and damage to civic amenities, such as excessive noise and littering. After giving the government and social environment—i.e., the community—standing as bearers, the need diminishes for a separate principle to justify criminalizing activities that are not harmful to single individuals but have been supposed to be harmful to the government or community.

We present our exclusions and delve into their significance at the close of this section, but we note here that we regard perpetrators as bearers in our applications of the framework and, with very few exceptions, rate the severity and incidence of the harms they incur along with all others equivalently. We then assign priority rankings to those harms just as we do the rest, but we report them as harms to perpetrators, so that the policy community can decide whether and how to treat them in policy-making.

Harms can arise from damages to functional integrity, material support, reputation, or privacy and autonomy, but not all types of harm are relevant to all bearers. Following von Hirsch and Jareborg (1991), who, themselves, draw from Sen (1987), we treat these interest dimensions as representing capabilities or paths to attaining a certain quality of life, specifically the "standard of living," or, by analogy, an entity's "institutional mission" or the environment's "sustainability," which we discuss in Section 4.4. By including material support as a direct path, we also depart from Sen, who does not consider means as equivalent to capabilities; however, by framing such means as purely instrumental, we depart only slightly.

We attempt to allocate harms to their ultimate bearers, taking account of the individuals, businesses, NGOs, and other entities that compose a community, but recognize that some harms are partly or wholly communal and apportion them to the environment—either social or physical—as an independent bearer of harm. In this regard, we differ from Kopp and Besson (2009) and Dorn and van de Bunt (2010) who take an aggregative approach to "systemic" harm. In Kopp and Besson (2009, 312), for example, systemic harms would include societal harm (e.g., corruption of public officials), community harm (e.g., neighborhood disintegration and the impairment of the business community), and certain economic harm (e.g., market distortions, lack of competition, and barriers to entry). Our approach, however, requires additional care in allocating the harms that Kopp and Besson and others would call systemic.

We also acknowledge that, in some instances, we are only reaching as far as the near-ultimate bearers of harm, irrespective of any communal effects. For example, one could take the position that most, if not all, harms borne by the private sector and government are borne ultimately and to varying degrees by particular individuals, such as shareholders, employees, taxpayers, and residents. Given the practical realities of data availability and analytical complexities, it would be difficult, perhaps impossible, to derive all such results at the individual level.

Our decision to cast a wider net than "individuals" stems largely from our experience working across disciplines and with related literatures. For example, one of us, Greenfield, has worked with economic models (e.g., Burfisher 2011) that provide roles for private-sector entities, government, and the physical environment, albeit typically attempting to capture the pass-through of effects to individuals or households. In addition, notwithstanding legal theory's almost exclusive focus on the harms to individuals (see, e.g., Roxin 2006, 8–47, for Germanic exceptions), our examination of legal history (e.g., Berman 1983; Riggsby 2016), legal theory (e.g., Duff, 2007; Hefendehl et al. 2003), critical criminology (e.g., Henry and Milovanovic 1996, 102–5; Presser 2013), green criminology (e.g., White 2013), restorative justice and regulatory theory (e.g., Braithwaite 2002; Drahos 2017), international criminal justice (Daly and Proietti-Scifoni 2011; Karstedt 2014), and the governance of security (e.g., Buzan, 1983; Johnston and Shearing 2003) also influenced the choice. We discuss the literatures and the lessons we have drawn from them in Chapter 2, but note here that leading thinkers as well as the policies, jurisprudences, and practices in each field acknowledge the interests of private and public entities, communities, and the physical environment with its nonhuman inhabitants as worthy of protection, thus supporting the case for the broader perspective.

Harms to Individuals

We delineate the types of harms to individuals much as von Hirsch and Jareborg (1991) delineate them—in terms of damages to particular interest dimensions—but note a handful of differences in a crosswalk between their dimensions and ours. Von Hirsch and Jareborg (1991, 19) set out four interest dimensions, consisting of physical integrity, material support and amenity, freedom from humiliation, and privacy or autonomy, which we have recast as functional integrity, material support, reputation, and privacy and autonomy.

We expand "physical integrity," which we rename "functional integrity," to encompass physical, psychological, and intellectual damages, among which we also consider the psychological consequences of affronts to dignity.[13] Sen (1987) uses "functioning" as a term of art whereas we use "functional" more colloquially, to encompass a range of capabilities that make it possible to proceed effectively in life, business, etc. The inclusion of psychological losses is consistent with Sen (1987, 26–7) and accords with the prevailing opinion of the drug-related harm literature.[14] For examples, see MacCoun and Reuter (2001), MacCoun et al. (1996), MacDonald et al. (2005), Newcombe (1992) and our discussion in Section 3.2. Victimologists, such as Spalek (2017) and public health researchers, such as Oram et al. (2012), also suggest the relevance of the psychological and emotional impact of crime (see Section 3.3). Nussbaum, a philosopher and distinguished professor of law and ethics, refers (1997, 287; 2003, 41) to the capabilities of "senses, imagination, and thought," "emotion," and "practical reason" as components of a larger list of capabilities that pertain to quality of life.

Physical, psychological, and intellectual damages can take a variety of forms and arise independently or jointly. Physical incursions can range from death, at one extreme, to momentary pain or discomfort, at the other. Psychological damages, which can be almost as wide-ranging, might occur along with physical injuries or separately. They might arise from humiliation, which von Hirsch and Jareborg treat as a separate interest dimension, and from affronts to dignity. Similarly, an intellectual damage might be coupled or uncoupled. An individual might be beaten to the point of permanent cognitive loss or, as might occur in the trafficking of minors, denied access to education.

[13] Our initial applications of the framework to cocaine and human trafficking do not include intellectual damages.

[14] In a break from his earlier writing, Sen (1987, 27) argues that "Being psychologically well-adjusted may not be a 'material' functioning, but it is hard to claim that achievement is of no intrinsic importance to one's standard of living. In fact, any achievement that is rooted in the life that oneself leads (or can lead), rather than arising from other objectives, does have a claim to being directly relevant to one's standard of living." Von Hirsch and Jareborg (1991, 23), however, omit psychological harm as "too much of a catchall to be of help."

In our framing of "material support"—which von Hirsch and Jareborg refer to as "material support and amenity"—we too cover a spectrum of conditions, ranging from bare subsistence to modest comfort and luxury, but we also consider the implications of distinguishing between means and capabilities. Although we include material support in our evaluative space, we see it as a stepping stone and, in our ratings of the severity of damages, assess the extent to which material damages would impinge on the individual's ability to function.[15] Following Sen (1987), we view material support as instrumental and, in our applications, address the consequences for analyses that cross borders and cultures.

Damages to "reputation"—a category of our own initiative, but deriving from legal precedent (e.g., McGonagle 2016)—arise from actions or events affecting others' view of the individual. They might involve instances of mistreatment or exploitation, as could occur in cases of human trafficking, or stem from instances of physical abuse or mere association, but they cannot emerge unless a third party, community, or larger society becomes aware of the episode. For example, if only the victim and attacker know an attack has occurred, it cannot have a reputational effect. However, if others become aware of the attack, it might affect their opinion of the victim, potentially resulting in loss of respect, confidence, or trust, depending on the circumstances.

We group violations of "privacy and autonomy" together, as closely related but conceptually distinct phenomenon.[16] A violation of privacy, such as an unauthorized entry or the control of personal documents, such as a passport, might occur in a burglary, kidnapping, or case of human trafficking. Some such events could also entail a related, but additional loss of autonomy. A violation of autonomy would restrict an individual's ability to function independently and might occur in conjunction with a violation of

[15] Clark (2006, 3) provides a useful synthesis, "we must consider how well people are able to function with the goods and services at their disposal." As a practical matter, Clark (2005) and others who have applied Sen's approach appear to start with activities and commodities, which they trace to functionings and, by extension, the living standard. Perhaps most famously, the Human Development Index (HDI), which is rooted in Sen's work on capabilities, includes income directly along with life expectancy and schooling (see Human Development Index (HDI) | Human Development Reports (undp.org)).

[16] Von Hirsch and Jareborg (1991) refer to this interest dimension as "privacy or autonomy" and tend to refer to privacy and autonomy synonymously. In our initial applications of the framework to cocaine and human trafficking, we did not draw a distinction either and, in some publications, we omitted the term autonomy entirely. Having become better acquainted with Sen's catalogue of work on freedom, we have since come to value the distinction and incorporate it in our research.

privacy, as in a case of kidnapping, but it could occur separately or in conjunction with violations of other interests. Physical or psychological abuse or intellectual deprivation might also result in a diminution of autonomy.

Autonomy presents conceptual challenges, because it is tied to privacy and it is also a close cousin of "freedom," which underlies Sen's notion of capabilities. In effect, freedom wears two hats in Sen's underlying work.[17] In the first instance, he treats freedoms as the bedrock of his capabilities-based approach; for example, in his early writing, he describes capabilities as "notions of freedoms, in the positive sense: what real opportunities you have regarding the life you may lead" and, in later essays, as "the freedom to attain different kinds of alternative lives" (Sen 1987, 36; 2008, 23). However, he also values freedom in its own right, for its intrinsic importance, "Acting freely and being able to choose may be directly conducive to well-being, not just because more freedom might make better alternatives available" (Sen 1993, 39).[18] Our evaluations of autonomy give due credit to that intrinsic value.

Referring back to Chapter 2 (Section 2.5), we note that our four interest dimensions closely match the interests that Adam Smith ([1763], 1896, 5) and, more recently, Buzan (1983, 19–20) single out in their discussions of threats to individual security. In addition, turning to Chapter 3 (Section 3.2) we also acknowledge several similarities (and a few differences), in relation to Doyal and Gough's (1991) theory of human needs along the lines of Gough's (2014) comparison of their theory with Nussbaum's (2003) and Sen's work (2009).

Harms to Other Bearers

We reinterpret the interest dimensions, to the extent necessary, to create analogies for the private sector, government, and the environment.

Each of the four interest dimensions is relevant to the private sector and government, but not without some adaptation. We equate the functional integrity of a business, NGO, or public agency with its operational integrity rather than its physical, psychological, or intellectual integrity. Does a criminal activity cause damages that interrupt, interfere with, or prevent

[17] Clark (2005, 1343) provides a good discussion of this point and additional citations.

[18] Recall that Sen (1987, 29; 1993, 36–8) defines the standard of living as a subset of well-being.

an entity from producing or providing goods or services? We treat material support largely as directly observable effects on balance sheets, income statements, budgets, etc. For example, a business, NGO, or public agency that bears the costs of repairing equipment damaged in the commission of a crime or unwittingly compensates employees who engage in criminal activities on-the-clock, experiences a material loss. Such entities might also suffer a loss of privacy; for instance, through unauthorized access to and possible misuse of the entity's premises or sensitive or proprietary information. Unauthorized access might occur in cases of burglary or tax fraud, during which business documents, official documents, and other data are especially vulnerable. Corruption that leads an entity down an operational path that it would not otherwise choose, might also damage the entity's autonomy. Damage to a business, NGO, or public agency's reputation can occur under a variety of circumstances, including those involving an employee, official, or representative's engagement in crime, but we contend that such entities also experience some reputational loss whenever rule or law breaking occurs with sufficient notoriety to leave the impression of weakness. Ultimately, a reputational effect might track to a loss of respect, confidence, or trust in an institution much as it did for the individual, if other individuals, a community, or a larger society become aware of the underlying event or its aftermath.

One could reasonably argue that losses to a business or other entity's functionality, privacy, autonomy, and reputation ultimately boil down to matters of material support. For example, accessing and misusing an entity's sensitive or proprietary information might render the entity less able to pursue its institutional interests and impinge on its finances. As suggested previously, one could also take this line of reasoning a step further and argue that all or nearly all harms to entities, regardless of their type, eventually pass through to individuals. But, making those connections through a chain of evidence presents practical challenges.

For the environment, in both its social and its physical manifestations, we limit the analysis to functional integrity, consisting of physical, operational, and aesthetic integrity. The remaining dimensions of harm—material support, reputation, and privacy and autonomy—are either inapplicable or duplicative because they would emerge elsewhere in the taxonomy, as with respect to individuals, etc. Not all environmental harms are strictly communal and it might be possible to trace some damages to other bearers, but in many settings, including those in which property rights are ill-defined, that attribution is infeasible, at least empirically.

Concerns about the physical environment could encompass mistreatment of nonhuman animals and plant life; pollution of air, water, soil, noise and light; inaccessibility of open spaces; and obstruction or destruction of landscapes (e.g., Brisman and South 2017; Presser 2013; White 2010, 2013). At the start of a cocaine supply chain, which we explore in Chapter 6, fertilizers, herbicides, and other pesticides that growers apply to coca, the plant from which cocaine derives, might contaminate ground water and waterways; at the end, drugs might find their way into water in human waste (van Nuijs et al. 2009).

Concerns about the social environment include public nuisance, social fragmentation, and community disassociation. In addition to impinging on the physical environment, as they sometimes do, drug dealing and prostitution might also, for example, create a persistent public nuisance, resulting in the de facto appropriation of public spaces in some neighborhoods. Research in the UK by Innes (2004) and Bottoms (2006) has shown that even minor incivilities, such as "youths hanging around," litter, and graffiti can generate widespread concern, because they are perceived as signals of a lack of neighborhood safety. The anti-social behaviour orders (ASBOs), the hybrid civil–criminal preventive orders the UK introduced in 1998, were intended to tackle these incivilities. As discussed in Section 2.2, von Hirsch and Simester (2006) and other scholars (e.g., Bottoms 2006; Duff 2007) resort to the "offense principle" to justify the criminalization of these incivilities, because they do not admit harm to communities. However, if individuals are social creatures, as long recognized by anthropologists (e.g., Fortes 1983) and stressed, within criminology, by Bottoms (2006), and if social participation constitutes a basic human need (e.g., Barbalet 1998; Doyal and Gough 1991), we believe it is justified to conceive of the social environment or community as a bearer of harm in itself. This position is also in line with Feinberg's (1984, 63) inclusion of harms to the community and Duff's (2007, 140–1) conceptualization of crimes as "public wrongs" that concern the whole polity and affect not only individual, but also collective interests.

As discussed below in this section, whether a harm to the social environment—or any other bearer—materializes as perceptible or noteworthy might depend on its accumulation. In this legal arena, Bottoms (2006, 262) refers to Field's (2003, 44–5) notion of persistence: "each single instance does not by itself warrant a counter legal challenge ... it is in its regularity that anti-social behaviour wields its destructive force." (See also Feinberg, 1984, 64.)

Although especially difficult to capture, the framework can also be used to assess the social harms of widespread corruption, endemic failures to enforce laws, and other significant "dysfunctionalities," as in the case of the state crimes that fall within the competence of international tribunals (e.g., Karstedt 2014; see also Section 2.3). Harms of such kind impinge on the community's collective efficacy, which, according to Sampson (2012) incorporates both a static "social cohesion" and "trust" dimension and a more action-oriented "willingness to intervene" dimension. At a local level, for example, a neighborhood might cease to be a "neighborhood" beyond the coincidence of geography. However, we assume that the harms of these dysfunctionalities cannot emerge without substantial awareness of the activities, as we do in our assessments of the reputational harms of the same activities and events.

Responses of Taxonomy to Challenges of Normativity, Infinitude, and Causality

In our construction of the taxonomy, we have tried to account for some of the challenges of normativity,[19] infinitude, and causality, the last of which also has a dedicated step of the assessment process, "investigating the causality of harms" (Section 4.5).

Recognizing the inherent normativity of labeling something harmful, we spell out what we mean by harm and proceed transparently. In some instances, addressed later in this section, we set limits on the legitimacy of bearers and interests, by explicitly excluding certain losses from consideration; however, for the most part, we allow policy-makers the latitude to decide whether certain consequences of criminal activities should be treated as harmful and whether certain individuals (e.g., perpetrators) or entities should be deemed legitimate bearers.

Acknowledging the problem of infinitude, we have attempted to construct a broad and inclusive taxonomy, but do not claim that it—or its use—is exhaustive. Moreover, we acknowledge that some of our exclusions, addressed below, necessarily limit the scope of our assessments.

One particular way in which the taxonomy manifests breadth and inclusivity is in its accommodation of complex criminal undertakings, involving

[19] We use the term "normativity," here, as shorthand to encompass challenges of morality, cultural and socioeconomic variability, and legitimacy.

multiple interrelated activities. The taxonomy makes room for complexity and it is especially well suited to handling it. The taxonomy can be used, for example, to identify the harms associated with:

- a "primary activity" of interest, such as cocaine or human trafficking
- one or more "accompanying activities," such as violence, corruption, or money laundering,[20] which might support or occur along with the primary activity or an enabled activity and
- one or more "enabled activities," such as drug dealing and use, that occur downstream and are at least partially made possible by the primary activity.

When we identify harms associated with an accompanying activity, such as violence, we consider only those events that relate directly to the primary or enabled activity. For example, we include harms associated with assaults that occur in the context of the act of cocaine trafficking, such as those involving traffickers, facilitators, or any other individuals who are drawn into the activity, but we do not include harms associated with assaults that involve the same people—or their associates—that occur in other contexts. Note that "accompanying"—like "enabled"—is a relative term and that an activity might be treated as an accompanying activity in one situation, but as a primary or enabled activity in another, depending on the principle or underlying activity of interest in a particular harm assessment.

The decision to include accompanying activities, particularly violence, further opens the possibility of characterizing perpetrators as bearers of harm, potentially as outright victims. Victimologists have long recognized striking similarities between victim and offender populations and, in the case of violent crime, frequent overlap (e.g., Fattah 1992, 32–3). The not-uncommon practice of prosecuting victims of human trafficking as criminals (e.g., for their roles in sex work or their status under laws of immigration) contributes to the conflation of concepts and difficulties of discernment (e.g., International Women's Human Rights Clinic 2015).

Lastly, our taxonomy does not presume causality; instead, acknowledging the complexities of attribution, it establishes associations between harms and activities. On that basis, it might lessen the potential for misattribution. The causal link between an activity or event and a harmful

[20] We provide working definitions of violence, corruption, and money laundering in Appendix A.

outcome might be strong or weak, depending on the circumstance, and is the topic of analysis in the final step of the assessment process (Section 4.5). Some harms, such as the material losses or damages that occur in an act of theft or vandalism, emerge directly from an activity or event. Other harms are remote (e.g., Ryberg 2004, 64–6) or accumulative (Feinberg 1984, 225–7); that is, they are spatially, temporally, or behaviorally "distant," as in the case of drug trafficking and use, or they arise only if the act that triggers the harm is combined with other similar acts, such as repeated cases of anti-social behavior and incivility or minor tax fraud. Still others derive not from the activity but from some combination of policies, including the activity's legal status, and particular law enforcement practices (Caulkins et al. 2011). Harm might depend totally or partially on policies but also on the socioeconomic setting in which the activities generating them take place. Bottoms (2006) and others have shown, for example, that the most economically deprived areas tend to suffer most from incivilities.

Exclusions in Our Applications

Notwithstanding our emphasis on breadth and inclusivity, we adopted a small set of exclusions in our initial applications of the framework to cocaine and human trafficking, some of which speak to issues of the legitimacy of bearers (i.e., their standing) or interests. We explain our decisions in this section, but we also note some recent deviations from past practice in our more-recent assessment of coca cultivation and processing in Colombia.

First, we limited our assessments to first-order effects. We did not, for example, include the ripple effects of harms borne by one individual on another (e.g., when harm to a parent results in harm to a child) or other "second generation costs" (Miller et al. 1996, 11). This approach is not inconsistent with our focus on the ultimate or near-ultimate bearers of harms. In tracing harms to those bearers, we are identifying the "pass through" of first-order effects from one entity or individual to another, not the accrual of second-, third- or nth-order effects. Similarly, we excluded the dynamic effects of experience and did not contemplate the potential for criminal activities in one period to affect those in another, as might occur if offenders build up capabilities or develop networks that they can employ in future crimes.

As a related matter, we also followed von Hirsch and Jareborg (1991, 11) and Sen (1987, 26–7) and treated the standard of living as "self-regarding," meaning that it pertains only to the nature of one's own life.[21] For example, we did not include indirect psychological damages, which Sen (1987, 27) characterizes as "one's misery at the sorrow of another."

Second, we excluded any gains, material or otherwise, from criminal activities. Although advocating "full accounting" as an aspirational goal and policy imperative (Greenfield and Paoli 2012), we focused on gross harms in our initial applications to cocaine and human trafficking in Belgium (Paoli et al. 2013; Greenfield et al. 2016) and elsewhere, after determining that the gross and net results would not be vastly different, given our focus and scope.

Third, as a related matter, we excluded any losses of "ill-gotten gains"; any losses of illegally acquired or inherently illegal possessions that might occur, for example, when one criminal steals another's gun or drug cache; and any damages to wholly illegal enterprises or shell companies, established purely for purposes of illegal business.

Fourth, we excluded law-enforcement costs. This decision goes against frequent practice in the cost-of-crime literature (e.g., Cohen 2005), but it is not without precedent in the criminological literature. The logic behind our decision rests on concerns about vicious cycles: if law-enforcement costs were added, then the criminal activities that policy-makers and law-enforcement agencies already prioritize most heavily—as reflected, for example, in the agencies' budgets—could look more harmful than other activities that they prioritize less heavily.[22] As Levi and Burrows (2008, 294) observe, "if one includes the costs of responses to crime as part of the 'costs of crime', the less that is done about them, the lower are the 'costs of crime'." Likewise, the more that is done, the higher the costs. Funding, which reflects a society's perceptions of and concern about harm (Dorn and van de Bunt 2010, 9), does not measure harm directly. Moreover, it might be difficult to pull apart the costs of addressing particular forms of crime as many costs are borne through common, shared pots of funding.

Fifth, and for similar reasons, we excluded costs that individuals and private-sector entities incur to protect themselves from crime. As above, inclusion could result in a vicious cycle, based in perceptions and concerns, and estimation might be next to impossible. Prevention costs are not solely

[21] For more on this point, see the discussion in a note in Section 4.2.

[22] Heaton (2010, 3, footnote 2) addresses this concern in a different context, relating to analyses of the benefits and costs of programs that increase enforcement, but he suggests that the practical effects of including them are modest because they represent a small share of total costs.

a function of the inherent toxicity of crime, but they are also a function of the perceptions and concerns of individuals and entities. A business, for example, might incur security expenses for three reasons: an internal desire to hedge risks, the demand from employees and customers for particular protections, and government regulation mandating certain security measures (Jackson et al. 2007, 34–5). Regardless of the individual's or entity's reasons, their decision to spend more or less to protect against a crime would suggest more or less harm and, thus, be self-fulfilling. Moreover, individuals, and often businesses and NGOs, do not assess the threats of each criminal activity separately, making it impossible to identify, let alone estimate, the costs of efforts to prevent a particular activity. Insomuch as businesses lump their prevention costs with other general compliance and technology costs, it would be difficult to disentangle them empirically (Levi and Burrows 2008, 310).

We did not, however, exclude remediation, repair, or replacement costs. Examples include the costs of treating violence-related injuries in hospital emergency rooms, providing shelter to victims of human trafficking, and repairing misused assets or covering increases in related insurance premiums. Some of these costs, such as those associated with healthcare, might fall at least initially on the government, but would be borne ultimately by taxpayers.

With the foregoing taxonomy and these exclusions, we gave standing in the earlier assessments to:

- all individuals who experience harm directly, be they victims or perpetrators, unless the harm derives from the loss of ill-gotten gains or illegally acquired or inherently illegal possessions, as might be true of guns or drugs
- all entities that experience harm directly, be they private or public, unless the entities have been established solely for illegal purposes, such as wholly illegal enterprises or shell companies, or the harms can be traced to other, ultimate bearers
- all elements of the social and physical environment that incur harm directly, unless the harms can be traced to other, ultimate bearers.

In Chapter 6, where we present a new harm assessment of coca cultivation and processing in Colombia, we deviate from some of those practices. In particular, we take a step toward full accounting and attempt to capture some of the gains from illegal activities, such as coca growers' income from coca cultivation and processing. In the spirit of "fullness"—and for consistency—we also consider some losses of ill-gotten gains (i.e., coca-derived income), losses of illegally acquired or inherently illegal possessions (e.g., coca), and harms to wholly illegal operations, insomuch as coca dominates a grower's agricultural pursuits. To embark on full accounting, we might be said to be taking a position on legitimacy that strays from a purely legalistic perspective. More generally, we recognize that national laws cannot always be used as the exclusive criteria for establishing legitimacy; for instance, if one were assessing harms in an authoritarian context (see Section 3.4) or if a country's laws did not fully recognize a class of bearers, such as the physical and social environment. In such cases, international laws, such as those founded on UN declarations, might serve as an appropriate complement for establishing the legitimacy of claimants and interests.

4.4 Two Scales and a Matrix

We use one ordinal scale to rate the severity of harms, another ordinal scale to rate the incidence of harms, and a matrix that combines the scales to rank and prioritize harms. Our approach to severity draws from both the criminal-law and national-security literatures—namely, von Hirsch and Jareborg (1991) and Greenfield and Camm (2005), respectively—but our approach to incidence, including our use of the matrix, draws only from the latter. Although intending to remain true to the spirit of these references, we have introduced a handful of modest—and hopefully clarifying—changes in wording, structure, and interpretation.

The Severity Scale

The severity of a harm can be "catastrophic," "grave," "serious," "moderate," or "marginal" (Table 4.2), rated on the basis of common benchmarks for individuals, entities, and the environment, respectively. We treat each level of harm as representing a range of negative outcomes—more like a bandwidth than a point estimate.

Benchmarks and ratings for individuals

For individuals, the benchmark for evaluating the severity of damages and harms is the standard of living. Following von Hirsch and Jareborg (1991,

Table 4.2 Benchmarks and levels for rating severity for different bearers

Severity Rating	Individuals	Entities	Environment
	Level of living standard at which damage occurs	Level of mission attainment at which damage occurs	Level of sustainability at which damage occurs
Catastrophic	1°. Subsistence	1°. Viability	1°. Viability
Grave	2°. Minimal	2°. Minimal	2°. Minimal
Serious	3°. Adequate	3°. Adequate	3°. Adequate
Moderate	4°. Enhanced	4°. Enhanced	4°. Enhanced
Marginal	Negligible damage at any level	Negligible damage at any level	Negligible damage at any level

Sources: Authors' adaptation of Greenfield and Paoli (2013) and Paoli et al. (2012, 2013), drawing from von Hirsch and Jareborg's (1991) living-standard approach and their notation (1°, 2°, etc.).
Notes: Entities refers to both the private sector and government.

17–19), we delineate four living-standard levels into which crime can intrude and yield harm. Specifically, one can have the capabilities to attain just "subsistence" or, with steadily progressive improvement, a "minimal," "adequate," or "enhanced" quality of life. We, like von Hirsch and Jareborg, gauge intrusions in relation to the average individual in a particular context, a point that we take up again later. Subsistence implies survival, but with maintenance of only "elementary human capacities to function" that amount to "barely getting by" (von Hirsch and Jareborg 1991, 18). By contrast, an enhanced quality of life implies some satisfaction or luxury beyond mere adequacy. To illustrate, von Hirsch and Jareborg (1991, 19) suggest a Swedish individual's ownership of a small summer cabin, which they describe as commonplace in their prosperous socio-economic context.

Harms, then, involve "a taking away" (von Hirsch and Jareborg 1991, 18)—through damages—at one of those four levels. Consequently, in this schema, intrusions upon subsistence, which would impede or prevent survival, are the most damaging.

In Table 4.2, the first four severity ratings (catastrophic, grave, serious, and moderate) correspond to intrusions at each of the four living-standard levels. To illustrate, a catastrophic harm from damages to an individual's physical integrity would occur at the level of subsistence, implying death or a fully disabling physical impairment, such as a coma. At the other end of the spectrum, marginal damages do not encroach substantially at any level.

Von Hirsch and Jareborg (1991, 21–2) highlight the importance of "temporal perspective" in adjudicating severity. They suggest a medium-term perspective of about a year or slightly longer, "Living-standard judgments are addressed to the overall quality of someone's life, and this suggests a considerably longer temporal perspective than the highly variable quality of experience from day to day," but they rule out longer-term perspectives, such as a decade, as "too reductive." Though, as we note vis-à-vis the environment, a longer-term perspective might be necessary in some instances. Von Hirsch and Jareborg (1991, 22) also distinguish between the duration of a crime and the duration of its effects, "A physical assault, and its immediate trauma, may soon be over; yet if the experience was painful or humiliating enough, it may still matter in evaluation of, say, the quality of a whole year's experience."

A corollary of using the living standard as a benchmark is that some interest dimensions are inherently more "basic"—that is, more apt to cut into subsistence—than others: whereas the violation of an individual's functional integrity can result in a catastrophic harm, the violation of his or her reputation cannot (von Hirsch and Jareborg 1991, 21).

Benchmarks and ratings for entities

We apply the same five-tiered scale to the harms to other bearers, but we use an analogy for the standard of living for the private sector and government. Recalling that the term "living standard" refers to various capabilities, we assess the harms to an entity in relation to its ability to fulfill its mission, defined as the entity's raison d'être. Mission statements, often short and to the point, have become common among businesses, NGOs, and, in many countries, public agencies. According to Entreprenuer.com, "A mission statement defines what an organization is, why it exists, its reason for being."[23] A list of 50 mission statements for "top" nonprofits (TopNonprofits 2018, n.p.),[24] includes examples that range from a few to many words: at one end, TED offered "Spreading ideas" and, somewhat longer, the Rotary Foundation offered "To enable Rotarians to advance world understanding,

[23] Accessed from https://www.entrepreneur.com/encyclopedia/mission-statement (accessed May 25, 2018).

[24] Accessed from https://topnonprofits.com/examples/nonprofit-mission-statements/ (accessed May 25, 2018); as of October 18, 2021, the working link is https://topnonprofits.com/mission-statements/.

goodwill, and peace through the improvement of health, the support of education, and the alleviation of poverty." Turning to public agencies, the UK's National Crime Agency describes its role as "to protect the public from the most serious threats by disrupting and bringing to justice those serious and organised criminals who present the highest risk to the UK."[25] The national security literature (see, e.g., US Department of the Army 2014, 1–4) speaks to mission directly and literally in its assessments of the risks of "mission degradation" and "mission failure."

Admittedly, some mission statements amount to image crafting, but the underlying concept of an entity's raison d'être still holds.

Benchmarks and ratings for the environment

Our approach to benchmarking and rating environmental harms is still evolving. In our initial assessments of cocaine and human trafficking, environmental harm was a relatively minor concern and, as a consequence, we did not have a reason to explore it fully. Although we contemplated adapting the standard of living for nonhuman animals and invoking "sustainability" for the collective parts of the social and physical environments, we had little opportunity to test either approach. However, in Chapter 6, where we introduce a new assessment of harms associated with coca cultivation and processing in Colombia, environmental concerns loom large. In that assessment, we revisited our approach and worked with sustainability, though our focus, by design, is on the physical, not the social, environment.

Although scholars and public agencies have written extensively on the meaning of "sustainability," we highlight just a few definitions and point to the United Nations General Assembly (2015) for recent examples of programmatic use, in its "Sustainable Development Goals" for climate, ecosystems, cities, and communities. In 1987, the Brundtland Commission's report for the United Nations offered what might be among the most visible definitions of the term, with its call for development that meets the needs of present and future generations (see Chapter 2, Section 2.5, and Appendix A), but it is just one of many definitions. Basiago (1995) offers five different disciplinary perspectives on the meaning of sustainability, consisting of biological, economic, sociological, planning, and ethical. For example, he describes the biological and economic perspectives as concerned with, on

[25] Accessed from https://www.nationalcrimeagency.gov.uk/who-we-are/our-mission (accessed May 26, 2018).

the one hand, preserving natural assets for future generations, with particular regard to biodiversity, and, on the other hand, properly accounting for the value of natural resources in measures of national income.

For our purposes, we propose "the ability to persist"—an inherently long-term proposition—as a compact variant that parallels our benchmarks for harms to individuals and entities, though we come back to valuation in Chapter 6. So, for the environment, von Hirsch and Jareborg's medium-term perspective might be too short to capture relevant harms. In Chapter 6, we investigate particular concerns about degradation of the physical environment, specifically from deforestation and pollution. At one end of the spectrum, we ask if a forest and its inhabitants can just persist, even in some reduced form; at the other end, we ask if they can thrive, as much as they would naturally, without human intervention. Whereas sustainability, so defined, posed a reasonable benchmark for assessing damages to functional integrity, as a physical and operational matter, we have not yet found a comparable approach for dealing with aesthetic integrity and do not address it in Chapter 6.

At this stage, we have made more progress developing our approach to benchmarking physical harm than our approach to social harm, which plays a modest role in the applications in this book. However, when we turn to social harm with our full attention, we might look to the United Nations General Assembly (2015) goals for cities and communities, possibly integrated with Sampson's (2012) well-honed concept of collective efficacy, for guidance.

Approach to standardization

In assessing harms to individuals, we attempt to estimate the standard impact of a criminal activity on the living standard of an individual, assuming, as do von Hirsch and Jareborg (1991, 4), that "injury occurs to someone who is neither especially vulnerable nor resilient" in the context of the society under consideration. In Sen's (1987, 29) lexicon, this would amount to a "standard evaluation."[26] Thus, we do not distinguish between the effects

[26] Sen (1987, 29) compares two evaluative methods, self- and standard evaluation: "Self-evaluation would tell us what the person would judge to be his standard of living in comparison with other positions (in line with his own valuations), whereas standard evaluation places that person's living conditions in a general ranking in terms of some social standard (as it is reflected by commonly accepted values in the society)." He further notes (p. 30), "If contemporary standards are widely shared ... then the two sets of answers may typically not diverge ... "

of an event on the basis of an individual's specific life circumstances; for example, we would treat the loss of a single pay check identically, regardless of the particular victim's wealth, as we would the loss of one's entire pension or retirement savings.[27] In each case, we might ask how an average person, earning an average income would fare under each circumstance, in which case the loss of pay would be uniformly less concerning—with a lower severity rating—than the loss of the pension or savings. In the United States, the former might entail moderate harm whereas the latter might entail serious or even grave harm. In our application of the framework to coca cultivation and processing in Colombia (Chapter 6), we consider the economic consequences of growing coca relative to per capita gross domestic product (GDP) in that country, suggesting that an average person would earn an average income in that context.

For other bearers, we might consider the level of analysis. A division of a local public agency or private manufacturer—or the entire agency or company—might be heavily affected by corruption, whereas the totality of "the Government" or an industrial sector remains fundamentally intact. The same also applies to the environment. A neighborhood might be heavily affected by a particular crime, whereas the encompassing city or province, taken as a whole, might suffer little damage. Given the impossibility of typifying all such entities, we might delineate subclasses when different kinds of bearers in a class are affected.

- For businesses and NGOs, we could, for example, distinguish between small-, medium-, and large-scale entities or between local, sectoral, or economy-wide effects.
- For government, we could consider harms to local, regional, and national agencies and, for governing bodies, more generally, supranational agencies.
- For the environment, already specified as either social or physical, we might introduce local, regional, national, or global distinctions.

In our assessments of the harms of cocaine and human trafficking in Belgium (Chapter 5, Greenfield et al. 2016), we conducted case-by-case

[27] Scholars also debate whether the punishment meted out for a crime should reflect and be calibrated upon the different subjective experiences of those who are punished. However, the predominant view is that punishment should be meted on objective grounds, although the convicted person's personal circumstances might be taken into account in debating the role of mercy. See Gray (2010) for a review of the debate and rejection of the subjectivist standpoint.

assessments of the harms to the private sector and government and, in our assessment of harms of coca cultivation and processing in Colombia (Chapter 6), we considered environmental harms at subregional-to-national levels, but this much refinement might not be feasible or necessary in all cases.

Cross-cutting and differentiated effects

In many instances, the same criminal activity can impinge on more than one interest dimension and it can do so to varying degrees. The only clear exception is the catastrophic harm associated with a murder because the victim, upon death, is no longer able to experience a material, reputational, or other loss directly. Other scenarios are more complicated. An act of violence, for example, can affect a victim's functional integrity and reputation, but it can do so differently. If the act produces major injuries that merit hospitalization and impinge on an adequate standard of living, the harm from those physical damages would be regarded as "serious." If the same act of violence has only a modest effect on how others view the victim, the harm from those reputational damages would be regarded as "moderate" or even "marginal."

Moreover, criminal activities, even if referred to singularly, as "violence," "corruption," or "money laundering," can take vastly different forms. In our analyses, we try to define each of these and other "accompanying activities" specifically enough to align them with the accrual of particular harms and, if necessary, create activity subcategories, potentially corresponding to the aforementioned "harming event."[28] For example, in the case of the violence that accompanies human trafficking, we considered episodes of threatening behavior, assaults of varying degrees, and kidnapping, rape, and murder separately, though we list them together under the rubric of "violence" in our final assessments. Similarly, we can create subcategories for corruption, such as "petty" and "grand," to reflect the differences between low-level bribes and payments to high-level officials, and for money laundering.

Admittedly, it can be challenging to decide how finely to parse an activity, hence harms, and then how to characterize evidence consistently across different activities or forms of crime. Indeed, one could parse activities so finely as to designate an arbitrarily large number of harms for any issue of concern. Over the course of our analyses, we have settled on

[28] This discussion departs slightly from our prior publications. We elaborate further on our approach and its implications for evaluating incidence, below.

particular conventions, some specific to our evaluations of accompanying and enabled activities, which we discuss in this and later chapters.

The Incidence Scale

For incidence, we also use a five-tiered scale. Harms can emerge "continuously," "persistently," "occasionally," "seldom," or "rarely." If a type of harm is irrelevant to a specific activity in a given context, we deem it "not applicable." For example, in our Belgian cocaine-trafficking assessment, we found no evidence of damages to the physical environment during import; hence, we regarded such environmental harms as not applicable in that context.

To support comparative assessments of harms across different forms of crime, we find it necessary to consider the "overall" incidence of harm, which depends not just on the extent to which the harm occurs in relation to a particular activity, but on the extent to which the activity, itself, occurs. A criminal activity might always produce serious harm but, if the activity occurs rarely, the harm can emerge only rarely.

In practice, we address two distinct components of incidence:

- the incidence of the criminal activity, and
- the incidence of the harm in relation to that criminal activity.

We refer to the latter as the "within-activity" incidence.

To arrive at an estimate of the overall incidence, we must somehow combine the two components. Faced with a range of options, we have chosen to follow the national security literature (e.g., Greenfield and Camm 2005, drawing from US Department of the Army 1998 and US Department of the Army, Marine Corps, Navy, and Air Force 2001; and, more recently, US Department of the Army 2006, 2014) and treat incidence, roughly speaking, as indicative of probability. On that basis, the combination is conceptually multiplicative (see Box 4.1), involving two components that lie somewhere on a "zero-to-one"-like continuum, and the overall rating cannot be greater than the rating of the lesser of the two components.

To be more concrete, our assessment of cocaine trafficking in Belgium indicated that body packing—the practice of ingesting drugs to conceal them during transport—yields catastrophic harm "rarely."[29] Because

[29] A drug-filled packet might break inside a smuggler's body and cause a fatal overdose.

Box 4.1 Incidence, Conditionality, and Complex Crimes

In effect, we treat the within-activity incidence like a conditional probability, defined as the probability that the harm or harms occur (e.g., the harm of a serious beating) given that the underlying activity occurs (e.g., cocaine trafficking).

For a single primary activity (p) and a single harm (h), we can represent overall incidence as:

Inc(h) = Inc(p) × Inc(h, given p)

Where:[30]

Inc(h) = the overall incidence of the harm

Inc(p) = the incidence of the primary activity

Inc(h, given p) = the incidence of the harm in relation to the primary activity, i.e., the "within-activity" incidence, given the occurrence of the primary activity.

To evaluate scenarios involving complex crimes, one could create a chain of ratings, leading from an underlying primary activity, such as cocaine trafficking, to the harm associated with an accompanying activity, such as violence, corruption, or money laundering; an enabled activity, such as drug dealing or use; or even an activity that accompanies an enabled activity.

For a single primary activity (p) and a single accompanying activity (a), which has a single related harm (h), we can represent the overall incidence as:

Inc(h) = Inc(p) × Inc(a, given p) × Inc(h, given a)

Where:

Inc(h) = the overall incidence of the harm

Inc(p) = the incidence of the primary activity

Inc(a, given p) = the incidence of the accompanying activity, given the occurrence of the primary activity

Inc(h, given a) = the incidence of harm in relation to the accompanying activity, given the occurrence of the accompanying activity.

The same approach would hold for an enabled activity, but we would substitute "e" for "a" in our notation. In the case of multiple accompanying or enabled activities, we could use subscripts to designate each (e.g., a_i, where i = 1 to N, for each of N such activities), effectively creating branches on a tree that starts with the single, primary activity, p.

30 We use non-mathematical notation (e.g., "Inc(h)") for readability.

trafficking occurs persistently, our estimates of the overall incidence could be no greater than the estimate of the within-activity incidence, which is "rarely." In theory, we would "multiply" persistently by rarely for the catastrophic harm and arrive at an overall rating that could be somewhat lower than rarely, but, in practice, as we are working with qualitative bandwidths not point estimates, we could not justify—or support—this level of precision and chose to assign the within-activity incidence, rarely, as an approximate result. By comparison, we found that some reputational damages occur continuously and, in those cases, the incidence of trafficking, which is lower, constrained the overall rating.

As a practical matter, we tend to treat the lesser of the activity and within-activity incidence as the over overall incidence in our ratings. We recognize that this procedure might result in an upward bias in our assessments, but it might also offset the countervailing downward influence of "the dark figure of crime," referring to instances of the activity or of the related harm that remain unknown or unreported. On balance, the push and pull could be a wash.

However, in some instances, a difference in units of measure (e.g., tons, kilograms, or grams) or level of analysis (e.g., local, regional, or national) or the spatial, temporal, or behavioral distance between events and outcomes is such that this interpretation requires rethinking. For example, drug dealing can occur in units so much smaller than trafficking—grams as compared to kilograms or tons—that the frequency of dealing is not, practically speaking, bound by the incidence of trafficking over the relevant range of analysis. In these instances, we evaluate the incidence of the activity—and related harms—separately.

In general, we try to minimize the need to create chains of ratings (Box 4.1) by defining accompanying activities narrowly enough to create a one-to-one correspondence between the activity and each of its related harms.[31,32] We do so, in part, by creating subcategories for some activities, including violence and corruption. On that basis, a harm would always occur along with the accompanying activity and the within-activity incidence would be "continuous," which would be roughly equivalent to describing the occurrence of the harm as certain in the event of the accompanying activity. To extend the probability analogy in Box 4.1, we need only

[31] The longer a chain, the greater the potential to overstate the incidence of a harm, if, as suggested above, we choose to treat the lower-bound estimate as the final estimate.

[32] The activity can give rise to many different harms, framed in terms of type, bearers, etc., but, in each case, the correspondence between the activity and harm would be lock step.

go so far as to calculate the incidence of the accompanying activity given the underlying primary activity, and then, for each harm, multiply that incidence by "one."

Severity and Incidence in the Priority Matrix

Our matrix (Table 4.3) jointly considers the severity and incidence—specifically, the overall incidence—of harms to provide an initial basis for prioritizing them.[33] The matrix is symmetric, implying that we weigh severity and incidence equally, but other options are possible. Taken in combination, the severity and incidence ratings can suggest different priorities than a severity or incidence rating taken in isolation. For example, a grave harm might seem to merit more attention than a moderate harm, but if the grave harm occurs rarely and the moderate harm occurs continuously, the moderate harm might merit more attention than the grave harm.

We treat these prioritizations as initial: to rank harms more definitively, one would need to weigh the costs of implementing measures to address them.

That an interest dimension is more or less "basic" does not affect the design or application of the matrix; rather, it affects the placement of harms in the matrix. Violations of functional integrity can engender more severe harms than violations of reputation, potentially placing them closer to the top of the matrix, but, as the foregoing comparison of grave and moderate harms suggests, the relative ranking of the violations will still depend on their incidence.

The combination of our two scales can also account for accumulative harms (Section 4.3), albeit with possible limitations involving exposure over extended periods (Chapter 5, Section 5.6). In the context of harms to the social environment, we noted the relevance of the accumulation of antisocial behavior that mattered only if persistent and recurring, but we can point to examples concerning other activities and bearers. In the case of corruption, for example, the occasional involvement of a low-level employee of a transportation company in cocaine trafficking might cause only marginal harm to the company's mission. However, if numerous employees engage in corrupt acts, even if they are all low-level, the company's operational

[33] This matrix differs slightly from those found in our prior publications. For a comparison of difference and a brief discussion of implications, see the notes that accompany Table 4.3.

Table 4.3 Matrix for prioritizing harms

Severity	**Incidence**				
	Continuously	**Persistently**	**Occasionally**	**Seldom**	**Rarely**
Catastrophic	VH	H	H	MH	M
Grave	H	H	MH	M	ML
Serious	H	MH	M	ML	L
Moderate	MH	M	ML	L	L
Marginal	M	ML	L	L	VL

Sources: Authors' adaptation of Greenfield and Camm (2005, 48), drawing from US Army (1998), US Army et al. (2001), and other US military doctrine, and Paoli et al. (2012, 2013).
Notes:

VH = very high priority; H = high priority; MH = medium high priority; M = medium priority; ML = medium low priority; L = low priority; VL = very low priority.

This matrix differs slightly from those found in our prior publications. Specifically, medium harms now span the diagonal rather than medium-high harms, we have eliminated "high-medium" harms, we have introduced "medium-low" harms, and we have redesignated the highest-ranking harms as "very high" and the lowest ranking harms as "very low" for purposes of symmetry and differentiation. In addition, we now refer to the highest incidence rating as "continuously," instead of "always." As a consequence of these changes, the labels—but not the relative positions—assigned to the rankings presented in this book (see, e.g., Chapter 5) differ somewhat from those presented previously (see, e.g., Paoli et al. 2013).

integrity, reputation, and perhaps also its privacy and autonomy might be endangered.

Responses of Scales and Matrix to Challenges of Standardization, Measurement, and Commensurability

We cannot make individuals, entities, or the environment homogeneous, when they are not and, as a result, we cannot fully overcome the challenge of standardization in a broad-based empirical assessment. But we can address it partly by typifying individuals (von Hirsch and Jareborg 1991) for the society under consideration (Sen 1987), and by delineating levels of analysis for other bearers. An individual is a more-or-less "average" person within a particular society, but what is average in one society might not be average in another, a point that we take up in Chapter 5; private and public entities might be treated as "small," "medium," or "large" or as "local," "regional," "national," or "supranational"; and elements of the social or physical environment can be assessed locally, regionally, nationally, or globally.

Arguably, we have done better with measurement. Our framework admits qualitative evidence and invokes a simple ordinal rating scheme; consequently, it does not require quantification, allows a more expansive data collection, and might also ease the burden of measurement. We gladly quantify that which we can quantify appropriately, such as episodes of violence, numbers of fatalities, revenues from drug or human trafficking, and costs of material losses, and will use that information in our evaluations. Moreover, as we address in Chapter 6, regarding deforestation, we welcome attribution of economic value to resources that have been left "off the books" previously, if the attribution sheds light on the accrual or distribution of harms. But we are not dependent on numbers and can proceed without them. This flexibility buys us the freedom of employing alternative methods of analysis and formally incorporating qualitative insights; we do not, so to speak, leave any credible information on the table. For example, following drug-policy scholars (e.g., Nutt et al. 2010) and others, we accept expert judgment as valid but acknowledge its limitations.[34] Different experts might—and often do—have different opinions, rooted in their disciplines and experience. Therefore, we recommend triangulating expert opinion with observations from other sources.

We would be remiss, however, if we did not explain our use of hedging language in the preceding paragraph. In particular, we say that our approach "might" ease the burden of measurement, not that it "would" ease that burden. Simply relaxing the demand for numbers cannot eliminate the difficulties of data evaluation and, in some ways, it could amplify them. Were we to assign numbers, such as monetary units, to everything in our assessments, we might be able to combine them seamlessly.[35] However, as discussed in Chapter 3, attempts to reduce all harms to monetary or other units entail their own challenges and imply the exclusion of any harms—and they are not insignificant—that cannot be so reduced.

We can also claim progress in addressing the challenge of commensurability. Our approach allows comparisons of a broad range of harms among

[34] In our assessments, we admit other experts' professional judgment but try to avoid our own. Although we cannot be accused of codifying our opinions as fact, this stance might lead us to underreport some harms.

[35] We are also aware that ordinal scales are not without controversy and have considered the debate on the relative merits of four- and five-point scales in developing our scales.

individuals and, to a lesser extent, within the classes of private-sector entities, government, and the environment, but not across classes. Different types of harms to individuals are held to a common benchmark, as are different types of harms to a private-sector entity, government, or the physical environment, which enables within-class comparisons, but damages to an individual's standard of living, an entity's mission, and the environment's sustainability are not readily comparable.[36] These cross-class differences do not necessarily imply an impasse for policy-making, but they can yield ambiguity. In some cases, clear patterns will emerge from the rankings that can suggest a focus of attention for policy-making, or the rankings are clear-cut and can inform policy-making directly; on other occasions, the results might be murky and uninterpretable, without assigning societal weights to the harms to the different bearers. Likewise, we cannot readily aggregate or compare harms, even within classes of bearers, without a more precise scoring system.[37]

Various scoring options could facilitate within-class aggregation and comparisons, for instance, by assigning numbers to each tier and adding or multiplying them together to arrive at overall, numeric assessments. These simple methods would maintain the symmetry of severity and incidence by weighting them equally, but each raises interpretive concerns, such as those regarding the relative importance of harms residing at the center or edges of the matrix. Moreover, one might reasonably say that transforming tiers and bandwidths into point estimates is fundamentally inconsistent with the underlying premise of "tiers" and "bandwidths" and could engender overconfidence in falsely precise distinctions among harms.

Thus, we face a dilemma. We can be more, if falsely, precise and take commensurability further—while satisfying any craving for numbers—but we run the risk of undermining the foundation of our approach.

Nevertheless, with or without a more precise scoring system, our approach offers the benefit of enabling users to harvest all available information, be it quantitative or qualitative, about the harms of an activity and, lacking need for large data sets or elaborate statistical methods, the potential advantage of speed. Absent an extensive data collection, one can exploit the facts on the ground to conduct a rapid, yet systematic, assessment.

[36] In this regard, we are no worse off than those attempting monetization and other forms of quantification in that we can still use quantitative information to make the same partial comparisons they make. See Heaton (2010) for an overview of the cost-of-crime literature and Chapter 3 of this book for our critical discussion.

[37] E.g., we cannot state unequivocally whether a set of 10 low-priority, 7 medium-priority, and 1 high-priority harm is better or worse than a set of 12, 4, and 2.

4.5 The Assessment Process

The harm assessment process is a series of steps that draws together the foregoing tools, implements an additional tool (a data template) that we introduce shortly, and involves data collection, sorting, and analysis (Figure 4.1). The final step, the investigation of causality, does not benefit from a tool, but proceeds as a two-stage exercise.

In summary, we:

- use a data template to articulate the business model or script
- use the taxonomy to identify, sort, and classify possible harms
- use the ordinal scales to evaluate the severity and incidence of harms
- use the matrix to rank and prioritize harms
- investigate the causality of harms in a two-stage exercise.

In Chapters 5 and 6 we illustrate the harm assessment process with applications to cocaine trafficking, human trafficking, coca cultivation and processing and compare the results. Here, we summarize the process, focusing most closely on its start, with the creation of the business model or script, and its conclusion, with the investigation of causality.

Articulating the Business Model or Script

We begin the process by articulating a "business model" or "script" for the activity under consideration. In cases of mafia-like organized criminal activities or farm-level investment and production activities, as per coca growing, one might imagine an actual model of strategy, operations, or decision-making, involving an identifiable entity or unit that engages in commerce. In other circumstances, the notion of a business model could be either too formal or inadequate to describe a criminal activity that is not economically oriented, hence the inclusion of "script." Taking the approach developed by Sieber and Bögel (1993) and Huisman et al. (2003) in studies of organized crime in Germany and the Netherlands, respectively and, more generally, by Cornish (1994; see also Leclerc 2014), our renderings of the business model or script depict the typical patterns, logistics or modus operandi of the criminal activity. The depiction can characterize the activity by phase, such as import or recruitment in cases of trafficking, and, for complex crimes, by the functions and modes of accompanying and enabled activities.

In effect, this step of the process provides essential building blocks of information for subsequent steps of the assessment process.

To facilitate articulation, we suggest using a data template to collate evidence from criminal justice records, interviews, academic and grey literatures, media reports, and other sources. We present a highly simplified version of the template in Table 4.4, using cocaine trafficking to illustrate the premise, and present another such version in Chapter 6.

Our template allows us to go beyond the standard "script analysis," as it is known in criminology, which merely identifies the "sequence of actions

Table 4.4 Simplified illustration of the data template

Activities	Characterization					
	Events[d]	Participants[e]	Resources	Venues	Time frame	Data sources[f]
Primary[a,b]						
• Cocaine trafficking						
Enabled						
• Cocaine dealing						
• Cocaine use[c]						
Accompanying[b]						
• Violence						
• Corruption						
• Money laundering						

Source: Authors' analysis.
Notes:

[a] For definitions of technical terms, see Appendix A, "Glossary of Terms."

[b] In our assessments of cocaine trafficking in Paoli et al. (2013) and Chapter 5, we identified import and wholesale distribution or export as two separate phases of the primary activity and we identified several subcategories of each accompanying activity.

[c] Not included in assessments in Paoli et al. (2013) or Chapter 5.

[d] Consequences can be listed with events or separately in another column.

[e] Individuals, entities, or elements of the social or physical environment that are directly involved in an activity, either actively or passively, potentially including perpetrators, victims, law enforcement officials, witnesses, etc.

[f] Data sources could include criminal justice records, interviews, academic literature, etc.

adopted prior to, during, and following the commission of a particular crime" (Leclerc 2014, 15). With this tool, researchers can systematically record data on all events related to a certain activity (e.g., all instances of drug trafficking or production) in a certain context. They can also assemble information about the participants, made up of all the individuals, entities, or elements of the social or physical environment that are involved in the activity, either actively or passively (e.g., as traffickers, recipients of bribes, police officers, or witnesses); the resources that participants use to engage in the activity, ranging from guns to land; and the venues where and time frames in which particular criminal activities occur and harms emerge.

The data template is a very recent addition to our toolkit.[38] Over time and with repeated applications, we have found a need for a checklist and data repository to better ensure that we touch on all the relevant issues in each assessment and think about them similarly. We suggest working with this or a comparable structure to promote comprehensiveness and consistency across analyses and, by implication, to uncover gaps in knowledge.

Identifying Possible Harms

In this step, we identify possible harms; by singling out harms that are plausible, given what we have learned from depicting the criminal activity. This is a scoping exercise that also serves an analytical purpose. The exercise involves sorting harms by primary, accompanying, and enabled activities and classifying harms according to type and bearer, using the taxonomy. Earlier, we framed harm as a bundle of attributes; namely, (1) activity, including a harming event; (2) type, by interest dimension; (3) bearer; (4) severity; and (5) incidence. In this step of the assessment process, which addresses the possible not the actual, we concern ourselves with the first three attributes, consisting of the activity, the type of harm, and the bearer of harm. In the next step, which turns to the actual, we might find insufficient evidence of severity or incidence to support a rating or ranking, but at this point, we cast a wide net.

Both Sen and the national security literature suggest the importance of considering the range of the possible. Sen (1993, 32–3) analyzes capabilities

[38] We did not use the template to collate data in our analyses of cocaine and human trafficking in Belgium or in our assessment of coca cultivation and processing in Colombia, which was less formal and data-intensive.

in two phases, "identification" and "evaluation," by asking, first, "What are the objects of value" and, second, "How valuable are the respective objects." He frames identification as a necessary step in the analytical process, because it defines the evaluative space, but also notes that the former question is an elementary aspect of the latter insomuch as it assigns "positive weights" to particular objects. Thus, the act of identification is an analytical effort, not just a descriptive one. Similarly, Greenfield and Camm (2005, 47; see also Figure 2.2) outline a well-known five-step risk-management process that begins with "identify hazards" and, through applications to military affairs (2005, 50–3), demonstrate the importance of naming as an analytical exercise. Through the act of naming, they are able to group concerns and trace patterns and relationships among them.

Evaluating the Severity and Incidence of Harms

Next, we evaluate the severity and incidence of each harm deemed "possible," using the scales and methods that we set out in Section 4.4. Whereas we identify possible harms on the basis of plausibility, we confine our evaluations of severity and incidence to the evidence of realization found in official records, interviews, academic and grey literatures, media reports, etc. As such, a harm that we cited as "possible" might not materialize in this step with a rating.

Ranking and Prioritizing Harms

Taken together, the ratings of incidence and severity provide a basis for preliminarily establishing policy priorities.

While our approach facilitates the systematic assessment of wide-ranging harms, it does not, as we noted previously, fully allow either direct comparisons of harms across different classes of bearers or, without further scoring, the aggregation of harms within a particular class of bearers. Moreover, lacking information about the relative costs of addressing harms, we cannot, even within classes and with additional scoring, grant definitive ranks.

Nevertheless, we can examine the broad sweep of rankings and draw insight from their distribution: for example, in our assessment of the harms of cocaine trafficking in Belgium we found that the harms associated with that activity most notably involve, but are not limited to, individuals who, themselves, are traffickers or dealers.

Investigating the Causality of Harms

The investigation of causality occurs in two distinct analytical stages, neither of which implements a template, taxonomy, scale, matrix or other tool.

First, we consider the distance between harms and the primary activity. The harms of enabled activities, for example, constitute remote harms, not only because they are spatially or temporally distant from the primary activity, but also because they are mediated by the choices and behavior of other actors who were not participants in the primary activity. In the case of cocaine trafficking in Belgium, the harms of dealing are immediately adjacent to those of trafficking, but they can accrue in different places and times than those of trafficking and are mediated by the choices of others, including dealers and facilitators, along the supply chain. The harms of use are yet further distant. Von Hirsch and Jareborg (1991, 33–4) suggest discounting harms to account for varying distance; however, without objective criteria for developing a formula, we report such harms as we find them, comment on the degree of distance, and leave it to others in the policy community to decide whether and how to view them in policy decisions.

Second, we examine the extent to which the harms associated with a criminal activity are intrinsic to that activity or arise from policy, including the prohibition of the criminal activity, and related law-enforcement practices. As noted by Maltz (1990, 41–8), one activity, such as theft or human trafficking, might cause harm, whether it is illegal or legal, while another activity, such as drug trafficking, might cause harm in part or whole because it is illegal.[39] We are not arguing for treating previously excluded law-enforcement costs as a harm of crime, but rather, for considering whether policy or its expression through law enforcement might be the underlying source of harm. We carry out this assessment using counterfactual reasoning, a common approach to testing the validity of claims of causation in the social sciences and in historical studies (Calhoun 2002; Reiss 2009),

[39] See also Akerlof and Shiller (2015) and Anielski and Braaten (2008, 81–99) for a discussion of gambling.

by asking what might have happened had the policy or related law enforcement practices not been in place. Insomuch as the analysis singles out policy as the source of harm, the analysis might also suggest a point of leverage for policy-makers to reduce harm. If a policy poses harm to a society, who better than a policy-maker to change it? That said, finding evidence of policy-induced harm would not, alone, provide enough insight to design a particular policy reform. For example, one would also need to consider the policy's extant benefits and the effects of a proposed reform on those benefits.

Unless germane to policy decisions, we do not, however, explore the causal links between criminal activities, their harms, and specific characteristics of the broader socioeconomic and environmental context. In some of our earliest applications, including that to cocaine trafficking in Belgium, we did not regard this exploration as necessary; however, in other circumstances, we have had to dig deeper and examine socioeconomic and environmental factors that can play a part in the emergence of harms. For example, in the case of human trafficking in Belgium (Greenfield et al. 2016), we looked at the ways in which migration policy and poverty might contribute to the severity and incidence of harm and, in our assessment of coca cultivation and processing in Colombia, we found that land tenure and terrain mattered. With limited attention to context, we do not attempt to establish the ultimate causes of crime in all circumstances nor aim to develop a full causal model, which would require listing all the possible causes of a certain outcome, such as a crime event or harm (e.g., Cartwright and Stegenga 2011).

In Section 4.3, we noted that our taxonomy does not presume causality, which might reduce the odds of misattribution, but it is in this final step of the assessment process that we come closest to addressing the challenge of causality full on.

The relevance of causality has also been set forth in related literatures, but from somewhat different perspectives. Much as MacCoun and Reuter (2001) and MacCoun et al. (1996) look to the primary sources of drug-related harms, Greenfield and Camm (2005, 47–8) conclude that establishing the root cause of a bad consequence affecting a military mission or other national security operation is essential. Absent knowledge of that cause, a policy-maker might erroneously weigh the pros and cons of different mitigations or controls and, potentially, suggest a remedy that will leave a hazard in place or make matters worse.

4.6 Concluding Remarks

In presenting the tools of our framework and explaining the assessment process, we have identified methods of addressing the challenges of harm assessment and, whenever relevant, spelled out the limitations of those methods. Although some challenges cannot be overcome fully—for example, we cannot escape normativity, eliminate all the influences of the "dominant political morality," or force homogeneity on heterogeneous individuals, institutions, etc.—we can address substantial elements of each. (Table 4.5 presents a summary.) In some instances, however, we face conceptual and technical trade-offs. For example, the decision to proceed qualitatively forecloses the possibility of making all harms commensurable across all classes of bearers. Yet, even in that arena, we offer a partial

Table 4.5 Means of addressing conceptual and technical challenges

Challenge	Approach
Normativity	• Framework operates with explicit criteria for legitimacy of bearers and interests and with transparency
Infinitude	• Taxonomy claims to be encompassing, not exhaustive • Taxonomy accommodates harms of complex crimes that entail primary, accompanying, and enabled activities
Causality	• Taxonomy does not presume causality • Assessment process includes two-stage investigation that considers remoteness and counterfactuals
Standardization	• Scales apply to average individuals and levels (e.g., local, regional, etc.) of institutions and the environment
Measurement	• Scales exploit quantitative and qualitative evidence in "bandwidths," not point estimates
Commensurability	• Matrix, inclusive of underlying taxonomy, scales and benchmarks, enables comparisons of harms within classes of bearers and of the distribution of harms across classes of bearers, with the potential to establish patterns of accrual over disparate forms of complex crime

Source: Authors' adaptation of Greenfield and Paoli (2013).
Notes: We use the term "normativity" here as shorthand to encompass challenges of morality, cultural and socioeconomic variability, and legitimacy.

solution, by proposing benchmarking as a basis for making comparisons of harms to bearers within particular classes.

All told, we contend that our framework—with its tools, processes, and transparency—rises to meet the challenges of normativity, infinitude, causality, and so forth, to assess that which we intend it to assess, but the confirmation will rest on our applications.

In Chapters 5 and 6, we present and discuss applications of the framework to cocaine trafficking in Belgium, with comparisons to other trafficking activities in Europe, and to coca cultivation and processing in Colombia, which together represent the end and beginning, respectively, of an illegal, if not entirely illicit, supply chain. We undertook the first application as a full-blown assessment of harms in a largely familiar arena, whereas we attempted the second, our most recent joint application, as a rapid assessment of particular harms in a somewhat less familiar arena. Each tested the framework in its own way; provided new insight to harm and policy; presented challenges, some unique to the application and some not; and suggested methodological responses. Through those applications, we hope that the framework will come to life and that our methods will become clearer.

5

An Application of the Framework to Cocaine Trafficking in Belgium (with Comparisons to other Applications to Drug and Human Trafficking in Europe)

5.1 Introduction

In this chapter, we use our seminal application of the harm assessment framework to cocaine trafficking in Belgium to walk through the steps of the assessment process and, with the benefit of hindsight, we comment on our experience with the application. For insight to the reliability and robustness of the approach, we also compare the results to those of an assessment of the same activity, cocaine trafficking, in another country, the Netherlands, and an assessment of another activity, human trafficking, in the same country, Belgium. Taken together, the three applications demonstrate the merits of the approach across settings and some of the challenges still confronting it. The chapter draws from Paoli et al. (2013), "The harms of cocaine trafficking: Applying a new framework for assessment," and, in its comparative elements, from our work on cocaine trafficking in the Netherlands (e.g., Paoli et al. 2015) and on human trafficking in Belgium (Greenfield, et al. 2016).[1] The objective of the Belgian assessments, funded partly by the Belgian Federal Science Policy Office, was to focus specifically on harms that accrue within Belgium from trafficking.

[1] We refer to Greenfield et al. (2016), Paoli et al. (2013), and Paoli et al. (2015) as "our" work, but they would not have been possible without the contributions of our co-authors, Andries Zoutendijk and Loes Kersten.

Assessing the Harms of Crime. Victoria A. Greenfield and Letizia Paoli, Oxford University Press. © Victoria A. Greenfield & Letizia Paoli 2022. DOI: 10.1093/oso/9780198758174.003.0005

The chapter has benefitted from some of our ongoing efforts to simplify and routinize the assessment process and from recent changes in our priority matrix (see Table 4.3). Although we have not attempted to superimpose our newly developed data template (see Table 4.4) on the underlying data collections for any of our prior assessments, we have more systematically bundled, unbundled, and evaluated the harms of cocaine trafficking in Belgium and reranked them using the latest version of the matrix. For those reasons, the results presented in this chapter do not map identically to those presented in Paoli et al. (2013), but they flow more logically and faithfully from the principles of estimation set out in Chapter 4.[2] As previously, we define "drug trafficking," cocaine or otherwise, as encompassing all transportation and marketing activities occurring prior to retail and refer to retail-level activities, by sale or barter, separately as dealing (see Appendix A).

In our application to cocaine trafficking in Belgium, we assessed harms associated with all the principal phases and modes of the primary activity, cocaine trafficking; a directly enabled activity, dealing; and a set of accompanying activities, consisting of violence, corruption, and money laundering, potentially relevant to the primary and enabled activity. The harms of cocaine use, which trafficking also enables, are more remote than those of dealing and were beyond the scope of our assessment and its supply-side orientation. Moreover, we confined the analysis to harms that accrue in Belgium as a matter of both research objectives and practicality, because we relied heavily on Belgian data sources.

In Sections 5.2–5.4, we describe the research design and data collection for our work on cocaine trafficking in Belgium and walk through the assessment process, starting with the articulation of the business model and ending with an investigation of causality. In Section 5.5, we sum up the main findings and methodological lessons from this application. In Section 5.6 we broaden our perspective, by briefly summarizing the key findings of our applications to cocaine trafficking in the Netherlands and human trafficking in Belgium, comparing the findings from these applications to those of our first application, and then drawing out additional methodological lessons.

[2] With these changes in the matrix, we might apply a different label to a harm, e.g., "medium" or "low," but the relative ranking of the harm would be the same.

5.2 Research Design and Data Collection

To support our assessment of harms associated with cocaine trafficking in Belgium, we undertook an extensive data collection and analysis, spanning the period 2003–11, that largely involved primary sources from the Belgian criminal justice system and interviews with criminal justice experts and perpetrators.

First, we analyzed raw extracts from the data files for the 81 criminal proceedings pertaining to cocaine trafficking that were opened by the Belgian prosecutor's offices in Belgium from 2006 to 2008 and included in the organized-crime database of the Belgian Federal Police.[3] Cases that are recorded in that database must meet the criteria of the official Belgian definition of organized crime, which is drawn from the German BKA's (Federal Police Office's) definition and is very broad (BKA, Bundeskriminalamt 2009, 8). The database includes nearly all of the major cases of wholesale cocaine trafficking investigated by the Belgian police, but provides just very basic, standardized information about each case. On the basis of a questionnaire that includes several questions about attempted or effective use of violence and corruption, the central police headquarters collects information from the field officers directly responsible for the investigations. Unsurprisingly, the data present problems of "the dark figure of crime." Police can only gather information on known cases and they tend to collect evidence of the main charge (i.e., cocaine trafficking) but not necessarily of associated activities. Presenting a further limitation, the police do not update the database systematically after they initially record information about a case.

Second, we culled information from a set of 52 closed criminal proceedings that the same Belgian prosecutor's offices opened between 2003 and 2009.[4] We examined the proceedings partly (n = 8) in their full form

[3] Several years after completing this analysis, we learned that the Belgian police might have assigned unique identifying codes to some duplicate files, implying the potential for double counting some cases in our assessment. Any differences in ratings would depend on whether, on average, the duplicative cases entailed greater or fewer harms than the rest. If they were not very—and systematically—different, the incidence of harms, hence ratings, would be about the same.

[4] We refer to the full cases with the codes Case-Full-1 to -8; long summaries with the codes Case-LS-1 to -31; and short summaries with the codes Case-SS-1 to -13. We collected both the short summaries and the data from the organized-crime database directly from the headquarters of the Belgian Federal Police. On the basis of the latter, we selected the three judicial districts with the largest numbers of cocaine trafficking cases, consisting of Antwerp, Brussels, and Ghent, and, in each of those three districts, analyzed the full proceedings at court and the extensive summaries provided to us by the local police.

at the courts; partly (n = 31) as extensive or long (15- to 100-page) summaries written by the police at the end of the investigations; and partly (n = 13) as short (4- to 8-page) summaries. The proceedings overlap with the organized-crime database (39 of the 52 cases appear in both sources), but they span more years, include some cases that did not involve organized crime, and contain more information about each case.

We tend to treat the two sources—the organized-crime database and the set of 52 criminal proceedings—separately because of differences in structure and content and use them to corroborate each other. We generally refer to the 81 data files as "the organized-crime database" or "the database" and to the 52 proceedings as "our sample" of cases.

Third, we conducted interviews with 18 criminal justice experts and 12 convicted drug traffickers or dealers. The criminal justice experts consisted of six police officers, three customs officers, a public prosecutor, three police analysts, four money-laundering specialists, and a prison doctor. The convicted criminals were inmates in Belgian prisons who, to varying degrees, had direct experience in cocaine trafficking or dealing.[5] Two convicts dealt in grams on the retail market; two trafficked in 50- to 200-gram lots just prior to retail; four imported or exported 1- to 5-kilograms lots; and four imported or exported 15- to 300-kilograms shipments.

Fourth, we turned to "predigested" material, by reviewing official reports, such as the extensive biannual government reports on organized crime (Dienst voor het Strafrechtelijk Beleid 2008), and statistics (e.g., Federale Gerechtelijke Politie OA Airport Team Zware Criminaliteit (FGP-Airport) 2010), the scholarly literature, and media accounts. Although we limited our collection of primary data to Belgian sources, we also reviewed academic and policy analyses undertaken in nearby countries, such as the Netherlands and the United Kingdom (UK), and in the United States. In those instances, we extrapolated from the results and, if necessary, made adjustments for Belgian circumstances.

Given our objectives and reliance on Belgian sources, we conducted a "single country" assessment and did not assess harms accruing to bearers outside of Belgium.

Although we recognize that time passes and conditions change, we have not attempted to extend our analysis beyond the 2003–11 period of Paoli et al. (2013), as this would constitute a monumental—and largely

[5] We refer to our criminal justice interviewees with the codes Int-CJ-1 to -18 and to the traffickers or dealers with the codes Int-Of-1 to -12.

infeasible—undertaking; however, we point to instances in which more-recent statistics, reports, or anecdotal evidence either confirm our findings or suggest a need for revision and we offer observations on the implications of that evidence in our concluding remarks. Here, we note growing concern for the harms of cocaine trafficking and related activities in Belgium (e.g., van Horenbeek and van den Broek 2018), but caution against engaging in moral panics (Paoli 2017).

In this application, as in our others of the same era (e.g., Greenfield et al. 2016; Paoli et al. 2015), we considered harms of all types to all classes of bearers and we adopted the exclusions that we outlined in Chapter 4; for example, we conducted a "gross" analysis of harms in which we disqualified any ill-gotten gains or losses thereof.

5.3 The Business Model of Cocaine Trafficking in Belgium

The business model that emerged from the data for 2003 to 2011 consists of two phases of trafficking (first, import and, second, wholesale distribution or export), occurring via sea, air, and land; two enabled activities (dealing and use); and three accompanying activities (violence, corruption, and money laundering), as depicted in Figure 5.1. We address imports by sea, air, and land separately, because the modes accrue harms differently.

We describe each of these activities, phases, etc., below and address the relevance of accompanying activities to each with one noteworthy exception. Although we identify cocaine use as an enabled activity, we do not assess harms associated with use in this chapter. That assessment would be necessary for a complete analysis of policy options, but it was beyond our scope.

Import

In our period of analysis, cocaine entered Belgium primarily via the port of Antwerp (hereafter "Antwerp port"), which is the second-largest port in Europe (Port of Antwerp 2010), and the country's two international airports, particularly Brussels International Airport (hereafter "Brussels airport"). Cocaine was also smuggled into Belgium via land, largely from the Netherlands. The Antwerp port's dominance in Europe's sea trade has

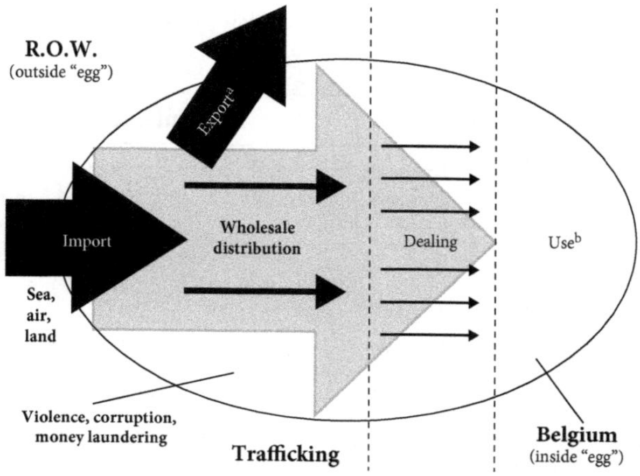

Figure 5.1 Graphical representation of business model for cocaine trafficking and related activities in Belgium

Source: Authors' adaptation of Paoli et al. (2013).

Notes:

R.O.W. = rest of world.

[a] Export might entail some wholesale or distributional activities prior to transit.

[b] We did not study cocaine use.

helped to make Belgium a key transit point for cocaine. In 2006, the US Department of State (2006, 320) reported "an official estimate of 20 tons [of cocaine] entering the port each year," but added that "the actual number is believed to be considerably higher." Belgian officers were more cautious in pinning down a number (Int-CJ-3, -8) but some (e.g., Frans 2010) believed the US estimate was too low. A few years later, the US Department of State (2010, 143) suggested that about 25 percent of the cocaine that moves from South America through Europe eventually transits Belgium, which could amount to at least 30 tons annually.[6,7]

[6] We made this calculation on the basis of UNODC (2010c) consumption estimates for Europe and without accounting for seizures. UNODC (2010c, 71) reports 124 tons of pure cocaine consumed in the "EU/EFTA" (i.e., European Free Trade Association, including also Iceland, Liechtenstein, Norway and Switzerland) region in 2008: 25 percent of 124 is 31 tons. If including East and South-East Europe, we would add 25 percent of the 13 tons of cocaine consumption reported for those regions, bringing the total to 34 tons. If one were to adjust the figures for seizures, the flows would be even larger.

[7] More-recent reports suggest that more cocaine is either flowing through or attempting to flow through Antwerp port than in our period of analysis. Seizures of cocaine at Antwerp port in 2018 and 2019 were about 51 tons and 64 tons, respectively, according to *Belga* (2020), compared with 2.5 tons in 2008 (Table 5.1; see also Colman et al. 2018).

Table 5.1 Numbers of large-scale cocaine seizures and amounts seized in Belgium (2005–8)

Year	Number of seizures					Amount of cocaine seized				
	Total	Antwerp port		Brussels airport		Total	Antwerp port		Brussels airport	
	n	n	%	n	%	Tons	Tons	%	Tons	%
2005	n/a	6	n/a	57	n/a	9.2	2.9	31.5	1.7	18.5
2006	174	22	12.6	108	62.1	3.9	2.1	53.8	0.7	17.9
2007	188	14	7.4	133	70.7	2.5	1.2	48.0	0.7	28.0
2008	168	38	22.6	94	56.0	3.9	2.5	64.1	0.9	23.1

Source: Authors' adaptation of Paoli et al. (2013), based on data from Centrale Dienst Drugs (2010).
Notes:
n = number; % = percentage; n/a = not available
Large-scale cocaine seizures are defined as those weighing more than half a kg.

On a much smaller scale, Brussels airport accounted for the lion's share of cocaine smuggling by air. The airport has good connections with most large Latin American and Caribbean countries and with several African countries (e.g., Benin, Congo, Ghana, Sierra Leone, and Togo) that have served as cocaine transshipment points en route to Europe. From 2005 to 2008, Antwerp port and Brussels airport accounted for 50 percent to 87 percent of the cocaine seized in wholesale amounts[8] in Belgium (Table 5.1).

A comparison of transit estimates, seizure amounts, and consumption estimates suggests that substantially more cocaine entered Belgium than was consumed there. Consumption data are notoriously weak (Paoli et al. 2009), but two very different methods of estimation yield roughly consistent ballpark figures. Whereas a sewage-water analysis (van Nuijs et al. 2009) suggested that Belgium's aggregate annual consumption might amount to about 1.75 tons, our own analysis of United Nations Office on Drugs and Crime (UNODC) data on prevalence suggested a figure of about 2.5 tons. Extrapolating from the European School Survey Project

[8] Defined as seizures larger than half a kg. Wholesale seizures, so defined, accounted for the overwhelming majority of the overall quantities seized (UNODC (2010b).

on Alcohol and Other Drugs, UNODC (2010c, 285) estimates a past-month prevalence of 1.2 percent in the Belgian adult population, ages 15 to 64 years. Given a population estimate of 6.9 million Belgian residents between the ages of 15 and 64 (Central Intelligence Agency 2010), the 1.2 percent prevalence rate implies about 82,800 current users. We then multiplied the number of users by the UNODC estimate of the average amount consumed by each user, which is 30.2 grams of pure cocaine per year (UNODC 2010c, 71), to arrive at the 2.5-ton figure. Large-scale seizures alone, ranging from a low of 2.5 tons to a high of 9.2 tons from 2005 to 2008 (Table 5.1), would match or exceed either consumption figure, even after adjusting for differences in the purity of cocaine in the measures. In other words, transshipment dominated.

Transit by sea

An overview of traffic at Antwerp port hints at the challenges of interdiction at this and similar entry points. Advertising 160 kilometers of quayside available for loading and unloading and 5.3 million square meters of warehousing, the port handled upwards of 150 million tons of freight in a year during our time frame,[9] hosted tens of thousands of port calls, and described itself as the "supermarket of Europe," with trade flowing from the major cocaine producing countries and their neighbors (Port of Antwerp 2010).

Cocaine shipments that transited Antwerp port typically ranged from a few kilograms to several tons. The largest seizure on record in Belgium up to the end of our data collection weighed 3 tons and was found in a banana container in 2002 (*Belang van Limburg* 2002; Int-CJ-8). Four years later, Dutch authorities intercepted 4.6 tons of cocaine in Rotterdam that were bound for Antwerp (*De Volkskrant* 2005).[10] All of our sources, including three known traffickers (Int-Of-2, -6, -7), indicate that cocaine shipments were frequently or most often hidden in containers.[11]

Out of our sample of 52 proceedings, 40 were initiated by the Antwerp prosecutor's office between 2003 and 2009. In at least 15 of these 40 criminal

[9] More recently, the Port of Antwerp (2018a) has handled more than 200 million tons of freight annually.

[10] In 2012 and 2017 record amounts of cocaine, 8 tons and 7 tons, respectively, were seized at the port, in both cases hidden among bananas (Openbaar Ministerie 2012; Politie 2018).

[11] The methods do not seem to have changed since then, but the quantities smuggled in each shipment have tended to become larger. That is why, according to van Horenbeek and van den Broek (2018), the number of annual seizures at the port has remained fairly stable.

proceedings, dock and other port workers were involved in retrieving cocaine from either a ship or a container (Case-LS-1, -2, -7, -11, -12, -13, -16, -17, -18, -20, -21, -22, -26, -27, -29; see also US Department of State 2010). An informant (Int-Of-7) with direct experience smuggling cocaine through the port reported that dock and other port workers sometimes facilitated operations.

In most instances, we found that port workers were bribed. Their payoffs varied from €1,000 to €30,000 per operation, depending on their tasks (Case-LS-16, -21). On some occasions, such as Case-Full-5, dock workers might have entered a ship, picked up one or more bags, and delivered them to a vehicle or driven them to a safe house. Alternatively, they might have ensured that the right container stood on a predetermined spot or provided information about its location (Int-Of-7). At other times, dock workers delivered discharge documents to traffickers, informing them exactly when and where a ship would arrive (e.g., Case-LS-16).

Container technicians, especially those who repair and maintain refrigerated containers, were also involved in cocaine extractions. Refrigerated containers with compartments for electronics and cooling equipment often are used to transport fruit and other perishable goods that are shipped from cocaine-producing countries in Latin America to Belgium. Technicians typically have free access to those compartments and can remove bags or packages at will. In nine of the Antwerp cases, smugglers used such refrigerated containers to hide the cocaine (Case-LS-10, -19, -25 and Case-Full-8 show only the retrieval of cocaine; Case-LS-2, -7, -16, -21, -29 also show the involvement of container technicians). Two of our interviewees (Int-Of-6, 7) also confirmed this practice.

Sailors or other ship staff, such as mess employees, were implicated in smuggling in six Antwerp cases (Case-LS-2, -20; Case-SS-8 -9, -13; Case-Full-8). They delivered bags with cocaine to a person who either waited on the dock or entered the ship.

Whereas a few low-level ship or port workers might have been corrupted, the evidence suggests that the managers and owners of shipping and logistics businesses were usually unaware of misuse. We did not, for example, find evidence of a shipowner's or captain's complicity in any of the cases in our sample or in our interviews with experts and perpetrators. Likewise, it appears that the containers used for shipping cocaine were usually rented from legitimate logistics companies without their knowledge of illegal activities. In the unlikely event that a manufacturing or service company was drawn into investigations, the company also seemed to lack awareness of misuse. In 3 of the 40 Antwerp cases, the companies' managers or owners did play a knowing role, but, in those cases, the companies were just front companies, without additional purpose (Case-LS-3, -9, -24). An informant with direct experience in this business (Int-Of-7) stressed that smugglers tend to prefer hiding cocaine in the cargo of large legitimate manufacturing businesses that have a good reputation, carry out high-frequency shipments, and are unaware of "hitch-hiking."

We found modest evidence of violence—either threats or use—in the import of cocaine through Antwerp port. Six of the 40 Antwerp cases (Case-LS-1, -2, -17, -21, -30, -31) provide evidence that some traffickers had threatened their accomplices. In Case-LS-3, the Turkish individual who had organized the shipment was compelled to stay with the Colombian and Ghanese owners of the cocaine, while the 600 kilograms were loaded off the ship. In six cases, partially overlapping with those documenting the threat of violence (Case-LS-1, -2, -7, -14, -18, -26), authorities found small firearms (handguns) during searches or arrests. (The presence of firearms, even if suggestive, does not constitute evidence of explicit use of violence.) Traffickers also emphasized the nonviolent nature of high-level cocaine smuggling, especially by sea: they all noted that the larger the shipments, the less violent is the business (Int-Of-2, -3, -4, -5, -6, -7, -9, -11). Two of them described violence as occurring "hardly ever" or "very rarely" during import (Int-Of-2, -5).

We found little or no evidence of the threat or use of violence against government officials along sea routes in our sample of cases, in the organized-crime database, or from our interviewees.[12] Further suggesting a low risk of encountering violence, a law-enforcement officer indicated (Int-CJ-3) that the Belgian police hardly ever use firearms to arrest traffickers.[13]

Corruption of Belgian government officials along sea routes appears to have been a minor concern. An interviewee described a 2009 investigation (Int-CJ-8 with telephone updates in July 2011), in which a customs officer's partner was accused of cocaine trafficking. The officer was cleared of facilitation and retained; the trial against the officer's partner was still pending at the time of our data collection. In the course of a 2010 operation,

[12] We refer to the database in our discussion of the business model, but we reserve a fuller discussion of that source for the analysis in Section 5.4 because it—the source—does not distinguish between phases or modes of trafficking as we do in this section and, thus, we cannot parse the content of the database accordingly.

[13] More-recent sources do not suggest an increase in the use of violence in the import of cocaine via sea routes (see, e.g., van Horenbeek and van den Broek 2018).

Table 5.2 Cocaine couriers and body-packers arrested at Brussels airport and main departure airports (2006–9)

	2006	2007	2008	2009
Cocaine couriers arrested	164	116	87	39
Main airports of departure[a] (≥ 8 arrests)	Conakry, Abidjan, Caracas, Cancun, Dakar, Banjul	Conakry, Dakar, Banjul, Lome	Conakry, Punta Cana	Punta Cana
Body-packers[b]	85	47	37	17

Source: Authors' adaptation of Paoli et al. (2013), based on data from FGP-Airport (2010).
Notes:

[a] Conakry, Dakar, Banjul, and Lome are the capitals of Guinea, Senegal, Gambia, and Tome, respectively; Abidjan is the largest city of the Ivory Coast; Punta Cana is in the Dominican Republic.

[b] The category of body-packers includes cocaine and heroin couriers; however, the ratio of the number of heroin to cocaine seizures at Brussels airport is about 1:10, implying that most of the body-packers carried cocaine (FGP-Airport 2010).

the Belgian police also arrested a member of the Royal Marechaussee, a Dutch military police force, who had taken part in a smuggling operation at Antwerp port (Mos 2010).[14,15]

Transit by air

According to police statistics (FGP-Airport 2010; Table 5.2 of this chapter), most cocaine smuggled via air reached Brussels airport from Western Africa or Latin America. The statistics also show a sharp decline in the number of cocaine couriers arrested, from 164 in 2006 to 39 in 2009. We are unaware of any reduction in detection efforts and none of our interviewees could explain the decline definitively.[16]

14 A low-level custom officer working at the port was arrested in late 2012 for facilitating the import of at least 10 tons of cocaine, including the 8 tons seized in October of that year, and was later sentenced to 14 years of imprisonment (see, e.g., van Horenbeek and van den Broek 2018). Less than a handful of other cases of corruption have come to the fore since then (e.g., *De Standaard* 2021).

15 The available evidence suggests that private yachts were also used for ocean crossings, but not frequently. In case Case-LS-6, for instance, some evidence was found that two 40-foot sailing boats had entered the Belgian port of either Zeebrugge or Nieuwpoort. According to a witness, each vessel carried 250 kg of cocaine, but no cocaine was seized.

16 Judging by the lack of media attention, the decline of both the quantities seized and the number of couriers arrested has likely continued since the end of our data collection. The most

The Belgian Federal Police (FGP-Airport 2010) do not keep detailed statistics on smuggling techniques via air for each type of illegal drug, but three techniques stand out. First, drugs might be hidden inside luggage. Second, couriers might hide small cocaine packets—or "balls"—*in* their bodies, either by swallowing them or inserting them in their rectum or vagina (so-called "body-packing"). Third, couriers might hide drugs *on* their bodies, either under their clothes or inside their shoes. While a few kilograms can be hidden in luggage—as demonstrated by the seizure of about five kilograms of cocaine in the luggage of couriers coming from Congo, Cameroon, and Togo (e.g., Case-Full-4, -6)—body-packers and other couriers cannot ordinarily carry more than one or two kilograms on each trip, as one of our informants, himself a body-packer, confirmed (Int-Of-10).

Of the three techniques, body-packing was and is the most dangerous, but the technology has improved and lethal accidents have become more uncommon. In the approximate period of our analysis, two body-packers died en route to or upon arriving at Brussels airport, when drug-filled balls exploded in their bodies (Int-CJ-4).[17]

If cocaine was hidden in luggage, it was usually retrieved by the courier, who brought the luggage out of the airport and consigned it to a trafficker, typically without involving the cooperation of airport personnel. In 2007 and 2008, though, in two partially overlapping investigations, 13 employees of the main baggage-handling company at Brussels airport were arrested because they were suspected of participating in a number of cocaine smuggling operations. In the first case, the luggage came from several African countries; in the second case, from the Dominican Republic (*Dernière Heure* 2007; *De Standaard* 2007; Int-CJ-1, -11; Case-Full-2, -3). The baggage handlers extracted marked suitcases that contained cocaine from airplanes and delivered the suitcases to a contact person waiting in a car at the airport parking deck. They received up to €10,000 per operation (*Dernière Heure* 2007; Int-CJ-9).

Other smuggling options, albeit reported infrequently, include hiding cocaine in air cargo or leaving the cocaine on a plane and having cleaners

recent media account we have found online was dated 2014 and reported a further decrease in the quantities seized at Brussels Airport. Accordingly, 420 kg were seized in 2011, 550 kg in 2012, and 160 kg in 2013 (*HLN* 2014).

[17] See Zaitch (2002, 149–50), for a related discussion of trafficking in the Netherlands.

or catering personnel pick it up. In the period 2006–9, the Belgian Federal Police identified seven instances of cocaine transportation by air cargo (FGP-Airport 2010). In one proceeding (Case-Full-1), a cocaine trafficker approached a few employees of a large logistics company—based in Brussels airport—and asked if they wanted to extract packages from the secured logistical network that allowed the company to skip border controls at entry points. The employees were promised €10,000 to €50,000 per week, but they refused the offer and informed their supervisor. Ultimately, the trafficker was arrested (Int-CJ-1, -9; Case-Full-1). Logistics companies might have been misused more passively by people who sent cocaine in packages from cocaine-producing or transit countries. This occurred in Case-LS-4, in which a group of Dutch individuals asked their contact(s) on the island of Curacao in the Caribbean to send packages containing about 600 grams of cocaine to addressees in Antwerp.

Cocaine was also smuggled into Belgium with private planes. One of our interviewees (Int-Of-6) used a private plane to move cocaine from Ghana to France. Law-enforcement data suggest that this method was not very common; however, it might be underreported.

In none of these instances was there any evidence that the senior staff of airport or other logistic companies were aware of—let alone had accepted or participated in—the misuse of their companies or facilities by traffickers.

We found less evidence of the threat or use of violence along air routes than along sea routes. It seems plausible that workers (couriers and bribed airport employees) involved in smuggling operations were threatened to ensure their compliance; however, our sources, including our interview with a body-packer (Int-Of-10), provided little evidence of threats. The interviewee added, speaking from personal experience, that traffickers often select couriers with financial problems that make them more dependent. In Case-Full-2, a driver in charge of transporting bags of cocaine from the airport to a warehouse reported being "ripped"; that is, robbed of drugs at a gunpoint. However, the police officer in charge of the investigation doubted the reliability of the account (Int-CJ-9).

The corruption of government officials also appears to have been quite limited in this context. In our period of analysis, two members of the law-enforcement community emerged as possible facilitators along air routes

(Case-Full-2, -3). The suspects, a police officer and a police trainee, were closely related to a group of traffickers by ethnic and friendship ties, but it was yet unclear whether the small intelligence tips the police officer delivered concerned cocaine trafficking (Int-CJ-1, -9). Although the criminal case was still pending at the time of our data collection, both suspects had been fired.[18]

Transit by land

The third possible mode of import is by land, including transit by both roads and railways. Much less information was available on land transit than on sea or air, as there are many possible entry points and Belgian land borders are not patrolled.

All of the evidence from our sample of cases (e.g., Case-Full-7), our interviews with experts (Int-CJ-3, -7, -10), and Belgian and US reports (e.g., Federale Politie België 2008; US Department of State 2007, 360) suggests that most cocaine smuggled into Belgium by land, in either small or large lots, arrived from the Netherlands. Several of the traffickers who we interviewed also bought large quantities of cocaine in the Netherlands (Int-Of-3, -4, -5, -9). Still, cocaine also arrived by land from other countries. In Case-LS-16, for example, several multi-kilogram lots of cocaine were smuggled by car from Paris to Antwerp. In Case-SS-10 a private yacht was used to transport 1,200 kilograms of cocaine from Venezuela to Spain; later, the cocaine was distributed by land and 300 kilograms arrived in Antwerp (see also Naesen and Demeyer 2005). However, any of these routes might be underassessed in official analyses because Belgian land borders are effectively open.

Traffickers sometimes used rental cars or vans to transport cocaine from and to the Netherlands and other European countries, apparently without the knowledge of the rental companies. We found evidence of this practice in two cases (Case-LS-1, -5) and two interviews (Int-Of-3, -11), but found no corresponding evidence of harms.

We did not find any specific information on the threat or use of violence or corruption along land routes.[19]

[18] The media has not reported any other cases of drug-related corruption at Belgian airports since then.

[19] The media has not reported any significant changes concerning land routes in recent years.

Wholesale Distribution and Export

Belgian authorities have limited information on wholesale distribution and export, but our sources consistently suggest that the cocaine entering Belgium often journeyed to the Netherlands. According to an Antwerp police officer (Int-CJ-3), the overwhelming majority of the cocaine ("95 percent") entering Antwerp port was bound for the Netherlands. Although this estimate was unverifiable, Dutch authorities admitted (Korps Landelijke Politiediensten 2005) that the Netherlands had become a hub in the European illegal drug market. In eight cases in our sample (Case-LS-1, -2, -9, 20; Case-Full-1, -2, -3; Case-SS-2), we found evidence that cocaine seizures were intended for transshipment to clients in Amsterdam or, less frequently, elsewhere in the Netherlands. As both criminal justice experts (Int-CJ-2, -3, -10) and traffickers (Int-Of-2, -3, -4, -5, -6, -7, -9) explained, the wholesale load was often exported to the Netherlands, unpacked and cut, and then part of it would re-enter Belgium for domestic use, while the rest was shipped to other countries.

According to both law enforcement officers and traffickers (Int-CJ-3; Int-Of-8), Antwerp seemed to be the center of wholesale distribution in Belgium because of its port and its proximity to the Netherlands. Lots to be distributed in Belgium were, depending on their size, brought to warehouses or private premises, where they were split, cut, and repackaged for further distribution. The cocaine packages initially imported by airport couriers might have been sold to dealers, but two or three more transactions could occur before the larger loads imported by sea or land reached the retail market (Int-CJ-10).[20]

None of our sources documents corruption of either businesses or government agencies in export or wholesale distribution, but the threat or use of violence seemed to be more common in this phase than during import. We found repeated evidence of "rip-deals" at the wholesale- and middle-market levels: after a few successful exchanges, a trafficker would order a lot of cocaine larger than usual and then rob his supplier at gun point. Case-LS-31 involved an especially serious swindle. A Belgian citizen who mediated the sale of four kilograms of cocaine was taken hostage by the buyers,

[20] The role of Antwerp's drug traffickers in wholesale distribution seems to have grown since the end of our data collection, possibly because some Antwerp-based import facilitators allegedly have started taking payment "in kind," with cocaine, instead of in cash (e.g., *Humo* 2017; Sauviller 2017).

threatened with a gun, and assaulted. The traffickers and dealers whom we interviewed concurred that rip-deals were the most likely way to encounter the threat and, more rarely, use of violence in the cocaine business (Int-Of-3, -5, -6, -7, -8, -9, -11). One interviewee (Int-Of-9) also admitted to carrying out rip-deals. Except for such swindles, traffickers and law enforcement officers (e.g., Int-CJ-8) agreed that the level of violence in the Belgian cocaine market was low.

In general terms, the organized-crime database, confirmed the interviewees' perceptions: among the 81 cocaine trafficking cases represented in that database, we found evidence of one kidnapping or hostage taking (the same episode that was reported in Case-LS-31) and six assaults of any kind (Table 5.3). The organized-crime database also associated two murders or manslaughters with trafficking, but we do not include them in our assessments. One episode took place outside of Belgium and was not relevant to our assessment and, according to the law-enforcement officer in charge of the investigations (contacted by telephone in June 2010), the other was unconfirmed in subsequent investigations.[21]

Dealing

To the extent that Belgian dealers purchased cocaine in Belgium during our period of analysis, they often did so in Antwerp, which had become a locus for domestic distribution, but dealers—and users—often went to the Netherlands to buy cocaine (Int-Of-3, -4, -9).

As in other countries, two separate retail markets coexist in Belgium: dealers sell cocaine (and other illegal drugs) on the street and in private settings. By whatever means, retail transactions must have been occurring routinely, as 82,800 Belgians were consuming about 1.75–2.5 tons of cocaine in gram-denominated lots, annually.[22]

The street or "open-scene" market was dominated by ethnic minorities and, specifically, recent migrants who often lacked legal residency or job permits. In Brussels and Antwerp (Int-CJ-11, -12), much as in Frankfurt

[21] A drug-related murder occurred in late 2012, when a Dutch wholesaler was killed in front an Antwerp hotel allegedly as retribution for stealing 200 kg of cocaine from other traffickers. Since then, other shootings, at least two kidnappings, and many grenade explosions have been recorded in Antwerp, leading the local press to speak of a "drug war" and "Moroccan drug mafia" (e.g., *Humo* 2017; Lefelon 2018; Sauviller 2017; Heymans et al. 2019).

[22] See the discussion of these numbers in Section 5.3, under "import."

Table 5.3 Episodes of violence in Belgium associated with cocaine trafficking (2006–8) (as reported in Belgian Federal Police's organized-crime database)

Identity of Target	Nature of Violence										
	Direct threat	Menacing presence	Threat of acquaintance	Malicious phone call	Rumor mongering	Blackmail	Assault	Murder/ manslaughter[a]	Kidnapping/ hostage taking	Other	Total
Own criminal group affiliate	22	3	3	1	0	2	5	1	1	3	41
Other criminal group affiliate	2	1	1	0	0	0	0	1	0	0	5
Informant	0	0	2	1	1	0	0	0	0	0	4
Perpetrators, including informants, subtotal	**24**	**4**	**6**	**2**	**1**	**2**	**5**	**2**	**1**	**3**	**50**
Individual/firm's representative	2	1	1	1	0	0	1	0	0	0	6
Politician/political party affiliate	0	0	0	0	0	1	0	0	0	0	1
Police officer	1	0	0	0	0	0	0	0	0	0	1
Magistrate	1	0	0	0	0	0	0	0	0	0	1
Nonperpetrators, private and public, subtotal	**4**	**1**	**1**	**1**	**0**	**1**	**1**	**0**	**0**	**0**	**9**
Other	0	1	0	0	0	0	0	0	0	0	1
Total	**28**	**6**	**7**	**3**	**1**	**3**	**6**	**2**	**1**	**3**	**60**

Source: Authors' adaptation and expansion of Paoli et al. (2013), based on data from Federale Politie (2010).

Notes:

The organized-crime database reports 60 episodes of violence distributed over 37 of 81 proceedings for the years 2006–8.

[a] We do not include these murders or manslaughters in our analysis. The organized-crime database lists them, but one episode took place outside of Belgium and was not relevant to our assessment and the other was unconfirmed in subsequent investigations.

and Milan (Paoli 2000), they were mostly Northern and Southern Africans. Undocumented migrants are especially vulnerable and, according to the accounts of some policemen, their employers can mistreat and oblige them to sell drugs, sometimes also threatening their families in their home countries. In Charleroi, two undocumented migrants reportedly asked for help from the police (Int-CJ-10). Although they were less visible, native-born Belgian addicts also functioned as street dealers.

In other urban contexts, street dealing creates a public nuisance, principally in disadvantaged neighborhoods; however, at the time of our data collection this seemed to be unusual in Belgian cities which had little tolerance for open drug scenes. None of Brussels' neighborhoods stood out as traditionally associated with drug sales (Decorte et al. 2004, 12). Decorte et al. (2004) carried out a detailed study on drug-related nuisance throughout the country; in a survey of 3,700 individuals "less than 1 percent of the nuisance reported was regarded as drug-related" (p. 157, our translation)—an assessment largely confirmed by Decorte et al.'s ethnographic fieldwork in Antwerp and Charleroi and our interviews (Int-CJ-10, -11, -12).

Cocaine is also, perhaps primarily, dealt in private or "closed-scene" settings. Research on drug markets in cities across Europe suggests that dealers in these settings typically are indigenous to the countries in which they deal or are second- or third-generation immigrants (Paoli and Reuter 2008).[23] An extended study of cocaine use in Antwerp (Decorte 2000), involving interviews with 111 users, provides little evidence of criminal professionalization among closed-scene dealers. Users most often reported acquiring cocaine from friends or a single, regular dealer, whom they visited at home or who delivered to their home. Less than 10 percent of users bought cocaine on the street (Decorte 2000, 218–19).

None of our sources indicates that either open- or closed-scene dealing required or engendered government or private-sector corruption. In closed-scene dealing, dealers misused some cafés and discotheques as sales venues, but without evidence of the managers or owners' complicity. In street dealing, dealers supplying or supervising street workers sometimes rented flats to hide and "cut" cocaine (Int-CJ-10, -11).

Violence—other than threatening or intimidating behavior, as cited—also seemed to occur infrequently, particularly in the closed-scene settings where cocaine exchanges are embedded in trusted relationships. Swindles happened on the street and among street dealers and their cocaine suppliers,

[23] Paoli and Reuter (2008) report on ethnic minorities and drug trafficking across Europe.

but they did not often involve the explicit use of violence. According to police officers working in Brussels and Antwerp (Int-CJ-10, -11, -12), police hardly ever found guns in the possession of street dealers and their cocaine suppliers.

Money Laundering

We found no official estimates of the revenues of cocaine trafficking in Belgium and, hence, potential laundering, but a UNODC report (2005, 131) allows some scoping of the Belgian retail market. According to that report, consumers in Western and Central Europe used 107.4 tons of cocaine in 2003, valued at $17,328 million at retail. Rough estimates of annual Belgian consumption—1.75 tons (van Nuijs et al. 2009) and 2.5 tons (our estimate, based on UNODC 2010c)—suggest that Belgium could have accounted for about 2 percent of that market. On that basis, if average retail prices in Belgium were not very different from those elsewhere in Europe, Belgium's retail stake could have amounted to almost $350 million.[24]

A considerable fraction of trafficking revenues—possibly the majority of import revenues—appears to have gone to other countries. Of the 660 cocaine traffickers associated with the 81 cases in the organized-crime database, over 60 percent were born outside of Belgium, mainly in the Netherlands (8.3 percent), Turkey (6.7 percent), Morocco (4.2 percent), and Ghana (3.2 percent); presumably, they repatriated some revenues to their countries of origin (Federale Politie België 2010). Belgian offenders also held part of their ill-gotten earnings outside Belgium to avoid detection (Int-Of-6, -7). Several criminal proceedings offer evidence of these practices. In four investigations (Case-SS-1, -4, -8; Case-LS-8), cocaine trafficking profits were moved via banks and money-transfer companies to Afghanistan and Turkey, Brazil, Costa Rica and Brazil, and Nauru, respectively. In Case-LS-6, the profits flowed through an underground banking scheme in real estate projects in Dubai.

It seems unlikely that the financial flows associated with cocaine trafficking had a substantial effect on the Belgian economy in aggregate or

[24] This estimate might be too high because it combines data from a 2009 report (van Nuijs et al. 2009) and a 2010 report (UNODC 2010c) for Belgium and a 2005 report (UNODC 2005) for elsewhere in Europe: during that interval, the European market grew, at least in terms of tonnage. However, it might also understate revenues, because it does not account for cocaine imports meant for re-export.

locally. The value of the retail cocaine market probably amounted to about a tenth of a percent of Belgium's overall economic activity[25] and we found no evidence that traffickers were able to affect any sector of Belgium's legal economy. One trafficker (Int-Of-7) laundered his profits, which were up to €100,000 per operation, through his second-hand car company. In another episode, one of the biggest Belgium-based traffickers known—who, however, dealt primarily with hashish and heroin—bought a beauty salon in Antwerp for his ex-wife and invested part of his profits in a tourist resort in Thailand (van der Aa 2009). Our evidence indicates that the money kept in Belgium was used mostly to buy real estate or spent on luxury goods and lifestyles (e.g., Case-Full-2; Case-SS-4; Case-LS-7, -20; Int-Of-9).

Surprisingly, large sums were kept in cash and hidden at home (e.g., Case-LS-20) and, in one case, under the suspect's bed (Case-Full-2). Although money laundering typically involves "hiding," "obscuring," or "concealing," we treat this practice separately and refer to it as "physical concealment" (see Appendix A).

These investment patterns might also reflect the small-scale of many cocaine trafficking enterprises active in Belgium during our period of analysis. Contrary to the assertion of the US Department of State (2010, 143) that "the flow of cocaine to Belgium is mainly controlled by Colombian organizations with representative[s] residing in Africa and Europe," the Belgian data suggest otherwise. Colombians were just one of the nationalities involved in wholesale trafficking and were ranked as the seventh-largest group (with Albanians and Filipinos) in the list of cocaine traffickers found in the organized-crime database in the period 2006–8. Nor did Colombians play a major role in the proceedings in our sample. Case-LS-7, one of the few relevant cases, described a Colombian arriving in Antwerp to take control of a container of cocaine parked in the port. Some Colombian trafficking organizations might have owned the drugs, but the Belgian police have difficulty establishing ownership, not least because many large shipments are destined for the Netherlands. There is no doubt, however, that small and ephemeral trafficking enterprises were also at work, often composed of Belgian and Dutch nationals (e.g., Case-LS-1, -8, -9; for similar

[25] According the World Bank (World Development Indicators, downloaded, May 20, 2011), Belgium's gross domestic product in 2003 was $311,192 million in current dollars. Above, we estimated that its retail cocaine market might have amounted to almost $350 million in that same year.

findings regarding trafficking in the Netherlands, see van Duyne and Levi 2005, 127–33).[26]

5.4 Walking through the Assessment Process

Working with the business model, we walk through the remaining steps of the harm assessment process.[27] As noted previously, our assessment excludes harms incurred outside of Belgium and those associated with cocaine use in Belgium.

Identifying Possible Harms

In this step, we identify the possible harms for each phase of the primary activity (cocaine trafficking) and the activities that accompany it (violence, corruption, and money laundering) and then we repeat the process for the enabled activity (dealing). That a harm appears in Table 5.4, which shows the results of this exercise by class of bearer and type for each activity, does not imply that it occurs to any great extent, only that it is plausible, given what we learned about the primary, enabled, and accompanying activities from the data for our period of analysis. By extension, the absence of a harm from Table 5.4 suggests its implausibility.

To illustrate our approach, we highlight a few examples of plausible harms and implausible harms. Speaking to the plausible or "possible," the business model suggests that body-packers might suffer physical and psychological losses from accidental overdoses, whereas traffickers, dealers, facilitators and, much less likely, government workers could suffer harms from damages to their physical or psychological integrity if they encounter

[26] More-recent media reports (e.g., de Coninck 2014) and journalists' books (e.g., Sauveller 2017) report the presence of more stable drug-trafficking groups operating on Belgian soil, many of which are allegedly composed of second- and third-generation migrants, frequently of Moroccan descent. While we could not check the trustworthiness of such statements, the pattern of money laundering does not seem to have changed much since the end of our data collection. For all of 2017, for example, the Antwerp section of the Federal Police reported the seizure of assets worth €10 million, much of which is said to consist of properties in Morocco, luxury goods and cars (Lefelon 2018).

[27] At this point in the chapter, readers might notice a shift in tone; whereas we described events in the business model in the past tense, we describe the assessment process in the present tense.

Table 5.4 Possible harms in different phases of cocaine trafficking, dealing, and accompanying activities

Harms to/associated with	Trafficking		Dealing	Money laundering	Corruption	Violence	Bearers
	Import	Export/ Wholesale Distribution					
Harms to individuals, specifically to their:							
Functional integrity							
Loss of life	X (air)	n/a	n/a	n/a	n/a	n/a	Body-packers, i.e., if drug balls cause fatal injuries, by exploding and leading to overdose
Other physical, psychological, and intellectual	X (air)	n/a	n/a	n/a	n/a	n/a	Body-packers, i.e., if drug balls cause nonfatal injuries
	n/a	n/a	n/a	n/a	n/a	X (I, E/ D, R)	Traffickers, dealers, couriers, facilitators, and less plausibly government officials or representatives, i.e., if targeted by threat or use of violence
Material support	X (air)	n/a	n/a	n/a	n/a	X (I, E/ D, R)	Ancillary to functional harms (health)
	n/a	n/a	n/a	n/a	n/a	X (I, E/ D, R)	Traffickers, dealers, couriers, facilitators, and others, i.e., if targeted by threat or use of violence, specifically blackmail
Reputation	n/a	n/a	n/a	n/a	n/a	X (I, E/ D, R)	Traffickers, dealer, couriers, facilitators, and less plausibly government officials or representatives, i.e., if targeted by threat or use of violence, specifically detectable
Privacy and autonomy	n/a	n/a	n/a	n/a	n/a	X (I, E/ D)	Traffickers, i.e., if kidnapped or confined

Continued

Table 5.4 *Continued*

Harms to/associated with	Trafficking		Dealing	Money laundering	Corruption	Violence	Bearers
Harms to private-sector entities, specifically to their:							
Functional integrity	X	X	n/a	n/a	X (I)	n/a	Transport or import businesses, e.g., if corrupt officials or employees or traffickers misuse assets
Material support	X	X	n/a	n/a	X (I)	n/a	Ancillary to functional harms (property) Independent of functional harms (property)
Reputation	X	X	n/a	n/a	X (I)	n/a	Transport or import businesses, e.g., if corrupt officials or employees or traffickers misuse assets, even if businesses are unaware of exploitation at time of occurrence
Privacy and autonomy	X	X	n/a	n/a	X (I)	n/a	Transport or import businesses, e.g., if corrupt officials or employees or traffickers misuse assets
Harms to government, specifically to its:							
Functional integrity	n/a	n/a	n/a	n/a	X (I, E/D, R)	n/a	Government agencies, i.e., if officials or representatives engage in corrupt practices, including neglect of duties
Material support	X (air)	n/a	n/a	n/a	X (I, E/D, R)	X	Ancillary to functional harms (health)
	n/a	n/a	n/a	n/a	X (I, E/D, R)	n/a	Government agencies, i.e., if paying wages associated with neglect of duties

Reputation	n/a	n/a	n/a	n/a	X (I, E/D, R)	n/a	Government agencies, i.e., if officials or representatives engage in corrupt practices, including neglect of duties
	X	X	X	X	X	X	Government, overarching, if law breaking implies it cannot enforce its laws
Privacy and autonomy	n/a	n/a	n/a	n/a	X (I, E/D, R)	n/a	Government agencies, i.e., if officials or representatives engage in corrupt practices, including neglect of duties
Harms to the environment, specifically to its:							
Functional integrity							
Physical environment	n/a	n/a	n/a	n/a	n/a	n/a	Physical environment
Social environment	n/a	n/a	X	n/a	n/a	n/a	Social environment, local, e.g., if dealing creates public nuisance
	X	X	X	X	X	X	Social environment, overarching, e.g., from endemic failures to enforce laws, widespread corruption, or other dysfunctionalities

Source: Authors' adaptation of Paoli et al. (2013).
Notes:

X = applicable; n/a = not applicable; I = import; E/D = export or wholesale distribution; R = retailing/dealing.

violence. By contrast, we found nothing in the evidence to suggest the relevance of harms to Belgium's physical environment and regard them as not applicable (n/a) in Table 5.4. Cocaine found in sewage water might, at least speculatively, enter and affect the environment, but it enters from cocaine use, not trafficking. Similarly, we found nothing in any of our sources to suggest harms from money laundering, apart from those to the Belgian government's reputation or the social environment.

Although not apparent in Table 5.4, we also exclude harms to manufacturing and service businesses, because the few businesses that were found to be involved in cocaine trafficking were front companies, established solely for illegal purposes.

Evaluating the Severity and Incidence of Harms

Whereas we identified possible harms on the basis of plausibility, we limit our evaluations of severity and incidence to evidence of realization during our period of analysis (i.e., 2003–11). As explained in Chapter 4, we do not tally an actual harm if we lack credible evidence of a harming event. For that reason, a harm that we deemed possible earlier in the assessment process might not obtain a severity or incidence rating here.

We begin by evaluating the incidence of the primary activity—namely, cocaine trafficking. Recalling the 30-ton-per-year estimate of Belgian throughput and given the variability of shipment quantities (ranging from grams to tons) and the frequency of seizures, we describe trafficking as a "persistent" activity. Using the 30-ton figure and an average seizure amount for all points of entry of 19 kilograms per seizure,[28] we estimate that smuggling occurs at an average rate of slightly over four episodes a day. If, instead, we distinguish between small- and large-scale smuggling operations, defining small-and large-scale by the average seizure amounts at Brussels airport and Antwerp port, respectively (i.e., 7 kilograms and 78 kilograms at each location), we find that small-scale operations occur about three-and-a-half times a day and that large-scale operations occur more than five times a week. Accounting for smaller-scale operations suggests even higher frequencies.

Given vast differences in units of measure in cocaine trafficking and dealing, we treated the incidence of dealing separately, without reference to that of trafficking. Dealing, which involves hundreds of

[28] Calculated using the data in Table 5.1 from 2006 to 2008.

thousands—possibly even millions—of gram-denominated transactions each year, occurs at least persistently, if not continuously.[29]

Next, we evaluate the severity and "within-activity"[30] incidence of the harms of each primary, enabled, and accompanying activity, with the already-noted exception of cocaine use. If the harm is tied to an accompanying activity, we define that activity in sufficiently specific terms to establish a one-to-one correspondence between that activity and each associated harm by creating subcategories of activities for violence, corruption, etc. that call out particular kinds of harming events. In the case of violence, the subcategories ranged from threats or intimidation to kidnapping, to murder and manslaughter.

In theory, we should multiply the within-activity incidence by the incidence of cocaine trafficking—or dealing—to arrive at the overall incidence (Box 4.1), which can be no greater than each of its parts. However, in most instances multiplying the within-activity incidence by "persistently" or "persistently-to-continuous" were it possible, would not result in a readily discernible difference between the overall and the within-activity incidence. It would be as if we were multiplying by something close to "1." For that reason, our ratings of within-activity incidence tend to stand as our ratings of overall incidence. We note a few exceptions, below, in the cases of damages to government reputation and the social environment.

Table 5.5 provides a synthesis of our evaluation of the harms associated with cocaine trafficking, dealing, violence, corruption, and money laundering, ordered first by class of bearer, then by type, and then by priority or ranking.[31]

[29] Consider two simplistic approaches to estimating the number of transactions, neither of which is likely to produce a correct answer, but both of which suggest large numbers. First, taking the prior consumption estimate of 1.75–2.5 tons, annually, and converting it to grams (i.e., 1.75–2.5 million grams), could easily imply hundreds of thousands or more of gram-denominated transactions each year. Second, if an average consumer were to purchase cocaine about once a month, then Belgium's 82,800 consumers, taken in combination, might encounter their dealers almost a million times in a year. The actual numbers of transactions could be lower and not all retail transactions are, strictly speaking, enabled by Belgian trafficking—e.g., some Belgian dealers and users purchase cocaine in the Netherlands—but dealing would appear to occur very often.

[30] The within-activity incidence, as defined in Chapter 4, is the incidence of harm in relation to an activity.

[31] The results in this chapter are generally consistent with, but not identical to those in Paoli et al. (2013). For example, the labels—but not the relative positions—assigned to the priority rankings—e.g., "high," "medium," and "low"—differ in some instances because of recent changes in our priority matrix (Table 4.3). In addition, we now refer to the highest incidence rating as "continuously," not "always." Improvements in our approach to bundling, unbundling, and evaluating observations, including a more systematic approach to parsing them, have also given rise to differences in the number of harms and the ratings and rankings of those harms. In this chapter, we have adhered more closely to the estimation principles set out in Chapter 4.

Table 5.5 Evaluation of harms associated with cocaine trafficking in Belgium

	Severity	Incidence	Priority	Activities, events, and consequences	Bearer
Harms to individuals, specifically to their:					
Functional integrity					
• Loss of life	Catastrophic	Rarely	$M_{i,p}$ [a]	Trafficking (import, air), body packing and overdose (fatal), death	Perpetrators (traffickers, body-packers)
• Other physical, psychological, and intellectual	Grave	Rarely	$ML_{i,p}$	Trafficking (import, air), body packing and overdose (nonfatal), permanent disability or similar	Perpetrators (traffickers, body-packers)
	Grave	Rarely	$ML_{i,p}$	Violence in trafficking,[b] assault and battery (mayhem), permanent disability or similar	Perpetrators (traffickers)
	Grave	Rarely	$ML_{i,p}$	Violence in trafficking, kidnapping or confinement (sustained), permanent disability or similar	Perpetrators (traffickers)
	Grave	Rarely	$ML_{i,p}$	Violence in dealing, assault and battery (mayhem), permanent disability or similar	Perpetrators (suppliers and dealers)
	Serious	Rarely	$L_{i,p}$	Trafficking (import, air), body packing and overdose (nonfatal), nonpermanent health consequences, meriting hospitalization or similar	Perpetrators (traffickers, body-packers)
	Serious	Rarely	$L_{i,p}$	Violence in trafficking, assault and battery (major), nonpermanent health consequences, meriting hospitalization or similar	Perpetrators (traffickers)

Serious	Rarely	$L_{i,o}$	Violence in trafficking, assault and battery (major), nonpermanent health consequences, meriting hospitalization or similar	Nonperpetrators (private and public)
Serious	Rarely	$L_{i,p}$	Violence in dealing, assault and battery (major), nonpermanent health consequences, meriting hospitalization or similar	Perpetrators (suppliers and dealers)
Moderate	Rarely	$L_{i,p}$	Trafficking (import, air), body packing and overdose (nonfatal), nonpermanent health consequences, meriting out-patient care or similar	Perpetrators (body-packers)
Moderate	Rarely	$L_{i,p}$	Violence in trafficking, assault and battery (limited), nonpermanent health consequences, meriting out-patient care or similar	Perpetrators (traffickers)
Moderate	Rarely	$L_{i,p}$	Violence in dealing, assault and battery (limited), nonpermanent health consequences, meriting out-patient care or similar	Perpetrators (suppliers and dealers)
Marginal	Rarely–seldom	$L_{i,p}$	Violence in trafficking (except import), assault and battery (petty), negligible health consequence	Perpetrators (traffickers)
Marginal	Rarely–seldom	$L_{i,p}$	Violence in dealing, assault and battery (petty), negligible health consequence	Perpetrators (suppliers and dealers)

Continued

Table 5.5 *Continued*

	Severity	Incidence	Priority	Activities, events, and consequences	Bearer
	Marginal	Rarely	$VL_{i,p}$	Trafficking (import, air), overdose (nonfatal), negligible health consequences	Perpetrators (traffickers, body-packers)
	Marginal	Rarely	$VL_{i,p}$	Violence in trafficking (import), assault and battery (petty), negligible health consequence	Perpetrators (traffickers)
• Only psychological or intellectual	Marginal	Occasionally	$L_{i,p}$	Trafficking (import, air), threats or intimidation and health risks, anxiety or similar	Perpetrators (traffickers, body-packers)
	Marginal	Occasionally	$L_{i,p}$	Violence in trafficking, threats or intimidation, anxiety or similar	Perpetrators (traffickers)
	Marginal	Occasionally	$L_{i,p}$	Violence in dealing, threats or intimidation, anxiety or similar	Perpetrators (suppliers and dealers)
	Marginal	Seldom	$L_{i,o}$	Violence in trafficking, threats or intimidation, anxiety or similar	Nonperpetrator (private and public)
	Marginal	Rarely	$VL_{i,p}$	Violence in trafficking, kidnapping or confinement (brief), anxiety or similar	Perpetrators (traffickers)
Material support	Serious	Rarely	$L_{i,p}$	Violence in trafficking, threats or intimidation (blackmail), substantial financial impairment	Perpetrators (traffickers)
	Serious	Rarely	$L_{i,o}$	Violence in trafficking, threats or intimidation (blackmail), substantial financial impairment	Nonperpetrators (private and public)

Reputation	Moderate	Rarely	$L_{i,p}$	Violence in trafficking, assault and battery (major or mayhem), third-party awareness, loss of respect, confidence, or trust	Perpetrators (traffickers)
	Moderate	Rarely	$L_{i,p}$	Violence in dealing, assault and battery (major or mayhem), third-party awareness, loss of respect, confidence, or trust	Perpetrators (traffickers)
	Marginal	Rarely–seldom	$L_{i,p}$	Violence in trafficking (except import), assault and battery (petty or limited), third-party awareness, loss of respect, confidence, or trust	Perpetrators (traffickers)
	Marginal	Rarely–seldom	$L_{i,p}$	Violence in dealing, assault and battery (petty or limited), third-party awareness, loss of respect, confidence, or trust	Perpetrators (suppliers and dealers)
	Marginal	Rarely	$VL_{i,p}$	Violence in trafficking (import), assault and battery (petty or limited), third-party awareness, loss of respect, confidence, or trust	Perpetrators (traffickers)
Privacy and autonomy	Serious	Rarely	$L_{i,p}$	Violence in trafficking, kidnapping or confinement (sustained), loss of liberty for duration of event	Perpetrators (traffickers)
	Marginal	Rarely	$VL_{i,p}$	Violence in trafficking, kidnapping or confinement (brief), loss of liberty for duration of event	Perpetrators (traffickers)

Continued

Table 5.5 *Continued*

	Severity	Incidence	Priority	Activities, events, and consequences	Bearer
Harms to private-sector entities, specifically to their:					
Functional integrity	Marginal	Occasionally	$L_{ps,\ bus}$	Corruption in trafficking, employees' involvement (asset misuse or negligence), interference with operations	Businesses (local)
Reputation	Marginal	Occasionally	$L_{ps,\ bus}$	Corruption in trafficking, employees' involvement (asset misuse or negligence), community awareness of employees' involvement, loss of respect, confidence, or trust	Businesses (local)
Privacy and autonomy	Marginal	Occasionally	$L_{ps,\ bus}$	Corruption in trafficking, employees' involvement (asset misuse or negligence), breach or systems, records, or similar	Businesses (local)
Harms to government, specifically to its:					
Functional integrity	Marginal	Rarely	$VL_{g,le}$	Corruption in trafficking, government officials' involvement (asset misuse or negligence), interference with operations	Law enforcement, customs, other public agencies
Material support	Moderate	Rarely	$L_{g,med}$	Trafficking (import, air), treatment of body-packers' overdoses (fatal and nonfatal), resulting in permanent disability, meriting hospitalization, or similar, associated operating costs	Medical facilities
	Moderate	Rarely	$L_{g,med}$	Violence in trafficking, treatment of assault and battery (major or mayhem), associated operating costs[c]	Medical facilities

	Moderate	Rarely	$L_{g,med}$	Violence in dealing, treatment of assault and battery (major or mayhem), associated operating costs[c]	Medical facilities
	Marginal	Rarely–seldom	$L_{g,med}$	Violence in trafficking (except import), treatment of assault and battery (petty or limited), associated operating costs[c]	Medical facilities
	Marginal	Rarely–seldom	$L_{g,med}$	Violence in dealing, treatment of assault and battery (petty or limited), associated operating costs[c]	Medical facilities
	Marginal	Rarely	$VL_{g,med}$	Violence in trafficking (import), treatment of assault and battery (petty or limited), associated operating costs[c]	Medical facilities
	Marginal	Rarely	$VL_{g,med}$	Trafficking (import, air), treatment of body-packers' overdoses (nonfatal), meriting no more than out-patient care or similar, associated operating costs	Medical facilities
Reputation	Marginal	Persistently–continuously	M_g	Dealing (repeated law breaking), societal awareness of failure to enforce law, perceived absence of authority and weakness, loss of respect, confidence, or trust	Government (overarching)
	Marginal	Persistently	ML_g	Trafficking and accompanying activities (repeated law breaking), societal awareness of failure to enforce law, perceived absence of authority and weakness, loss of respect, confidence, or trust	Government (overarching)

Continued

Table 5.5 *Continued*

	Severity	Incidence	Priority	Activities, events, and consequences	Bearer
	Marginal	Rarely	$VL_{g,le}$	Corruption in trafficking, government officials' involvement (asset misuse or negligence), societal awareness of officials' involvement, loss of respect, confidence, or trust	Law enforcement, customs, other public agencies
Harms to the environment, specifically to its:					
Functional integrity	Marginal	Persistently–continuously	$M_{e,s}$	Dealing (repeated law breaking), societal awareness of dysfunctionality, loss of social cohesion	Social environment (overarching)
	Marginal	Persistently	$ML_{e,s}$	Trafficking and accompanying activities (repeated law breaking), societal awareness of dysfunctionality, loss of social cohesion	Social environment (overarching)
	Marginal	Occasionally	$L_{e,s}$	Dealing, public nuisance	Social environment (local)

Source: Authors' adaptation and revision of Paoli et al. (2013).
Notes:

M = medium priority; ML = medium low priority; L = low priority; VL = very low priority; i = individual; p = perpetrator; o = other, nonperpetrator; ps = private sector; bus = business; g = government; le = law enforcement; e = environment; s = social.

[a] Subscripts indicate class and, if relevant, subclass or specific characteristics of bearer.

[b] Analysis pertains to any or all phases and modes of trafficking, unless noted otherwise, e.g., "trafficking (import, air)."

[c] Treatment of perpetrators and nonperpetrators, as needed.

Harms to individuals

We find that cocaine trafficking, dealing, and the accompanying activities, together, yield moderate to catastrophic harms to individuals in Belgium "rarely" and yield marginal harms "rarely" to "occasionally."

Body-packing can involve damages to individuals' physical and psychological integrity, including their dignity, with attendant harms that range from marginal to catastrophic, and it is the only trafficking-related activity that yields a catastrophic harm (i.e., death) to the body-packer. According to our sources, deaths occur exclusively during or immediately subsequent to air transit, both of which we treat as occurring "in Belgium." Given evidence of two such deaths in our approximate period of analysis, we assess the incidence of the catastrophic harms of fatal overdoses as rare among body-packers (Int-CJ-4).

Our assessment is consistent with several near-contemporary studies carried out in other countries (the UK and Italy), which find that cocaine body-packers rarely incur lethal or very serious complications. In a study conducted at Heathrow airport (1996–9), 7 of 180 identified body-packers needed surgical interventions and none died (Bulstrode et al. 2002). In Italy, 161 body-packers arrested at Milan airport (1999–2000) were observed in the nearby emergency room: 15 complained of colicky pain; 10 recovered with food deprivation and medical treatment; and 5 required surgery (Pidoto et al. 2002). Lacking such observations on the consequences of body-packing in Belgium, we rely on these studies to conclude that body-packing might yield additional marginal to grave harms, but also rarely.

As discussed previously, we found little evidence that acts of violence result in more-than-marginal harms from functional damages; specifically, one case in our sample (Case-LS-31) involved a hostage taking during a wholesale transaction and had grave implications. According to criminal justice officers and traffickers, assaults happened "hardly ever" during import (Int-Of-2, -5) and "very rarely" at the wholesale and retail levels (e.g., Int-CJ-8 and Int-Of-9). The organized-crime database of the Belgian Federal Police lists six assaults in addition to the hostage taking (Table 5.3). Lacking information on the types of assaults and not being able to allocate them by phase of operations, we triangulate the data with evidence from other sources and conclude that the use of violence rarely yields moderate to grave damages to individuals' physical and psychological integrity, including dignity.

As none of our sources provides relevant evidence of murder or manslaughter, we do not associate trafficking-related violence with catastrophic harm.

The use of violence, particularly minimally intrusive "petty assaults," could also result in marginally harmful functional damages, but we have even less evidence to work with in making this assessment. Most of our sources, including traffickers (Int-Of-2, -3, -4, -5, -6, -7, -9, -11), suggest that petty assaults occur at most rarely—and possibly never—during import, but the story is less clear further down the supply chain. The database includes six "assaults," but neither the database nor our sample specifically references "petty assaults." However, law-enforcement agencies might underreport minimally intrusive assaults because the agencies either lack awareness of minor episodes or do not record them (Int-CJ-7, -8 with law-enforcement officers). Offenders rarely report petty assaults; nevertheless, they mention rip deals repeatedly (Int-Of-3, -5, -6, -7, -8, -9, -11). These swindles generally involved malice or threats, but sometimes involved physical contact. Evidence of swindles on the street and among dealers, bare as it is, also suggests minimal use of violence. Lacking the grounding for a singular estimate, we regard the marginal harms to individuals from damages to their physical integrity as occurring rarely to seldom after import.

Criminal-justice sources and traffickers suggest that threats occur at least occasionally; thus, marginal harms from associated damages to individuals' psychological integrity and dignity, absent a physical component, can also occur at least occasionally. Threats and rip deals are mentioned just four times in our sample (Case-LS-2, -31), but the database references 48 incidents of threatening behavior and blackmail in trafficking (Table 5.3) and, as noted above, offenders often mention rip deals (Int-Of-3, -5, -6, -7, -8, -9, -11). Dealers also encountered and, at times, report threatening and intimidating behavior (Int-CJ-10). Other marginal psychological harms might accrue to body-packers who faced risks of overdose and to traffickers who experienced brief periods of confinement (Case LS-3).

Research on other nations presents similar findings; for example, from Pearson and Hobbs (2001, 42), "violence and killings attract police attention and leave traces, as well as attracting retaliation. Violence is therefore strictly 'bad for business'" (see also Dorn et al. 2005; Reuter and Haaga 1989).

Up to this point, we have not carefully distinguished harms to perpetrators from harms to other individuals; however, evidence from the organized-crime database suggests that violence in trafficking largely involves perpetrators, consisting of members of the trafficking groups under investigation, members of rival trafficking groups, and some police informants. Perpetrators, so defined, were identified as victims in 50 of the 60 violent episodes reported in the database (Table 5.3). Of the 10 other victims of violence (one police officer, one magistrate, six private persons or business representatives, one politician, and one "other"), nine were threatened and one, an employee of a legitimate business, was assaulted (see also Int-Of-2, -3, -4, -5, -6, -7, -9, -11). On that basis, we find that nonperpetrators who encounter trafficking experience threats seldom and assaults rarely.[32] Having evidence of one assault of a nonperpetrator and lacking information about the details of that event, we assign it a rating at the midpoint—"serious"—of our severity scale.

Additional to the psychological implications of blackmail, we also acknowledge the financial implications and the potential for harms to material interests. In trafficking, we found evidence of three episodes of blackmail, two involving perpetrators and one involving a politician (Table 5.3), suggesting that perpetrators and others encounter blackmail in trafficking, but rarely. As above, we found no specific information about the events and, so, we assign them ratings at the midpoint of the severity scale.

Either the threat or use of violence associated with cocaine trafficking in Belgium could affect individuals' reputations, but we limit our assessments to instances of physical contact, likely to leave visible traces, such as bruises, because other instances might not come to light. The incidence of such intrusions varies by type of assault, from rarely to seldom. Given the medium-term perspective of the living-standard approach—von Hirsch and Jareborg (1991, 21–2) suggest an interval of about a year or slightly longer—we rate the effect of an assault on one's reputation as marginal to moderate.

Lastly, a kidnapping or hostage taking, as was reported in Case-LS-31 and the database, would imply a serious loss of privacy and autonomy whereas the brief confinement reported in Case-LS-3 would imply a marginal loss. Having found only one such example of either form of captivity, we regard both incursions as occurring rarely.

[32] As the database provides information on trafficking, but not specifically on dealing, we cannot use the database to parse the harms to nonperpetrators that encounter dealing. Although we found evidence of threats to street dealers' family members, those threats occurred in the dealers' home countries.

Harms to private-sector entities

Our sources indicate that private-sector corruption occasionally involves damages to businesses' operational integrity and reputation that yield marginal harms.

Employees of shipping and logistics businesses participated in cocaine smuggling through Antwerp port in 19 of the 40 of the criminal proceedings initiated by the Antwerp prosecutor's office (15 cases of port workers, including container technicians and 4 ship staff members: Case-LS-1, -2, -7, -11, -12, -13, -16, -17, -18, -20, -21, -22, -26, -27, -29; Case-SS-8 -9, -13; Case-Full-8).[33] Some offenders and criminal justice officers (Int-Of-7; Int-CJ-7, -9) confirmed the repeated involvement of port workers. We found less evidence of corruption at Brussels airport. Two cases from the sample (Case-Full-2, -3) document import facilitation by employees of baggage-handling companies. We found no evidence of corruption of professionals, business managers, or senior staff in any of the cases in our sample, apart from the managers of front companies (Case-LS-3, -9, -24).

The organized-crime database provides additional, but limited insight to private-sector corruption. The database reports 29 episodes of efforts to corrupt public and private individuals, spread over 21 of the 81 cases; of those 29 episodes, 18 specifically involved private individuals, business personnel, or lawyers and another 7 were reported as "others" (Table 5.6). However, the database does not distinguish between attempted and effective corruption; for example, the intended recipient of a gift might reject the offer.

Any of these episodes could have touched on the businesses' operational integrity, reputation, privacy, or autonomy. Given the not-insubstantial share of cases involving corruption and the confirming perspectives of some offenders and officers, we regard the incidence of harms from damages to these interest dimensions as occasional; however, because the cases appear to have involved low-ranking employees, we rate the harms as marginal.

Although we attribute actual harms to the foregoing episodes, the misuse of a business' facilities or assets need not convey harm. As already noted, these same businesses and some other transportation and manufacturing companies are also misused episodically by traffickers who exploit facilities

[33] In four more cases (Case-LS-10, -19, -25 and Case-Full-8), cocaine was found in a refrigerated container but the law-enforcement agencies could not identify the technicians who were supposed to pick up the cocaine.

Table 5.6 Episodes of possible corruption in Belgium associated with cocaine trafficking (2006–8) (as reported in Belgian Federal Police's organized-crime database)

Identity of target	Nature of possible corruptions						
	Money	Gift	Sexual favor	Promise	Manipulation	Unknown	Total
Individual/firm's representative	9	1	2	1	2	0	15
Lawyer	1	0	1	0	1	0	3
Private individuals, subtotal	**10**	**1**	**3**	**1**	**3**	**0**	**18**
Politician/political party affiliate	0	0	0	0	1	0	1
Customs official	0	0	1	0	0	0	1
Other public agency or institution	1	0	0	0	0	1	2
Public-sector representatives, subtotal	**1**	**0**	**1**	**0**	**1**	**1**	**4**
Other	**4**	**0**	**0**	**0**	**3**	**0**	**7**
Total	**15**	**1**	**4**	**1**	**7**	**1**	**29**

Source: Authors' compilation of data from Federale Politie België (2010).
Notes: The organized-crime database reports 29 episodes of possible corruption distributed over 21 of 81 proceedings for the years 2006–8.

or assets without the businesses' awareness and without publicity or interference. Absent public knowledge, that misuse cannot have a reputational effect; absent interference, it cannot have an operational effect. Moreover, if, as we observe, traffickers transport cocaine by ship or airplane or in a container or rental car without any access to the businesses' private records, proprietary information, etc., or the cocaine circulates in the public areas of sea ports and airports along with other cargo and luggage, then the traffickers misuse the assets without violating privacy or autonomy.

We did not find any evidence of harms from damages to private-sector entities' material interests during our period of analysis.

Harms to government

Few law-enforcement officers, one of whom was a trainee, or other public officials, have been implicated in cocaine trafficking operations in Belgium.[34] The investigations concerning law-enforcement officers (Case-Full-2, -3) were ongoing at the time of our data collection, but the evidence indicated that the officers' and trainee's roles had been, at most, minor, likely yielding only slight damage to the Belgian police or customs agency. Similarly, a case involving two customs officials (Int-CJ-8), one of whom was cleared, suggests minor consequences. The experts in Antwerp and Brussels, traffickers (Int-Of-7, -9), and foreign sources (US Department of State 2010, 143) concurred that no other such cases of cocaine-related corruption had come to the fore. Here too, the organized-crime database provides additional, but limited insight to corruption. Of the 29 episodes of efforts to corrupts, both public and private, 4 involved public-sector representatives (a politician, a customs official, and two public employees, respectively), and, as noted above, another 7 episodes involved "others" (Table 5.6). Thus, we regard the operational and reputational damages of corruption as yielding rare and marginal harms to the Belgian government, specifically to its law-enforcement, customs, and other public agencies.

More generally, we argue that the reputation of any government, writ large, suffers at least slightly, whenever it appears unable to enforce one of its laws, such as a law prohibiting cocaine trafficking or dealing. This harm might be marginal, but it always occurs when law breaking leaves the impression that a government lacks authority. Given that cocaine trafficking through Belgium occurs with some notoriety, it seems reasonable to suggest

[34] This was true at the time of publication of Paoli et al. (2013).

that it would call the Belgian government's authority into question, if just marginally. However, because cocaine trafficking occurs "persistently" and not "continuously," the overall incidence of this harm to the Belgian government is "persistently." Although dealing might garner somewhat less notoriety than trafficking it is, nevertheless, a well-documented, unsavory activity; hence, we describe it similarly as inflicting marginal reputation harm, but as doing so "persistently-to-continuously," as per its incidence.

Lastly, given the public provision of emergency medical care in Belgium, the government would likely bear most of the immediate material burden of treating trafficking-related overdose and assault cases. Not having undertaken an analysis of the costs of specific medical services, we speculate that the damages would range from marginal, for petty or other assaults and overdoses, requiring no more than outpatient care, to moderate, for more-damaging assaults and overdoses, requiring further medical treatment. Tracking the incidence of the underlying assaults and overdose episodes, we conclude that the government would incur marginal costs rarely during import and rarely to seldom in all other phases of trafficking and dealing; it would incur moderate costs rarely. Eventually, however, the government will pass this cost on to Belgian taxpayers; in this context, the government is the near-ultimate bearer of the harm, but not the ultimate bearer.

Harms to the environment

As addressed in Chapter 4, we also consider the possibility that widespread corruption, endemic failures to enforce laws, and other substantial "dysfunctionalities" can be socially harmful. In this assessment, we did not observe widespread corruption and, hence, would not claim it as a dysfunctionality, but failures to enforce laws were persistent for trafficking, persistent-to-continuous for dealing, and visible for both. In this assessment, we rate the severity of the damages associated with those failures as marginal and the incidence as persistent and persistent-to-continuous, paralleling the incidence of the activities or events—and reputational harms—with which they would co-occur.[35]

Dealing might generate additional harm to the social environment as a matter of nuisance, marginally and no more than occasionally. Open drug

[35] Although the within-activity incidence is "continuous," as it was in the case of nonenforcement and reputation, the overall incidence cannot be greater than persistent or persistent-to-continuous, depending on whether the harms emerge from trafficking or dealing.

scenes were not tolerated in Belgian cities and most socially integrated users—the large majority of all users—bought their cocaine in closed-scene settings (e.g., Int-CJ-10). Insomuch as street dealing occurs, it is largely inconspicuous because dealers do not want to attract law-enforcement attention. Moreover, Decorte et al. (2004) indicate that drug-related nuisance is uncommon in Belgium and is associated primarily with the presence of addicts, not their suppliers.

We find no evidence of harm to the physical environment from cocaine trafficking, dealing, or any of the accompanying activities.

Ranking and Prioritizing Harms

Next, we turn to prioritization. As shown in Table 5.5, few of the harms associated with cocaine trafficking in Belgium in our period of analysis rank more than "low" and none more than "medium." Among the harms to individuals, we rank the catastrophic loss of life generated by body-packing as only a medium priority because it happens rarely. Similarly, we rank the grave but rare harms from damages to individuals' physical and psychological integrity that arise from disabling assaults and overdoses and kidnappings as medium-low priorities. Among the harms to other bearers, just those to the Belgian government and the social environment that emerge from repeated law breaking rank above "low." Although we regard the harms as marginal, they happen persistently and persistently-to-continuously.

Our rankings support prioritization, within limits. For example, while our approach facilitates the systematic assessment of wide-ranging harms, it does not, as addressed in Chapter 4, fully allow the aggregation of harms within a particular class of bearers or direct comparisons of like types of harms to different classes of bearers. Nevertheless, the distribution of harms across bearers is telling: we find that perpetrators, consisting of cocaine traffickers, in various capacities, and dealers, accrue the majority of all harms to individuals.

Finally, we note again that we treat the overall incidence of most harms, other than some to the government's reputation and environment, as roughly equivalent to the within-activity incidence. Strictly speaking, each harm should be viewed as occurring somewhat less frequently because neither trafficking nor dealing occurs "continuously": trafficking occurs "persistently" and dealing occurs "persistently-to-continuously." The differences should not affect the harms' relative rankings, except in relation to some reputational and environmental effects, but it could affect prioritizations vis-à-vis other criminal activities.

Investigating the Causality of Harms

The investigation of causality occurs in two stages.

In the first stage, we assess the distance between harms and cocaine trafficking, which is the primary activity in this assessment. Of all the harms listed in Table 5.5, only those associated with dealing, an enabled activity, and the violence, etc. that accompanies dealing, are remote—that is, they can accrue in different places and times than the harms of cocaine trafficking and are mediated by the choices of others along the supply chain—but they are located immediately adjacent to the harms of trafficking.

Second, we assess the extent to which harms either are intrinsic to cocaine trafficking, dealing, and the accompanying activities or arise from policy and related law-enforcement practices. Most if not all of those harms appear to derive—once subjected to counterfactual reasoning (Calhoun 2002)—from the legal status of cocaine and its enforcement. There would be little or no body-packing and less corruption and violence if cocaine could be imported into, distributed in, and exported from Belgium legally. However, we cannot rule out corruption and violence entirely because, even in a legal regime, black or gray markets would likely develop outside what might be imagined as a highly regulated system. Similar conclusions have been reached in other countries. MacCoun and Reuter (2001, 105–12), for example, find that "tough enforcement is responsible for much of the observed damage" associated with trafficking in the United States.

Although we did not assess the harms of cocaine use in this exercise, we offer two observations on their causality. First, harms associated with use are even more distant from trafficking than those of dealing. They depend not just on the intervening actions of dealers, but also on those of users.[36] One might ask whether and to what extent they should be attributed to

[36] They might also be said to depend partly on the intervening actions of emergency responders, healthcare providers, and others, but the same could be said of the harms of trafficking and dealing.

trafficking. Von Hirsch and Jareborg (1991, 33–4), for example, consider discounting harms that occur solely through a victim's consent and explicitly mention drug use, but they propose no formula for calculating the discount.[37] Second, there is no doubt that some use-related harms arise from the inherent properties of the drug;[38] however, policy, including modes of enforcement, and other economic, social, and cultural factors can play a part in determining the ultimate consequences. For example, a policy of prohibition—and all it might entail—will affect the price and quality of cocaine, which, in turn, can affect consumption and its effects. Some users shift from snorting to injecting to increase their satisfaction from expensive, diluted drugs (e.g., Decorte 2000, 158–73).

Having linked most of the harms associated with cocaine trafficking to policy and related practices, we caution against overinterpretation. Without conducting a complete assessment of trafficking *and* use, we cannot say—and do not try to speculate on—whether the balance of the harms resulting from cocaine, itself, and those produced by the drug's legal status or particular law enforcement practices is positive or negative (see also MacCoun and Reuter 2001, 127). Still, realizing that a policy or practice gives rise to harm provides policy-makers and law-enforcement officials with an opportunity. In New York, for example, changes in local policing led to a radical decline in drug-related killings, even if drug consumption, and presumably dealing, remained stable (Zimring 2012, 191–3). Similarly, recent drug-market interventions in High Point, NC, and elsewhere (e.g., Corsaro et al. 2012; Saunders et al. 2016), have focused on tactics to reduce crime associated with dealing.

5.5 Summing Up Our Assessment of Cocaine Trafficking in Belgium

Although national and international law-enforcement agencies (e.g., Federale Politie België 2006; Europol 2013, 2017) often take the harms of drug trafficking for granted, our assessment indicates that cocaine trafficking, as distinct from use, generated few notable harms in Belgium during our period of analysis. Our assessment also shows that most of the

[37] As noted in Chapter 4, we do not apply discounts in our analyses.

[38] For a brief review of the health consequences of cocaine use, see European Monitoring Center for Drugs and Drug Addiction (2009, 65–6).

harms to individuals accrued to traffickers, dealers, or their facilitators, oftentimes as a consequence of violence that accompanies trafficking, and that a majority of all harms arose from the legal status of cocaine and law enforcement practices.

More recent evidence that we acknowledged throughout the text, suggests that the incidence of cocaine trafficking in or through Belgium might be even greater now than during our period of analysis and that accompanying violence might be more severe and frequent, though not necessarily occurring in greater proportion to trafficking, itself. The amounts of both trafficking and violence might have risen, but whether the increases in violence have been proportionally greater than those of trafficking is uncertain. In an updated analysis we might feel yet more comfortable calling cocaine trafficking in Belgium a "persistent" activity, but we might need to elevate the rankings of some harms associated with violence.

Concerning policy implications, we cannot argue against cocaine's illegality solely on the basis of our assessment, as it does not encompass use, but we can still point to our findings as evidence of policy's role in shaping harms and an opportunity for reforms to reduce violence in the context of illegality. Even without examining use, the current application indicates the value of the framework as an evidence-based, systematic tool to focus policy-making attention and resources on actual instead of perceived harms.

Our first application of the framework also yielded methodological lessons. Most importantly, it has shown that the framework can cope effectively with most of the conceptual and technical challenges that we discussed in Chapters 3 and 4.

This application, as the framework, itself, acknowledges the *normativity* of harm assessment, starting with fundamental issues of the bearers' standing and the legitimacy of interests. A striking result of the application, as noted above, is that nearly all harms to individuals accrue to perpetrators. In our assessment, we treated harms to law breakers and law-abiding citizens equivalently, though excluding losses of ill-gotten gains, of illegal possessions, and to wholly illegal enterprises, but policy-makers could do otherwise. For example, one might try to limit the analysis to harms born by parties who are not directly—and willingly—involved in the criminal act, but the lines between perpetrators and victims in this and other settings can be blurry.[39] Moreover, many crime and drug-control policies are

[39] In Chapter 4, we address this issue more generally.

intended to reduce harms from damages to the physical integrity of all participants in a criminal activity, regardless of their role (e.g., Council of the European Union 2004, 2005).

We addressed the challenge of *infinitude* in ways that both limited and expanded our reach. On the one hand, we focused on supply, per se, and considered only the first-order effects of each activity. Consequently, we cannot weigh in on the ultimate effects of trafficking or the broader societal implications for illegality, as one might if they linked trafficking to harms associated with cocaine consumption and probed further. We also assessed the harms within Belgium, thereby excluding any harms in other countries, and within a specific period of time. On the other hand, we assessed not only the harms associated with the primary activity of cocaine trafficking, but also those related to dealing and major accompanying activities, consisting of violence, corruption, and money laundering, increasing considerably both the scope and policy relevance of our assessment from a supply-side perspective.

As for *causality*, we investigated it, by gauging both the remoteness of harms and their dependence on policy, rather than presumed it. In so doing we uncovered the roles of policy and related law enforcement practices in producing harm.

We dealt with the challenge of *standardization* by conducting what Sen (1987, 29) calls a "standard evaluation" (see Chapter 4), which means assuming that the affected individuals are "average" and do not differ radically in their vulnerability or resilience. Similarly, we regarded private-sector and government entities generically, because the actual harms for each were few and distinguishing among small, large, local, or national entities would not—in this specific application—have added much value.

Regarding *measurement*, we harvested both quantitative and qualitative information, thus including harms that cannot be quantified easily, but found that admitting qualitative evidence can create its own challenges when words do not fall neatly into a rating system. In this application, it was easier to assign ranks at the extremes of the severity and incidence scales—marginal and catastrophic—than to assign ranks in the middle. Over time, we have become more precise in our delineations of assaults (see Appendix A) and developed rules of thumb that aid in this purpose, but the data are not always good enough to support the rules. Yet, even were we able to assign perfect ranks to all harms, policy-makers would still need to decide how to prioritize the harms that accrue to different classes of bearers.

Lastly, on *commensurability*, our first assessment met our expectations, by providing a comparison of harms within classes of bearers and a distribution of harms across classes of bearers from which we could consider policy implications. Despite the unavoidable incommensurability of harms across classes of bearers, our rankings singled out harms that deserve policy attention, regardless of the different bearers and interests affected.

On balance, this first application of our framework suggests the larger potential of the framework for providing evidence-based, systematic assessments of wide-ranging crime-related harms to individuals, private-sector and governmental entities, and the environment, including harms that cannot be quantified easily. In the next section, where we compare the results of this assessment to two others—cocaine trafficking in the Netherlands and human trafficking in Belgium—we begin to establish the framework's applicability to wide-ranging harms and to disparate activities.

5.6 Findings and Lessons from Other Applications in Europe

In this section, we draw further insight from two other applications of the framework conducted in Europe; one (Greenfield et al. 2016) involving human trafficking, also in Belgium, and the other (Paoli et al. 2015) involving cocaine trafficking in the Netherlands.[40] These applications and the first application covered similar periods, starting in the early 2000s, and employed criminal justice sources and interviews, but the human-trafficking assessment drew additionally from nongovernmental organizations (NGOs) reports and the public-health literature.

By selecting applications that exhibit a degree of geopolitical and temporal consistency, we were better able to control, loosely speaking, for the social and political climate, economic conditions, etc.; compare the results; and explore issues of reliability and robustness, in terms of replicability and stability, respectively. To explore reliability, we would look for whether the same crime in similar venues generates similar results; in the case of robustness, our interest is in whether or how well the framework holds up in an application to a very different form of crime, albeit in the same country. In

[40] For results from an application to cannabis production in the Netherlands, see Paoli et al. (2015).

particular, we can use the results of the applications to cocaine trafficking in Belgium and in a neighboring country (i.e., the Netherlands) to "test," so to speak, for reliability and we can use the results of the application to a different activity (i.e., human trafficking) in Belgium to test for robustness. Arguably, human and cocaine trafficking have little in common beyond the term "trafficking."[41]

We were encouraged to find that the results of the two cocaine-trafficking assessments—Belgian and Dutch—are similar and the differences potentially explicable, suggesting that the framework is both reliable and sufficiently "perceptive" to pick up modest difference in circumstances. As was true in Belgium, cocaine trafficking in the Netherlands, generated a small set of harms across bearers and tended to affect perpetrators, including traffickers and dealers, more than other individuals.[42] Among the noteworthy differences, Paoli et al. (2015) found evidence of rare catastrophic violence in the Netherlands, which Paoli et al. (2013) did not find in Belgium at about the same time, but still involving perpetrators, particularly traffickers.[43] They also found additional rare, but marginal harms to businesses and government from money laundering. Differences in the two countries' market functions might drive some of the differences in the results; for example, although both countries were and still are major entry points for cocaine into the European Union (EU), Dutch traffickers tend to play a greater role in wholesale distribution than Belgian traffickers and as a consequence, they might experience more transactions, implying greater risk of violence all else equal. Not surprisingly, in the Netherlands too, the

[41] In our assessment, we worked primarily with the United Nation's (2000, 2) definition of human trafficking: "[T]he recruitment, transportation, transfer, harbouring or receipt of persons, by means of the threat or use of force or other forms of coercion, of abduction, of fraud, of deception, or the abuse of power or of a position of vulnerability or of the giving or receiving of payments or benefits to achieve the consent of a person having control over another person, for the purpose of exploitation."

[42] Though largely supporting of these findings, Paoli et al. (2015) assess harms of cannabis cultivation in Belgium and find evidence of low- and medium-low-priority harms to the material interests of nonperpetrators, including individuals, businesses, and government agencies that suffer damages to rental properties on which cannabis cultivation occurs, experience electricity theft, or incur dismantling costs.

[43] The extent of violence associated with cocaine trafficking in the Netherlands has been reported to have increased since the end of our data collection and some stakeholders have expressed heightened concern (see, e.g., Boffey 2018). However, in a 2017 study on contract killings, the Dutch Ministry of Security and Justice found no major differences in incidence, reporting 20 to 30 contract killings yearly over the last few decades, primarily from drug-trafficking-related conflicts (van Gestel and Verhoeven 2017).

Table 5.7 Cases of human trafficking in Belgium, by form of human trafficking (2006–10)

	Cases reported by the police				Criminal proceedings opened by prosecutor's office			
	2006	2007	2008	Total	2008	2009	2010	Total
Sex trafficking	26	118	115	259	141	189	175	505
Production of pornography with minors	3	19	14	36	n.a.	n.a.	n.a.	n.a.
Labor trafficking	45	283	182	510	202	173	136	511
Forced begging	2	11	15	28	12	10	5	27
Removal of organs	n.a.	n.a.	n.a.	n.a.	1	1	1	3
Forced crime	2	8	10	20	30	20	20	70
Total	78	439	336	853	386	393	337	1116

Sources: Authors' adaptation of Greenfield et al. (2016), based on data from Dienst mensenhandel (2008a, 5; 2008b, 4); Centrum voor gelijkheid van kansen en voor racismebestrijding (2011a, 66).
Notes: n.a. = not applicable.

majority of the harms accrue from the legal status of cocaine and law enforcement practices.

The results of the application to human trafficking are quite different, as one might expect from a considerably different activity. Whereas human trafficking victims, largely of foreign origin, experience multiple and sometimes very serious, grave, or even catastrophic harms, the overall dimensions or scale of human trafficking in Belgium appeared to be modest, in terms of the numbers of victims (Table 5.7) and analogous immigration statistics (Centrum 2011b, 22; Kaizen and Nonnemann 2007, 125) and relative to cocaine trafficking. Nevertheless—amidst an apparent decline in exploitation and the use of violence in Belgium, particularly in sex trafficking—the harms of human trafficking still exceeded those of cocaine trafficking in volume and severity.[44] Moreover, most of the harms to victims,

[44] For a direct, equivalent comparison of results, see Greenfield et al. (2016) and Paoli et al. (2013).

including the most severe, were a direct consequence of the activity, not its legal status.

Even so, government policies can affect the severity and, possibly, the incidence of harms to human trafficking victims. For example, restrictive policies on immigration have helped shape an environment in which non-EU citizens can pay smugglers exorbitant fees to enter Belgium, thereby opening the door to debt bonding, which is a cornerstone of exploitation in human trafficking. Were those policies less restrictive and the services of clandestine smugglers, some of whom turn out to be traffickers, no longer valued, these individuals could buy an ordinary bus ticket and might avoid being drawn into an exploitative arrangement. Evidence of changes in sex-trafficking patterns during our period of analysis and improvements in treatment of Bulgarian and Romanian sex-trafficking victims since their countries' accession to the EU, suggest that potential victims who have better options, more bargaining power, and lack need of smugglers can steer clear of the most heinous forms of sex trafficking or trafficking *tout court*. To an unknown extent, general advances in socioeconomic conditions in the victims' countries of origin and, perhaps less so, prevention campaigns against sex trafficking might also contribute to reductions in trafficking, exploitation, and violence (for a review, see van der Laan et al. 2011).

In summary, the severity of harms from human trafficking rate substantially higher than those of cocaine trafficking, as one might imagine, given the odious nature of the crime, but the overall incidence is much lower. Moreover, in the case of human trafficking, the victims bear the brunt of the harms, rather than the perpetrators, and the legal status of the activity matters less than broader policy concerns, such as those of immigration.

Speaking partly to the robustness of the framework, we were able to draw five additional methodological lessons from the human-trafficking assessment, some but not all tying back to challenges that we discussed in Chapters 3 and 4 and earlier in this chapter.

First, the human-trafficking assessment demonstrated the practical difficulties of standardization and benchmarking, especially with regard to individuals.[45] Such standardization can be difficult, in part, because the hurtfulness of a crime can depend on a victim's circumstances, including whether they have specific health concerns or are living in poverty. Moreover, our benchmark for individuals (i.e., the standard of living) might

[45] Some of the same issues arise in relation to entities.

require different empirical content, depending, for example, on the country of analysis. As recognized by Sen (1987), the means necessary to achieve the same living standard can vary markedly depending on the wealth and cultural sophistication of the society—or between the victims' countries of origin and exploitation. A further complication is that human-trafficking victims, especially those who cross borders, can be partially suspended between two worlds. Many victims still regard their meager financial rewards as attractive because they assess them by the values and parameters of their countries of origin and, as a result, might not identify themselves as victims.

Second, as was true of cocaine trafficking, we found it easier to assign ratings at the extremes of the severity and incidence scales than in the middle, but the assignments, including some closer to the endpoints, were even more difficult because the data were weaker. In the assessment of human trafficking, we had fewer means to overcome the data deficiencies and less confidence in our snapshot, including our understanding of the basic parameters of the problem. To mitigate the risk to our characterization of the crime, we reached beyond our usual criminal justice sources and drew from NGO reports and the public-health literature and, to address our uncertainty regarding the ultimate magnitude of the crime, we also examined the sensitivity of our results to the incidence rating. Specifically, we took "seldom" as a starting point and considered alternative results for "occasionally" and "persistently," in which cases the criminal activity looked predictably worse.

Third, the application to human trafficking highlights the role of incidence in prioritization. Despite the serious nature of many of the harms and their persistence in relation to trafficking, most obtained low priorities in our initial assessments because human trafficking occurred infrequently. Whereas accounting for the overall incidence of harms makes it possible to conduct comparative assessments across different forms of crime, we recognize that the incidence of the underlying activity might not be a concern in all circumstances. If, for example, a country determines that it has a particular interest in combating human trafficking because it will not tolerate coercion and human degradation, then policy-makers might find it appropriate to rank harms and allocate resources solely on the basis of the within-activity incidence—the incidence of the harm in relation to the activity. In that way, the approach would still provide a systematic means of establishing priorities to combat of human trafficking, taken on their own merit.

Fourth, the ongoing and prolonged nature of some harms associated with human trafficking presented a different analytical challenge. In cocaine trafficking, the crime event and many or most of the associated harms are discrete and nonrecurring; in human trafficking, by contrast, some harms might occur repeatedly over a period of months or years or emerge long after the event, as can be true of some sexually transmitted diseases. On that basis, one might describe the few-hundred annual victims as daily victims over the period of their exploitation or beyond, suggesting persistent or continuous and long-lived, accumulative harms, but higher ratings might then overstate the incidence of human trafficking in relation to other crimes, including cocaine trafficking, and might require an extended temporal horizon. An alternative might be to account explicitly for the matter of "exposure" in the assessment of severity or to treat exposure as a third metric. For example, we might—or perhaps should—rate repeated, ongoing beatings of a particular intensity as more severe than single or intermittent episodes of equal intensity.

Fifth, insomuch as the incidence of human trafficking is knowable and society values its relevance, this application demonstrates the feasibility of comparing harm across different kinds of criminal activities, at least by classes of bearers. Focusing on individuals, the harms of human trafficking outranked those of cocaine trafficking, notwithstanding the probable difference in incidence between the two activities. In the case of "persistent" cocaine trafficking, only the catastrophic and grave harms that emerged from body-packing and violence against traffickers yielded rankings greater than "low."[46] Reassessing the harms of human trafficking with a higher activity incidence (i.e., "occasionally" or "persistently") served to reinforce the relative harmfulness of human trafficking.

5.7 Concluding Remarks

To close the chapter, we offer a small number of overarching observations that cut across all three trafficking assessments and speak further to the utility of our approach.

Our cocaine- and human-trafficking assessments suggest the broad applicability of the framework to disparate, complex criminal activities, and its policy relevance. The human-trafficking assessment drew further

[46] See Greenfield et al. (2016) and Paoli et al. (2013) for directly comparable findings.

attention to known conceptual and technical challenges, set out in previous chapters and apparent in the drug-trafficking assessments, and also pointed to others, but the framework did not unravel in a new setting; rather, it provided a basis for comparing harms across two very different forms of crime and provided a similar degree of policy insight in each case. Viewed as a package, these applications suggest that systematically and empirically assessing the harms of crime can yield policy-relevant results, some of which, such as those pertaining to policy's role as a harming agent and to the overall dimensions of human trafficking, might contradict popular wisdom.

Human trafficking, like drug trafficking, has been established as a leading priority in the policy community (e.g., European Council 2010; Ministeries van Binnenlandse Zaken en Justitie 2012, 14–15; and Europol 2013, 39) without regard to either the severity or incidence of harms. If our assessments of the harms of these activities were approximately correct for our period of analysis, the results suggest the value of developing a more focused approach to directing resources to the most harmful dimensions of the crimes and to more carefully uncovering policy's role in contributing to those harms.

That said, as implied throughout our discussions of normativity, infinitude, and causality, the framework is not intended to provide policy-makers with a simple recipe for optimal resource allocation. They must weigh at least some findings for themselves, as the decision cannot be made with scientific rules and methods alone.

We revisit our methodological findings in Chapter 7, where we reflect on lessons from these applications and from the application presented in the next chapter on harms at the start of a cocaine supply chain, specifically in Colombia.

6 An Application of the Framework to Coca Cultivation and Processing in Colombia

6.1 Introduction

In this chapter, we continue our exploration of the harms of the drug trade, but we shift perspectives from the end to the start of a supply chain; that is, from a country that consumes cocaine, such as Belgium, to a country that produces it, namely, Colombia. We turn our attention to a source country to improve our understanding of the accrual of harms in a global market that spans borders and continents and to further test the framework with differences in activities, venue, and analytical conditions.[1]

We selected Colombia because of its prominence as the world's leading supplier of coca—the agricultural commodity from which cocaine derives—which implied a potentially rich evidence base for a rapid assessment, and because it provided an opportunity to investigate new methodological terrain. For decades, the environmental and economic consequences of Colombia's engagement with coca have been subjects of extensive data collection, research, and debate. Previously, we have proposed sustainability as an environmental benchmark and espoused full accounting (Greenfield and Paoli 2012), but, until embarking on this assessment, we had not yet tested either idea.

Similarly, we had not yet tested our framework's capacity for quick-turn analysis (Greenfield and Paoli 2013, 11–12) and, to that end, we have undertaken a less comprehensive harm assessment for Colombia than for Belgium, with a less extensive data collection. Working with data and analyses from official, scholarly, and media outlets, available at the time of our research in 2017, we focused on harms involving the physical environment

[1] See Paoli et al. (2009) for a discussion of the global character of drug markets.

Assessing the Harms of Crime. Victoria A. Greenfield and Letizia Paoli, Oxford University Press. © Victoria A. Greenfield & Letizia Paoli 2022. DOI: 10.1093/oso/9780198758174.003.0006

and material support, and dealt with fewer activities, aiming for completion in about 12 weeks.[2] We drew a loose circle around farm-level cultivation and processing, which we deemed "primary," and the violence, corruption, and money laundering that accompany them in-country. Although we reference off-farm processing, trafficking, and conflict, we did not emphasize them.

We also reflect further on the framework's robustness, by considering how well it works in a substantially different setting and with reliance on data collected, analyzed, and reported for other purposes, all with the intention of relatively quick completion.

In Sections 6.2–6.5 of this chapter, we offer a primer on the scope, technology, and vocabulary of cocaine production and efforts to stop it; describe our analytical approach; articulate a grower's business model; assess particular harms, involving the physical environment and material support; and investigate causality and policy's role in shaping harms. In Section 6.6, we sum up our topical and methodological findings and, in Section 6.7, we offer concluding remarks on the risks and rewards of conducting an assessment rapidly.

6.2 The Lay of the Land

To orient our readers, this section provides a brief introduction to the technology of coca cultivation and processing and an overview of drug-control policies of importance to growers' cultivation and processing decisions.[3]

Cocaine is a psychoactive alkaloid found in the leaves of coca, a shrub that has grown in the Americas, Mexico, Indonesia, and the West Indies (Biondich and Joslin 2016). Taken together, three South American countries—Colombia, Peru, and Bolivia—account for the vast majority of the world's coca cultivation, hence, cocaine supply. Over the past few decades, Colombia and Peru have taken turns ranking first among the three, but they have no contemporary rivals.[4] Less than a decade ago, the United Nations

[2] See Section 6.3 for a more information about the timing—and time frame—of our research.

[3] For our purpose, coca "cultivation" encompasses planting ("investment"), maintenance, harvesting, and abandonment or removal ("divestment"), whereas "production" includes maintenance, harvesting, and processing (e.g., from coca leaf to paste), but not investment or divestment (see Appendix A).

[4] According to EMCDDA and Europol (2010, 9), nineteenth- and early twentieth-century Dutch, German, and Japanese pharmaceutical firms sourced coca for legal, industrial cocaine

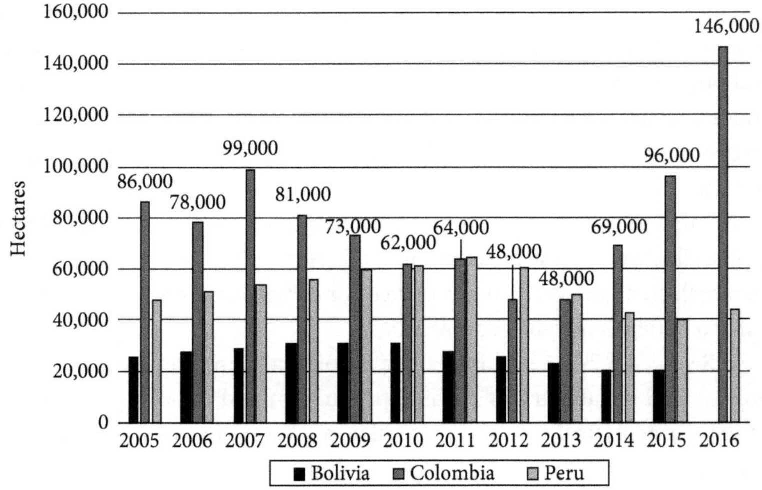

Figure 6.1 Bolivian, Colombian, and Peruvian coca cultivation

Source: Data compiled by authors from UNODC (2017, Part 2, 58) and UNODC and Government of Peru (2017).

Notes:

Data on cultivation in Bolivia for 2016 not available at time of research.

UNODC and Government of Colombia (2010) reported cultivation in 2009 for Colombia as 68,000 hectares, but UNODC and Government of Colombia (2011, 8) and later UNODC publications report that cultivation as 73,000 hectares to adjust for small plots.

UNODC (2017, Methodology, 29) discusses data comparability.

Office on Drugs and Crime (2011, 7) described market leadership as a pendulum swinging from Colombia to Peru and Bolivia, but since 2013, cultivation in Colombia has increased to the point that it exceeds cultivation in Peru and Bolivia combined (Figure 6.1).[5]

As a general matter, coca yields a leaf crop, along the lines of tea, spearmint, or bay leaf, and has a productive life expectancy of 10 years or more, so that the decision to cultivate coca—typically as a "stand" on a plot of land—can look much like an investment decision (Greenfield 1991).[6]

production from plantations located on islands (e.g., Java and Formosa) that were part of the Dutch and Japanese colonial empires.

[5] In the years since we undertook this assessment, cultivation in Colombia has reached new record levels, but might be plateauing. See UNODC (2020, Part 3, 21–4), for a discussion of data through 2018.

[6] Coca is a perennial, which means that its life cycle can extend over several or even many years.

Growers incur an initial "capital cost" when they plant the shrub and they reap "returns" when they harvest the leaves over time. The shrub's productivity or yield, hence the expected path of returns, follows an age-dependent trajectory of ascent and descent that depends partly on cultivation practices and growing conditions, including market forces, policy, and security. Modest harvests are usually possible within a year of planting, but coca might not reach its full productive potential for about four or five years. Mature shrubs can remain at their peak for several years, but their productivity will decline eventually and, when harvests are no longer worthwhile, because the yields no longer justify the costs of labor and other inputs, a grower might choose to stop producing or "divest" by removing the stand or abandoning the plot altogether.

Upon harvest, coca growers can sell the leaves to middlemen for processing or process the leaves first and then sell the derivatives.[7] Processing can occur in roughly three stages of progressive complexity, capital intensity, and risk that, with aid of various chemicals, transform the leaves to coca paste, then to cocaine base, and then to cocaine hydrochloride, which is commonly referred to as cocaine (see, e.g., US Drug Enforcement Administration [DEA] 1993; European Monitoring Centre for Drugs and Drug Addiction [EMCDDA] and Europol 2010). Whereas coca growers in Colombia often produce coca paste and sometimes produce cocaine base, they almost never produce cocaine, which typically occurs in "labs" in Colombia or other countries (United Nations Office on Drugs and Crime [UNODC] and Government of Colombia 2017, 65).[8] Cocaine eventually makes its way to consumers in the Americas, in Europe, and elsewhere.

Coca leaf is listed on Schedule I of the United Nations (UN) Single Convention on Narcotics Drugs, 1961, but it is not unambiguously illegal (see, e.g., Biondich and Joslin 2016; Plowman 1986; EMCDDA and Europol 2010). Its history as a legitimate "whole leaf" commodity dates back thousands of years and has been documented in archeological studies in Chile, Ecuador, and Peru. The leaf, consumed as a beverage or chewed,

[7] Fresh coca leaves must be dried—or processed—shortly after harvest to avoid fungal activity, fermentation, and deterioration (DEA 1993, n.p.; Greenfield 1991, 12). Dry leaves might survive 2-3 months, but lose potency over time (Greenfield 1991, 27); van Dyke and Byck (1982, 130) offer this observation on the early colonial period, "if coca leaves retained their potency after drying and long travel as successfully as tobacco leaves and coffee beans do, the role of coca in European and North American society might be quite different from what it is today."

[8] UNODC and Government of Colombia (2017, 65) report that traffickers export cocaine base to countries in Central America or Europe for the final stage of processing.

is nonaddictive, mildly energizing, and known for its medicinal properties and nutritive value.[9] Common traditional uses include treatment of altitude sickness, oral infections, digestive ailments, and hunger and fatigue and are still permissible in some countries.[10] Biondich and Joslin (2016, 3) note that medical interest in whole leaf coca in Europe and the United States in the nineteenth century diminished rapidly when a handful of chemists isolated cocaine. Unwittingly, they unleashed an addictive psychoactive drug, leaving present-day policy-makers to seek controls through domestic and international programs that target cultivation, processing, and distribution.[11]

Efforts to reduce or eliminate drug-crop cultivation generally involve some combination of carrots and sticks, such as those found in rural development and crop eradication programs, respectively.[12] The former ranges from narrowly framed crop-substitution programs (e.g., swapping coca for various food or industrial crops), to broadly based alternative-livelihoods programs (e.g., promoting agricultural and non-agricultural pursuits and educational opportunities). Historically, eradication of various drug crops across continents and countries has included forced, voluntary, and quasi-voluntary efforts, using mechanical—oftentimes manual—or chemical means in different settings.[13] Over a period spanning at least a decade, aerial spraying or fumigation featured prominently in Colombia, especially under a US-funded program known as Plan Colombia, but it has been suspended there, at least temporarily, and outlawed elsewhere, including Bolivia and Peru.[14] Each approach targets growers' incentives to cultivate drug crops, by trying to reduce the relative appeal of illegal activities.

[9] For more on coca's nutrient value, see Plowman (1986).

[10] Bolivia and Peru still allow some traditional and personal coca use. In addition, Bolivia has a reservation clause under the UN's Single Convention, relieving it of various international requirements for criminalization. (See EMCDDA and Europol 2010, 9; Rosen 2015, 10.) Speaking to legality in other contexts, there are specific exemptions for using coca as a flavoring (i.e., in coca cola), so long as the leaf has been decocanized. For more on the history of coca and coca cola, see Elmore (2016).

[11] Sigmund Freud drew attention to cocaine with *On Coca*, and Albrecht Erlenmeyer, a German physician and psychiatrist, accused him of having "unleashed 'the third scourge of humanity'" (van Dyke and Byck 1982, 131).

[12] This paragraph draws heavily from Greenfield et al. (2017, 742).

[13] A "quasi-voluntary" program might include an option for farmers to remove crops in exchange for payments, coupled with a threat of forced and unfunded removals at a later date.

[14] According to Mejía and Posada (2008) and Sherret (2005), Colombia's aerial efforts predated Plan Colombia's initiation in 2000, but they intensified under the program. For more on Plan Colombia, see, e.g., Beittel (2017) and Beittel and Rosen (2017) and the later discussion in this chapter.

Drug-control policy has also targeted the precursor chemicals, such as hydrochloric and sulfuric acids, acetone, and other solvents and potassium permanganate that growers and middlemen use to convert coca leaves to paste, base, and cocaine (EMCDDA and Europol 2010, 14).

Colombia's drug-control policy has undergone change, stemming partly from a partial agreement, reached between the Colombian government and the Revolutionary Armed Forces of Colombia (known as FARC, for Fuerzas Armadas Revolucionarias de Colombia), in 2014, and reinforced in the Peace Accord of 2016. Key supply-side features of Colombia's 2015 counternarcotics strategy include (Beittel and Rosen 2017, 6–7):

- social investment and institutional reform (e.g., construction of roads, provision of electricity and water utilities, and access to health care and education)
- crop substitution and development support (e.g., food security programs, technical and financial assistance for households that abandon drug-crop cultivation, and land titling)
- enhanced interdiction, investigations, and prosecutions (e.g., destruction of laboratories; seizure of cargoes and precursor chemicals; and effective detention of drug traffickers)
- a strategy to address drug cultivation in Colombia's national parks and to protected territories of Afro-Colombian and indigenous communities.

In addition, the Colombian government suspended aerial spraying, citing health and other concerns,[15] but it left the door open and, according to Beittel and Rosen (2017, 7), "Forced manual eradication by the government, however, remains a tool to assure compliance from those who do not commit to voluntarily removing their illicit crops" (see also Casey 2017).

Adding uncertainty, Colombia's president at the time of our assessment seemed poised to "upend" those policy developments and take an "aggressive" stance against drugs in the tradition of those who advocated for Plan Colombia (Faiola 2018).[16] His administration was actively seeking to reinstate aerial spraying, but was meeting with court challenges.

[15] These concerns spanned borders and have led to legal action (Beittel and Rosen 2017, 9). Specifically, Ecuador filed a case in 2008 before the International Court of Justice in The Hague, claiming health and environmental harms from spray drift over its border with Colombia, and settled out-of-court in 2013 for $15 million in financial compensation and a formally imposed ban on spraying within 10 km of the border.

[16] Here and throughout this chapter, we use the term "uncertainty" somewhat colloquially.

In recent years, coca cultivation in Colombia has increased substantially (Figure 6.1 and Appendix B),[17] but the longer-term effects of suspending aerial spraying and refocusing on alternative livelihoods and other development support are still unfolding. Crop substitution has had a checkered past in Colombia and internationally (see, e.g., Greenfield et al. 2015a, Appendix E), but we present evidence on development efforts in Section 6.5 that suggests a potentially constructive role for assistance. Moreover, while the longer-term effects of policy changes may depend on the Colombian government's delivery on promises of development support, some observers contend that those promises have led growers to increase—or even commence—coca cultivation to obtain that support later down the road (see, e.g., Casey 2017; Kraul 2017; *The Economist* 2017; UNODC and Government of Colombia 2017, 14).[18]

6.3 Approach to Analysis

This application of the framework to coca cultivation and processing in Colombia is both like and unlike our prior applications to cocaine and human trafficking (e.g., Paoli et al. 2013; Greenfield et al. 2016). Among the similarities, it is a single-country, supply-oriented application in which we first develop a business model, to assemble the underlying facts that are necessary for our analysis, and, then, undertake the analysis. Likewise, we did not assess harms beyond Colombia's borders or harms associated with drug consumption. Among the differences, we opted for a rapid and partial assessment, with less emphasis on data collection and, for most but not all purposes, a narrower aperture in relation to the types of activities and harms under consideration.

Regarding the data for our business model, we did not analyze raw data or gather new data, as we have previously, but we relied on material from official reports and statistics; scholarly research crossing varied disciplines, including ecology, geography, and economics; and media accounts, spanning the early 2000s to mid-2010s.[19] To identify sources, which we refer

[17] Appendix B provides data on coca cultivation, yields, prices, etc. with data through 2016, as available at the time of the assessment. For cultivation data through 2018, see UNODC (2020, Part 3, 21–4).

[18] See Greenfield (1991) for a formal economic model of a policy in Bolivia that might have had such effects.

[19] By "early 2000s," we mean years at the start of the decade, beginning with the year 2000. Our period of analysis in this assessment encompasses that of the Belgian cocaine trafficking

to broadly as "the literature," we searched on coca cultivation, Colombia, glyphosate, and other key words or terms, using standard academic search engines for publications, and we combed UNODC, EMCDDA, and other agency and nongovernmental organization (NGO) websites.[20]

Of the many UNODC sources we enlisted, we drew especially from the agency's annual cultivation surveys (UNODC and Government of Colombia 2017, etc.) and from *Características Agroculturales de los Cultivos de Coca en Colombia, 2005–2010* (UNODC and Ministry of Justice and Law 2010).[21] The latter includes information on two phases, 2005 and 2006–10, of a study that addressed coca cultivation and processing in seven regions, consisting of Putumayo-Caquetá, Central, Orinoquía, Pacífico, Sierra Nevada, Meta-Guaviare, and Catatumbo.[22]

As for our aperture, we concentrated on activities at the start of the supply chain (i.e., cultivation and processing that occur on-farm), and harms to the physical environment, particularly in relation to decisions about the use of land, fertilizers, herbicides, and other pesticides sold as agrochemicals, and processing chemicals.[23] Although we discuss the environmental effects of glyphosate, a common component of herbicides that has featured prominently in Colombia's forced eradication programs,[24] we do not weigh in on human health. We also consider, with broader brushstrokes, some implications of coca cultivation and processing for individuals' material support, drawing attention to the relevance of full accounting.

Thus, whereas our prior assessments looked across all classes of bearers and types of harm, this assessment addresses a subset. For the physical environment, we evaluate functional harms, using sustainability as a benchmark for an amalgam of physical and operational integrity.[25] By contrast, we took a broader view of material concerns than previously, by considering

assessment and, at one point, we had hoped to trace a continuous supply chain with concurrent data, but that ambition remains unfulfilled.

[20] We completed our primary searches for academic and other sources, which included material from past projects, in 2017, but occasionally we also cite material that we encountered thereafter—such as data from more recent versions of UNODC publications—and have augmented our discussions accordingly.

[21] Following Paoli et al. (2009), we work mostly with UNODC data on coca cultivation and processing.

[22] We could not locate comprehensive reports on any later phases.

[23] We refer collectively to industrially produced fertilizers, herbicides, and other pesticides as "agrochemicals," but not all such agricultural inputs are produced industrially.

[24] For the remainder of this chapter, we refer primarily to forced eradication, unless stated otherwise.

[25] We do not address aesthetic integrity.

losses *and* gains and taking our first step toward full accounting. For example, coca growers could incur losses from price inflation and extortion, sometimes taking the form of bribes to officials or protection payments to intermediaries, but they could also gain from additional income. As a consequence, we made different decisions about exclusions (Chapter 4, Section 4.3) and decoupled legitimacy from legality, treating as de facto "legitimate" some ill-gotten gains (i.e., coca-derived income), illegally acquired or inherently illegal possessions (e.g., coca), and losses thereof as well as harms to wholly or mostly illegal (i.e., coca-growing) enterprises.

To start, we articulate a business model for coca cultivation and processing in Colombia that emphasizes farm-level or "on-farm" activities but references others. In this assessment, we used the business model template as a tool for parsing activities as "primary," "enabled," etc., but not to collate data as we would for an assessment with a larger data collection. By filling in the activities in the template as shown in Table 6.1, we were able to think through some of the thornier issues of delineating primary, enabled, and accompanying activities. We have also filled in the row for "investment" to illustrate its intended use.

After setting out the business model, we explore coca cultivation and processing through the lens of harm assessment, focusing on implications for the physical environment and material support. We address drug-control policy, especially eradication, in a dedicated discussion of causality and policy's role in shaping harms, but, inevitably, we touch on concerns about policy sooner in the assessment. As a practical matter, much of the research on coca and policy—like their reality—is intertwined.

6.4 The Business Model of Coca Cultivation and Processing in Colombia

As evident in Table 6.1, we treat coca cultivation and processing that occur on-farm as primary activities and processing that occurs off-farm and trafficking as enabled activities.[26] We also treat conflict as an enabled activity, insomuch as growers' pay "taxes"—as bribes or protection payments—that help to finance conflict or insurgents and paramilitary forces engage

[26] Alternatively, we could have drawn the line at cultivation and treated all processing as enabled; however, the on- and off-farm distinction provided a cleaner break for decision-making and technology.

Table 6.1 Illustrative use of data template for coca-related business model

Activities	Characterization					
	Events[c]	**Participants**	**Resources**	**Venues**	**Time frame**	Data sources[d]
Primary[a]						
• Coca cultivation						
- Investment	Land clearing, site preparation, and planting, including use of agrochemicals and resulting, e.g., in loss of forest cover, soil erosion and runoff, and agrochemical contamination	Growers, physical environment, adjacent communities, distant communities	Land, labor, seeds or plantlets, water, equipment, agrochemicals	Plots located in rain forests, on park land, along rivers, and elsewhere, held with or without title	Approximately 2000–16	Academic, governmental (e.g., Colombian), multilateral organizations (e.g., World Bank), NGOs, and press
- Maintenance						
- Harvest						
- Divestment						
• Coca processing						
- Leaf-to-paste (on-farm)						
- Paste-to-base (on-farm)						

Continued

Table 6.1 *Continued*

Activities	Characterization					
Enabled						
• Coca processing						
- Leaf-to-paste (off-farm)						
- Paste-to-base (off-farm)						
- Base to cocaine (off-farm)[b]						
• Trafficking						
• Conflict						
Accompanying						
• Violence						
• Corruption						
• Money laundering						

Source: Authors' analysis.
Notes:

[a] For definitions of technical terms, see Appendix A, "Glossary of Terms."

[b] For all practical purposes, this activity only occurs off-farm.

[c] Consequences can be listed with events, as some are here, or separately in another column.

[d] In a full application, this column would include specific citations or references.

directly in production and marketing, but recognize that conflict might also be a driver of cultivation and processing.[27] We identify violence, corruption, and money laundering as accompanying activities, as we have previously, but with a slight difference. In the Colombian context, we deal with violence largely as an activity that accompanies conflict outside of agricultural activities, though both conflict and violence can occur in other ways, on- or off-farm, and can also result from drug-control policy, as we address later.[28] Corruption and money laundering can also occur along the entire supply chain and, as a consequence, can accompany on- or off-farm activities, but corruption might be relevant earlier in the supply chain than money laundering. Growers might need to bribe officials to avoid crop eradication, but only late-stage processers and traffickers might accumulate enough income to warrant laundering.

In Figure 6.2, we depict the full suite of primary, enabled, and accompanying activities, but in the remainder of this section, we emphasize on-farm activities.

UNODC and Ministry of Justice and Law (2010, 21–3) offer a typology of "coca producers" that consists of "agricultural producers," growers who cultivate coca and other agricultural products; "cocaleros," growers who are tied to the drug industry, but not to agriculture by ancestry or tradition; and "rural day laborers," hired workers who might stay within a particular region or move among regions, as market forces and other circumstances dictate. Agricultural producers might be more inclined to sell coca leaves to middlemen for processing and cocaleros might be more inclined to engage in processing, but we refer to both as growers or farmers and draw distinctions between them only when our sources do so clearly and purposefully.

Elements of Coca Growers' Decisions

In stylized terms, the coca grower's business model involves three kinds of decision: (1) a planting or "investment" decision, with choices about the location and size of the stand, the density and variety of coca, and so forth;

[27] In this assessment, we are concerned with conflict as a political phenomenon, involving insurgents, paramilitaries, and government forces. For discussions of the use of this term, see, e.g., Beittel (2017), Cárdenas and Rozo (2008), Holmes and Gutiérrez de Piñeres (2006), and Holmes et al. (2006).

[28] In our work on cocaine trafficking in Belgium, we focused largely on perpetrator-to-perpetrator disputes, so that violence accompanied trafficking, the primary activity, and dealing, an enabled activity.

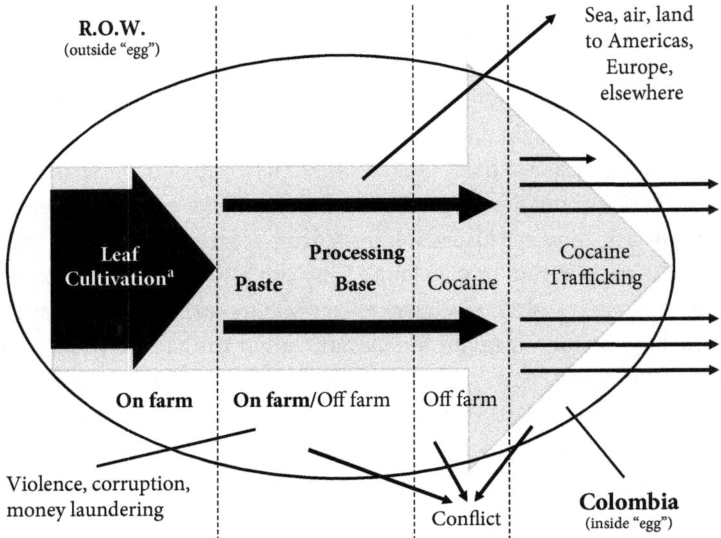

Figure 6.2 Graphical representation of business model for coca cultivation and processing and related activities in Colombia
Source: Authors' analysis.
Notes:
R.O.W. = rest of world.
[a] We emphasize on-farm activities, as represented inside the "egg," with text in bold font.

(2) a series of age-dependent "production" decisions, relating to maintenance, harvests, and processing, that can recur over a few or several years; and eventually (3) a "divestment" decision that can also entail reinvestment.[29,30] Ultimately, these decisions, mediated by the effects of disease, weather, and other sources of uncertainty, will yield coca and, by extension, income for coca growers and laborers.

The planting decision, like any other investment decision, is forward looking. A grower must glance a few or several years ahead to decide whether returns from harvests are likely to justify initial expenditures on planting, both in absolute terms and relative to other options. If a grower intends to process coca leaf to coca paste or cocaine base, their decisions

[29] Recall that "cultivation" covers investment, maintenance, harvesting, and divestment, whereas "production" covers maintenance, harvesting, and processing, but not investment or divestment (see Appendix A).
[30] Economists refer to this as a vintage capital model (see, e.g., Greenfield 1991).

about planting could also depend on their expectations regarding returns from those products.

As a practical matter, a coca grower decides at the outset where, how, and what to plant and on how much land. The grower might, for example, choose between planting coca on land—titled, leased, or otherwise claimed—that has been cleared previously or still requires clearing and is either near to or far from home. As we discuss elsewhere in this chapter, a grower might choose a location that is remote and inaccessible to protect their investment from detection and destruction or located near a river for access to water, if engaging in processing, and for ease of transport. For a given parcel, a grower must also consider how much land to allocate to coca as compared to other crops (e.g., for own consumption or local sale).

With varying degrees of awareness and rigor, growers make these kinds of decisions subject to their expectations about a broad range of growing conditions, including socioeconomic and environmental factors, policy, security, and household-specific circumstances (Greenfield et al. 2015a), over the projected life of the stand that can play a part in determining the crop's absolute and relative income-earning potential. Among the socioeconomic factors, a grower might weigh expectations about the prices of coca and alternatives and the costs of labor, fertilizer, pesticides, and taxes, including bribes and protection payments, but they might also weigh concerns for morality, legitimacy, conflict, and violence.[31] In addition, policy could come into play through expectations about eradication or development programs.

Moreover, actions that a grower takes at or plans to take after planting can affect the grower's calculus, largely through their implications for the productivity and yield of the stand. For example, decisions about planting, such as the density and variety of shrubs, will bear on a shrub's productivity and affect the stand's income-earning potential, as will decisions about production, including harvest intensity, input use, and other aspects of land management (UNODC and Ministry of Justice and Law 2010, 61, 76–80).

After planting the coca, growers must decide each year, as conditions unfold, how much labor, fertilizer, herbicide, and other pesticide to use to maintain the stand, how often and much leaf to harvest, and how much leaf

[31] See, e.g., Angrist and Kugler (2008), Dávalos-Álvarez (2016), Ibanez and Carlsson (2010), Ibanez and Martinsson (2013), Rincón-Ruiz et al. (2013a, 2013b) for research on coca farmers in Colombia and Greenfield et al. (2015a, 2017) for research on opium poppy farmers in Afghanistan.

to process, with what mix of chemicals and other supplies. Those production decisions will depend on many of the same factors, policies, and household circumstances as the investment decision but over a shorter horizon.

The coca grower's decisions about production and, eventually, the decision to stop producing entirely, by divesting, will also depend partly on the stand's age, because a shrub's productivity will vary as it ages (i.e., first increasing, then peaking, and then decreasing) (see Section 6.2). Growing conditions, ranging from prices to security, can also affect the timing of divestment and subsequent decisions about reinvestment. For example, if the price of coca is falling with no expectation of recovery, a grower might divest sooner and choose an alternative.

A grower's land-tenure arrangement—title, lease, or other claim—might also affect decisions about planting, production, and divestment, possibly by altering his or her perception of the relevant time frame for decision-making. For example, a grower with well-defined and secure property rights on titled land might take a longer-term view and favor land-management practices that maintain plant and soil health than a grower who lacks those rights. Along such lines, titling might also lead some growers toward formal market activity.[32]

Finally, coca growers must contend with uncertainty. Prices fluctuate, storms strike, diseases spread, and eradication programs, conflict, and violence can damage or destroy crops, disrupt production, or endanger personal safety, with substantial departures from expectations. As a result, the decisions that growers make about investment, production, and divestment will also depend on their attitudes toward risk and, relatedly, their objectives. For example, a "risk averse" grower who needs, above all, to feed their family, might allocate more of their land to producing food crops—for subsistence—and less to coca than another.[33]

Evidence on Coca Growers' Decision-Making

In this section, we review the evidence on growers' decision-making and related outcomes, including harm, starting with those on investment.

[32] For evidence post-dating this assessment, see Muñoz-Mora et al. (2018).

[33] Ibanez and Carlsson (2010) and Ibanez and Martinsson (2013) model growers' goals and attitudes toward risk.

Location of landholdings

Coca cultivation has occurred in over 20 Departments in Colombia, but it tends to be concentrated among far fewer. Since 2012, Nariño, Putamayo, and Norte de Santander have accounted, together, for half or more of all cultivation and, in 2016, their cumulative share was over 60 percent. (See Figure 6.3 for a map of Colombia.) Other prominent Departments have included Cauca and Caquetá, which ranked fourth and fifth, respectively, in 2016. Looking back over a longer period (2001–16), Nariño and Putamayo have tended to be market leaders, but the data indicate a decline in regional

Figure 6.3 Map of Colombia

Source: Beittel (2017).

concentration over the mid-to-late 2000s and a resurgence in the mid-2010s, largely tracking aggregate growth, which Nariño has dominated.

The historical data also point to the impermanence of declines and the potential for cultivation to shift back-and-forth across Departments. A Department, such as Norte de Santander, might fade from view in one decade and reappear as a leader in another.

See Appendix C for details of the data.

Rincón-Ruiz and Kallis (2013, 67–9) warn, however, that the story of coca's migration is not one of shifts alone, but also of diffusion throughout territories. In particular, they find that aerial spraying, which we address below with causality and policy, led to displacement and relocation and to diffusion across municipalities. Moreover, a considerable amount of new cultivation has emerged on frontier land and, less so, in national parks, to avoid detection and counter measures that previously included aerial spraying, which was prohibited in the parks. As of 2010, Colombian growers were tending about 62,000 hectares of coca—as compared to about 91,970 hectares of cocoa and 650,000 hectares of coffee—and were occupying about 3,675 hectares of the country's 12.6 million hectares of park land (UNODC and Ministry of Justice and Law 2010, 14; Appendix B and Figure 6.4 of this book). Aerial spraying has since been suspended and the incentive to occupy parks might have diminished, but, as of 2016, coca had

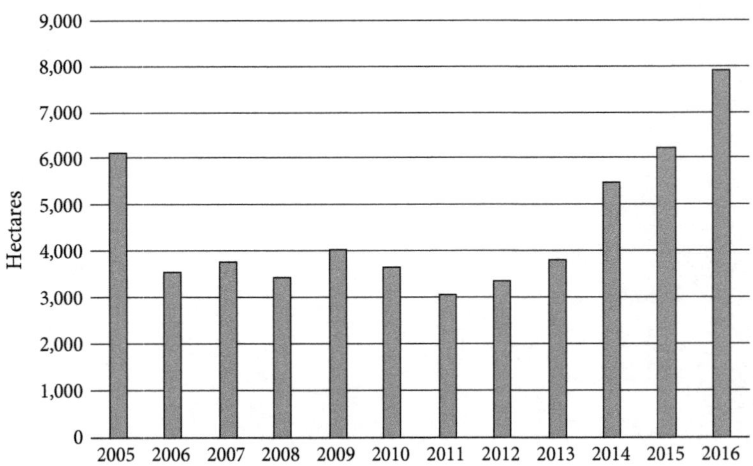

Figure 6.4 Coca cultivation in national parks (Hectares measured as net coca cultivation, at year's end)

Sources: Data compiled by authors from UNODC and Government of Colombia (2006–17).

spread to a total of 7,889 hectares of park land, roughly in line with the increase in total cultivation.

Dávalos et al. (2009, 384), who report on Putumayo and Caquetá, conclude that, "most frontier smallholders driving coca deeper into the forest are second- and third-generation locals" and that displaced smallholders, possibly from other frontier areas, likely constitute the remainder.[34]

Characteristics of landholdings

Many, but not all, coca growers in Colombia cultivate their crops on a few hectares or less. At the time of the UNODC and Ministry of Justice and Law (2010, 11) study, landholdings ranged from 0.25 to 95.6 hectares, with smaller landholdings accounting for a larger share of all production units. In that same era, UNODC and Government of Colombia (2009, 6) reported that about 59,300 households cultivated coca on about 81,000 hectares at year's end, implying an average of 1.37 hectares of coca per household. UNODC and Government of Colombia (2017, 11–12) report 106,900 households with 146,000 hectares, implying the same average, but masking variation in intervening years (Appendix B and Figure 6.5).

More often than not, farmers, including coca growers, in Colombia hold land informally. According to UNODC and Ministry of Justice and Law (2010, 13), 66 percent of farmers occupied their land without title, 13 percent owned their land with title, 17 percent leased their land, and the rest fell into other categories, including partnerships, as of the mid-to-late 2000s. The same study (p. 11) also suggests that informality affects growers' decisions about land use, claiming that some landholders view land as a speculative asset.[35]

Allocation of landholdings

Consistent with a degree of risk aversion and concerns for meeting basic needs, coca growers, particularly those whom UNODC and Ministry of Justice and Law (2010) call "agricultural producers," appear to allocate some of their land to legal agricultural pursuits, including subsistence, even if they lean heavily on coca for cash income.[36] Dávalos et al. (2009,

[34] For a different perspective, see UNODC and Ministry of Justice and Law (2010, 24–5).

[35] Consistent with this premise, more-recent research (Muñoz-Mora et al. 2018) finds that informality increases risk taking and correlates with coca growing.

[36] See Ibanez and Carlsson (2010) and Ibanez and Martinsson (2013) for different perspectives.

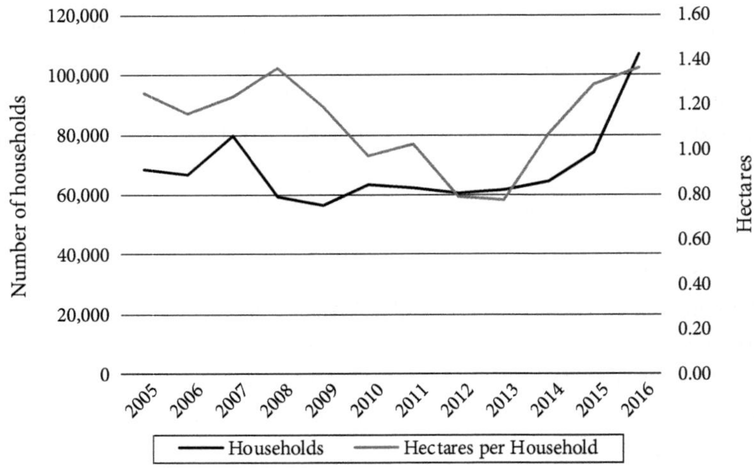

Figure 6.5 Coca-growing households and hectares of coca cultivation per household (Hectares per household measured from net coca cultivation, at year's end)

Sources: Data compiled by authors from UNODC and Government of Colombia (2006–17).

382) report that smallholders in most coca-growing regions do not or cannot produce coffee, flowers, bananas, or oil palm for export, but might produce cassava, plantains, legumes, or other fruits for household consumption and local markets. According to Carrillo González (2014), some affluent households in Caquetá produce a combination of coca, rubber, and livestock (p. 209), but others might grow yucca, plantain, other fruits, and hold a few cows for milk (p. 215).[37]

According to UNODC and Ministry of Justice and Law (2010), agricultural producers—as distinct from "cocaleros"—allocated about 82 percent of their operations to coca in 2005, declining to about 60 percent in 2010 (p. 19) with a commensurate decline in coca's contribution to their incomes (p. 33), and, in some instances, they might engage in mono-cropping.[38]

[37] See Rincón-Ruiz and Kallis (2013, 71) for further evidence of subsistence agriculture and livestock ownership across regions. Henman and Metaal (2009, 17) also describe subsistence practices, noting that collocating coca with legal crops can benefit the cultivation of those crops, e.g., by stabilizing soils.

[38] Accordingly, the total number of hectares in coca declined from 85,750 hectares to 62,000.

About 77 percent of all plots including those of cocaleros were dedicated to coca alone (pp. 75–6).

Use of labor and other agricultural inputs

Coca cultivation, especially harvesting, is inherently labor intensive. At harvest, growers must hand pick or "pluck" the coca leaf and may need to hire seasonal workers to help them, depending partly on the availability of household labor and the size of their stand. According to Mejía and Posada (2008, 4), the labor requirement for harvesting a hectare of coca is up to 300 man-days, which is at least as labor intensive as opium poppy, another notoriously labor-intensive drug crop, and considerably more labor intensive than many typical bulk commodities (see, e.g., Greenfield et al. 2015a, Appendix B). Growers can apply fertilizers, herbicides, and other pesticides to boost yields and control pests, which might raise or lower the labor requirement on balance. Whereas the increase in yields from healthier plants and less competition in the fields might imply more labor at harvest, chemical treatments that discourage weeds and pests might imply less labor at other times.

UNODC and Ministry of Justice and Law (2010, pp. 3, 88–91), which report use of various agrochemicals, reference or highlight:

- many fertilizers and cite "Triple 15" (nitrogen, phosphorous, and potassium at 15 percent, each) as especially popular among solid fertilizers (pp. 3, 88–9)
- widespread use of paraquat-based Gramoxone®—70 percent of growers post-2005—and lesser use of glyphosate-based Roundup® as herbicides (pp. 3, 89–90).
- substantial use of Látigo® and Tamaron®, among other pesticides, which the World Health Organization has classified as "extremely dangerous" (pp. 3, 90–1).

UNODC and Ministry of Justice and Law (2010, 87) also indicate a decline in coca growers' use of agrochemicals, possibly related to the risk of crop loss at that time, but also—and perhaps more likely—because of higher costs and lower returns (UNODC and Government of Colombia 2017, 86) (See also Appendix B and Figure 6.6). While UNODC (2006, 63) depicted coca maintenance as relatively resource intensive, UNODC (2016, 90) suggests that coca growers use agrochemicals more or less on a par with farmers of other tropical crops.

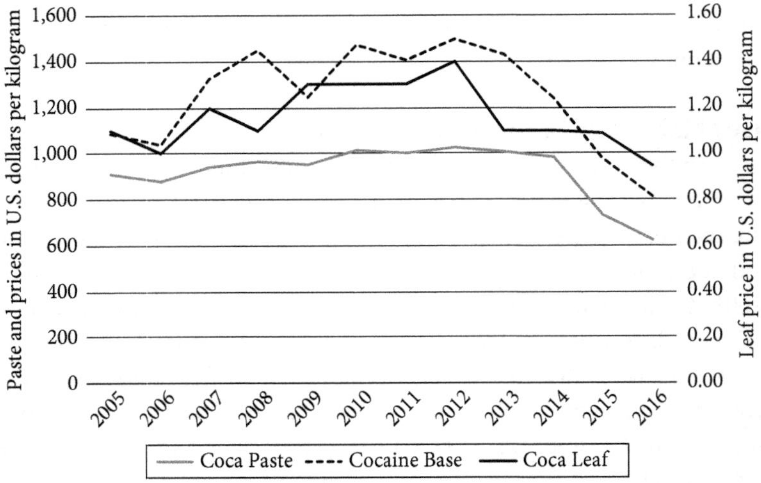

Figure 6.6 Prices of coca leaf, coca paste, and cocaine base (Prices measured in US dollars, current value, per kilogram)

Sources: Data compiled by authors from UNODC and Government of Colombia (2006–17).

Harvest intensity, yields, and lifecycles

Growers' decisions on harvest intensity appear to track data on age.[39] UNODC and Ministry of Justice and Law (2010, 77) indicate that growers typically harvest young stands (e.g., less than one to two years) twice per year and harvest mature stands (e.g., four to five years) four or more times per year. A young stand might yield less than 4,000 kilograms per hectare, whereas a mature stand might yield more than 5,000 (p. 77). At the time of the study, harvests per year averaged about four and a half and the annual yield per hectare averaged about 4,600 kilograms (p. 44), but yields differ by region and have risen modestly since then (Appendix B and Figure 6.7).[40]

Growing conditions in Colombia might favor early divestment, which might in turn suggest less attention to sustainable land-management practices than otherwise. UNODC and Ministry of Justice and Law (2010) report a 4- to 10-year life cycle as typical, but that is much shorter than in some other environments and eras, and Harden (2006, 256) reports some abandonment and relocation after two or three growing seasons, "to gain fertility and evade authorities."[41]

39 Plots may include young and old shrubs.

40 Yields have continued to increase since our assessment (UNODC 2020, Part 3, 22).

41 Well-maintained plantations in Bolivia can remain productive for up to 40 years (Plowman 1986, 13).

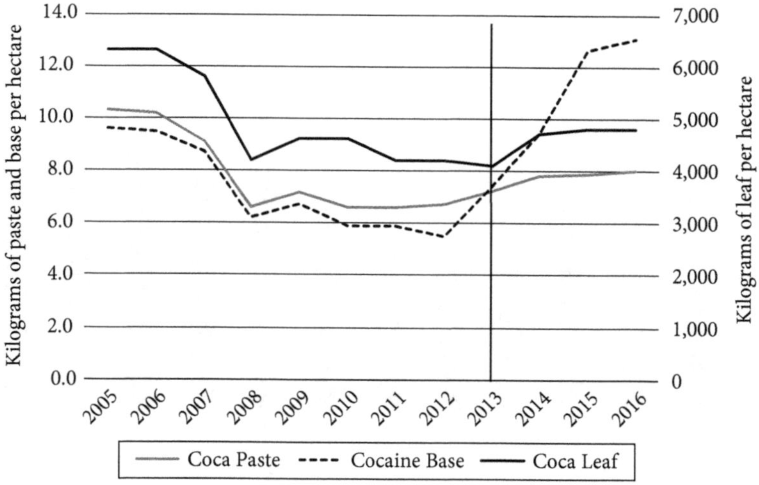

Figure 6.7 Yields of coca leaf, coca paste, and cocaine base (Yields measured in kilograms per hectare)

Sources: Data compiled by authors from UNODC and Government of Colombia (2006–17).
Notes: Coca paste and cocaine base yields for 2013 are averages of the 2012 and 2014 yields for each, because data for the coca paste and cocaine base yields for 2013 are not available. However, UNODC and Government of Colombia (2014, summary fact sheet, n.p.) caution, "Manufacturing data presented from 2013 has been adjusted within this report and is not comparable to data published within the 2012 report." For more information, see UNODC and Government of Colombia (2014, 119–23).

Processing activities

As noted previously, growers who seek to capture value added along the supply chain often engage in the earliest stages of processing, sometimes engage in later stages, but almost never engage in the last stage. Reports on processing in Colombia dating back as far as DEA (1993) indicate a consistently moderate-to-high degree of farm-level involvement in paste production, in part to avoid transporting leaves. Between 2005 and 2016, the share of coca growers producing coca paste averaged 31 percent, ranging from a low of 22 percent in 2009 to high of 39 percent in 2016 (UNODC and Government of Colombia, 2006–17; Appendix B and Figure 6.8 of this book). By contrast, farm-level involvement in the next stage of processing has been substantial at times, but has dwindled. Between 2005 and 2016, the share of coca growers producing cocaine base reached a high of 37 percent in 2008 and fell to a low of 1 percent in 2015 (UNODC and Government of Colombia, 2006–17; Appendix B and Figure 6.8 of this book).

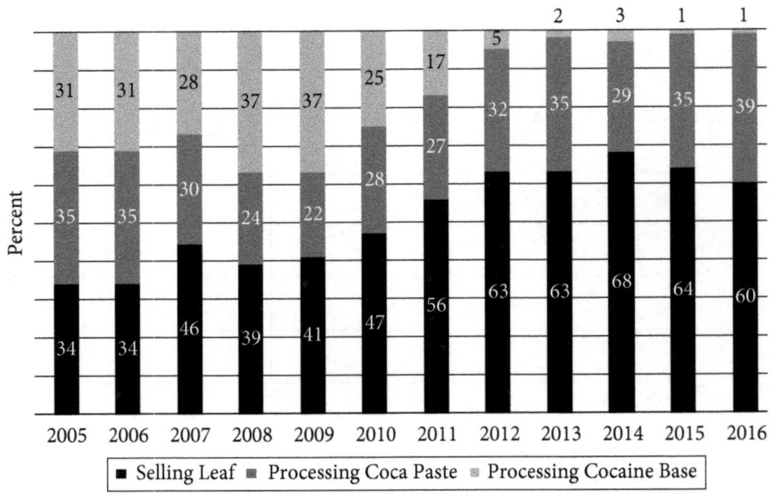

Figure 6.8 Division of labor (Division of labor measured as percent of growers engaging in each activity)

Sources: Data compiled by authors from UNODC and Government of Colombia (2006–17).

Notes: Data for 2007 have been apportioned to sum to 100 percent.

UNODC and Ministry of Justice and Law (2010, 51–4) warn against generalizing about chemical use in processing, citing a lack of standardization of quantities and concentrations and differences in purity, but they cite common use of sulfuric acid, ammonia, sodium bicarbonate, caustic soda, gasoline, and potassium permanganate, depending on the extent of processing, and they suggest an opportunity for water and soil contamination. Such contamination might occur through improper use or dumping. Likely compounding the risks of water contamination are the reinforcing needs to use water for processing and to use rivers for transportation, both of which might imply co-location of processing with waterways.

Indicative of incentives to engage in processing, UNODC and Government of Colombia (2006–16) report the potential gross income per hectare from each stage of production, measured by the amount of income a grower would obtain from growing just leaves or processing them to just paste or base on a hectare of land. For 2008, which is within the period of analysis of the UNODC and Ministry of Justice and Law (2010) study,[42] UNODC and Government of Colombia (2009, 55) report potential

[42] We chose 2008 as our reference year for this period because it has the most complete, best documented, and least idiosyncratic data among the years.

gross income from selling just unprocessed leaves, from processing leaves through to paste, or from processing leaves through to base of $4,620, $6,360, and $8,990 per hectare, respectively. In 2008, 39 percent of growers sold leaves, 24 percent sold paste, and 37 percent sold base, but the share producing base declined sharply in later years.

In the mid-2010s, the yields on coca leaf, coca paste, and cocaine base rose, but associated prices fell. On balance, data on potential gross income from coca and its derivatives for that period (Appendix B), suggest vacillating and slightly lower figures for leaf and paste and a much higher figures for base, which has all-but vanished from coca growers' portfolios. In view of the possibility of higher returns, the drop-off in base production among growers begs the question, "why has it dropped off?" Evidence, albeit scant, of higher cocaine base yields among middlemen processors, suggests that they might be squeezing out growers and claiming the value added for themselves. UNODC and Government of Colombia (2017, 64) note that off-farm processors have higher productivity from larger-scale production and better use of supplies.

Risk and risk management

To make decisions about coca investment, production, and divestment, growers must consider the usual possibilities of price fluctuations, bad weather, plant disease, etc., and, depending on their location and other factors, the less usual possibilities of eradication, conflict, and violence.[43] Among the latter, the threat of eradication stands out as oriented toward, if not necessarily limited to, drug-crop cultivation and the threats of conflict and violence might be greater in regions of illegal cultivation and trade than elsewhere (see, e.g., Angrist and Kugler 2008; Chouvy and Laniel 2007; Dávalos-Álvarez 2016; Rincón-Ruiz and Kallis 2013). The interaction among these factors, including growers' decisions, generate harms.

Whether coca growers face more uncertainty than other farmers is unclear. Coca growers face a range of agricultural concerns, regarding crop prices, weather, and disease, that could be more or less pronounced, and might suffer distinctively from some threats, such as that of eradication, but they could also benefit from market surety and access that other farmers lack. Speaking to the threat of aerial spraying, Rincón-Ruiz and Kallis (2013, 70–2, 75) characterize fumigation as indiscriminate because

[43] See Greenfield (1991), Greenfield et al. (2015a), Ibanez and Carlsson (2010), and Ibanez and Martinsson (2013).

it affects not just coca, but also the legal crops growing with or near it and, thus, poses a threat to legal crops too. Ironically, Gonzáles (2014) suggests that some coca growers had opted for coca because of its resilience to fumigation.[44] However, with the suspension of fumigation and shift to manual eradication methods, which should be better targeted, these dynamics might change.

Still, Dávalos et al. (2009, 382) suggest that coca is, on balance, less risky economically than other crops and Rincón-Ruiz and Kallis (2013, 75) cite the relative stability and security of income and employment as "most appealing." That said, coca growers have a history of planting different kinds of crops—and raising livestock or engaging in other agricultural and nonagricultural off-farm activities—to diversify and mitigate risks of income loss, food deficits, or lack of shelter (UNODC and Ministry of Justice and Law 2010, 34). In addition, Palacios (2012) finds that coca growers are less likely to experience forced displacement from conflict zones than farmers who plant less labor-intensive crops, though, as we discuss later, Dion and Russler (2008, 414–15), Rincón-Ruiz and Kallis (2013, 71–2), and others report a strong statistical relationship between eradication and displacement.

Market participation and farmgate incomes

Reflective of coca growers' decisions on investment, production, and divestment, UNODC in various configurations of authorship and co-authorship provides data on households' participation in illegal cultivation and processing and incomes for our period of analysis (Appendix B), that encapsulate growers' decisions and can provide insight to offsetting gains from engagement in cultivation and processing.

UNODC and Government of Colombia (2009, 6, 55–6) report gross farm-level income from coca and derivatives of about $623 million in 2008, with $155 million from leaf, $137 million from paste, and $332 million from base (Appendix B and Figure 6.9).[45] The total amounted to about $7,700 per hectare, $10,500 per household, and $2,600 per capita, spread over about

[44] Dávalos et al. (2009, 385) describe various risk-mitigation tactics that include using native trees and co-located legal crops to hide or shelter coca. See also UNODC and Ministry of Justice and Law (2010). More recently, research from Muñoz-Mora et al. (2018) suggests that coca might be riskier than legal crops in an environment of forced eradication, but it does not test for this risk explicitly.

[45] Recall, we chose 2008 as our reference year because of the data's completeness, documentation, and consistency.

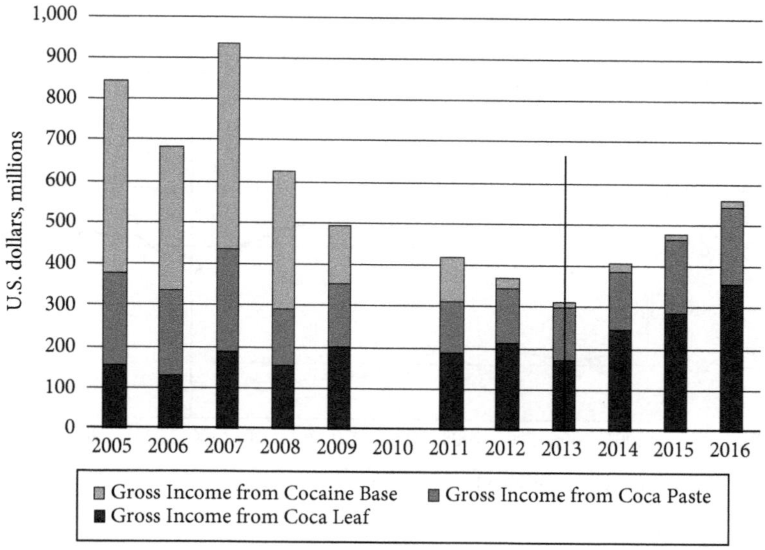

Figure 6.9 Gross income at farmgate from coca and derivatives, by product (Income measured in US dollars, millions, current value)

Sources: Data compiled by authors from UNODC and Government of Colombia (2006–17).

Notes: Data not available for 2010. Regarding later years, UNODC and Government of Colombia (2014, summary fact sheet, n.p.) caution, "Manufacturing data presented from 2013 has been adjusted within this report and is not comparable to data published within the 2012 report." For more information, see UNODC and Government of Colombia (2014, 119–23).

81,000 hectares, 59,300 households, and 238,000 individuals, respectively, compared with per capita gross domestic product (GDP) of about $5,400 (Appendix B and Figure 6.10).[46]

As of 2016, UNODC and Government of Colombia (2017, 11–12, 87) report that land use and participation had increased dramatically, to about 146,000 hectares and 106,900 households, amounting to over 530,000 individuals, but the total farmgate value of production was about $560 million ($356, $186, and $18 million from leaves, paste, and base, respectively). On that basis, gross incomes per hectare, per household, and per capita, fell to about $3,840, $5,240, and $960, respectively, compared with GDP per capita of about $5,800.[47]

[46] Data on GDP downloaded from https://data.worldbank.org/indicator/NY.GDP.PCAP.CD (accessed May 10, 2018).

[47] The $960-per-person figure comes from UNODC and Government of Colombia (2017), but our calculation from the underlying data is $1,047 per person.

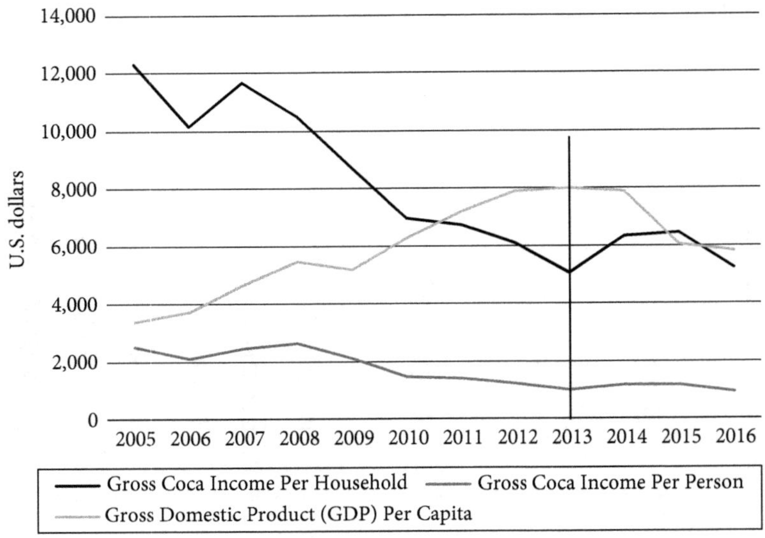

Figure 6.10 Gross income at farmgate from coca and derivatives per household and individual and gross domestic product per capita (Income measured in US dollars, current value)

Sources: Data compiled by authors from UNODC and Government of Colombia (2006 through 2017).

Notes: To calculate gross coca income per person for 2006, we use the number of households for 2006 and the average number of persons per household for 2005 and 2007 to arrive at a total number of persons, the divisor, because data for the average number of persons per household in 2006 are not available. Regarding later years, UNODC and Government of Colombia (2014, summary fact sheet, n.p.) caution, "Manufacturing data presented from 2013 has been adjusted within this report and is not comparable to data published within the 2012 report." For more information, see UNODC and Government of Colombia (2014, 119–23).

The potential for gross income from cocaine base rose in the mid-2010s, but growers produced less of it and obtained less of their total farmgate income from it, which might help to explain their dwindling incomes. Coca growers might have scraped by on coca when they were garnering a substantial share of their income from higher-value-added processing activities, but, in later years, a grower who depended largely on coca for cash income would have been living at just over the World Bank's $2.00 a day standard for poverty, without considering costs of production. While the average grower's gross coca-related income was about 50 percent of Colombia's per capita GDP in 2008, it dropped to 20 percent in 2016.

From 2005 to 2016, land use, household participation, and income from coca varied considerably, but coca's share of Colombia's overall and agricultural economies remained small to modest, at well under 0.5 and 5 percent, respectively (Appendix B).

Further downstream, those who engage in later stages of processing and trafficking and obtain greater returns might seek to launder their income and have been said to purchase real estate or land, potentially driving up prices of each, and embark on ranching and pasturing, at some cost to the environment, to do so.

6.5 Coca Cultivation and Processing through the Lens of Harm Assessment

In this assessment, we draw a loose circle around farm-level activities, focus on harms to the physical environment and consider damages to material support, primarily in relation to individuals. As per the tools and process of the framework (Chapter 4), we identify possible harms before turning to actual harms, causality, and the role of policy.

Identifying Possible Harms

Looking back at the business model, we see potential for harm to the physical environment at each juncture: (1) at planting (e.g., if growers clear-cut forest); (2) in production (e.g., if growers use agro- and processing chemicals to boost yields, control pests, and process coca); and (3) at the point of divestment, depending partly on what comes next (see Table 6.2).

In addition, the ubiquity of informal land-tenure arrangements coupled with the threat of eradication, whether chemical or manual, might exacerbate those harms, by creating mutually reinforcing incentives to prefer immediate returns, eschew sustainable cultivation practices, abandon stands sooner, and establish new ones in remote, ecologically fragile areas. Concerns about conflict, violence, and displacement could make matters worse, whether more or less pronounced for coca growers. On balance, these factors might discourage growers from taking the long view and lead them to pursue what Henman and Metaal (2009, 19) refer to as seemingly "predatory" cultivation practices.

Table 6.2 Possible harms and offsets in coca cultivation and processing and related activities

	Physical Environment's Functional and Aesthetic Integrity		Individuals' Material Support	
	Harms from/to (–)	**Offsets from/to (+)**	**Harms from/to (–)**	**Offsets from/to (+)**
Primary activities				
• Coca cultivation				
- Investment	Forest cover loss, soil erosion, runoff, and agrochemical contamination of soils and water; carbon and particulate emissions	n/a	Resource diversion; inflation in real estate and land prices, input prices, and other costs of living; income dependence; income inequality; diminished productivity	Additional income, net of initial investment and production costs, including wages
- Maintenance and harvest	Agrochemical contamination of soils and water	n/a	See investment	See investment
- Divestment	If replanted in situ or elsewhere, see investment, maintenance, and harvest	If abandoned, possibility of recovery and regeneration	n/a	n/a
• Coca processing[a] (on-farm)	Chemical contamination of soils and water		See investment	See investment

Enabled and accompanying activities				
• Conflict and violence[b]			Disruption, displacement, and protection payments	n/a
• Corruption			Bribes	n/a
• Money laundering[c]	Forest cover loss, soil erosion, and runoff, including damages to plant and wildlife; carbon release and particulate emissions	n/a	Inflation in real estate and land prices	n/a
Bearers	Forests, soils, water, air, and climate, via loss, contamination, and emissions, including ancillary harms to other wildlife, potentially across local, regional, and national boundaries	Forests, soils, water, air, and climate, depending on extent of recovery and regeneration, including ancillary gains to other wildlife, potentially across local, regional, and national boundaries	Coca growers, residents of local community, adjacent communities, region, or nation	Coca growers, hired labor, agrochemical and processing chemical suppliers; local entrepreneurs, responding to increased demand for goods and services

Source: Authors' analysis.

Notes:
n/a = not applicable.

[a] This row includes processing from leaf to paste and from paste to base.

[b] We did not attempt to disentangle the joint effects of conflict and violence.

[c] Harms from money laundering are more likely to accrue with later stages of processing.

As evidence of such pressures, we might expect to see growers in Colombia curtailing cultivation sooner than elsewhere and we have. Recall that UNODC and Ministry of Justice and Law (2010) report a typical lifecycle of just 4–10 years and Harden (2006) reports some abandonment and relocation as early as 2–3 years.[48]

We also see potential for material damages, for example, if coca supplants other pursuits that might have led to better outcomes, if costs of living rise because of coca booms, if growers become overly dependent on coca for cash income, if coca impedes productivity, or if officials or intermediaries demand bribes or protection payments.

Further into the business model, those "taxes"—and direct returns from processing and trafficking—could support conflict and violence, which might disrupt economic activity and result in additional material losses. They, especially the direct returns, might also entail money laundering that exacerbates inflation, and, in some instances, redoubles environmental damages, if, for example, dirty money flows into ranches and pastures.

Lastly, if coca diverts income from legal channels, Colombia—the government and, eventually, individuals—could experience material losses from forgone tax revenue, but only if Colombian authorities would have collected and dispersed the funds more productively.

However, we also note the possibilities of recovery (e.g., through regeneration on abandoned plots) and economic gains, through thousands of households' and laborers' additional income.

Thus, in this assessment, the story might include some "positives."

In the next step of the assessment, we turn our attention to actual outcomes for the physical environment and material support, primarily that of growers. To assess environmental harms, we draw largely from ecologists, geographers, economists, and others who have conducted studies on the effects of coca on land use, habitats, and wildlife and have addressed the effects of development on growing decisions and environmental outcomes. Our discussion of economic considerations draws from economic narratives and empirical evidence found in official, scholarly, and media sources. Although we touch unavoidably on drug-control policy, insomuch as it

[48] In an exchange post-dating our assessment, a colleague noted that growers have been retaining stands longer, partly because peace negotiations have resulted in less conflict and fewer drug-control efforts. This observation would seem to support our assessment of conflict and policy as having contributed to truncated lifecycles during our period of assessment. For a related and potentially confirming observation on more-recent land-management practices and the age structure of coca, see UNODC (2020, Part 3, 22).

influences the context of growers' decision-making, we reserve a fuller discussion of the role of policy for our investigation of causality. For example, we probe the extent to which policies on eradication underly certain cultivation and production decisions largely as a matter of causality, not as part of our initial evaluation of environmental harms.

Evaluating Harms from Environmental Damages

Here, we examine evidence on the effects of farm-level decisions about investment, production, and divestment on the physical environment, specifically in terms of deforestation and pollution. Some have portrayed coca growing as "ecocide,"[49] but the still-evolving and sometimes contradictory evidence is not as compelling as the moniker. Whereas Dávalos et al. (2009, 382) once described coca as "the single most important driver of deforestation in the country," Dávalos et al. (2011) present newer statistical work, covering much of Colombia's northern Andes, Chocó, and Amazon forests, and take a more nuanced stance.

The literature suggests that engagement with coca, especially through cultivation alone, inflicts harms that might be less onerous than those of other plausible economic activities and that simple comparisons, aggregate statistics, and generalities might be misleading.[50] Although much of the literature concludes, at least implicitly, that coca cultivation might not be as bad as the alternatives—to paraphrase, "it could be worse"—it is not clear that the other activities are really alternatives, that coca is really less damaging, or that lessons learned in one context (such as a region, municipality, or biome) apply broadly to others.[51] In addition, coca cultivation and coca processing might pose different risks insomuch as coca processing—to coca paste and cocaine base—could entail greater damages relating to chemical use and disposal.

[49] See Henman and Metaal (2009, 16), for examples of the use of this term and see National Police of Colombia (2014) and Wortham (2007–8) for perspectives that lean in this direction.

[50] Empirical research provides evidence of coca-induced deforestation, ecosystem fragmentation, and ecosystem loss, but it suggests that cattle ranching, pasture, and other activities pose a greater threat to environmental sustainability (see, e.g., Armenteras et al. 2006, 2011, 2013a, 2013b; Chadid et al. 2015; Dávalos et al. 2009, 2011, 2014, 2016, esp. 979–80; Etter et al. 2006b; Rincón-Ruiz et al. 2013a, 2013b; UNODC 2016).

[51] A biome "is a large community of vegetation and wildlife adapted to a specific climate," such as a grassland, forest, or tundra. See https://www.nationalgeographic.org/encyclopedia/biome/ (accessed September 2, 2021).

In all, coca might use resources differently in different locations or precede rather than replace some activities; moreover, it might occupy fewer hectares, but take a greater toll on its surroundings at different stages of cultivation and production.

Deforestation

With those complexities in mind, we find that the harms associated with coca-induced deforestation could range from serious to catastrophic because, in the extreme, they epitomize nonsustainability, and from rare to persistent, depending on the location and the level of analysis, be it national, regional, municipal, or biome-specific. Colombia, which is larger than France and Germany combined, covers immensely varied terrain. For example, damages to parts of the Pacific region, including areas of previously untouched tropical rainforest, might occur persistently, even if damages to the entire region occur just occasionally or less. With those ratings, the harms would rank from a low to high priority, depending on the context.

In the pages that follow, we present the evidence, starting with that on the extent of coca-induced deforestation, which speaks partly to the incidence of harms, but note that deforestation occurs in the context of prohibition and damages might stem, as we address later in this chapter, at least as much from policy incentives as other drivers.

Extent of forest cover loss

Coca might account for a small share of all the deforestation in Colombia, but interplay with other activities might obscure its role. A study of a 12.4-million-hectare area in Colombia found that about 5 percent of the forest loss that occurred from 2001 to 2006 could be attributed directly to coca cultivation and a follow-on study found an even lower rate through 2012 (UNODC (2016, 87) (see also UNODC 2016, 88, Table 4). Along similar lines, Armenteras et al. (2013b, 5–4) conclude that coca contributed to deforestation in northwestern Amazonia from 2000 to 2009, but less so than other land uses, including pastures. However, Holmes and Gutiérrez de Piñeres (2006) link ranching to traffickers and money laundering, which might, then, redirect attention back to coca, and Chadid et al. (2015) suggest that land in the San Lucas mountain range might have been cleared first for coca, before it became pasture.

Identifying marked differences across contexts, Armenteras et al. (2013a) examine the relationship between coca and deforestation rates nationally and in the Amazonian, Caribbean, Oronoco, and Pacific regions from 1990 to 2005 and find that coca was a statistically significant factor in the Caribbean and Orinoco regions, but not in the other regions or nationally. Armenteras et al. (2011, 2013a), Rincón-Ruiz et al. (2013a, 2013b, 2016), and others also present findings on regional and other contextual differences in deforestation patterns.

Although the bulk of the evidence points to coca's relevance to deforestation, not all of it agrees. For example, Sánchez-Cuervo and Aide (2013) do not detect a statistically significant relationship between coca and changes in forest cover at the national, biome, or other scales, but, instead, identify important roles for other environmental conditions and for other sociodemographic variables, including armed conflict. Without supporting data, Henman and Metaal (2009, 17) suggest that coca growers tend to avoid virgin woodlands out of practicality and, instead, clear regenerating scrubland to plant coca.

Effects of locational decisions

Some authors point to coca's expansion along waterways and into remote, untouched forest and fragile ecosystems, and cite dangers of fragmentation. Armenteras et al. (2006) note that colonization and fragmentation tend to follow the areas' waterways, consistent with dependence on fluvial transportation, as they point out, and a need for water to process coca. Rincón-Ruiz et al. (2013a, 27–8) identify a shift toward cultivation in areas with more natural forest cover, which they associate with fumigation policy, and a greater tendency to cultivate in areas with lower road density. Moreover, Rincón-Ruiz et al. (2013b, 107) find coca cultivation mainly affects forest habitats and call out expansion into regions, such as the Pacific, where coca had not grown before. Chadid et al. (2015) also find that coca, more so than pasture, tends to push into new frontiers, with forest losses in areas closer to rivers and, as Rincón-Ruiz et al. (2013a) imply, is less susceptible to detection (e.g., further removed from other crops, in remote mountainous zones, and farther from existing settlements).[52]

Damage can manifest in the loss of forest cover, itself; the loss of wildlife it supports directly, in situ; and the loss of wildlife it supports indirectly, in now-fragmented, formerly contiguous habitats in biologically diverse and ecologically sensitive areas (see, e.g., Álvarez 2002; Brain and Solomon

[52] Similarly, Dávalos et al. (2014, 72) find that coca does not expand in accessible areas and prefers municipalities with a high percent of forest cover to those that have been deforested.

2009, 943–5; Fjeldså et al. 2005; Rincón-Ruiz et al. 2016, 63–4; Quimbayo Ruiz 2008, 7). According to Rincón-Ruiz et al. (2016, 63–4), 84 percent of coca crops in Colombia are concentrated in 4 of the country's 34 biomes, largely in tropical rainforests along the Pacific, "a region considered one of the country's, and the world's, most important in terms of biodiversity."[53] The potential for fragmentation-induced damage also suggests that aggregate data do not tell the whole story because small plots can have large impacts.

The duration of harm

When a grower removes forest cover to grow coca, the damage might be long lived, and catastrophic or nearly so for the forest, but not necessarily permanent.

Dávalos et al. (2011, 1221) and Rodríguez et al. (2012, 126), who, in combination, cover substantial terrain, find little or no evidence of forest regeneration (see also Dávalos 2001, 72; Etter et al. 2006a, 80–1; Rincón-Ruiz and Kallis 2013, 70), but other scholars do. For example, Armenteras et al. (2013b, 5, 8) describe coca's nomadic existence in Amazonia—growers abandon stands in one location and move to another—but almost a third of the land planted in illicit crops in 2001 was forested again in 2009. They conclude, "Over time, the cultivation of illicit crops advances into intact forests, promoting further destruction" but "these areas are later abandoned, leading to forest regeneration (p. 8)." Notably, Armenteras et al. attribute coca's transience—only 1.3 percent of the stands in place in 2001 remained in place in 2009—to pressures from eradication, not to aging (pp. 5, 7). Sánchez-Cuervo et al. (2012, 10) also find evidence of recovery, "It is possible that we are detecting the first stages of natural regeneration (i.e., shrubs) following the eradication of these illicit crops."

However, even if regeneration occurs, Sánchez-Cuervo and Aide (2013, 1064) point out that hectares of new and old forest are not equivalent.[54] Moreover, regeneration might not undo the damages of any fragmentation of ecosystems that preceded it.

In addition, Harden (2006, 256), Solomon et al. (2007a, 88–9), and others cite the deleterious and potentially long-term effects of water run-off and soil erosion from clearing forests, which might be exacerbated by proximity

[53] See Quimbayo Ruiz (2008) for more on the relevance of Colombia's "megadiverse" physical environment.

[54] See Solomon et al. (2007a, 96) for a related discussion of recovery times.

to rivers and other waterways; particulate and carbon emissions; and species loss. Although outside the scope of a single-country assessment, these harms would almost certainly reach beyond Colombia; for example, the implications of forest loss for climate change are literally global.

Coca in relation its alternatives

Whether statements like "it could be worse" make sense in this context depends partly on whether the alternative for a particular plot is to remain in forest or shift into another use and likely differs by locale. For example, Amenteras et al. (2013b, 4–5) and Davalos et al. (2014, 67) suggest that pasture either has or might have replaced coca in some settings, but whether pasture would have taken hold without coca's prior entry is debatable. Chadid et al. (2015) cast some doubt on the premise of pasture as a likely alternative, when they find that pasture gravitates toward less remote and more accessible areas than coca and most typically consolidates—rather than provokes—change. Though, others (e.g., Holmes and Gutiérrez de Piñeres 2006) who have linked ranching and pastures to traffickers and money laundering, suggest ties to coca.

Other activities, like ranching and pasturing, might be worse over all, largely because their incidence is greater, but, if they are not competing for land, the relative difference does not lessen concern for coca's impact on the physical environment, especially if coca precedes pasture or promotes it, eventually, through money laundering.

Water and other pollution

Here, we focus largely on what we have learned about coca cultivation, processing, and pollution, specifically in relation to the use of agro- and processing chemicals. Data on the use of those chemicals and related studies of toxicity suggest considerable opportunity for environmental damages, but we fell short on concrete evidence of actual damage and could not rate or rank associated harms. Clearly, some commonly used agro- and processing chemicals, including gasoline and other precursors, have the potential to damage the physical environment,[55] but surprisingly little is known about the dimensions of the threat and whether damages occur.

In our rapid assessment, we found much less research on pollution from growing or processing coca than on the use of glyphosate to control coca. Although we cannot rule out that we missed or misinterpreted evidence,

[55] See also Quimbayo Ruiz (2008, 6–9) for commentary on industrial product use.

Henman and Metaal (2009), UNODC (2016), and others also suggest a deficit of research on production effects.[56] We draw insight from studies of glyphosate-based products that, although geared toward investigating the consequences of aerial spraying, might shed light on its use among farmers as an herbicide, from other studies of pesticide toxicity, and, to a lesser extent, from a broader environmental literature.[57]

We found opposing strands of research on glyphosate-based products.[58] One strand (e.g., Bernal et al. 2009; Brain and Solomon 2009; Solomon et al. 2005, 2007a, 2007b) leaves the impression that the products are relatively and perhaps even absolutely benign. For example, Solomon et al. (2007a) compare hazard ratings for glyphosate-based products and 16 other chemical products used to cultivate illegal crops and report both low ratings for the former and substantially higher ratings for some of the latter. (See also Henao Muñoz et al. 2015). Another strand of research (e.g., Relyea 2005a, 2005b, 2012; Relyea and Jones 2009; Relyea et al. 2005), suggests greater scope for harm, albeit in studies of North American amphibians and from combinations of ingredients, but not necessarily from glyphosate, per se, or alone.[59]

More recent academic reviews of effects across agricultural settings (e.g., Bai and Ogbourne 2016; Saunders and Pezeshki 2015; van Bruggen 2018), do not rule out harm. In addition, we would direct the reader to various court proceedings.[60]

Regardless of their positions on the absolute or relative risks of glyphosate-based products, participants in the debate (e.g., Brain and Solomon 2009; Solomon et al. 2007a; Relyea and Diecks 2008) report findings on other pesticides that might elicit concerns about their use. In addition, more recent work on the toxicity of common pesticides to amphibians (e.g., Triana et al. 2017) also suggests some potential for harm.

[56] Long preceding our efforts, Joyce (1999, A75–A77) commented on the lack of studies.

[57] Although we conducted searches on "glyphosate," "environment," and "Colombia" to identify major strands in the literature on glyphosate, we did not conduct a comprehensive literature review. Some highly visible researchers in this arena have faced considerable criticism. Washington Office on Latin America (2008, 20–22) and Transnational Institute (2005) present critiques of Solomon et al. (2005), the authors' foundational report, voicing concerns about breadth, methodology, and impartiality, and Bernal et al. (2009) and others provide critical commentary on Relyea's work.

[58] For an overview of competing views, see also Rincón-Ruiz and Kallis (2013, 70–1).

[59] Relyea has also identified negative health effects for amphibians from exposure to different combinations of insecticides and herbicides, including glyphosate (e.g., Relyea 2004, 2009; Relyea and Diecks 2008).

[60] See, e.g., those in the aforementioned Ecuadorian case and in the European Union.

Ultimately, the environmental consequences of production are unclear.

Henman and Metaal (2009), alone, argue that coca-growing helps maintain species diversity and stabilize soils (p. 17), but concede, "Real costs . . . accrue to the environment by the increasing use of industrial products in both boosting coca yields and processing coca into coca paste" (p. 18). According to the authors (p. 18), coca growers of the mid-2000s widely employed agrochemicals to increase productivity, but there was little research on the effects, let alone education or outreach on proper use. Chemical use might have diminished since then (see, UNODC and Ministry of Justice and Law 2010, 87; UNODC and Government of Colombia 2017, 86), but it has not stopped altogether nor have educational efforts commenced. For its part, UNODC (2016, 90–1) raises the specter of environmental harm in coca processing from dumping byproducts and unused chemicals, including gasoline, but it suggests that a combination of high rainfall and reuse of chemicals can mitigate. Insomuch as either agro- or processing chemicals can affect river health, coca's tendency to spread along waterways (Armenteras et al. 2006; Chadid et al. 2015) could also create an opening for damage.

Speaking again in relative terms, Henman and Metaal (2009, 16–19) contend that other tropical crops are worse polluters (see also Quimbayo Ruiz 2008), but UNODC (2016, 90), citing survey data on comparative agrochemical use, suggests rough equivalence.

Considering Harms from Material Damages

Observers in academia, policy-making, and the press, have characterized coca growing alternatively as a blight on Colombia's economy or as a vital source of income for rural households and laborers, each suggesting consequences that could add negatively or positively to a ledger of material support. Among the negatives, Thoumi (1995) has been quoted as saying, "the drug trade has in fact weakened the country's economy by fostering violence and corruption, undermining legal activity, frightening off foreign investment, and all but destroying the social fabric."[61] Less forcefully, Angrist and Kugler (2008), Cárdenas and Rozo (2008), Holmes and Gutiérrez de Piñeres (2006), Holmes et al. (2006), Navarro (2013), and others discuss

[61] Quotation from Thoumi (1995) as reproduced in Holmes et al. (2006, 158).

different paths to negative consequences, if not blight. However, in this domain, the evidence is often a narrative—a story about outcomes, peppered with illustrative anecdotes or statistics—and might speak more to "possible" than to "actual" harms. Although we cannot truly evaluate both sides of the ledger, we can consider each side through those narratives and a small set of surveys and other studies that present indicators of outcomes. We find enough evidence of losses and gains to justify the premise of full accounting and can imagine arriving at a literal "net" in a longer-term project, with some quantification and monetization.

Here, we trace a series of potential paths to harms. Along mostly direct paths, the literature questions whether coca growing diverts resources or expand incomes, drives inflation, creates income dependence, or impedes productivity. Along mostly indirect paths, it raises the specters of conflict violence, and corruption, as disruptive and draining.

Resource use and income effects

The literature suggests the possibilities of negative or positive income effects, depending on whether resources are diverted from "good" to "bad" purpose.[62] If, for example, coca were to supplant an economically preferable crop, the income differential or opportunity cost from diverting land, labor, and other resources to growing coca would constitute a material loss. As the argument goes, coca might gain such undeserved prominence, if traffickers can sway farmers with protection schemes, market assurances, cash advances, or other coca-oriented incentives (Kraul 2017). Alternatively, coca growing could yield gains if un- or minimally productive land can be put to use, un- or underemployed workers can find jobs, and households can obtain higher incomes, all implying additionality, not diversion. If, by contrast, coca replaced another crop when that crop was no longer economically preferable (e.g., because the costs of producing it rose or the market price fell), we would view the incremental gains from coca as additional income. Taking the counterargument a step further, coca might, as Dávalos (2009, 382), Casey (2017), and Kraul (2017)[63] suggest, fill a void for

[62] Holmes and Gutiérrez de Piñeres (2006, 107) tease out both sides of the argument, using coffee as an illustrative example, though empirical evidence on coffee's viability in coca-growing locales calls this into question.

[63] Casey (2017) also hints at displacement, describing a dwindling labor supply at a government-sponsored sugar-cane processing plant, but this might also constitute replacement.

growers. In that case, coca growers would not divert resources to ill-effect, they would use the resources to create income.

Offering evidence of gains, various survey results suggest that coca yields additional income for growers, over all. UNODC and Ministry of Justice and Law (2010, 21) report that 58 percent of survey respondents said that poverty and unemployment had been factors that led them to enter coca fields. The study (pp. 28–9) cites "profitability" as the main reason (30 percent) that agricultural producers—as distinct from cocaleros and laborers—offer for including coca in their agricultural portfolios, followed by "there are no more options" (25 percent), "easy market" (22 percent), and "regional custom" (21 percent). Similarly, the study (p. 26) finds that poverty and unemployment have been leading causes of relocation among immigrants in coca-growing regions. On that basis, farm-gate income from coca and its derivatives, amounting to about $623 million in 2008 and $560 million in 2016, is at least partly additional.

Moreover, UNODC and Government of Colombia (2006–17) survey data suggest that coca-growing supports rural incomes for a non-trivial and increasing number of households and, by extension, individuals (Appendix B and Figure 6.5). In 2016, the number of coca-growing households reached 106,900, implying about 535,000 associated individuals, not counting the "floating" populations of day laborers. Some of that income might spread to adjacent areas; for instance, UNODC and Ministry of Justice and Law (2010, 35) indicate that nearly 40 percent of agricultural producers have accumulated enough wealth from coca growing to acquire homes in areas or urban centers near their operations. In addition, local shopkeepers and service providers stand to gain from additional business.

Nevertheless, agricultural producers are ambivalent about growing coca and say they would do more of something else if they could. According to UNODC and Ministry of Justice and Law (2010, 36–7), 77 percent of agricultural producers would have liked to stop cultivating coca and, instead, draw income from other agricultural activities, but 95 percent of agricultural producers had not received institutional support for crop substitution.

All told, the story is likely additive, if unsatisfying, for many growers. However, additivity neither implies a windfall nor rules out negative consequences.

The data on gross incomes from coca and derivatives suggest a meager existence for the average coca-growing household and its members, even if coca is their best option. In the mid-2010s, the annual average gross income for an entire coca-growing household, consisting of about five members, barely kept pace with per capita GDP (Appendix B and Figure 6.10). As growers' participation in higher-value-added activities, especially base processing, ebbed (Appendix B and Figure 6.8), their incomes shrunk (Appendix B and Figure 6.10).

In a statistical analysis of 14 coca-growing Departments, Angrist and Kugler (2008) find the rise in coca cultivation in Colombia in the 1990s "generated only modest economic gains in rural areas" (p. 191) and seems unlikely to have raised overall standards of living in growing areas (p. 210). The authors propose (p. 210), "[t]he absence of wider gains may be due to the fact that coca has few links with other sectors, or to extortion on the part of insurgents and paramilitary forces and the fact that coca finances a conflict that reduces economic activity."

Inflation

Other losses might stem from inflationary effects, e.g., from rising demand for agricultural land, agro- and processing chemicals, housing, and consumer goods and services that distorts local markets. For example, growers might bid up the prices of chemicals whereas traffickers, seeking to cleanse illegally earned income, might bid up real estate or land prices. Relatedly, Holmes and Gutiérrez de Piñeres (2006, 108–9) cite concerns that "The effect of coca on landownership exacerbates an already unequal distribution of income in Colombia."

Along these lines, we found scattered evidence of negative effects. For example, rising demand for housing and homes could drive up local real estate prices. Navarro (2013), who studies the relationship between cocaine exports and urban housing markets in Bolivia and Colombia, finds that cocaine exports have had a "profound" effect on pricing, but mainly through money laundering that accompanies drug trafficking. Similarly, Holmes and Gutiérrez de Piñeres (2006, 108) cite striking estimates of traffickers' agricultural landholdings, which they report as dedicated mostly to ranching. More recently, UNODC and Government of Colombia (2017, 86) discuss inflated costs of agrochemicals and labor and high costs of living, but without supporting data (see also, Healy 1986).

Income dependence

Favoring a single cash crop, be it coca or any commercial commodity, might create susceptibility to market fluctuations or downturns, but the evidence against coca is not compelling. Although coca growers lean heavily on coca—Kraul (2017) describes "completely narcotized" municipalities—they mitigate risk by allocating land to legal crops and livestock for local sales and household consumption and might fare better depending on coca for cash income, than on other exports crops (Dávalos et al. 2009, 382; Carrillo González 2014, 215; Henman and Metaal 2009, 17; Rincón-Ruiz and Kallis 2013, 71; UNODC and Ministry of Justice and Law 2010). As addressed in Section 6.4, Dávalos et al. (2009, 382) and Rincón-Ruiz and Kallis (2013, 75) portray coca as a relatively low-risk and appealing option, economically speaking, and Gonzáles (2014) suggests that coca is a relatively resilient crop.[64]

Broader productivity effects

The evidence on productivity is ambiguous, but noteworthy. Cárdenas and Rozo (2008, 17) lay blame for crime and related economic damages at the feet of coca cultivation, arguing that "the increase in crime and the subsequent reduction in productivity were the result of an increase in the production of illicit crops." By contrast, Holmes et al. (2006) and Holmes and Gutiérrez de Piñeres (2006, 104) find that "Colombia's economic problems stem more from political violence than the drug trade in itself."[65] If Cárdenas and Rozo (2008) are correct, the economy-wide toll could be large. They find that the annual growth in output or GDP per worker fell from 1.55 percent between 1955 and 1979 to 0.8 percent between 1980 and 2005 (pp. 14–15).

Conflict, violence and, corruption

More and less directly, coca growing might also impede economic activity by contributing to conflict, violence, and corruption in a vicious and, perhaps, two-way cycle. Compounding the obviously disruptive effects of conflict and violence, growers could be drawn into that cycle, by making protection payments that help to finance conflict and violence. These, in turn, foster insecurity that favors coca, partly because of those payments, which, in turn, displaces other crops, and so on. Insurgents or paramilitary forces might reinforce the cycle if they actively promote coca cultivation through cash advances or other coca-oriented incentives, as noted above,

[64] A more thorough investigation could compare, e.g., the variance of coca and other commodity prices.

[65] Holmes and Gutiérrez de Piñeres (2006, 109) also raise the possibility of export-induced "Dutch Disease," explained nontechnically in *The Economist*, at https://www.economist.com/blogs/economist-explains/2014/11/economist-explains-2. (accessed March 1, 2018).

or engage directly as middlemen processors or traffickers (Kraul 2017),[66] at which point they would be reaping returns of their own, not just skimming others'.[67] The effects of corruption, which can occur anywhere along the supply chain, could be felt through nonproductive spending on bribes, etc.—which represents another form of resource diversion—and through institutional dysfunctionality.

To conclude, we note that "negatives" and "positives" are not mutually exclusive and can sometimes operate across interest dimensions, as the interrelatedness of income effects and conflict, violence, and corruption suggests. Similarly, material gains might yield environmental losses (e.g., through deforestation) that, in turn, entail offsetting negative economic consequences. However, Basiago (1995, 113) cautions against a "false dichotomy between the economy and the environment." He cites Repetto (1992) as contending that environmental damages, such as deforestation, can hurt earning potential, and that, if we valued natural resources in national income accounting, we might find there is no trade-off between the economy and environment. If economic losses were attributed to environmental degradation, they might constitute losses to individuals or private or public entities, depending on the circumstances, but, howsoever allocated, they could be substantial and offsetting, mirroring the damages to the physical environment, cited above.

Policy might play its part too, because programs intended to subdue coca might also lead to material harm—for example, by damaging coca and legal crops or giving rise to disruptive conflict and violence—but we address those consequences with causality. Speaking more broadly, we have connected coca cultivation and processing to environmental and material consequences, but the question remains, "Are the harms associated with coca really harms of coca?"

Investigating Causality and Policy's Role in Shaping Harms

Clearly, we cannot rule out coca as a proximate source of harm—when a grower clears forest cover or releases chemicals into a river, there is no

[66] Kraul (2017) also reports direct involvement of Mexican drug trafficking syndicates.

[67] Evidence on the shift of base-processing income from growers to middlemen (Section 6.4 and Figure 6.9) might have concerning implications for financing, conflict, and violence.

distance between the activity and the harm—but some harms are "remote," and some might rest on others' shoulders entirely.[68]

Palacios (2012), like many others, attributes harms in coca-growing areas not to coca, but to policy to reduce or eliminate coca, pointing specifically to aerial spraying and quoting the Bishop of Tumaco: "Fumigation does not end the business, it destroys land, ruins people, damages legal crops and animals" (p. 136). Similarly, Palacios blames migration on crop eradication (p. 137), not on crop establishment; Dion and Russler (2008, 415) find a positive relationship between eradication and displacement; and Armenteras et al. (2013b, 7) attribute the spread of coca to eradication.

Rincón-Ruiz and Kallis' (2013) conclusions, based on case studies, interviews, and statistical work on 1,125 municipalities from 2001 to 2008, are stark (p. 61):

1. "Fumigation has not eradicated, but displaced coca production to other regions."
2. "Fumigation in Colombia displaces production to areas of primary forest of great environmental significance."
3. "Fumigation causes negative health impacts but these are contested and hard to verify."
4. "Fumigation is associated with increased human displacement."
5. "Less developed communities, including indigenous and Afro-Colombian communities, are disproportionately impacted by fumigation and coca displacement."

They find that fumigation also diffuses coca cultivation and that cultivation often returns later, even if at a lower level, "This creates a negative spiral of fumigation and cultivation that affects more and more territories and people." Data showing ebbs and flows in Departmental cultivation provides corroborating evidence (see Section 6.4 and Appendix C). In addition, Rincón-Ruiz et al. (2016, 63–4) find that aerial spraying pushed coca into new areas, including some of Colombia's most socially and physically vulnerable areas.

Rincón-Ruiz and Kallis (2013, 72) highlight two displacement-promoting factors. First, fumigation destroyed cultivation and forced the part

[68] A remote harm is spatially, temporally, or behaviorally distant from an activity under consideration.

of the population that was economically dependent on both coca and traditional crops to move, and, second, because of its nonselectivity, it impacted the traditional crops of families that were not involved in coca, affecting their food security and forcing them to migrate too. The extent to which these harms would emerge from manual eradication remains to be seen, but it stands to reason that even a well-targeted eradication campaign could elicit displacement and, as we address below, contribute to disruptive conflict and violence.[69]

However, the evidence on eradication and forest cover is not unambiguous. Amenteras (2013b), Dávalos et al. (2009 and 2016), Dion and Russler (2008), Rincón-Ruiz and Kallis (2013), and Rincón-Ruiz et al. (2016) collectively link eradication to deforestation and migratory pressures on ecologically sensitive, protected, and frontier land; Dávalos et al. (2011, 1224–5) find no connection between eradication and rates of deforestation; and, as noted above, Sánchez-Cuervo et al. (2012, 10) link eradication to reforestation.

As we try to reconcile these findings, it seems likely that results can differ by location or over time, but more studies than not indicate negative outcomes for forest cover.

Turning to other harms to the physical environment, the story is less clear. In Section 6.5, we presented competing perspectives on the harmfulness of glyphosate-based products, as used previously for aerial spraying and still as an herbicide. Some studies, including Bernal et al. (2009), Brain and Solomon (2009), and Solomon et al. (2005), suggest less cause for concern, by finding, for example, that aerial spraying is no more or even less environmentally threatening than cultivating coca, but others, including Relyea and co-authors, do not.

Lastly, Henman and Metaal (2009, 18–19) blame overplanting, soil depletion, and increasing use or misuse of industrial fertilizers and pesticides on eradication's incentives, claiming that eradication has made agriculture more predatory because growers must get what they can from their shrubs before eradicators destroy them. The authors also point to a lack of education on the proper use and disposal of agro- and processing chemicals. Lending credibility to claimed pressures of immediacy on cultivation decisions, one can connect evidence on coca's transience and abbreviated

[69] See Greenfield et al. (2015a, Appendix E) for a discussion of findings in the literature.

lifecycle with eradication (see, e.g., Armenteras et al. 2013b; Harden 2006). Without claiming causality, we also note that UNODC (2016, 90) reports less use of agrochemicals among coca growers in an era of less threat of eradication.

On that basis, one could take policy attribution further, by arguing that some or much of the degradation of the physical environment that emerges from planting and production tracks ultimately to policy. For example, if coca were not illegal, growers would not seek out remote land nor would they necessarily lack adequate guidance on fertilizers or other agrochemicals. Similarly, growers might hold stands longer and with greater attention to sustainability, absent the threat of eradication. On that basis, policy lurks in the background as an underlying cause of damage when coca replaces forests and chemicals contaminate water or soil.

In the economic domain, we found scattered evidence of coca-induced harms, e.g., through inflation, and of gains in households' income, even if meager, and we could not rule out an indirect path from coca, to crime, to economy-wide damages, via productivity effects (Cárdenas and Rozo 2008). Thus, what could constitute the most far-reaching material harm is a remote harm, implying that we cannot "pin it" on coca directly and there might be opportunities for intervention further along the causal chain. In addition, money laundering, an accompanying activity, might distort local real estate or land markets, but it might be more closely associated with later stages of processing and trafficking, also implying temporal, spatial, and behavioral distance. Some such effects might double back on the physical environment, as when traffickers engage in ranching to launder profits and further deplete or degrade forests.

Drug-control policy could also come to bear in this domain.

If the income from coca growing is additive, a policy that eliminates or disrupts the activity could take its toll on growers, but the policy might inflict greater harm if it destroys legal crops concurrently or entails other unintended consequences. Rincón-Ruiz and Kallis (2013, 70–1) describe negative associations between fumigation and legal agriculture, rural livelihoods, and human health and other scholars, some of whom they cite, address the issues more directly or statistically. For example, Messina and Delamater (2006, 127) find that aerial spraying in Putumayo "has the unintended consequences of defoliating not only coca but contiguous and interspersed native forest and food crop parcels" and Rozo (2014, 4) finds a noteworthy relationship at the municipality level between the share of area sprayed and the poverty rate.[70] Casey (2017) provides corroborating anecdotal evidence of a farmer who voluntarily replaced coca with cocoa, only to lose the latter to fumigation.

Although we have confined our discussions of conflict, violence, and related material consequences to the "enabled" realm of insurgents and paramilitary forces, we are aware that they can occur elsewhere, up and down the supply chain, and accompany policy. With the suspension of aerial spraying, more enforcement must occur on the ground and, while manual eradication might be better targeted, it can also create or exacerbate conflict. Kraul (2017) and *The Economist* (2017) report eradication-related conflict and violence in coca-growing areas, with harms flowing from enforcement officers to farmers and from farmers to enforcement officers. For example, Kraul (2017) describes a clash between farmers and antinarcotics police, that left 7 farmers dead and 21 wounded, and another in which farmers overpowered 50 police, held 12 as hostages for a day, and seized their weapons.

Drug-control policy cannot be held harmless in this assessment. At a time when aerial spraying was a prominent policy instrument in Colombia, drug-control policy, itself, was an instrument of damage and, in an era of manual eradication, it still appears to elicit damage in forced contexts. The government's decision to suspend aerial spraying might imply fewer or less onerous damages going forward, if it holds under new leadership, but reports of clashes suggest that drug-control policy will continue to serve as a harming agent.

And, what of the net effects of policies to reduce or curtail coca cultivation? Specifically, do they serve their intended purpose, even if they entail harms?

On the relationship between eradication efforts and the total area of coca cultivation in Colombia, the verdict from the economics, geography, and ecology literatures is still out. In the economics literature, Dávalos-Álvarez (2016), Dion and Russler (2008), Ibanez and Carlsson (2010), Ibanez and Martinsson (2013), Mejía et al. (2017), and Rozo (2014) find negative effects, though sometimes just partial,[71] whereas Moreno-Sanchez et al. (2003) and Reyes (2014) identify positive effects. Rouse and Arce (2006)

[70] Rozo (2014, 4) also identifies substantial effects on infant mortality, school dropout, and homicide rates.

[71] E.g., Rozo (2014, 4) finds a quarter hectare reduction in coca for one hectare sprayed and Mejía et al. (2017, abstract) find just a 2–3 percent reduction.

find that eradication reduces cultivation in the Andes, overall, but not in Colombia. Moreover, they and Reyes (2014) find that increases in cultivation in Colombia have tended to offset reductions in Bolivia and Peru. Of particular relevance to deforestation and other environmental damages, Moreno-Sanchez et al. (2003, 381–2) find that cultivation increases as eradication efforts intensify and that "[f]armers appear to compensate for eradication by cultivating crops more extensively."

Similarly, geographers and ecologists, including Rincón-Ruiz and Kallis (2013), give reason to pause and reflect on the likelihood of "successful" eradication efforts.

Offering potential to offset some of the negative consequences of eradication and alleviate pressures to grow coca, we identify development assistance measures, including land titling, that are part of Colombia's current drug-control strategy, but we do so with a measure of caution. Land titling, which is cited in Colombia's strategy as a development component, could create incentives for farmers to take the long view and adopt healthier land-management practices, especially if it coincides with the suspension of aerial spraying. Creating permanency through titling might promote economic development and environmental sustainability, but is less apt to succeed if other policy measures impose countervailing incentives.

In addition, the literature highlights poverty and development deficits as drivers of coca cultivation, suggesting the potential benefit of reducing both, but with its own caveats. Whereas Rincón-Ruiz et al. (2013a, 31) find that municipal development negatively influences coca cultivation across regions and time, Dávalos-Álvarez (2016, 127), who studied 440 municipalities from 2001 to 2010, finds a negative relationship between social investment, infrastructure, and human capital investment and new coca, hence loss of forest cover, but not between alternative development and new coca. In work across Colombia's forests, Dávalos et al. (2011, 1224–5) consider factors that "mediate the relationship between coca cultivation and deforestation rates" and highlight pervasive poverty, inadequate rural development, and economic pressures to clear forests to support migrants. However, they also warn that efforts that improve access to frontier lands without easing those pressures, could accelerate forest losses (see also Dávalos et al. 2016; UNODC 2016, 82–3).[72]

[72] Fergusson et al. (2014) and Sánchez-Cuervo and Aide (2013) address the role of conflict.

Casey (2017), Kraul (2017), *The Economist* (2017), and others also suggest caution regarding poorly designed development efforts and credibility deficits.

The weight of the evidence strongly suggests that policy to control coca through eradication, especially aerial spraying, inflicts its own wounds and might do more harm than good, but efforts to promote economic development—which might, secondarily, reduce cultivation—are not meritless. However, we cannot say whether "more harm than good" would emerge as a final verdict from a more comprehensive empirical assessment, because it would need to address the functional, material, reputational, and other types of harms to all bearers that could be associated with cultivation or processing and the activities that accompany or follow them.

6.6 Summing Up Our Assessment of Coca Cultivation and Processing in Colombia

This assessment was a learning experience in relation to our subject matter and for what it could and could not tell us about harms. For example, our exploration of causality pointed more forcefully to policy as a harming agent than previously, but contextual variation, reflecting Colombia's megadiversity, confounded our efforts to rate and rank harms. Findings on deforestation, pollution, and economic effects might hold up in one location but not in another and the results of solid empirical analyses were sometimes ambiguous or contradictory. Nevertheless, we drew together evidence from wide-ranging sources for viewing under a common lens and have insights to share from the results.

Turning first to our subject matter, we found that coca cultivation and processing entail both losses and gains for some bearers, even if varying and unranked. In material terms, coca growers, who are likely among Colombia's least wealthy citizens, are potential gainers from access to coca, as are hired laborers, but less so than the middlemen, including insurgents and paramilitary forces, who engage in higher-value-added processing and trafficking activities. Growers' and laborers' earnings might be essential to their material support, but the sums are not large and have declined over the years. Moreover, losses from inflation, productivity effects, and market disruptions suggest an uncertain balance. For the environment, losses from deforestation and pollution appear to dominate, even if some regeneration and recovery—albeit of uncertain value—could occur over the longer term.

At the same time, traffickers' enthusiasm for agricultural land has likely compounded environmental and material losses.

As was true of drug-control policy in Belgium and the Netherlands, drug-control policy in Colombia has played a leading role in causing or reinforcing harms. Over decades of aerial spraying, damages were direct and indiscriminate, with losses of income from coca and legal crops and environmental degradation from pressure to relocate to remote areas and national parks with no-spray rules and, perhaps, from chemical toxicity. Eradication risks likely encouraged coca's encroachment on remote, untouched, and fragile ecosystems, with ensuing forest-cover losses and fragmentation. Moreover, eradication, coupled with weak land-tenure incentives, might also push growers to seek short-term gains at the expense of long-term environmental and economic well-being. The evidence on shortened lifecycles, some attributed directly to eradication (Armenteras et al. 2013b; Harden 2006), is compelling. In an era of manual eradication, enforcement might be targeted better and provide less reason to enter parks, but other damages might persist and flow from on-the-ground conflict and violence. Although recent Colombian leadership has pressed for a return to aerial spraying, our analysis suggests that aerial spraying has taken its toll and warrants its own harm assessment.

Were we to attribute economic value to forest and other natural resources, as Repetto (1992) suggests, the material losses stemming from environmental degradation, be it coca- or policy-induced, could offset or outweigh other economic gains.

As for development assistance, the evidence suggests that even well-designed programs can undermine efforts to reduce coca and preserve forest cover, but they might still contribute positively to the policy landscape. For example, development assistance might help to ease transitions for growers seeking an exit ramp or losing income to eradication, and land titling could provide incentives that promote healthier land-management practices. Evidence on landholdings indicates that Nariño, Putumayo, and Norte de Santander are more heavily invested in coca than other Departments, potentially implying more need for easing.

Turning next to the framework, we found support for some lessons from previous assessments and gained new insight from working with principles of full accounting, addressing environmental concerns, and undertaking a partial and rapid analysis. As we walk through those lessons and insights, we relate them to the conceptual and technical challenges of normativity, infinitude, and so forth, as we did in Chapter 5, but with some thematic reordering.

The *normativity* of our task remained inescapable, but we encountered it anew through our decision to consider material losses and gains. To do so, we valued ill-gotten gains, illegal possessions, and associated losses and we recognized agricultural operations that would constitute wholly or mostly illegal enterprises. We did not set out to diminish or delegitimize Colombian law, but one cannot simultaneously argue for excluding ill-gotten gains, etc., on legal grounds and for full accounting and, in this application, the latter seemed necessary to understanding the societal consequences of coca and policy. Although we could not say whether the net consequences were positive or negative, we could articulate paths to gains and losses and, more concretely, speak to coca's part in supporting agricultural households and laborers and policy's part in thwarting them. However, having chosen to admit activities and interests outside the law, we would leave it to policy-makers to decide how to treat coca-derived income and related assets as we have other consequences for perpetrators in prior assessments.

Our first attempt to delve into harms to the physical environment also elicited methodological concerns that took different forms or were more striking than those in earlier assessments. For example, we had different and, perhaps, greater concerns about managing *infinitude* in this assessment, which we addressed to varying degrees of satisfaction. We found that treating Colombia as a mostly closed system, as we did for our trafficking assessments in Belgium and the Netherlands, simplified the analysis as it had in those assessments, but it sacrificed more insight. Harms from forest loss, fumigant drift, and chemical contamination could, as we acknowledged, spill over to Colombia's neighbors and beyond. The temporal perspective also mattered more—arguably, a one-year horizon as per von Hirsch and Jareborg (1991, 21–2) is fundamentally at-odds with the premise of sustainability—and so, for this assessment, we looked further ahead.

The challenge of *standardization* also manifested somewhat differently and more problematically in this context. We could not get a clear read on severity or incidence, in part, because there was too much variation in local conditions—in effect, there was no "average" environmental bearer across or within locales—and we lacked the resources to conduct additional empirical research to mitigate the variation. One could imagine homing in on the locales with the greatest ecological fragility or economic dependency on coca, or, in a longer-term study, sponsoring cross-locale data collections to support additional, controlled studies specifically for the sake of a harm assessment.

In this assessment, we also confronted the self-imposed limitations of a partial assessment, which, by design, meant we lacked visibility over the accrual and distribution of harms, even for cultivation and processing, and, at least as much as previously, could not calculate policy's net effect. Our analysis dealt with the incremental effects of a subset of activities on a subset of bearers, but not the totality of harms, even for those activities and bearers. While our investigation of *causality* pointed clearly to policy as a harming agent, with aerial spraying coming to the fore as environmentally and economically damaging, we could not say definitively whether such policy inflicted "more harm than good." To do so, would have required a more comprehensive empirical assessment, addressing a fuller range of bearers, interests, and activities that accompany or follow cultivation and processing.

Undertaking a rapid assessment raised new issues of *measurement*. We found it was possible to glean relevant evidence from others' data and research, but we could not expect their work to meet all our analytical needs. For example, the data or research might address an issue that touches on our issues, but is not "the" issue, as was true of the toxicity literature. Moreover, other researchers might not frame their work in a way that melds seamlessly with our analytical goals or methods. For example, they might not distinguish theoretically or empirically between the effect of a primary activity, such as coca growing, and enabled activities, such as trafficking. Cárdenas and Rozo (2008) attribute economic losses from crime and productivity effects to coca cultivation but omit steps in a casual chain that might point to other culprits.

Having rated and ranked a small set of environmental harms, we have less insight to *commensurability* from this assessment than from our others. That said, we suspect that if we had gotten further, we would have needed to think carefully and creatively about how to factor-in differences across and within locales, including what might be described as different, yet interrelated environmental constituents (i.e., forests, soils, and waterways).

Speaking directly to robustness, the framework transferred to Colombia and coca more comfortably than expected in some regards and less comfortably in others. Despite major differences in venues—Colombia does not look much like Belgium, environmentally or economically—the framework "made sense," at least for the activities and harms that we considered. Sustainability, as defined, holds meaning across venues, even if it might be valued differently in each, and material interests can be judged relative to domestic conditions, using a measure like per capita GDP, even if they differ. One society might care more or less about one type of harm than another, but the effect is still the effect, even if weighed differently. However, as implied above, the issue of legitimacy gave us something to ponder, along with the practical implications of borders, time, and contextual variability.

6.7 Concluding Remarks

To close this chapter, we offer a few final comments on the risks, rewards, and utility of rapid assessment, as they played out in this analysis.

On risks, we admit that attempting something rapid leaves little room for missteps or maneuvering, be it in making decisions about borders and temporal perspectives, judging data availability, or engaging with unfamiliar disciplines or literatures. Nevertheless, missteps can happen and in a rapid assessment may or may not resolve satisfactorily. For example, while we recognized the inadequacy of a one-year horizon at the outset and were able to adjust accordingly, we lacked the resources to extend our analysis across borders. However, even after recognizing the potential for spillovers, we believe that the benefits of a sharper focus (e.g., on a particular locale or biome) would still outweigh those of a wider reach.

In terms of familiarity with disciplines or literatures, to say that we knew nothing of this arena would be an overstatement—one of us, Greenfield, is an agricultural and resource economist, with an extensive record of research on drug-crop cultivation and policy—but to say that we know the arena across all domains, including some of immediate relevance to our assessment, would also be incorrect. For example, we knew little of research among geographers or toxicologists when we began this assessment. We hope that we "got it right *enough*" in their domains and that a fresh and cross-cutting perspective on long-lived issues can add value, but with humility we acknowledge likely deficiencies.

Turning to rewards, our efforts have shed light not just on the nature of harms, but also on policy's role in fostering them. Recalling that we undertook this assessment over a period of about 12 weeks, we believe that we were able to uncover substantial evidence of the harms "of" policy, sufficient to justify both this analysis and a distinct analysis of policy, itself, especially in view of recent attempts to resume aerial spraying in Colombia. Still, the policy story was not wholly negative in that we found promise in development assistance, including land titling.

7
The Case for Harm and Harm Assessment

7.1 Introduction

At the start of this book, we asserted the need for a "firm analytical foundation" for making normative decisions about criminal policy and the governance of security as it concerns crime and we claimed as our central aim to provide such a foundation and promote its use.

The goal of this chapter is to bring closure to our central aim and make the case for our harm assessment framework. To start, we review our main findings and accomplishments from each chapter and, then, we discuss methodological lessons from our assessments. We consider the viability of the framework in terms of its reliability and robustness, its implied validity across conceptual and technical challenges, and, ultimately, its usefulness. Next, turning to academia and related research, we suggest, first, expanding criminology's mission to include the study of harms and target harm reduction and, second, positioning harm assessment as a core task of the discipline. We argue that "starting from the end" (Paoli and Greenfield 2015) with the consequences of crime—and, potentially, other seemingly harmful activities—can benefit criminology and help it connect to broader societal debates on justice. Lastly, we discuss how taking on harm and its reduction with systematic, empirical assessments of the harms of crime—and other activities—can benefit criminal policy, the governance of security as it pertains to crime, and other spheres of public policy and, eventually, contribute not just to criminal justice, but to justice, overall.

The structure of this chapter follows accordingly. In the second and third sections, we consider our findings and accomplishments and highlight methodological lessons from Chapters 5 and 6. In the fourth and fifth sections, we explore the benefits of addressing harm in criminology,

Assessing the Harms of Crime. Victoria A. Greenfield and Letizia Paoli, Oxford University Press. © Victoria A. Greenfield & Letizia Paoli 2022. DOI: 10.1093/oso/9780198758174.003.0007

criminal and related policy, and other policy fields and, in the sixth section, we draw connections between our endeavor and the pursuit of justice.

7.2 Findings and Accomplishments

By exploring harm's place in legal history and theory, criminology, and related fields and by considering the relevance of harm and its reduction for criminal policy and the governance of security, we have demonstrated the centrality of harm, including its reduction, to crime, policy, and governance more or less explicitly in different eras and fora, but have also uncovered—and worked to fill—a substantial methodological gap.

In Chapter 2, we identified a well-marked, mostly clear trail of evidence of harm's relevance to crime in legal history and theory, dating back at least as far as Roman law and tracking to the present day via Beccaria, Smith, and Mill, but we found fewer signposts in criminology, where the trail was often indistinct. Beccaria, for example, proposed assessing crime for its damages and developing a scale of wrong actions. In contemporary criminology, we found less acknowledgment of harm in the mainstream, which tends to focus on the causes of crime, than we did along the edges, for example, among critical and green criminologists.

As for societal responses to crime, we found that the relevance of harm and harm reduction was more explicit and pronounced in phases of criminal policy dealing with criminalization, sentencing and punishment, and victims' assistance and restorative justice, than in those dealing with crime control and policing or crime prevention, but it was not entirely absent from the latter. Harm and harm reduction also play a part in deliberations on reparations in international criminal justice and, even more so, in the governance of security, albeit with little recognition from criminologists.

We also found that harm has gained prominence in formal policy statements, but neither harm nor its reduction has been conceptualized or implemented fully in any "phase" of criminal policy. Harm reduction tends to manifest differently across phases of criminal policy, with varying emphasis on harm prevention, mitigation, and remediation and without regard for consistency, leaving open the possibility that specific objectives and practices in one phase could undermine those in another, leading to more harm on balance.

In Chapter 3, we reviewed previous attempts to work with "harm" as an analytical device in criminology, criminal policy, and related fields.

Identifying few attempts in the criminological literature, we also considered analytical frameworks and empirical studies addressing drug-related harm, public perceptions of the seriousness of crime, the impact of criminal victimization, and the cost of crime. Although we found elements of an answer to Beccaria's proposal in each literature, we did not find a complete answer in any. Reflecting on these studies, we discussed the conceptual and technical challenges of assessing harm and argued that these challenges almost certainly have hindered progress toward harm assessment, but we did not view the challenges as insurmountable.

Reviewing the literature, analyzing documents, and, at the same time, evaluating the challenges of harm assessment prepared us to grapple with—and address—the challenges when we developed our own methodology, the harm assessment framework.

In Chapter 4, which is the nucleus of our endeavor, we presented our framework, the intended firm analytical foundation for decision-makers that is also our answer to Beccaria. The framework threads the needle of his proposal and the underlying conceptual and technical challenges, including those of measurement, in part, by admitting the inherent normativity of harm assessment and invoking both quantitative and qualitative methods. The framework, which "starts from the end," provides tools and a process to identify, evaluate, and rank harms and to carefully distinguish between harms that result directly from activities and harms that are remote or driven at least partially by policy choices and interventions. That distinction has led, as Chapters 5 and 6 demonstrate, to some of our most insightful empirical results.

Chapters 5 and 6 were devoted to empirical applications of the framework, consisting primarily of assessments of the harms of cocaine trafficking in Belgium and coca cultivation and processing in Colombia, respectively. The former also included comparisons to human trafficking in Belgium and cocaine trafficking in the Netherlands. In these chapters we demonstrated the viability of our framework in settings that differed markedly by venue, activities, and types of application. The first applications were more comprehensive and allowed sufficient time for data collection, compilation, and analysis; the second was partial and rapid. In each case, we gained insight into the nature of harms and the role of policy. For example, we found that policy constituted a prominent agent of harm in each application and, to varying degrees, refuted popular wisdom about the harmfulness of the underlying activities, which, in turn, suggested opportunities for harm reductions.

Each application yielded new, actionable knowledge. For example, in 2013, our assessment of cocaine trafficking in Belgium indicated considerable low-level corruption among the employees of logistic businesses that were active at the port of Antwerp, as would suggest the merit of developing integrity and screening programs, such as those that the Belgian government implemented in 2018 (Port of Antwerp 2018b; *De Standaard* 2020). More broadly, our human trafficking and coca cultivation and processing assessments suggested openings to reduce harms through immigration policy and development-assistance programs, respectively.

With those chapters, we have demonstrated harm's centrality to crime and societal responses, identified a substantial methodological gap, and taken steps to fill the gap. In the next section, we delve further into the methodological lessons from our applications, including those on broader applicability. Then, we are left to promote our harm-based approach, namely, the "harm assessment framework," as a systematic and empirical means to support decision-making and, perhaps, advance justice.

7.3 Methodological Lessons from Our Applications

In short, we have learned that harm—and its reduction—presents a compelling and powerful conceptual starting point for a firm analytical foundation, as posited in Chapter 1, and that systematic, empirical harm assessment can bear fruit, but it is also difficult and somewhat resource-intensive, even in a rapid assessment.

Regarding our conceptual starting point, harm offers a lens with which to evaluate criminal and related policy on wide-ranging activities. This lens is, on the one hand, rooted in history and consistent with contemporary trends in policy, and, on the other hand, capable of embracing normativity and transcending definitional ambiguities. With harm for a lens, we were able to forge a rigorous analytical path without stumbling over the definition of crime—or lack thereof—and irrespective of prior pronouncements of "criminality." Moreover, we have been able to operationalize harm to support a comprehensive assessment of crime's consequences across functional, material, and other interest dimensions of what might be said to constitute the main building blocks of contemporary society; namely, individuals, private and public institutions, and the social and physical environment. With reference to "harm reduction," we make our own normative leap when we identify harm prevention, mitigation, or remediation as a fundamental, though not always explicit, objective of criminal and related policy. For us, the logic is compelling: why else would we assess harm if not to reduce it or at least avoid increasing it? We study harm not for its own sake, but for that of making the world a less harmful place.

Turning to a closer examination of our framework's viability, defined broadly to encompass its reliability and robustness, implied validity across conceptual and technical challenges, and ultimate utility, our results have been encouraging.

Reliability and Robustness

Our applications in Chapters 5 and 6 highlighted different facets of reliability and robustness, as might be expected given differences in venues and activities. We found evidence of reliability and robustness in comparisons of results for the same activity (cocaine trafficking) in two different—but similar—environments (Belgium and the Netherlands), and of two different activities (cocaine and human trafficking) in the same environment (Belgium). Speaking to the framework's reliability, the assessments of Belgian and Dutch cocaine trafficking produced similar, but not identical results, as might be expected in similar, but not identical environments. The framework was able to detect subtle differences in consequences, without loss of replicability. In the assessments of cocaine and human trafficking, both in Belgium, the results diverged considerably, as befitting two activities that bear similarity largely in name alone, and showed the framework's robustness. Our application to Colombia, which entailed a yet more dramatic shift, stretched the framework, but did not break it. The framework encountered obstacles, such as those involving data adequacy and contextual variability, but, as we discuss below, the obstacles often had more to do with how we undertook the assessment than with the constitution and fortitude of the framework.

Validity across Conceptual and Technical Challenges

As for validity, we look back at how the framework handled the conceptual and technical challenges raised and recounted in Chapters 3 and 4 to consider whether our framework can, in fact, assess—identify, evaluate, rank, and investigate—that which we intend it to assess.[1] Touching lightly on our experience with each challenge, we start with normativity and conclude with commensurability, following the path of Table 4.5.

Having acknowledged the inherent *normativity* of our task at the outset, we have dealt with it as transparently as possible with explicit criteria for each assessment. That said, when we turned to Colombian coca and adjusted our criteria as a step toward "full accounting," a new concern emerged. In the cocaine and human-trafficking assessments, we excluded ill-gotten gains, illegal possessions, and so forth, but in this assessment we gave them standing. We believe this represented an analytical step forward, but in adjusting the criteria, we wondered whether we might have suggested inadvertently that some laws matter more or are more just than others. In the case of Colombia, we felt certain that we would sacrifice a full understanding of harms associated with coca cultivation and processing and related policy decisions had we chosen to exclude the gains from those activities, but we were not intending to take a moral stand on the country's laws.

In response to the challenge of *infinitude*, we built an encompassing taxonomy that can accommodate harms of complex crimes, but we do not claim that it is exhaustive and must still make decisions about where to draw the line in each assessment. For example, the potential for protracted harms, which first gave us pause in our assessment of human trafficking, came to the fore in our assessment of coca cultivation and processing and, in that case, we chose to extend our temporal horizon to align with our benchmark for the environment, sustainability. Similarly, the single-country approach that stood up imperfectly but acceptably in our applications to cocaine and human trafficking, was less satisfying in the context of coca cultivation and processing. We realized, in the latter, that damages could spillover from Colombia to its neighbors and beyond and, hence, drawing a line at the border could miss substantial harms.

The final step of our framework addresses *causality* directly, with a two-stage investigation of remoteness and policy that has served fruitfully across applications. In each assessment, we identified harms that were at least partially remote—meaning, distant from the primary activity—and

[1] The term "validity" can have different meanings across disciplines and methods. Here, we use it broadly to consider whether the framework manages the challenges we intend it to manage and, thus, by extension, can capture the consequences we intend it to capture.

examined the extent to which the harms associated with a criminal activity are intrinsic to that activity or arise from policy. Still, we note some tension in saving the investigation of causality for last, in that some well-informed readers have been quick to say preemptively, "hold on, that isn't *really* a harm of the activity, but of the policy," to which we have responded, "Perhaps, but we would not presume it to be true without evidence." Such exchanges further remind us why we try to say harms "associated with," not "of," until the evidence is in.

In all of our assessments, we faced more-technical challenges pertaining to standardization, measurement, and commensurability, including some relating to the implementation of our scales and others to the quality and suitability of data.

In a broad-based empirical study, some *standardization* (e.g., an average individual) is unavoidable, but not costless, as apparent in our assessments of human trafficking and coca cultivation and processing. If, for example, we only consider human-trafficking victims of average health, we might fail to learn that victims with certain underlying conditions require particular forms of support in recovery. Our benchmark for individuals—the standard of living—might also require different empirical content, depending, for example, on the country of analysis as well as the bearers' country of origin and actual residence. Along similar lines, we could not break through the variability in the Colombian landscape to draw firm conclusions about environmental harms without clearer regional or ecological delineations.

Recognizing that not everything that matters is amenable to *measurement*, our incidence and severity scales exploit quantitative and qualitative evidence in "bandwidths," not point estimates, and give equal weight to quantifiable and nonquantifiable information.

Nevertheless, some practical issues remain. In our assessments of harms associated with cocaine and human trafficking, for example, we raised concerns about subtle gradations of severity, accounting for ongoing exposure to harming events, such as beatings, and, even more so in the case of coca, data limitations. In the assessments of cocaine and human trafficking, we were able to cull existing criminal justice sources (e.g., cases and databases) and create data sets to suit our needs. The fit was not ideal and it left us with dark figures that hindered prioritization, but we had ample time to probe the data and were able to use them to construct internally consistent narratives. In the Colombian assessment, we lacked time to develop a well-calibrated data set and were less able to find existing sources to fit our purpose, which compounded the difficulty of telling a unified story.

We achieved enough in our first attempt at a rapid assessment to be cautiously optimistic about our framework's potential for quick-turn analysis (see also Peters and Paoli 2020), but this experience served to highlight the importance of rounding up the right data, along with realistic scoping and advance planning. With hindsight, we can see that we tried to do too much and, were we to start again, we would sharpen the focus and identify more ways to leverage our resources, including through partnerships with other researchers and subject-matter experts.

Finally, our framework tackles *commensurability* with benchmarks and rating scales that enable us to compare different types of harms within classes of bearers, such as individuals, and consider the distribution of harms across classes of bearers, such as individuals and the environment, even if it cannot support direct comparisons of harms across those classes. Given the impossibility of comparing the full range of harms to individuals and institutions, let alone the environment, no purely scientific procedure can decide whether, for example, violence in one domain matters more than violence in any other. However, we regard it as a further merit of the framework that it clarifies which steps can be carried out on the basis of scientific rules and methods alone and which cannot. Moreover, by accounting for incidence and severity, our matrix provides a basis for preliminarily establishing policy priorities among disparate crimes and, thus, circumventing some aspects of incommensurability.

Although we have not found a single, uniform way of dealing with all boundary-like issues, such as those of infinitude and causality, across applications, we offer practical suggestions for addressing them—largely through transparency and consistency—in the following section.

Utility in Relation to Policy Insight and Applicability

If one accepts the framework as reliable, robust, and valid, then judging its utility through our applications might be said to rest on whether it has rendered results that can inform policy and, eventually, reduce harm. On that score, all our applications yielded policy-relevant findings on the extent, distribution, and causes of harm that could contribute to changes in policy. The apparent dichotomy between policy statements and our empirical findings on the harms of cocaine trafficking in Belgium and the Netherlands and on the role of policy as a causal agent across contexts, strongly suggests the value of the framework as an evidence-based, systematic means to focus policy-making attention and resources on actual, instead of perceived, harms. Even in our application to Colombian coca, our results were instructive and, as much or more than previously, pointed to policy as a cause of harm, not just a response to harm.

Still, we note that applying the framework is, itself, an expertise-intensive activity, the utility of which depends partly on the user's proficiency. Using it well requires a solid understanding of the properties of the framework and a nontrivial investment in learning how to use it, along with the time to do so. The fact that no other such instrument exists is an indirect proof that there is no easy path to systematic, empirical harm assessment and that we are working to fill a gap, but, as we note below, we might still be able to make the path a little easier to travel.

In the following sections, we turn to more overt "promotion" of our work, both within the criminological community and in other spheres of societal debate and, to that end, we conclude here with early evidence of the framework's flexibility and applicability and a few thoughts on areas for continued methodological development and simplification.

Despite the difficulties and challenges, the framework has already stimulated and contributed to much research beyond that covered in Chapters 5 and 6. Edwards et al. (2013) draw from the framework to investigate policymakers and criminologists' perceptions of the seriousness and frequency of urban criminal problems. Adriaenssen (2017), Adriaenssen et al. (2019, 2020), and Paoli et al. (2020) rely on the framework to conceptualize crime seriousness, expound on its dimensions, and measure its perceptions through a population survey. Paoli et al. (2018a and b) have used the taxonomy and severity scale, to study the impact of cybercrimes through a survey of Belgian businesses. Relying on the framework, Peters (2020) has delineated the business model of piracy in the Gulf of Nigeria and Peters and Paoli (2020) have conducted a rapid assessment of the related harms, while Frederix (2018) has updated and expanded our earlier assessment of the harms associated with carrousel fraud in Belgium. Sheremeti (ongoing), in perhaps the broadest application to date, is using the framework to collect data on perceptions of harm among victims of state crime and other stakeholders in Kosovo and, with that data, will assess the harms of murder and rape in Kosovo and compare them with actual reparations and the reparations that victims of state crime actually need. The framework has also inspired research on the role of harm reduction in policy, itself. Kersten (2022), for example, is considering the relevance of harm and its reduction for the regulation of the meat sector in Belgium and for the recognition and prioritization of harms and bearers by policy-makers, private regulators, and stakeholders.

Regarding future work, we would like to press on with full accounting in different settings and are well aware of needs to hone our tools and process, as per the lengthier discussions of standardization, measurement, and commensurability in Chapters 5 and 6, but we are most eager to make harm assessment less burdensome—for academics and nonacademics—and, especially, to identify generalizable strategies and tactics for conducting rapid assessments. Along those lines, we might also look to developing tailored guidance, like that found in logic-modeling or program-evaluation handbooks (e.g., Taylor-Powell and Henert 2008; W.K. Kellogg Foundation 2004), that requires less immersion in the details of the framework.[2] Given our experience to date and the difficulty of assessing subtle gradations of severity, one might ask whether the framework could serve as a heuristic device in some research environments. In other recent studies, one author, Greenfield, has worked with less complicated matrixes—with fewer gradations—that we could try putting to use in our framework (see, e.g., Figure 7.1).[3]

While we would like to make harm assessment easier, we emphasize here, as in Chapter 5, that we did not design our framework to provide policy-makers with a simple recipe for decision-making, but, instead, to provide evidence for them to weigh in decision-making.

To end this section, we address a question that came to us from our anonymous reviewer, "how do we set boundaries in ways that do not introduce bias?" We referred to boundaries explicitly in our discussion of infinitude and causality, but decisions about standing and other aspects of scope—including what we called "exclusions" in Chapter 4—all involve boundaries of a kind and so speak to this question.[4] Early on, we set out criteria for legitimacy, drew a line at first-order effects, and chose a temporal perspective, all to establish such boundaries, but, with each new application, we encountered new stressors or puzzles, each requiring careful consideration and teaching us something about how to use our own creation.

[2] In Section 7.5, we also discuss the possibility of "notional" benefit–cost analysis.

[3] For another presentation of a four-quadrant matrix, see also United Nations Office on Drugs and Crime (2010a).

[4] In Chapter 3, we noted that all the challenges of assessment might be termed challenges of "counting," either figuratively or literally, insomuch as they raise the questions "what harms really 'count'?" and "how should we 'count' them, if we can?"

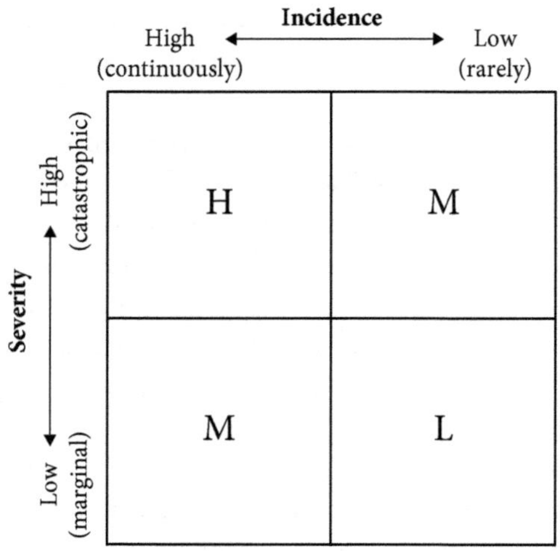

Figure 7.1 Four-quadrant matrix for prioritizing harms
Source: Authors' adaptation of National Academies of Sciences, Engineering, and Medicine (2018), Figure B.1, p. 148, which was developed for risk assessment.

Even in our assessment of cocaine trafficking in Belgium, which spanned all the "types" and "bearers" in our taxonomy, we could not cover everything and did not, for example, factor-in the harms of use. As a result, we could not argue for eliminating illegality to reduce violence solely based on our analysis, but could still suggest reframing policy and law enforcement to evoke less violence.

Although we cannot offer hard-and-fast rules, we offer three practical suggestions for approaching these concerns and an illustration:

- First, start each assessment with explicit criteria for what to include and exclude, consider the implied limitations, and document the reasons for and implications of any deviations, if or as they arise. Arguably, this first suggestion is no more than a restatement of our overarching stance on transparency in our assessments. As we found in our coca assessment, we could not get a full picture of material harms without full accounting, which meant relaxing a prior exclusion on returns from illegal activity, but we were clear about our decision and reasoning.
- Second, set boundaries that align consistently with the underlying research question. If, for example, a study seeks to understand harms

that cross a border, the assessment cannot stop at the border. This same fundamental principle applies equally to some of the other thorny issues we encountered, such as those regarding standardization. Taking an example from our work on human trafficking, a study that seeks to shed light on medical needs should account for the distribution of medical conditions among individuals. Simply put, conduct the assessment with borders, categories of bearers, etc., that make sense in the context or contexts under consideration.

- Third, if embarking on a comparative study of harms in multiple contexts, set boundaries that maintain as much consistency as possibly across venues, while still capturing the consequences that matter in each. The basic premise is to compare apples with apples, thereby preserving commensurability, and to avoid creating a situation in which harms look better or worse in one venue than another simply because of the choice of boundaries. This could mean looking more broadly, to consider other bearers, longer temporal horizons, etc., in one context than might be necessary if looking only at that context.

A more recent application of the framework to Nigerian piracy illustrates an approach to setting boundaries that balances concerns about feasibility and bias. In that case study, Peters and Paoli (2020) deviate from the single-country model of the early applications and consider incidents occurring in Nigerian waters as well as those occurring further offshore for completeness. In a planned replication of the study to piracy off Somalia, Peters and Paoli will implement the same geographical criterion for comparability across the two contexts. In the Nigerian application, they have also assessed harms to the affected businesses, distinguishing them by type, size, and nationality—a distinction that we have contemplated since 2013 but was unnecessary in earlier applications. Recognizing differences in the impact of piracy, Peters and Paoli have, for example, distinguished between different types of fishing businesses and between small-to-medium shipowners and operators, on the one hand, and usually foreign, large-scale vessel owners and operators, on the other, and then assessed the severity and incidence of the harms for each set of businesses. These delineations have revealed harms that are often neglected by policy reactions to piracy, which tend to be geared to protect the interests of "big business" (Lucia 2015, 20–3). Peters and Paoli's analysis shows that small, local fishing businesses are by far the most affected. These businesses experience rare catastrophic harm and seldom-to-occasional grave harms to their functional integrity because of piracy, violence, and property deprivation and damage. These harms, moreover, are not mitigated by insurance policies, which instead cover owners and operators of cargo vessels. Peters and Paoli make similar distinctions among the affected individuals and, along the same lines, conclude that the local fishermen suffer the most piracy-related harm, even if the underlying events are most likely to go unreported.

As this application to piracy demonstrates, the framework is flexible and can accommodate different boundaries defensibly, if they are clearly stated, well-reasoned, and applied consistently across comparative assessments. All in all, we contend that the framework can serve to assess and, eventually, reduce the harms of crime, even as we learn more about how to apply it in new contexts.

7.4 What Can "Harm" Do for Criminology?

Having established harm's centrality to crime, policy, and governance and recognized that many offenses have been labelled as "criminal" in contemporary societies precisely because of their harmfulness (Braithwaite and Pettit 1990, 2), we argue that criminology should include—and even embrace—the study of harms, target harm reduction, and position harm assessment as a core task of the discipline. In so doing, we are not seeking to overthrow the regime, but to build on its strengths and make it stronger, by expanding its mission and offering it complementary tools and a process—our framework—to support the expansion.

Box 7.1 compares our approach to those of other schools of criminology.

With this attention to harm, criminology's reach would extend from the manifestations and causes of crime, as per the mainstream, to the consequences of crime and, potentially—in tandem with other disciplines—other seemingly harmful activities.[5] Incorporating and extending victimology's approach, criminology would occupy a bigger tent that, with the use of our framework, could also encompass evaluations of policies and interventions for both their contributions to harm reduction and their effects on

[5] We are not suggesting that criminology should have dominion over—or even leadership in—the study of all harms. Clearly, other disciplines, such as those dealing with the environment, safety, health, and transportation, share an interest in and would claim the lead on harms in those fields, as is the case in national security, but criminology might, e.g., turn its gaze to activities thought to have substantial adverse consequences and bring empiricism to bear on decisions about criminalization (see Section 7.5).

Box 7.1 Where do we stand in relation to the main criminological schools?

We differ from mainstream criminology, with our focus on crime's consequences rather than its origins, but we stand by the mainstream's "fine tradition of careful observation of the natural and social worlds; of the scientist's duty to report his/her research data dispassionately, even if he/she find them personally unwelcome; and of the careful search for causes and explanation" (Bottoms 2008, 88). We too are committed to rigorous empirical analysis and dispassionate reporting, but, representing a substantial departure from the mainstream—and other schools—we explore the causes of crime's harms, not the causes of crime, itself.

In our work, we also draw insights from criminological schools that have challenged the mainstream "from the left and the right" (Laub 2004, 8). Following the traditions of "symbolic interactionism," "labelling theory," and, "constructivism," we recognize that crime is necessarily a social construction and, first of all, a legal category. By starting from the end and armed with our framework, we can systematically and empirically contribute to "deconstructing" the concept of crime. As we discuss below, our version of deconstruction—in terms of harms, interests, and bearers—could be used to learn whether the most harmful activities are criminalized or whether their harms are reduced by implementing criminal law.

However, unlike the most "radical" constructivists and postmodernists, we are committed to ontological realism—that is, to the existence of a world that we can perceive and investigate, even if imperfectly (Bottoms 2008). On that basis, we can turn to hard evidence and avoid leaning on the impromptu perceptions of polling respondents or policy-makers.

We also draw from critical criminologists' recognition of the normativity of the concept of crime and therefore of criminological research. In line with the critical tradition, our harm-based approach provides criminology and related fields with a clearer conceptual starting point (i.e., harm and its reduction) and has the ambition to connect with broader societal debates, not just with crime prevention and control or criminal justice. However, whereas Bottoms (2008, 92–3) accuses the critical criminologists of the 1970s of political advocacy, we are wary of such risk and aim to contribute dispassionately to policy deliberations (see Section 7.5).

We share victimologists' interest in the consequences of crime but aim at a systematic assessment of the overall impact of a criminal activity, going beyond victimologists' focus on traditional crimes and their individual victims.

Lastly, our approach gains from the insights of "neoclassical" or "administrative" criminology that emerged in the 1970s at the other end of the political spectrum. Consistent with routine activity and other opportunity theories (e.g., Mayhew et al. 1976; Cohen and Felson 1979), we begin with a concrete analysis of a criminal activity in a particular context and time and, like the proponents of situational crime prevention, we aim to influence policy deliberations and promote incremental change, but with attention to the causality of "harms," not "crime."

There are, however, three important differences between ours and the neoclassical approach to criminology. First, we treat harm reduction, rather than crime reduction, as the ultimate goal of criminal and related policy. We agree with Duff (2013) that "a system of criminal law" and by extension criminal policy cannot and should not only "prevent or reduce crime, since without the criminal law there would be no crimes—no conduct would count as criminal" (n.p.). Second, we have developed a methodology for systematically and empirically assessing harm. Third, whereas neoclassical scholarship has mainly evaluated specific, concrete policy interventions without considering contributions to broader policy goals (Bottoms 2008, 84–95), the interplay among policies, and differences in societal perspectives, we view the analytical leap as necessary. An intervention might reduce crime, but produce more harm than good (e.g., by stirring conflict and violence) after accounting for the full effects. Driven by this realization, we describe (Section 7.5) how harm assessment could be used to inform "notional" benefit–cost analyses of criminal policies.

particular interests and bearers. It would then be well positioned to explore whether some policies or interventions would contribute more to reducing harms than others, how effects span interests and bearers, and, perhaps, whether harm justifies criminalizing specific behaviors or activities.

Through this expansion, criminology might also better acknowledge and address harms of private- and public-sector entities that are dealt with outside criminal law, without claiming (see Sutherland 1945) that they are all crimes. In turn, criminologists might find new and creative ways of preventing and restoring harms outside criminal law that might lead them to develop innovative suggestions for improving policies that focus on criminology's more standard fare (Braithwaite 2000, 2002).[6]

The expansion could also help secure, and perhaps increase, the relevance and utility of criminological research against the backdrop of an ongoing shift from the "post-crime" orientation of criminal justice to the "pre-crime" orientation of security and risk preemption. According to Zedner (2007) and others, this shift risks depriving criminology of its subject matter and rendering it irrelevant, but, referring to Braithwaite's analogy (2000), attention to harm could spare criminology the fate of zoology after the development of new branches of biology. If the logic of risk management underpins the governance of security, including public and private approaches to dealing with crime-related threats (see Section 2.5), and even the rise of the regulatory state (e.g., Braithwaite 2000), then harm assessment, which addresses the substantive and "actuarial" components of risk, can provide an important contribution to related deliberations and debates. Indeed, our harm assessment framework, with its focus on severity and incidence, derives largely from the literature of risk management.

At the same time, criminology might employ harm assessment to critically question the appropriateness and effectiveness of interventions taken by private or public bodies to deal with crimes and crime-related security threats. While Braithwaite (e.g., 2000) and others (e.g., Shearing 1995; Shearing and Johnston 2005) have expressed confidence in the rise of self-regulation in the business world and the spread of restorative justice in local communities as practices of risk management, a systematic, empirical harm assessment would offer an independent, objective perspective on priorities and responses, including prevention and restoration. Kersten's (2022) project on the role of harm in the regulation of the Belgian meat sector, for example, shows that much policy and regulatory attention focuses on food safety, because businesses are keen on consumer trust, even if many food-safety violations do not entail serious harm (e.g., fraudulent substitution

6 See, e.g., Braithwaite and Drahos (2000) on dealing with harms of businesses.

of horse meat for beef). Other activities that inflict serious harms—for example to workers' health or animals' welfare—receive less attention.

Whatever constitutes the advantages and necessity of self-regulation and restorative justice, one could argue that democratic states should not leave private parties, with their own particular interests, the full power to decide, individually, which harms society, as a whole, should address. Similarly, relying more heavily on privately provided security services might be appropriate—and beneficial—in some, but not all contexts.

By focusing on and assessing harm, criminology could make more of its close connection with what Williams B (2005, 3, quoted in Bottoms n.d.) describes as the "first" political question in any society: that is, "the securing of order, protection, safety, trust, and the conditions of co-operation." According to Bottoms (n.d.), this connection already grants criminology a prominent place in the social sciences, but focusing additionally on assessing and reducing—preventing, mitigating, or remediating—harms, could help ensure that criminological theories and knowledge are not misused to secure just *any* order (see Walgrave 2013) and establish a firm commitment to broader societal goals of justice.

With great prescience, Stanley Cohen ([1979] 2016, 86) advocated for a paradigm shift in criminological thought and research in passionate, if polemical, terms:

> There should be a moratorium on nearly all types of standard criminological research and publication. Absolutely prohibited should be any research about the "causes" of crime and delinquency or the personal characteristics of criminals and delinquents . . . Instead, thought and research should be devoted to such questions as: differential perceptions of the seriousness of various crimes and the level of appropriate punishment, the degree to which certain forms of deviance can be tolerated without invoking the criminal sanction; the extent and nature of harm, victimization and damage by crime, the feasibility of decentralizing the justice system, the viability of forms of social control right outside the system . . . and so on.

Cohen's call for a moratorium on mainstream criminology is extreme and risks throwing away the baby with the bathwater but his proposed research program is as relevant today as in 1979. Whether labeled "zemiological," "criminological," or otherwise, such research, including the conceptualization and operationalization of harm, can, as we discuss in Section 7.5, benefit criminal and related policy, both within and "outside the system."

7.5 How Can a Harm-Based Approach Benefit Policy and Governance?

In this section, we show how our harm-based approach, with its emphasis on systematic, empirical assessment, can benefit criminal policy and the governance of security and contribute to deliberations in other policy and regulatory fields.

Benefits of Harm Assessment for Criminal Policy and the Governance of Security

Here, we walk through several examples of opportunities for constructive engagement with criminal policy and the governance of security as it concerns crime.

Establishing criminality

Taking a consequentialist perspective (Chapter 2, Section 2.2), one might use our harm assessment framework to consider whether specific activities warrant criminalization, even if a final decision on criminalization must account for other perspectives. Recall that Duff and Marshall (2014) identify two versions of the harm principle (see Chapter 2, Section 2.3): the "harmful-conduct principle" and the "harm-prevention principle."

Pursuant to the "harmful-conduct principle," one could use the framework to test whether an activity, criminal or not, is sufficiently harmful to be called out as "criminal." The assessment could, then, help answer what Duff (2010, 109) calls a "central question about criminalization." To paraphrase that question, when should society abstain from criminalizing some wrongs either because their harms are too trivial or because it is more important to ensure that the harm is repaired or compensated, presuming a trade-off?

In accordance with the "harm-prevention principle," one could use the framework to evaluate the extent of harms and, especially, the strength of the relationship between a harm and an activity. How severe, frequent, and remote are the damages associated with an activity and, to what extent could criminalizing the activity help prevent substantial harm? In some cases, an assessment might provide solid arguments for avoiding the excessive extension of the harm principle feared by some scholars (e.g., Harcourt 1999; Duff 2007) and for questioning the growing number of preventative offenses that have been introduced in recent years, especially but not only in counterterrorism (Ashworth and Zedner 2014; see Chapter 2, Section 2.4). If future applications of the framework were to entail full accounting and include the gains associated with activities, they could accommodate any repeated activity that, even if legal, is suspected of generating harms (e.g., tobacco or alcohol production and trade).

This is not to say that we advocate criminalization as a response to all harms of a particular intensity, but that the approach might afford a means to calibrate the policy response to harm and its enforcement. As Feinberg (1984, 35) contends, "any legal system determined to 'minimize harm' must incorporate judgments of the comparative importance of interests of different kinds so that it can pronounce 'unjustified' the invasion of one person's interest of high priority done to protect another person's interest of low priority."

Setting strategic and tactical priorities

Comparing harms across different types of already-criminal activities can provide initial evidence for setting strategic priorities in crime control and policing and crime prevention. One might, for example, rank criminal activities according to their harmfulness and, without ignoring low-hanging fruit or feasibility, look to address the highest ranking first.[7] The comparative assessment might also allow policy-makers to contrast current priorities, priorities that would emerge objectively from a systematic, empirical assessment, and the public's perceptions of priorities and initiate a public debate when rankings based on a systematic, empirical assessment and public perceptions diverge (see Adriaenssen et al. 2018).

As per Goldstein's "problem-oriented policing," a comparative assessment of harms might also help the police—along with others—identify the most serious problems facing a community and weigh competing interests (see Chapter 2, Section 2.4) to develop responses. While potentially drifting

[7] As we discuss later in this section, under "evaluating policies and interventions," such decisions should also involve consideration of costs.

beyond the purview—and competency—of policing, Goldstein (1990, 101) acknowledges that such decisions about priorities in policing should not be taken by the police alone, but "in the absence of sufficient in-depth analysis of what the police are expected to do, the questions—important as they are—are not being raised in the first place."

Identifying especially "harmful" perpetrators or "harmed" bearers—the "power few" in Sherman's (2007, 229) terminology—might suggest particular avenues of crime control and prevention and also help the responsible policy bodies set tactical priorities, possibly with less risk of stereotyping or profiling.[8] For example, the assessment process might reveal that certain types of perpetrators, distinguished by location or criminal affiliations, disproportionally engage in particularly harmful activities and suggest mitigations. The High Point Drug Market Intervention (e.g., Corsaro et al. 2012) took such an approach to reducing violence.

Harm assessment can also provide the evidence for establishing shared—strategic or tactical—priorities among the multiple public and private partners involved in the governance of security as it pertains to crime. The framework builds on risk-management methods that are familiar to businesses, police agencies (e.g., under the label of "threat assessment"—see Section 2.5), and national security agencies and could present a common analytical ground for partnerships.

Our framework's comprehensiveness represents a further advantage in the private–public governance of security. As it specifies a wide range of interests, including physical and material, and a host of potential individual, institutional, and environmental bearers, policy-makers can be clearer about which interests and bearers they are prioritizing in their roles as public officials; identify differences between their priorities and those of the private sector; and, if necessary, prompt their private-sector partners to pay due attention to broader societal concerns.

Reviewing sentencing guidelines and practices

An assessment of the severity of the harms of a crime, irrespective of their incidence, can yield evidence to review existing sentencing guidelines and practices. Recalling that "seriousness" in this debate consists of a combination of "harmfulness" and "culpability" (see Section 2.4), the assessment might supply an empirical gauge for judging the former and would do so

[8] Osborne and Wernicke (2003, 7) distinguish between strategic and operational priorities.

independently of prior policy decisions, public perceptions, and political imperatives. On that basis, it would represent a significant step forward from other recent efforts, including the Crime Harm Index (Sherman et al. 2016).

Strengthening remediation-oriented programs

A systematic, empirical assessment of the harms of crime to different classes of bearers, including businesses, nongovernmental organizations, government, and the environment, might also help strengthen current victim programs, restorative justice, and international criminal justice. It could expand the reach of both victim programs and restorative justice beyond traditional crimes and individual victims (e.g., Fattah 2010, 54–7; Letschert and van Dijk 2011) and, in all three fields, better acknowledge harms *of* private- and public-sector entities and harms *to* nonindividual bearers (e.g., Walgrave 2003, 61; White 2010; see Chapter 2, Section 2.4). In restorative justice and international criminal justice, the assessment could also provide a basis for proportionally aligning restoration and reparation, respectively, with harm. It would address concerns about proportionality that have been raised by restorative-justice scholars (e.g., Duff 2003), fulfill the United Nations' proportionality requirement, and help international courts set principled, evidence-based reparations (see Chapter 2, Section 2.4).

In addition, an assessment that takes the perspective of an "impartial spectator" (Sen 2009, 124, citing Smith [1790] 1976) could help policymakers identify and address a fuller range of the harms of a conduct—even if victims do not report them fully—and avoid unduly privileging the harms recounted by the most vocal victims.

Evaluating policies and interventions

Finally, our framework can support the evaluation of public policies and public and private interventions to address crime and crime-related security threats and feed into deliberations about future policies and interventions. A harm-based approach, such as ours, could be used to assess and compare the impact, including the unintended consequences and distributional effects, of different types of policies or particular interventions and to inform what we refer to as a "notional" benefit–cost analysis of the alternatives. We add the adjective "notional," because our framework does not require monetization or even quantification of the benefits (i.e., the gains from reducing harm); however, we do not use the term "qualitative" benefit–cost analysis, because we do not rule out the possibility of some quantification. For example, harms to individuals' and entities' material support and some environmental losses can—in some contexts—be expressed in monetary terms. Moreover, a full comparison of alternative policies or interventions, even if only notional, would still necessitate considering the costs of implementing each and some of those costs might be readily calculable.

As a practical matter, Greenfield and Paoli (2012, 11) delineate three layers of policy analysis, each with steps of its own:[9]

- First, one would need to establish whether a policy, after accounting for its positive and negative consequences, reduces harms on balance, by comparing conditions as they are and conditions as they would be with a change of policy. For example, if starting from a clean slate in a policy-free environment, one would first assess the harms of a yet-to-be-targeted activity and then consider the anticipated harms under a proposed policy, including those of the policy itself. To ascertain the effects of an existing policy, one would, instead, compare the harms under that policy with those in a policy-free environment. For any of these purposes, we advocate a truly "net" analysis of harms; meaning, an analysis that accounts fully for the negative and positive consequences of both the targeted activity and the proposed policy in each scenario. To look only at the negatives of a targeted activity or the positives of a policy option, would bias the results.
- Second, one would need to assess the overall effect of the policy relative to the resources needed to carry out the policy. Even if a policy generates a net "positive" vis-à-vis harms, the costs of the implementing the policy could be too high to justify acting. As addressed in Chapter 4, we would not treat control, response, or other implementation costs as harms in these analyses, but as "costs" to weigh against the "benefits" of reducing harms. We believe that resource-allocation decisions are not, themselves, measures of harm; rather, they are made—or should be made—in relation to society's understanding of and concern about the harm.
- Third, in the presence of multiple policy options, one would need to repeat the process and compare results across alternatives.

[9] The layers—first, second, and third—are the same as in Greenfield and Paoli (2012, 11), but we have adapted the accompanying text in each bullet for use in this book. For brevity's sake, we, like the underlying material, substitute "policy" for "policy and interventions."

Much of the analysis might be qualitative, but, as Greenfield and Paoli (2012, 11) note, it would still provide a systematic, empirical basis for policy evaluation. Moreover, the thought exercise, alone, could point to issues and concerns that otherwise might go unnoticed and escape the policy-making process. Greenfield and Paoli (2012, 12–13) offer a hypothetical example:

> To conduct a comprehensive, albeit largely qualitative, analysis of [the benefits and costs of] the current international drug-control regime, one might compare the baseline estimates of all harms under current policy to a no-policy scenario and then compare the notional "difference" to the implementation cost. If, for example, there were no coca-growing prohibitions or associated policy interventions, would deforestation worsen or lessen? [See Dávalos et al., 2009, 2011, for related discussions.] Adding another layer of complexity, one might seek to establish not just the balance of effects in relation to the implementation costs but the distribution within and across countries, including drug-consuming countries . . . one might [also] compare the incremental effects of discrete changes in policy against the baselines.

Speaking less hypothetically, one—or we—could extend the analysis in Chapter 5, to encompass use-related harms, and flesh out a fuller picture of the costs and benefits of illegality. Similarly, we could build on the analysis of coca cultivation and processing in Chapter 6, to begin a notional benefit–cost analysis of drug control and related policies.

As Greenfield and Paoli (2012, 11–12) suggest, the lens of harm assessment might lead us to uncover opportunities to address policy and outcomes more constructively. For example, Quimbayo Ruiz (2008, 1) proposes reducing harms associated with coca cultivation and processing, by furnishing rural communities with information and training to protect their health and the environment when they work with herbicides and other chemicals. While delivering conventional agricultural extension services might seem unusual in this context, the information and training would benefit all those—near and far—who otherwise would feel the ill-effects of the misuse or overuse of the herbicides and other chemicals. Greenfield and Paoli (2012, 12) also suggest that harm assessment can be used to better anticipate the consequences of new drug-control policies, programs, and interventions, drawing on the then-recent—and unexpected—story of cocaine flows from South America to Europe via West Africa as an example.

We—Greenfield and Paoli in various configurations—have been contemplating the idea of notional benefit–cost analysis since the start of our work in this area and, as suggested earlier, began to give it close consideration in Greenfield and Paoli (2012, 11–12). In the intervening years, one of us has actively pursued the idea in other fora, first, in an analysis of options for professional training programs (Greenfield et al. 2015b) and, next, in an analysis of options for policies to restrict access to precursor chemicals that are used to manufacture improvised explosive devices (National Academies of Sciences, Engineering, and Medicine 2018). Through that work, and exposure to others' work, we have gained confidence in our idea. In particular, we have learned that policy analysts can gain considerable insight into trade-offs among policy options, by drawing on the underlying tenets of benefit–cost analysis and without strict quantification, even if they cannot provide policy-makers with a "best" option in all cases.[10] In the same way, we would like to see more such undertakings in this realm, specifically, with support from the harm assessment framework.

In summary, systematic, empirical harm assessment can contribute to deliberations on criminalization, the establishment of priorities in crime control and policing, crime prevention, and the governance of security, sentencing and punishment, the improvement of our retributive and restorative responses to crime, and the development of more effective and accountable criminal policy. It might be true, as Robinson and Kurzban (2007, 1852) argue, that "the intuition that those who commit wrongs should be punished seems to be universal" and as Eisner et al. (2017, 61) show, that forms of "criminal justice" or "arrangements to deal with wrongs and deliver punishment" can be found in all large-scale societies, but intuition is not destiny.[11] Punishment has come about in many (increasingly milder[12]) forms, has been coupled with and even superseded by restorative interventions, and represents only one, if an essential, tool of criminal policy (see Chapter 2, Section 2.4; Garland 1990).

Against that backdrop, we believe that assessing the harms of crimes and policy, including interventions, can help rationalize the latter and

[10] Even US regulatory authorities (see, e.g., Office of Management and Budget 2003), which rely heavily on benefit–cost analysis, endorse qualitative reasoning and evidence, albeit as a supplement or last resort.

[11] Behavioral game theorists and evolutionary psychologists claim that "intuitions about modern mass-level criminal justice systems emerge from evolved mechanisms designed to operate in ancestral small-scale societies" (Petersen et al. 2010, 682).

[12] The death penalty and corporal sanctions have disappeared from most developed countries (see e.g., Durkheim [1900] 1969; Spierenburg 2013).

ensure that punishment and other tools of contemporary criminal policy are used to pursue broader societal goals (see Section 7.6), rather than becoming goals in themselves. With the modernization and consolidation of state authorities, individual revenge and family feuds have been superseded by third-party punishment, mediation, and regulation in much of the contemporary world. Thus, criminal policy reforms might continue with ongoing social change (Elias [1939] 2000; see also Walgrave 2013) and empirical, systematic harm assessment could support them.

Benefits of Harm Assessment in Other Policy Arenas

We have developed our framework to assess the harms of crimes and do not present any assessments of harms of legal or unregulated activities in this book, but we are confident that harm assessment can benefit other areas of public policy, as evident in Kersten's (2022) application to the Belgian meat sector. As Feinberg (1984, 31) notes, "criminal law is not the state's primary tool for the reduction of harm generally," and, according to Sparrow (2008), harm reduction constitutes a primary aim of policy in numerous fields, ranging from poverty alleviation, to antidiscrimination, to pollution and disease control.

While the applicability of our framework to those distant fields remains to be tested, we see strong potential for it to contribute to assessing damages in the many policy fields that admit tort litigations and, by extension, addressing criticisms of tort litigation and influencing policy-making. In close alignment with our specification of interest dimensions, tort law recognizes physical, emotional, economic, and reputational damages and violations of privacy, property, and constitutional rights.[13] The distinction between a tort and crime is not always clear-cut, but tort proceedings revolve around assessing damages and awarding compensation for damages (e.g., Coleman et al. 2015; van Dam 2013), suggesting an obvious role for harm assessment. From its modest beginning in the nineteenth century, the

[13] Torts are private wrongs, whereas crimes are public wrongs. Although both torts and crimes involve acts that cause injury or harm to another's person or property (see Chapter 2), complaints regarding the former are brought by the plaintiff or claimant in a civil-court proceeding.

regime of tortious liability has expanded greatly, reflecting the rise of industrialization, the growth of regulation, and modern societies' increased efforts to anticipate and manage risks. Today, tort litigations are admissible—and commonplace—for cases involving work safety and employment, health, transportation, and product liability as "an accepted part of the machinery of regulation which by now controls much of the economy" (Hedley 2013, 248).

Regarding criticisms of tort litigation, attention has focused largely on consistency and cost. Absent an authoritative system—beyond the codification of case law (e.g., Judicial College 2017)—across jurisdictions, there has been much debate on how damages are assessed and compensation is established (e.g., Quill and Friel 2016). Given the focus of torts on damages, our framework might contribute substantially to addressing those concerns. Moreover, in many English-speaking countries, unease has grown about the high cost of litigations, which some observers have attributed to a damaging "compensation culture" (e.g., Furedi 1999).[14] With such concerns in mind, a comprehensive assessment of the harms of different torts could help to determine which claimants' legal interests or capabilities have been harmed and restored through compensation and subsequently compare the damages to such interests or capabilities with the costs for states and insurers. While much media and political commentary tends to label increases in claims (either in number or monetary value) as "bad" and decreases in insurance costs as "good," a harm assessment can help determine—as Quill and Friel (2016, 3) and others suggest—"whether useful social goals are being advanced or retarded."

As for policy influence, systematic, empirical harm assessment might pinpoint the severity of damages, and, over time, uncover trends in the frequency and distribution, which, in turn, might suggest a role for policy. If, for example, damages to particular interests and bearers were to emerge consistently in a particular work environment or with particular modes of transportation, the trends might indicate a need for a policy intervention.

[14] In this context, compensation culture refers to the perception that the tort regime has conferred a structural advantage on plaintiffs, implying excessive wins, and that it has become too costly, as reflected in insurance premiums (e.g., Williams K. 2005; see also Quill and Friel 2016).

7.6 Diagnosing Injustice to Advance Justice

Ultimately, we see harm assessment as a "diagnosis of injustice" and as a means for "judging how to reduce injustice and advance justice" (Sen 2009, vii, ix). Our understanding of justice draws on Sen's work, which departs notably from Rawls's (1971) quest for perfectly just institutions, and largely conceives of justice as a matter of social realizations and, specifically, peoples' actual capabilities. Indeed, capabilities are at the heart of our conceptualization of harm, as we frame stakeholders' interests in term of paths to attaining a certain quality of life, a mission, or sustainability for individuals, private- and public-sector entities, and the environment, respectively (see Chapter 4, Section 4.3).

To clarify, Sen contrasts two concepts of justice in early Indian jurisprudence: the first concept, *niti*, relates to organizational propriety and behavioral correctness and the second, *nyaya*, relates to "the lives that people are actually able to lead" (2009, xv). Emphasizing *nyaya*, we adopt a realization-focused view of justice as the reduction—prevention, mitigation, or remediation—of manifest injustice or obstacles and, by extension, of harm. Moreover, following Adam Smith ([1763] 1896, 3), for whom "[t]he object of justice is the security from injury, and it is the foundation of civil government," we see justice and security, writ large, as closely intertwined, even if criminology often frames them in opposition (e.g., Brodeur and Shearing 2005).

If harm reduction, including prevention, is central to promoting both security and justice, the systematic, empirical assessment of the harms of crime can serve as a check on whether these objectives are being pursued effectively through criminal or other policy interventions. "Far too often . . . " Tirole (2017, 5) observes, "means and instruments . . . acquire a life of their own and lose sight of their true purposes. They can even end up working against the notion of the common good that justified them in the first place." Tirole, an economist, focuses on economic policy and institutions, but the same can be said of criminal policy and the governance of security as it pertains to crime. Referring specifically to criminal policy, Goldstein (1979, 236) warned that the police and other organizations suffer from the "means over ends" syndrome and he (1990, 147) sought new measures of effectiveness.

Effectiveness holds special meaning in criminal policy because the state intentionally metes out punishment, hence harm, to its citizens that can include, in the extreme, loss of privacy and autonomy over a lifetime through imprisonment or even death.[15] While defending the state's duty to punish, Tadros (2011, 1), a prominent contemporary jurist, admits that "punishment is probably the most awful thing that modern democratic states do to their own citizens" (see also, e.g., Hart [1968] 2008; Clear 1994). As Emile Durkheim ([1900] 1969, 52) noted at the turn of the twentieth century, "there is a real and ineluctable contradiction in avenging an offended human dignity, in the person of the victim, by violating the integrity of the person of the criminal." Criminal punishment, especially imprisonment, has a profound impact on citizens' lives that has no comparison in other policy arenas. Although unintended, the impact also reaches well beyond the convict, to his or her family and community (e.g., Travis et al. 2014), even if neither relatives nor communities are responsible for the crimes and resulting harms.

In addition, the institutions and practices of criminal policy, and most notably incarceration, are costly, in both absolute and relative terms. At one end of the spectrum, with an incarcerated population exceeding 2 million in 2017 (Maruschak and Minton 2020, 2), US corrections costs, including those of prisons and jails, were approaching $90 billion a year (Buelhler 2021, 4). In Europe, the incarcerated population is much smaller, but the costs are still considerable. According to statistics from the Council of Europe (Aebi and Tiago 2018, 112–4), France spent €2.7 billion per year on prison administration, Italy also spent €2.7 billion, Germany spent €3.1 billion, and Russia spent €3.9 billion, each ranking among the biggest spenders in 2017.[16] In some instances, such costs, expressed as per-inmate figures, could rival estimates of per capita gross domestic product (GDP).[17]

Given those peculiar harms and substantial costs, policy-makers might have a distinct obligation to specify the objectives of criminal policy and its interventions, including imprisonment; to determine whether the selected means are achieving those objectives; and to prevent the means—that is, criminal laws and the machinery of the criminal justice system—from

[15] Policy in other branches might inflict harm on state citizens, e.g., by restricting or imposing fines on various types of behavior, but, to our knowledge, none covers as many interest dimensions intentionally and to such possible extremes.

[16] The data for Germany are for 2016.

[17] For example, the cost of incarcerating a prisoner for a year might be as much or more than an average individual's contribution to their country's economy in a year. Based on Aebi and Tiago's (2018) data on daily costs for the detention of one inmate, World Bank data on GDP, and our calculations with mid-year exchange rates, the average annual cost per inmate in 2017 would exceed €39,000 in France, €48,000 in Italy, and also €48,000 in Germany, where per capita GDP in 2017 amounted to about €34,700, €29,000, and €39,900, respectively.

becoming objectives in themselves. If punishment can only "be justified in virtue of the good effects that it can have," as Tadros (2011, 2) argues, the evaluation cannot only be theoretical but must also be empirical. Assessing the harms of crimes—to qualitatively or quantitatively "estimate" the benefits of criminal policies and interventions in terms of harm prevention or mitigation—would constitute a first step.

We stress that we do not disregard the relevance of "procedural justice" to the legitimacy of criminal policy and criminal justice institutions (Tyler 2006), but it is not our central focus.[18] Without claiming harm as the sole criterion for developing or implementing any policy, we advocate for a "consequence-sensitive assessment" and, like the mythical Indian prince, Arjuna, whom Sen cites, we contend that "the results of one's choices and actions must matter in deciding what one should do" (Sen 2009, 210, 213).

7.7 Our Closing Argument

While our framework is our answer to Beccaria's centuries-old proposal for a measure of damages, promoting justice through harm reduction—consisting of prevention, mitigation, and remediation—would be our answer to the "why?" Kitcher (2001, 145), a philosopher of science, asks all scientists: "What is the collective good that we want inquiry to promote?" For us, the inquiry is our way of practicing "public criminology" (Loader and Sparks 2011) and "economics for the common good" (Tirole 2017). By taking up this cause, we might stand accused of partisanship, but offer Gouldner's (1973, 58) defense of objectivity:

> I do not regard partisanship as incompatible with objectivity. The physician, after all, is not necessarily less objective because he has made a partisan commitment to his patient and against the germ. The physician's objectivity is somehow vouchsafed because he has committed to a specific value: health. It is this commitment that constrains him to see and say things about the patient's conditions that neither of them may want to know.

[18] While we do not investigate, or discuss, the procedural aspects of criminal policy, we subscribe to Sen's (2009) idea of "comprehensive outcomes" that include not only the final outcome of a policy but also the way it is achieved and are capable of accommodating the fair treatment of the offenders and the public, and other procedural constraints.

Further developing Gouldner's analogy, we are convinced that the systematic, empirical assessment of harms can—and should—contribute to a thorough diagnosis of social ills, especially but not only criminal, even if neither physicians nor social scientists can decide, alone, on a course of action. Such decisions can only be the task of the patient or, in our case, a democratic society. Nonetheless, if democracy is understood as the "government by discussion" (Sen 2009, xiii, drawing on Mill), we hope that the systematic, empirical assessment of the harms of crime can contribute to the public debate and help prevent that debate from becoming hostage to populists' whims and shrewd politicians' tricks.

In medicine, few patients would claim the right to exclusive responsibility for either the diagnosis of their health problems or the evaluation of alternative therapies, even if the patient rightly controls the decision.[19] This book has been written with the hope that the diagnostic and evaluative evidence produced by systematic, empirical harm assessment achieves a similar status in normative debates on crime and security, is used routinely to inform deliberations on criminal and related—and even unrelated—policy, and, as a consequence, contributes to making our societies less harmful and unjust. In closing, we believe and have tried to persuade our readers that our harm assessment framework can provide a firm analytical foundation to support decision-making on criminal and related policy and contribute to policy that is more effective and accountable, all to the greater good.

[19] This statement seemed self-evident to us when we first wrote it, but societies' responses to the spread of Coronavirus 2019 (COVID-19) have challenged it. In this pandemic, we have time and again experienced the massive losses resulting from the neglect of expert advice.

APPENDIX A

Glossary of Terms

This glossary explains our use of technical vocabulary in this book. The explanations, many of which we crafted specifically for the purposes of the framework and its application, might not be appropriate in other contexts. Although we try to draw from commonly cited, widely available sources (e.g., the Organisation for Economic Co-Operation and Development (OECD), Transparency International, and the United Nations Office on Drugs and Crime), some of the words and phrases that appear in this glossary are used dissimilarly across academic disciplines and policy communities and among legal professionals, law enforcement officers, and other practitioners. In addition, some phrases, as noted below, are of our own design.

Accompanying activity (see also, enabled activity and primary activity). A term of our own design, referring to an activity that complements or occurs alongside a primary or enabled activity. For example, violence sometimes supports or occurs alongside cocaine trafficking, which was the primary activity in our assessment in Chapter 5. When we identify harms associated with an accompanying activity, we consider only those events that relate directly to the primary or enabled activity. For example, in Chapter 5, we considered harms associated with assaults that occurred in the context of the act of cocaine trafficking, such as those involving traffickers, facilitators, or other individuals who were drawn into trafficking, but we did not consider the harms of assaults that involved the same people—or their associates—in other contexts. Note that "accompanying" is a relative term and that an activity might be treated as an accompanying activity in one context, but as a primary or enabled activity in another, depending on the principle or underlying activity of interest in a particular harm assessment.

Accumulative harm. A harm that only arises if the act that triggers the harm is combined with similar acts of other (Feinberg 1984, 225–7) or of the same harming agent, such as repeated cases of antisocial behavior and incivility or minor tax fraud.

Activity (see primary, accompanying, or enabled activity).

Assault (see also, violence). The term "assault" can include or might even refer solely to the threat of injury without actual injury, whereas "battery" tends to indicate actual physical contact without consent (see, Cornell University Law School, https://www.law.cornell.edu/wex/assault and https://www.law.cornell.edu/wex/battery). Assault also may be viewed as "a lesser included offense of battery, meaning that assault merges into battery and that a defendant may be punished for one but not both crimes" (see, Cornell University Law School, https://www.law.cornell.edu/wex/assault_and_battery).

Table A.1 Severity of functional harms associated with assault and battery

Event	Consequences	Severity
Assault and battery (petty)	Insubstantial or no injuries that have negligible health consequences	Marginal
Assault and battery (limited)	Injuries that merit outpatient care, but not hospitalization	Moderate
Assault and battery (major)	Injuries that merit hospitalization, but are not permanently disabling	Serious
Assault and battery (mayhem)	Injuries that are permanently disabling, such as dismemberment, but not fatal	Grave
Murder or manslaughter	Death	Catastrophic

Note: We rate the functional harms of rape as "grave," similar to those of mayhem.

We take these differences into account in our assessments of violence and distinguish between threats or intimidation and explicit use—"threat or use," as shorthand—the latter of which includes verbal or psychological abuse that we term "assault (verbal or psychological)," and several different degrees of physical abuse, consisting of "assault and battery (petty)," "assault and battery (limited)," "assault and battery (major)," and "assault and battery (mayhem)."[1] For our purposes, an instance of "assault and battery (mayhem)" would result in a permanent disability, including but not limited to dismemberment and would obtain a "grave" severity rating; "assault and battery (major)" would result in injuries that merit hospitalization, but are not permanently disabling and would obtain a "serious" severity rating; and "assault and battery (limited)" would result in injuries that merit out-patient care (i.e., medical attention, but not hospitalization) and would obtain a "moderate" severity rating (Table A.1). An instance of "assault and battery (petty)" would result in insubstantial or no injuries, have negligible health consequences, and obtain a "marginal" severity rating. Although some individuals who experience petty assaults might seek medical treatment, medical treatment is not a necessary condition for the category "assault and battery (petty)." Lastly, we refer to assault and battery that results in death as "murder or manslaughter" and to rape and other sexual intrusions, respectively, as "assault (sexual, rape)" and "assault (sexual, other)."

Autonomy (see privacy and autonomy).

Battery (see assault).

Bearers. The individuals, entities (private-sector or government), or elements of the environment (social or physical) that suffer from harms.

Capabilities. Opportunities and freedoms to be or do (Sen 1987).

[1] We did not maintain these distinctions uniformly in our earlier work (e.g., Paoli et al. 2013).

Table A.2 Relationship between cultivation and production

Term	Coverage of term				
	Investment	**Maintenance**	**Harvesting**	**Processing**	**Divestment**
Cultivation	X	X	X		X
Production		X	X	X	

Claimant (see bearer).

Coca cultivation. Table A.2 shows the relationship between the terms "cultivation" and "production," as we use them in Chapter 6, with respect to investment, maintenance, harvesting, and processing activities. Whereas coca "cultivation" encompasses planting or "investment," maintenance, harvesting, and abandonment or removal, which we refer to as "divestment," "production" concerns maintenance, harvesting, and processing (i.e., from coca to coca paste, cocaine base, or cocaine), but not investment or divestment.

Cocaine dealing (see drug dealing).

Cocaine trafficking (see drug trafficking).

Corruption (see also, petty, grand, or political corruption and money laundering). Following the OECD (2008, 22), we define corruption broadly as the "abuse of public or private office for personal gain." In considering corruption we exclude companies set up solely for illegal purposes, as one might think of shell companies.

Crime. We define crime legalistically as "an intentional act or omission in violation of criminal law (statutory ad case law)" (Tappan 1947, 100). We note, though, that our framework can also be used to assess the harms of other activities thought to entail substantial adverse consequences, even if we have not assessed the harms of any such activities in this book.

Criminal policy (see also, governance of security). We use this term to cover various "phases" of policy-making and implementation that concern crime and involve, inter alia, developing and implementing strategies and tactics to deter people from committing crimes, identifying, sentencing, and punishing those who have already committed crimes, assisting victims, and temporarily or permanently incapacitating them to avert reoffending. As principal actors in the criminal justice system, police, prosecutors, courts, and prisons are chiefly responsible for implementing criminal policy, even if they also contribute to its development.

In this book, we focus on phases of criminal policy in which harm might play a part, consisting of criminalization, crime control and policing, sentencing and punishment, victims' assistance and restorative justice, and crime prevention, as well as international criminal justice. We omit a few other phases, such as the investigation of actual crimes and adjudication, because these phases primarily aim to establish culpability, and harm is less relevant for them. At times, we also use the phrase "criminal and related policy" to cover a broader set of concerns that could, for example, include policy on crime-related security threats.

Dealing (see drug dealing).

Drug dealing. All retail-level activities, including sale or barter, involving the psychoactive substances prohibited or controlled by the three United Nations Drug Conventions (United Nations 1961, 1971, 1988) and related national or jurisdictional legislation.

Drug trafficking. All transportation and marketing activities that occur prior to retail, which we define separately as "drug dealing," involving the psychoactive substances prohibited or controlled by the three United Nations Drug Conventions (United Nations 1961, 1971, 1988) and related national or jurisdictional legislation.

Enabled activity (see also, accompanying activity and primary activity). A term of our own design, referring to an activity that occurs "downstream" of a primary activity and is at least partially made possible by the primary activity. For example, cocaine dealing and use occur downstream of and cannot occur without some amount of cocaine trafficking, which was the primary activity in our assessment in Chapter 5. Note that "enabled" is a relative term and that an activity might be treated as an "enabled" activity in one context, but as a primary or accompanying activity in another, depending on the principle or underlying activity of interest in a particular harm assessment.

Entity (see private-sector entity or government).

Environment. In framing the environment, we delineate between the "social environment" and the "physical environment." We understand the social environment as consisting of the interactive regions (that is, relationships) between and among individuals and institutions and their associated cultural practices, including but not limited to communities. We define communities, in turn, as small or large social units of individuals who have something in common, such as norms, religion, or identity and are mostly, but not always, linked to specific place (e.g., a country, village, town, or neighborhood). Concerns about the social environment include public nuisance, social fragmentation and community disassociation.

We define the physical environment as "the naturally produced physical surroundings on which humanity is entirely dependent in all its activities (OECD 2008, 253)" and preliminarily encompass nonhuman animals and the whole bio- or ecosphere, while excluding human individuals, private- and public-sector entities, and their interrelationships. (For more on nonhuman animals, see also, individuals.) Concerns about the physical environment could include mistreatment of nonhuman animals and plant life; pollution of air, water, soil, noise and light; inaccessibility of open spaces; and obstruction or destruction of landscapes.

Governance of security (see also, criminal policy). The term "governance of security" encompasses but transcends criminal policy, both for its scope and for the actors involved. Regarding scope, it addresses crime-related security threats and security threats that are unrelated to, or broader than, crime, as in the cases of national security, environmental security, or food security. As for actors, it includes those in the public and private sectors, primarily businesses, and the numerous and multifaceted partnerships and networks that connect them.

Government. We define "government" broadly as consisting of all state entities (executive, legislative, or judicial), including local, regional, and national bodies, that exercise authority within the state territory (what the OECD terms "the government sector") and all other public entities or agencies including, for example, the central bank (see OECD 2008, 631). Our definition of government thus coincides with that of the "public sector" or "state sector."[2] If relevant to a particular assessment, we could extend the definition to include supranational entities and other publicly funded and managed bodies, such as those of the European Union and United Nations, or we could allocate them to their own class of bearers.

Grand corruption (see also, corruption and petty or political corruption). Following Transparency International (2009, 23), we first define "grand corruption" as "acts committed at a high level of government that distort policies or the central functioning of the state [in our terminology, government or public sector], enabling leaders to benefit at the expense of the public good." As in the case of petty corruption, we then extend the term "grand corruption" to private-sector entities and include the abuses of their board members and officers.

Harm. A multifaceted phenomenon or "bundle" of attributes, consisting of a negative outcome of a particular type (see also, interest dimension), severity, and incidence that emerges from a particular activity or set of activities and harming event, and is borne by particular individuals, entities, or the environment (see also, bearer).

Harm reduction. The prevention, mitigation, or remediation of harm.

Human trafficking. Following the United Nations (2000, 2) we treat "[T]he recruitment, transportation, transfer, harbouring or receipt of persons, by means of the threat or use of force or other forms of coercion, of abduction, of fraud, of deception, or the abuse of power or of a position of vulnerability or of the giving or receiving of payments or benefits to achieve the consent of a person having control over another person, for the purpose of exploitation" as the starting point for our analysis. In addition, in our assessment of the harms of human trafficking in Belgium, we considered the distinctions of Belgian authorities among five forms of related exploitation: prostitution and the production and distribution of pornographic materials; forced begging; organ removal; forced crime; and "letting victims work in conditions conflicting with human dignity" (Centrum 2006, 12–15).

Individuals. Thus far, we have implicitly equated "individuals" and "humans" and conceptualized nonhuman animals as either property of humans or part of the physical environment. If we were to undertake an assessment in which

[2] On the overlap and distinction between "government" and "state," two terms that have slightly different meanings in British and American English, see, among others, Robinson (2013).

nonhuman animals featured prominently, we could identify them separately as autonomous bearers, either by expanding this class of bearers to include nonhuman animals or by adding another class.

Interest dimension. A category of capability (i.e., functional integrity, material support, reputation, and privacy and autonomy) that is necessary for achieving a certain quality of life, in the case of individuals; mission, in the case of private-sector entities and government; or sustainability, in the case of the environment. The taxonomy specifies types of harms in relation to damages to the "interest dimensions" of each class of bearer. Functional integrity can apply in some form to all classes of bearers. Material support, reputation, and privacy and autonomy can apply to individuals, private-sector entities, and government, but not to the environment.

Living standard (see standard of living).

Mayhem (see assault).

Mission. An organization's reason for existing.

Money laundering (see also, corruption). According to the United Nations Office on Drugs and Crime and World Bank (2007, 13), "The crimes of bribery, corruption, and money laundering are inextricably linked; indeed, money laundering, understood as hiding or obscuring the source, ownership, control, and movement of assets, could be seen as the last link in a long chain of corrupt acts." Thus, money laundering may involve various forms of corruption or, in some instances, be seen as a manifestation of corruption, but, in our assessments, we most typically attribute the harm to money laundering to avoid double counting. Note that Transparency International (2009, 26) defines money laundering as, "The process of concealing the origin, ownership or destination of illegally or dishonestly obtained money by hiding it within legitimate economic activities," but others also include concealment within the illicit economy. In our analyses, we delineate smuggling and investment of the proceeds of crime and luxury consumption as forms of laundering, but we use the term "physical concealment" to connote literal hiding (e.g., under floor boards or in mattresses) as distinct from laundering.

Participants. Individuals, entities, or elements of the social or physical environment, that are directly involved in an activity, either actively or passively, potentially including perpetrators, victims, law-enforcement officials, witnesses, etc.

Petty corruption (see also, corruption and grand or political corruption). Following Transparency International (2009, 33), we first define "petty corruption" as "everyday abuse of entrusted power by low- and mid-level public officials in their interactions with ordinary citizens, who often are trying to access basic goods or services in places like hospitals, schools, police departments and other agencies." Pursuant to the definition of the OECD (2008, 22), which includes both public and "private office," we then extend the term "petty corruption" to private-sector entities and include the everyday abuse of entrusted power by low- and mid-level businesses' and non-governmental organizations' employees or representatives.

Physical environment (see environment).

Political corruption (see also, corruption and petty or grand corruption). Following Transparency International (2009, 35), we first define "political corruption" as "manipulation of policies, institutions and rules of procedure in the allocation of resources and financing by political decision-makers, who abuse their position to sustain their power, status and wealth." As in the case of petty corruption, we then extend the term "political corruption" to private-sector entities and the manipulation of their policies, institutions, and rules or procedures.

Primary activity (see also accompanying activity and enabled activity). A term of our own design, referring to the principle or underlying activity of interest in a particular harm assessment. In our assessments of the harms of cocaine and human trafficking, discussed in Chapter 5, those forms of trafficking are the primary activities.

Privacy and autonomy. We group violations of "privacy and autonomy" together, as closely related but conceptually distinct phenomenon. A violation of privacy, such as an unauthorized entry or the control of personal documents, such as a passport, might occur in a burglary, kidnapping, or case of human trafficking. Some such events could also entail a related, but additional loss of autonomy. A violation of autonomy would restrict an individual's ability to function independently and might occur in conjunction with a violation of privacy, as in a case of kidnapping, but it could occur separately or in conjunction with violations of other interests. Physical or psychological abuse or intellectual deprivation might also result in a diminution of autonomy.

Private-sector entity. A business or other nongovernmental organization.

Remote harm. A harm is remote when temporal, spatial, or behavioral distance separates conduct from consequences (Ryberg 2004, 64–6; Simester and von Hirsch 2011, 70–88). The harms of enabled activities, for example, constitute remote harms in relation to the primary activity, not just because they are spatially or temporally distant from the primary activity, but because they are mediated by the choices and behavior of other actors who were not participants in the primary activity.

Social environment (see environment).

Standard of living. The capability to attain a certain quality of life.

Standing. Standing, as a legal term, can be defined narrowly as the "capacity of a party to bring suit in court," which, in turn, depends on "the requirement that plaintiffs have sustained or will sustain direct injury or harm and that this harm is redressable" (Cornell University Law School, https://www.law.cornell.edu/wex/standing), but the term can also be used more generally to refer to the legitimacy of an individual or entity's stake in a particular matter. For example, Whittington and MacRae (1986, 1990) and Trumbull (1990) adopted the term in their essays on whether to include or exclude certain individuals in analyses of the costs and benefit of public policies and projects. We follow that literature and give standing to the individuals, entities, and environmental constituents whose harms we "count" in our assessments.

Sustainability. In broad terms, the ability to persist, and, as more narrowly applied to sustainable development, that which "meets the needs of the present without compromising the ability of future generations to meet their own needs" (Brundtland 1987, n.p.).

Trafficking (see drug or human trafficking).

Violence (see also, assault). We use the term "violence" to encompass a range of activities that can involve threats or intimidation, verbal or psychological abuse, and physical intrusion. In our assessments, we distinguish between threats or intimidation and explicit use—"threats or use" as shorthand—where use consists of verbal, psychological, or physical assault (alone or with battery), which we define by degree, and the possibilities of murder, manslaughter, kidnapping, and confinement. We recognize that drawing a distinction between threatening behavior and verbal or psychological abuse could require subjective interpretation, as threatening or intimidating language can, itself, constitute such abuse. Similarly, we describe blackmail as a form of threat or intimidation, but could have described it as use.

APPENDIX B

Data on Coca in Colombia

Table B.1, which constitutes the bulk of this appendix, provides data on coca cultivation, yields, prices, income, division of labor, and household participation in Colombia. The totals, multiples, and other manipulated figures in the table may not add or match up due to rounding error, but any substantial discrepancies between estimates as reported in the United Nations Office on Drugs and Crime (UNODC) and Colombian surveys that we cite and as calculated by hand, by us, from the underlying data in those surveys are noted throughout. All US dollars are in current (then-year) dollars.

Table B.1 Coca cultivation and related concepts in Colombia

	2005	2006	2007	2008	2009	2010	2011	2012	2013[1]	2014	2015	2016
Aggregate data												
Net coca cultivation (hectares)[2]	86,000	78,000	99,000	81,000	68,000[3]	62,000	64,000	48,000	48,000	69,000	96,000	146,000
Cultivation in National Parks												
• **Hectares[4]**	6,110	3,556	3,770	3,445	4,048	3,675	3,048	3,379	3,791	5,477	6,214	7,889
• **Percentage of total area of National Parks[5]**	0.05	0.02	0.02	0.02	0.03	0.03	0.03	0.03	0.03	0.04	0.04	n.a.
• **Percentage of net coca cultivation[6]**	7	5	4	4	6	6	5	7	8	8	6	5
Yields (kilograms per hectare)												
• **Coca leaf, fresh**	6,300	6,300	5,800	4,200	4,600	4,600	4,200	4,200	4,100	4,700	4,800	4,800
• **Coca paste**	10.3	10.2	9.1	6.6	7.2	6.6	6.6	6.7	7.25[7]	7.8	7.9	8.0[8]
• **Cocaine base**	9.6	9.5	8.7	6.2	6.7	5.9	5.9	5.5	7.45[9]	9.4	12.6	13.1[10]
Prices (US dollars per kilogram)												
• **Coca leaf, fresh**	1.1	1.0	1.2	1.1	1.3	1.3	1.3	1.4	1.1	1.1	1.09	0.95
• **Coca paste**	910	879	943	963	956	1,015	1,002	1,025	1,011	983	732	621
• **Cocaine base**	1,090	1,038	1,326	1,450	1,249	1,475	1,407	1,499	1,432	1,238	978	814
Potential gross income[11,12] (US dollars per hectare)												
• **Coca leaf, fresh**	6,930	6,300	6,960	4,620	5,980	6,020[13]	5,460	6,338	5,922	5,501	4,542	n.a.
• **Coca paste**	9,370	8,966	8,581	6,360	6,880	6,700	6,613	6,750	6,737	7,409	5,020	n.a.
• **Cocaine base**	10,460	9,861	11,536	8,990	8,370	8,700[14]	8,301	9,140	6,771	10,538	12,201	n.a.

Value added from processing coca leaf[15,16] (percentage difference)												
• **Coca paste**	35	44	23	38	15	11	21	7	14	35	11	n.a.
• **Cocaine base**	51	57	66	95	40	45	52	44	14	92	169	n.a.
Division of labor (percentage of growers)[17]												
• **Selling leaf**	34	34	46	39	41	47	56	63	63	68	64	60
• **Processing coca paste**	35	35	30	24	22	28	27	32	35	29	35	39
• **Processing cocaine base**	31	31	28	37	37	25	17	5	2	3	1	1
Farmgate value of coca leaf and derivatives[18] (US dollars, millions)												
• **Coca leaf, fresh**	153	129	187	155	200	n.a.	188	211	170	247	287	356
• **Coca paste**	224	206	249	137	153	n.a.	122	133	128	138	176	186
• **Cocaine base**	467	349	499	332	142	n.a.	109	26	15	22	15	18
• **Total**	843	683	934	623	496	443	420	370[19]	313[20]	408[21]	479	560
Total farmgate value as a percent of GDP[22]												
• **National**	0.7	0.5	0.5	0.3	0.2	0.2	0.2	0.2	0.2	0.3	0.3	0.4
• **Agricultural**	6	5	5	3	3	3	3	3	3	3	3	3

Continued

Table B.1 *Continued*

	2005	2006	2007	2008	2009	2010	2011	2012	2013[1]	2014	2015	2016
Household data												
Households engaging in cultivation[23]	68,600	67,000	80,000	59,300	56,900	63,700	62,400	60,600[24]	61,700[25]	64,500[26]	74,500	106,900
Persons associated with all households[27]	336,150	324,950[28]	383,000	238,347	233,688	310,130[29]	300,000	303,000	308,500	322,500	372,500	534,500
Persons per household[30] **(average)**	4.9	4.85[31]	4.8	4.0	4.1	4.9	4.8	5.0	5.0	5.0	5.0	5.0
Net cultivation per household[32] **(hectares)**	1.25	1.16	1.24	1.37[33]	1.20	0.97	1.03	0.79	.78	1.07	1.29	1.37
Gross income[34] (US dollars)												
• **Per household**[35]	12,300	10,194	11,675	10,508	8,710	6,950	6,731	6,106	5,073	6,326	6,430	5,239
• **Per person**[36]	2,500	n.a.[37]	2,440	2,616	2,120	1,427	1,400	1,220[38]	1,000[39]	1,160[40]	1,180[41]	960[42]
• **Per hectare of landholding**[43]	9,802	8,756	9,434	7,691	7,294	7,145	6,563	7,708	6,521	5,913	4,990	3,836
GDP per capita[44] **(US dollars)**	3,386	3,709	4,674	5,434	5,148	6,251	7,228	7,885	8,031	7,913	6,045	5,806
Addenda												
Eradication (hectares)												
• **Manual**	31,285[45]	41,346	66,392	96,003	60,565	43,804	35,201	30,456	22,121	11,703	13,473	18,227
• **Spraying**	138,775	172,025	153,134	133,496	104,772	101,940	103,302	100,549	47,052	55,532	37,199	0
• **Total**	170,060	213,371	219,526	229,499	165,337	145,744	138,503	131,005	69,173	67,235	50,672	18,227
Cocaine, potential production[46] **(metric tons)**	801	809	683	471	488	424	384	333	290	442	646	866

Sources: Eradication and potential cocaine production data are from United Nations Office on Drugs and Crime (2017, Part 2, 58–9) for 2005–14, unless noted otherwise and UNODC and Government of Colombia (2017, 11) for 2015 and 2016; per capita income data are from World Bank, https://data.worldbank.org/indicator/NY.GDP.PCAP.CD, downloaded on May 10, 2018; all other data are from then-year editions of the UNODC and Government of Colombia's, "Colombia Coca Cultivation Survey."

[1] UNODC and Government of Colombia (2014, summary fact sheet, n.p.) provide the following note, "Manufacturing data presented from 2013 has been adjusted within this report and is not comparable to data published within the 2012 report." For more information, see UNODC and Government of Colombia (2014, 119–23).

[2]Assessed net of eradication at year end, as reported in both then-year surveys and UNODC (2017, Part 2, 58–59), without discrepancies, unless noted otherwise.

[3]Reported as 73,000 hectares in UNODC and Government of Colombia (2011, 8) and later publications, including UNODC (2017), to adjust for plots smaller than 0.25 hectares.

[4]As reported in then-year surveys, without accounting for later revisions of up to 5% (+/-) to 2008, 2009, 2011, 2012, and 2014 estimates.

[5]Rounded to the nearest 100th for consistency across years.

[6]Rounded to the nearest whole percent for consistency across years.

[7]Hand calculated as the average of the 2012 and 2014 yields, because yield data for yields for 2013 are not available, but data might be noncomparable (see note 1).

[8]Extrapolated from tonnage estimates (UNODC and Government of Colombia 2017, 64), using the national average yield for fresh coca leaf of 4,800 kilograms per hectare.

[9]Hand calculated as the average of the 2012 and 2014 yields, because yield data for yields for 2013 are not available, but data might be non-comparable (see note 1).

[10]Extrapolated from tonnage estimates (UNODC and Government of Colombia 2017, 64), using the national average yield for fresh coca leaf of 4,800 kilograms per hectare.

[11]The amount of income that a grower could obtain from marketing only coca leaf, coca paste, or cocaine base, without deductions for costs of inputs.

[12]All figures as reported in then-year surveys, unless noted otherwise, but figures for 2012–16 do not align with simple calculations, using yield and price data.

[13]Shown in UNODC and Government of Colombia (2011, 59) as the product of the unrounded yield estimate, 4,632, and price estimate.

[14]This estimate and the corresponding value-added estimate do not match the estimates in UNODC and Government of Colombia (2011, 59), because the estimates in the report were based incorrectly on the prior-year price (i.e., $1,249 per kilogram), instead of the current-year price (i.e., $1,475 per kilogram) (see Tables 27 and 30).

[15]UNODC and Government of Colombia use the term "value added" for the percentage differences in gross income per hectare, or markup, if a grower were to produce and sell coca paste or cocaine base, as compared to selling leaf.

[16]As reported in then-year surveys for 2005–10, unless noted otherwise, and as hand calculated for 2011–16.

[17]All figures as reported in then-year surveys, but the shares for 2007 do not sum to 100.

[18]UNODC and Government of Colombia estimate farmgate value without deductions for costs of inputs.

[19]UNODC and Government of Colombia (2014, summary fact sheet, n.p.) report as $381 million, amounting to 0.2% of GDP and 3% of agricultural GDP.

[20]UNODC and Government of Colombia (2015, 12) report as $292 million, amounting to 0.2% of GDP and 2% of agricultural GDP.

[21]UNODC and Government of Colombia (2016, 12) report as $400 million, amounting to 0.2% of GDP and 3% of agricultural GDP.

Continued

Table B.1 *Continued*

[22]All figures as reported in the summary fact sheet with each then-year survey, rounded to the nearest 10th, which sometimes differed from figures as reported in the main text.

[23]Rounded to the nearest 100 for consistency across years.

[24]Reported as 65,300 households in UNODC and Government of Colombia (2014), without explanation for revision.

[25]Reported as 60,600 households in UNODC and Government of Colombia (2015), without explanation for revision.

[26]Reported as 67,000 households in UNODC and Government of Colombia (2016), to account for the latest available data from the Catatumbo and Central regions.

[27]As reported in then-year surveys for 2005–11 and as hand calculated for 2012–16, using data on numbers of households and estimates of persons per household from surveys.

[28]Hand calculated from the average of persons per household in 2005 and 2007 and the number of households in 2006, because data for persons associated with all households and persons per household for 2006 are not available.

[29]This estimate includes an adjustment for small plots and is not fully comparable with previous estimates (UNODC and Government of Colombia 2011, 59).

[30]As hand calculated for 2005–11, using data on numbers of households and persons from then-year surveys, and as reported in then-year surveys for 2012–16.

[31]Hand calculated as the average of 2005 and 2007, because data for 2006 are not available.

[32]All figure as hand calculated.

[33]This hand-calculated figure differs substantially from the estimate in UNODC and Government of Colombia (2009, 55), i.e., 1.2 hectares per household.

[34]Gross income per household and per person are estimated for coca and derivates, without deductions for costs of inputs.

[35]As reported in then-year annual surveys for 2005–10 and as hand calculated from survey data for 2011–16.

[36]As reported in then-year annual surveys for all years, with any substantial revisions or discrepancies between reported figures and hand-calculated figures noted separately.

[37]Hand calculated from the average of persons per household in 2005 and 2007 and the number of households in 2006, to arrive at a total number of persons, the divisor, because data for persons associated with all households and persons per household for 2006 are not available.

[38]UNODC and Government of Colombia (2014, summary fact sheet, n.p.) reported as $1,150 without explanation, but alongside revised income and household estimates.

[39]UNODC and Government of Colombia (2015, 11) reported as $1,040 without explanation, but alongside revised income and household estimates.

[40]As reported by UNODC and Government of Colombia (2015, 12, 64), but hand calculation is $1,265.

[41]As reported by UNODC and Government of Colombia (2016, 12, 60), but hand calculation is $1,286.

[42]As reported by UNODC and Government of Colombia (2017, 12, 87), but hand calculation is $1,047.

[43]All figures as hand calculated.

[44]Data on gross domestic product downloaded from https://data.worldbank.org/indicator/NY.GDP.PCAP.CD on May 10, 2018.

[45]This estimate and the corresponding estimate for aerial spraying are as reported in UNODC and Government of Colombia (2006, 6; 2007, 6).

[46]Estimated as 100% pure cocaine.

APPENDIX C

Where in Colombia Does Coca Grow?

Coca occupies a modest share of Colombia's land in cash crops, but more Departments than not feel its presence. In recent years, coca cultivation has occurred in over 20 of the 32 Departments in Colombia (Table C.1), with three (Nariño, Putamayo, and Norte de Santander) accounting for upwards of 60 percent of the country's total cultivation in 2016. Adding the cultivation of the fourth- and fifth-ranked Departments (Cauca and Caquetá), brings the cumulative tally to 78 percent and adding the sixth- through tenth-ranked Departments brings it to almost 98 percent.

A year-by-year examination of data from 2001 to 2016, suggests a slightly more complex story, with a decline in concentration over the mid-to-late 2000s and a resurgence in concentration in recent years, tracking aggregate production (Figure C.1). Although cultivation has increased recently among nearly all the top-ranking Departments, the increases have been greatest, proportionally, in the top-most-ranking Department, Nariño.

The historical data also suggest the potential for ebbs and flows with Departments—reductions in cultivation need not be permanent—and for cultivation to shift across regions and Departments, much as it does across countries. Among the clearest examples of ebbing and flowing, cultivation in Norte de Santander dropped from 9,145 hectares in 2001 to just 488 hectares in 2006, only to rebound over the next decade and regain a leading position in the Departmental rankings. Nariño and Putamayo have tended to be leaders throughout, but even Putumayo, has seen change. Cultivation in that Department fell from a high of 47,120 hectares in 2001 to a low of 4,386 hectares in 2004, ranking seventh, behind Meta, Nariño, Guaviare, Caquetá, Antioquia, and Vichada. By 2007, cultivation in Putumayo had risen to 14,813 hectares, but it waned and waxed again, before rising to 25,162 hectares in 2016. Similarly, Caquetá and other Departments have experienced their ups and downs as producers.

Table C.1 Coca cultivation by Department in order of rank as of December 31, 2016

	2001	2002	2003	2004	2005	2006	2007	2008	2009	2010	2011	2012	2013	2014	2015	2016
Nariño	7,494	15,132	17,628	14,154	13,875	15,607	20,259	19,612	17,639	15,951	17,231	10,733	13,177	17,285	29,755	42,627
Putumayo	47,120	13,726	7,559	4,386	8,963	12,253	14,813	9,658	5,633	4,785	9,951	6,148	7,667	13,609	20,068	25,162
Norte de Santander	9,145	8,042	4,471	3,056	844	488	1,946	2,886	3,037	1,889	3,490	4,516	6,345	6,944	11,527	24,831
Cauca	3,139	2,121	1,443	1,265	2,705	2,105	4,168	5,422	6,597	5,908	6,066	4,325	3,326	6,389	8,660	12,595
Caquetá	14,516	8,412	7,230	6,500	4,988	4,967	6,318	4,303	3,985	2,578	3,327	3,695	4,322	6,542	7,712	9,343
Antioquia	3,171	3,029	4,273	5,168	6,414	6,156	9,926	6,096	5,096	5,350	3,104	2,725	991	2,293	2,402	8,855
Guaviare	25,553	27,380	16,163	9,770	8,658	9,477	9,299	6,629	8,660	5,701	6,839	3,851	4,725	5,658	5,423	6,838
Meta	11,425	9,219	12,814	18,740	17,305	11,063	10,386	5,525	4,469	3,008	3,040	2,699	2,898	5,042	5,002	5,464
Bolívar	4,824	2,735	4,470	3,401	3,670	2,382	5,632	5,847	5,346	3,324	2,207	1,968	925	1,565	1,044	4,094
Córdoba	652	385	838	1,535	3,136	1,216	1,858	1,710	3,113	3,889	1,088	1,046	439	560	1,363	2,668
Chocó	354	0	453	323	1,025	816	1,080	2,794	1,789	3,158	2,511	3,429	1,661	1,741	1,489	1,803
Valle del Cauca	184	111	37	45	28	281	453	2,089	997	665	981	482	398	561	690	752
Vichada	9,166	4,909	3,818	4,692	7,826	5,523	7,218	3,174	3,228	2,743	2,264	1,242	713	511	683	699
Amazonas	532	783	625	783	897	692	541	836	312	338	122	98	110	173	111	167
Vaupés	1,918	1,486	1,157	1,084	671	460	307	557	395	721	277	254	184	109	33	97
Santander	415	465	632	1,124	981	866	1,325	1,791	1,066	673	595	111	77	26	21	37
Magdalena	480	644	484	706	213	271	278	391	169	121	46	37	37	9	7	35

César	0	0	0	0	0	0	0	5	0	0	0	13	13	10	32	26
Guainía	1,318	748	726	721	752	753	623	625	606	446	318	301	81	66	37	22
Boyacá	245	118	594	359	342	441	79	197	204	105	93	10	17	14	8	15
Arauca	2,749	2,215	539	1,552	1,883	1,306	2,116	447	430	247	132	81	69	25	17	9
La Guajira	385	354	275	556	329	166	87	160	182	134	16	10	6	0	0	0
Cundinamarca	22	57	57	72	56	120	131	12	0	32	18	0	0	0	0	0
Caldas	0	0	54	358	189	461	56	187	186	46	46	16	8	0	0	0
Total	144,807	102,071	86,340	80,350	85,750	77,870	98,899	80,953	73,139	61,812	63,762	47,790	48,189	69,132	96,084	146,139

Source: UNODC and Government of Colombia (2017, 214), Anexo 5, "Tabla 45, Serie histórica de cultivos de coca, 2001–2016, hectáreas."

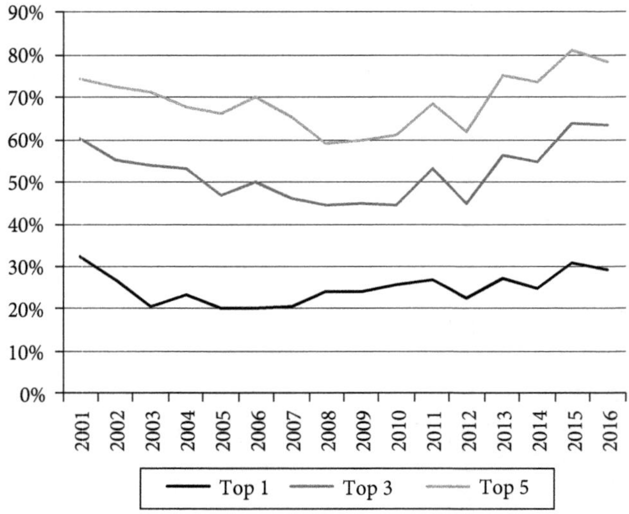

Figure C.1 Trends in the concentration of cultivation among Departments (Cultivation shares for the top 1, 3, and 5 Departments, respectively)

Source: Authors' analysis of data from UNODC and Government of Colombia (2017, 214), Anexo 5, "Tabla 45, Serie histórica de cultivos de coca, 2001–2016, hectáreas."

References

Abas, M., Ostrovschi, N.V., Prince, M., Gorceag, V.I., Trigub, C. and Oram, S. (2013). Risk factors for mental disorders in women survivors of human trafficking: A historical cohort study. *BMC Psychiatry* 13: 204. doi:10.1186/1471-244X-13-204.

Ackerman, F. and Heinzerling, L. (2002). Pricing the priceless: Cost–benefit analysis of environmental protection. *University of Pennsylvania Law Review*, 50, 1553–84.

Adams, J. (2003). Risk and morality: Three framing devices. In R. Ericson and A. Doyle (Eds.). *Risk and Morality* (pp. 87–103). Toronto, ON: University of Toronto Press.

Adriaenssen, A. (2017). *Publieke ernstpercepties van criminaliteit en het verband met televisiegebruik*. The Hague: Boom.

Adriaenssen, A., Karstedt, S., Paoli, L., and Visschers, J. (2019). Taking Crime Seriously: Conservation Values and Legal Cynicism as Predictors of Public Perceptions of the Seriousness of Crime. *International Criminal Justice Review* 29(4): 317–334.

Adriaenssen, A., Paoli, L., Karsedt, S., Visschers, J., Greenfield, V.A., and Pleysier, S. (2020). Public perceptions of the seriousness of crime: Weighing the harm and the wrong. *The European Journal of Criminology*, 17, 127–50.

Aebi, M.F., Akdeniz, G., Barclay, G., Campistol, C., Caneppele, S., Gruszczyńska, B., Harrendorf, S., Heiskanen, M., Hysi, S., Jörg-Martin Jehle, J.-M., Anniina Jokinen, A., Kensey, A., Killias, M., Lewis, C.G., Savona, E., Smit, E., and Þórisdóttir, R. (2014). *European Sourcebook of Crime and Criminal Justice Statistics 2014* (5th ed.). Helsinki: Academic Bookstore.

Aebi, M. F. and Tiago, M. M. (2018). SPACE I – 2018—Council of Europe Annual Penal Statistics: Prison populations. Updated June 11, 2019. Strasbourg, France: Council of Europe. Retrieved from https://wp.unil.ch/space/space-i/annual-reports/ (accessed October 19, 2021).

Akerlof, G. and Shiller, R. (2015). *Phishing for Phools: The Economics of Manipulation and Deception*. Princeton, NJ: Princeton University Press.

Alter A.M., Kernochan, J., and Darley, J.M. (2007). Transgression wrongfulness outweighs its harmfulness as a determinant of sentence severity. *Law and Human Behavior*, 31(4), 319–35.

Álvarez, M.D. (2002). Illicit crops and bird conservation priorities in Colombia. *Conservation Biology*, 16(4), 1086–96.

Angrist, J.D. and Kugler, A.D. (2008). Rural windfall or a new resource curse? Coca, income, and civil conflict in Colombia. *The Review of Economics and Statistics*, 90(2), 191–215.

Anielski, M. and Braaten, A. (2008). *The Socio-Economic Impact of Gambling (SEIG) Framework: An Assessment Framework for Canada.* Edmonton, AB: Anielski Management, Inc. Retrieved from http://www.anielski.com/Documents/SEIG%20Framework.pdf (accessed June 20, 2012).

Antkowiak, T.M. (2011). An emerging mandate for international courts: Victim centered remedies and restorative justice. *Stanford Journal of International Law,* 47, 279–332.

Armenteras, D., Rudas, G., Rodriguez, N., Sua, S., and Romero, M. (2006). Patterns and causes of deforestation in the Colombian Amazon. *Ecological Indicators,* 6, 353–68.

Armenteras, D., Rodríguez, N., Retana, J., and Morales M. (2011). Understanding deforestation in montane and lowland areas of the Andes in Colombia. *Regional Environmental Change,* 11, 693–705.

Armenteras, D., Cabrera, E., Rodríguez, N., Retana, J. (2013a). National and regional determinants of tropical deforestation in Colombia. *Regional Environmental Change,* 13, 1181–93.

Armenteras, D., Rodriguez, N., Retana, J. (2013b). Landscape dynamics in northwestern Amazonia: An assessment of pastures, fire and illicit crops as drivers of tropical deforestation. *PLoS One,* 8, art. e54310.

Ashworth, A. (2000). Is the criminal law a lost cause? *Law Quarterly Review,* 116, 225–56.

Ashworth, A. (2006). *Principles of Criminal Law* (5th ed.). Oxford, UK: Oxford University Press.

Ashworth, A. and Zedner, L. (2014). *Preventive Justice.* Oxford, UK: Oxford University Press.

Ashworth, A., Zedner, L., and Tomlin, P. (Eds.) (2013). *Prevention and the Limits of Criminal Law.* Oxford, UK: Oxford University Press.

Bagaric, M. (2000–1). Proportionality in sentencing: Its justification, meaning and role. *Current Issues in Criminal Justice,* 12, 143–65.

Bai, S.H. and Ogbourne, S.M. (2016). Glyphosate: Environmental contamination, toxicity, and potential risks to human health via food contamination. *Environmental Science and Pollution Research,* 23(19), 18988–9001.

Barbalet, J.M. (1998). *Emotion, Social Theory, and Social Structure: A Macrosociological Approach.* Cambridge, UK: Cambridge University Press.

Barona Vilar, S. (2005). Law, police and the practice of prosecution in Spain. In P.J. Tak (Ed.). *Tasks and Powers of the Prosecution Services in the EU Member States,* vol. I (pp. 405–28). Nijmegen, The Netherlands: Wolf.

Basiago, A.D. (1995). Methods of defining "sustainability." *Sustainable Development,* 33, 109–19.

Bauman, Z. (2000). Social uses of law and order. In D. Garland and R. Sparks (Eds.). *Criminology and Social Theory* (pp. 23–45). Oxford, UK: Oxford University Press.

Bayley, D.H. and Shearing, C.D. (1996). The Future of Policing. *Law & Society Review,* 30(3) (1996), 585–606.

Bazemore, G. and Walgrave, L. (1999). Introduction: Restorative justice and the international juvenile justice crisis. In G. Bazemore and L. Walgrave (Eds.).

Restorative Juvenile Justice: Repairing the Harm of Youth Crime (pp. 3–15). Monsey, NY: Criminal Justice Press.

Beard, J. (2017). Sentences of imprisonment for public protection. House of Commons Library Briefing Paper No. 06086. October 25.

Beccaria, C. ([1764, 1872] 1995). *On Crimes and Punishments and Other Writings*. Ed. R. Bellamy. Cambridge, UK: Cambridge University Press.

Beck, U. (1992). *Risk Society: Towards a New Modernity*. London, UK: Sage.

Becker, G.S. (1968). Crime and punishment: An economic approach. *Journal of Political Economy*, 76(2), 169–217.

Becker, H.S. (1963). *Outsiders: Studies in the Sociology of Deviance*. New York, NY: Macmillan.

Beirne, P. and South, N. (Eds.) (2007). *Issues in Green Criminology: Confronting Harms Against Environments, Humanity and Other Animals*. Cullompton, UK: Willan.

Beittel, J.S. (2017). *Colombia: Background and U.S. Relations*. CRS Report, R43813. Washington, DC: Congressional Research Service, November 14.

Beittel, J.S. and Rosen, L.W. (2017). *Colombia's Changing Approach to Drug Policy*. CRS Report, R44779. Washington, DC: Congressional Research Service, March 10.

Belang van Limburg, Het (2002). Grote drugsvangst in Antwerpse haven [The large drug seizure at Antwerp Port]. Retrieved from http://www.hbvl.be/Archief/guid/grote–drugsvangst–in–antwerpse–haven aspx?artikel=dbafd62e–c24f–4c40–87ef–7645b2e5f514 (accessed June 25, 2012).

Belga (2020). Coke blijft naar Antwerpen stromen [Coke continues to flow to Antwerp]. *Knack*. Retrieved from https://www.knack.be/nieuws/belgie/coke-blijft-naar-antwerpen-stromen/article-news-1594169.html (accessed August 7, 2020).

Bentham, J. (1843). *The Works of Jeremy Bentham, Principles of the Civil Code*. Edinburgh, UK: William Tait.

Berman, H.J. (1983). *Law and Revolution: The Formation of Western Legal Tradition*. Cambridge, MA: Harvard University Press.

Bernal, M.H., Solomon, K.R., and Carrasquilla, G. (2009). Toxicity of formulated glyphosate (Glyphos) and Cosmo-Flux to Larval Colombian Frogs 2. Field and laboratory microcosm acute toxicity. *Journal of Environmental Toxicology and Environmental Health, Part A*, 72(15–16), 966–73.

Biondich, A.M. and Joslin, J.D. (2015). Coca: A high altitude remedy of the ancient Incas. *Wilderness and Environmental Medicine*, 26, 567–71.

Biondich, A.M. and Joslin, J.D. (2016). Coca: The history and medical significance of an ancient tradition. *Emergency Medicine International*, doi:10.1155/2016/4048764.

Bjørgo, T. (2016). *Preventing Crime: A Holistic Approach*. New York, NY: Palgrave-Macmillan.

BKA, Bundeskriminalamt (2009). *Organisierte Kriminalität 2008 Bundeslagebild—Pressefreie Kurzfassung [Organized Crime 2008 Federal Situation Report—Public Summary]*. Wiesbaden, Germany: BKA.

Boffey, D. (2018, February 20). Netherlands becoming a narco-state, warn Dutch police. *The Guardian*. Retrieved from https://www.theguardian.com/world/2018/feb/20/netherlands-becoming-a-narco-state-warn-dutch-police (accessed 2 March 2018).

Bonger, W. ([1932] 1936). *An Introduction to Criminology*. London, UK: Methuen and Co.

Bottoms, A. (2002). Morality, crime, compliance and public policy. In A. Bottoms and M. Tonry (Eds.). *Ideology, Crime and Criminal Justice: A Symposium in Honour of Sir Leon Radzinowicz* (pp. 20–54). Cullompton, UK: Willan.

Bottoms, A. (2006). Incivilities, offence, and social order in residential communities. In A. von Hirsch and A.P. Simester (Eds.). *Incivilities: Regulating Offensive Behaviour* (pp. 239–80). London, UK: Hart.

Bottoms, A. (2008). The relationship between theory and empirical observations in criminology. In R.D. King and E. Wincup (Eds.). *Doing Research on Crime and Justice* (2nd ed., pp. 75–116). Oxford, UK: Oxford University Press.

Bottoms, A. (n.d.). *Criminology, Social Order and Compliance with Law*. Mimeo.

Bottoms, A. and Tankebe, J. (2012). Beyond procedural justice: A dialogic approach to legitimacy in criminal justice. *Journal of Criminal Law and Criminology*, 102, 119–70.

Bottoms, A. and Tankebe, J. (2017). Police legitimacy and the authority of the state. In A. du Bois-Pedain, M. Ulväng, and P. Asp (Eds.). *Criminal Law and the Authority of the State* (pp. 47–88). London, UK: Hart.

Boukli, A. and J. Kotze (Eds.) (2018). *Zemiology: Reconnecting Crime and Social Harm*. Cham, UK: Palgrave.

Brain, R.A. and Solomon, K.R. (2009). Comparison of the hazards posed to amphibians by the glyphosate spray control program versus the chemical and physical activities of coca production in Colombia. *Journal of Environmental Toxicology and Environmental Health, Part A*, 72(15–16), 937–48.

Boutellier, H. (2000). *Crime and Morality: The Significance of Criminal Justice in Post-Modern Culture*. Dordrecht, The Netherlands: Kluwer.

Braithwaite, J. (1990). *Crime, Shame and Reintegration*. Cambridge, UK: Cambridge University Press.

Braithwaite, J. (2000). The new regulatory state and the transformation of criminology. *The British Journal of Criminology*, 40, 222–38

Braithwaite, J. (2002). *Restorative Justice and Responsive Regulation*. Oxford, UK: Oxford University Press.

Braithwaite, J. (2004). Restorative justice and de-professionalization, *Good Society*, 13(1), 28–31.

Braithwaite, J. and Drahos, P. (Eds.) (2000). *Global Business Regulation*. Melbourne, AU: Cambridge University Press.

Braithwaite, J. and Pettit, P. (1990). *Not Just Deserts*. Oxford, UK: Oxford University Press.

Brand, S. and Price, R. (2000). *The Economic and Social Costs of Crime*. London, UK: Home Office.

Brisman, A. and South, N. (2017). Green criminology. In A. Liebling, S. Maruna, and L. McAra (Eds.). *The Oxford Handbook of Criminology* (6th ed., pp. 327–49). Oxford, UK: Oxford University Press.

Brodeur, J.P. and Shearing, C. (2005). Configuring security and justice. *The European Journal of Criminology*, 2(4), 379–406.

Brogden, M. and Nijhar P. (2006). Crime, abuse and social harm: Towards an integrated approach. In A. Wahidin and M. Cain (Eds.). *Ageing, Crime and Society* (pp. 35–52). London, UK: Routledge.

Brown, R. (2018). The Mexican drug war and early-life health: The impact of violent crime on birth outcomes. *Demography*, 55(1), 319–40.

Brundtland G.H. (1987). *Our Common Future: The World Commission on Environment and Development*. Oxford, UK: Oxford University Press.

Bruni, L., Comim, F., and Pugno, M. (2008). Introduction. In L. Bruni, F. Comim, and M. Pugno (Eds.). *Capability and Happiness* (pp. 1–15). Oxford, UK: Oxford University Press.

Bryen, A.Z. (2016). Crimes against the individual: Violence and sexual crimes. In P.J. Plessis, C. Ando, and K. Tuori (Eds.). *Oxford Handbook of Roman Law and Society* (pp. 322–31). Oxford, UK: Oxford University Press.

Buehler, E.D. (2021). Justice Expenditures and Employment in the United States, 2017. U.S. Department of Justice, Office of Justice Programs, Bureau of Justice Statistics, July. Retrieved from https://bjs.ojp.gov/library/publications/justice-expenditures-and-employment-united-states-2017 (accessed October 19, 2021).

Bulstrode, N., Banks, S., and Shrotria, S. (2002). The outcome of drug smuggling by "body-packers": The British experience. *Annals of the Royal College of Surgeons of England*, 84(1), 35–8.

Bureau of Justice Statistics (2017). Data Collection: National Crime Victimization Survey (NCVS). Retrieved from https://www.bjs.gov/index.cfm?ty=dcdetail&iid=245 (accessed February 25, 2018).

Burfisher, M. (2011). *Introduction to Computable General Equilibrium Models*. Cambridge, UK: Cambridge University Press.

Burton, K. (2007). Criminalisation: Applying a living-standard analysis to non-consensual photography and distribution. *Queensland University Technology Law and Justice Journal*, 7, 464–76.

Buzan, B. (1983). *People, States and Fear: The National Security Problem in International Relations*. London, UK: Harvester Wheatsheaf.

Cachet, A., de Kimpe, S., Ponsaers, P., and Ringeling, A. (Eds.) (2008). *Governance of Security in the Netherlands and Belgium*. The Hague: Boom.

Cain, M. and Howe, A. (Eds.) (2008). *Women, Crime and Social Harm: Towards Criminology for the Global Era*. Oxford, UK: Hart.

Calhoun, C. (2002). Counterfactual reasoning. In C. Calhoun (Ed.). *Dictionary of the Social Sciences (p.* 98). New York, NY: Oxford University Press.

Cameron W.B. (1963). Informal sociology: a casual introduction to sociological thinking. New York, NY: Random House.

Canton, R. (2017). *Why Punish? An Introduction to the Philosophy of Punishment*. Basingstoke, UK: Palgrave.

Cárdenas, M. and Rozo, S. (2008). Does crime lower growth? Evidence from Colombia. Commission on Growth and Development, Working Paper No. 30. Washington, DC: The World Bank on behalf of the Commission on Growth and Development.

Carrillo González, L. (2014). Social consequences of the cultivation of coca in Afro-Colombian communities in Caquetá: Analysis of the relationship among the illicit economy, the traditional farming practices, and their role in food security. *El Ágora USB Medellín–Colombia*, 14(1), 203–21.

Carson, E.A. (2018). Prisoners in 2016. Bureau of Justice Statistics, NCJ 251149.

Cartwright, N. and Stegenga, J. (2011). A theory of evidence for evidence-based policy *Proceedings of the British Academy*, 171, 289–319.

Casey, N. (2017, July 18). After decades of war, Colombian farmers face a new test: Peace. *The New York Times*. Retrieved from https://www.nytimes.com/2017/07/18/world/americas/colombia-cocaine-farc-peace-drugs.html (accessed November 28, 2017).

Cassese, A., Acquaviva, G., Fan, M., and Whiting, A. (2011). *International Criminal Law: Cases and Commentary*. Oxford, UK: Oxford University Press.

Caulkins, J.P. and Reuter, P. (1997). Setting goals for drug policy: Harm reduction or use reduction? *Addiction*, 92(9), 1143–50.

Caulkins, J.P. and Reuter, P. (2009). Towards a harm reduction approach to enforcement. *Safer Communities*, 8, 9–23.

Caulkins J.P., Reuter P., and Coulson C. (2011). Basing drug scheduling decisions on scientific ranking of harmfulness: False promise from false premises. *Addiction*, 106, 1886–90.

Cel voor Financiële Informatieverwerking (2009). 16de Activiteitenverslag 2009 [16th report of activities 2009]. Retrieved from http://www.ctif–cfi.be/website/images/NL/annual_report/2009_ctif_cfi_nl.pdf (accessed June 8, 2012).

Central Intelligence Agency (2010). *The World Factbook*. Retrieved from https://www.cia.gov/library/publications/the–world–factbook/ (accessed June 25, 2012). For more recent population estimates, see Central Intelligence Agency (2021). The World Factbook. Retrieved from https://www.cia.gov/the-world-factbook/ (accessed October 24, 2021)

Centrale Dienst Drugs and Federale Politie België (2010). Statistieken inbeslagnames cocaïne België. [Statistical data cocaine seizures in Belgium]. Unpublished memo.

Centrum voor gelijkheid van kansen en voor racismebestrijding (2006). *Mensenhandel–smokkel. Jaarverslag 2005 [Human Trafficking and Smuggling. Annual Report 2005]*. Brussels, Belgium: Centrum.

Centrum voor gelijkheid van kansen en voor racismebestrijding (2008). *Mensenhandel–Smokkel. Jaarverslag 2007 [Human Trafficking and Smuggling. Annual Report 2007]*. Brussels, Belgium: Centrum.

Centrum voor gelijkheid van kansen en voor racismebestrijding (2009). *Mensenhandel–Smokkel. Jaarverslag 2008 [Human Trafficking and Smuggling. Annual Report 2009]*. Brussels, Belgium: Centrum.

Centrum voor gelijkheid van kansen en voor racismebestrijding (2010). *Mensenhandel–Smokkel in een Schijn van Wettelijkheid. Jaarverslag 2009 [Human Trafficking and Smuggling in the Appearance of Legality. Annual Report 2009]*. Brussels, Belgium: Centrum.

Centrum voor gelijkheid van kansen en voor racismebestrijding (2011a). *Mensenhandel En Mensensmokkel: Sociale Fraude Bestrijden Is Mensenhandel*

Voorkomen. Jaarverslag 2010 [Human Trafficking and Human Smuggling: Fighting Social Fraud Is Preventing Human Trafficking. Annual Report 2010]. Brussels, Belgium: Centrum.

Centrum voor gelijkheid van kansen en voor racismebestrijding (2011b*). Migratie. Jaarverslag 2010 [Migration. Annual Report 2010]*. Brussels, Belgium: Centrum.

Centrum voor gelijkheid van kansen en voor racismebestrijding (2013). *Mensenhandel En Mensensmokkel: Bouwen Aan Vertrouwen. Jaarverslag 2012 [Human Trafficking And Human Smuggling: Building Trust. Annual Report 2012]*. Brussels, Belgium: Centrum.

Centrum voor gelijkheid van kansen en voor racismebestrijding (2014). *Mensenhandel: Bruggen Slaan. Jaarverslag 2013 van de Onafhankelijke Rapporteur Mensenhandel België [Human Trafficking; Building Bridges. Annual Report 2013 of the Independent Rapporteur on Human Trafficking in Belgium]*. Brussels, Belgium: Centrum.

Chadid, M.A., Dávalos, L.M., Molina-Escobar, J.M., and Armenteras, D. (2015). A Bayesian spatial model highlights distinct dynamics in deforestation from coca and pastures in an Andean biodiversity hotspot. *Forests*, 6, 3828–46.

Chalmers, J. and Leverick, F. (2014). Quantifying criminalization. In R.A. Duff, L. Farmer, S.E. Marshall, M. Renzo, and V. Tadros (Eds.). *Criminalization: The Political Morality of the Criminal Law* (pp. 54–79). Oxford, UK: Oxford University Press.

Chambliss, W.J. (1989). State-organized crime. *Criminology*, 27(2), 183–208.

Chambliss, W.J., Michalowski, R., and Kramer, R. (Eds.) (2013). *State Crime in the Global Age*. New York, NY: Willan.

Chouvy, P.-A. and Laniel, L.R. (2007). Agricultural drug economies: Cause or alternative to intra-state conflicts? *Crime, Law and Social Change*, 48, 133–50.

Christie, N. (1977). Conflicts as property. *The British Journal of Criminology*, 17(1), 1–15.

Christie, N. (1981). *Limits to Pain: The Role of Punishment in Penal Policy*. Oslo, Norway: Universitetsforlaget.

Christie, N. (1993). *Crime Control as Industry: Towards Gulags, Western Style?* London, UK: Routledge.

Clark, D.A. (2005). Sen's capability approach and the many spaces of human well-being. *The Journal of Development Studies*, 41(8), 1339–68.

Clark, D.A. (2006). *The Capability Approach: Its Development, Critiques and Recent Advances. GPRG-WPS-032*, Global Poverty Research Group. Retrieved from http://www.gprg.org/pubs/workingpapers/pdfs/gprg–wps–032.pdf (accessed November 24, 2015).

Clarke, K.M. (2015). We ask for justice, you give us law. In C. de Vos, S. Kendall, and C. Stahn (Eds.). *The Politics and Practice of International Criminal Court Interventions* (pp. 272–301). Cambridge, UK: Cambridge University Press.

Clarke, R.V. (2004). Technology, criminology and crime science. *The European Journal on Criminal Policy and Research*, 10, 55–63.

Clarkson, C., Cretney, A., Davis, G., and Shepherd, J.P. (1994). Assaults: The relationship between seriousness, criminalisation and punishment. *Criminal Law Review*, January, 4–20.

Clear, T.R. (1994). *Harm in American Penology: Offenders, Victims and Their Communities*. Albany, NY: State University of New York Press.

Clear, T.R. (2007). *Imprisoning Communities: How Mass Incarceration Makes Disadvantaged Neighborhoods Worse*. New York, NY: Oxford University Press.

Cohen, L.E. and Felson, M. (1979). Social change and crime rate trends: A routine activity approach. *American Sociological Review*, 44, 588–608.

Cohen, M.A. (1988). Pain, suffering and jury awards: A study of the cost of crime to victims. *Law and Society Review*, 22, 537–55.

Cohen, M.A. (2005). *The Costs of Crime and Justice*. London, UK: Routledge.

Cohen, M.A. and Piquero, A.R. (2009). New evidence on the monetary value of saving a high risk youth. *Journal of Quantitative Criminology*, 25, 25–49.

Cohen, M.A., Rust, R.T., Stehen, S., and Tidd, S. (2004). Willingness-to-pay for crime control programs. *Criminology*, 42, 89–110.

Cohen, S. (1972). *Folk Devils and Moral Panics: The Creation of the Mods and Rockers*, London, UK: Routledge.

Cohen, S. ([1979] 2016). Some modest and unrealistic proposals. *New Society*, March 29: 731–34. Reprinted in T. Daems (Ed.). *Outside Criminology: Selected Essays by Stanley Cohen* (pp. 79–87). London, UK: Routledge.

Cohen, S. (1988). *Against Criminology*. New Brunswick, NJ: Transaction.

Cohen, S. (1993). Human rights and crimes of the state: The culture of denial. *The Australian and New Zealand Journal of Criminology*, 26(2), 97–115.

Coicaud, J.M. (2013). Crime, Justice and Legitimacy: A brief theoretical inquiry. In J. Tankebe and A. Liebling (Eds.). *Legitimacy and Criminal Justice: An International Exploration* (pp. 37–59). Oxford, UK: Oxford University Press.

Coleman, J., Hershovitz, S., and Mendlow, G. (2015). Theories of the common law of torts. In E.N. Zalta (Ed.). *The Stanford Encyclopedia of Philosophy*. Retrieved from https://plato.stanford.edu/entries/tort-theories/ (accessed September 2, 2021).

Colman, C., de Middeleer, F., Spapens, A., van Nimwegen, S., Ceulen, R., Gerbrands, S., Paoli, L., and Roevens, E. (2018). *De Grens Voorbij: Belgische En Nederlandse Drugsmarkten In Beweging [Beyond the Border: Belgian and Dutch Drug Markets on the Move]*. The Hague: Boom.

Commission on Human Security (2003). *Human Security Now*. Washington, DC: Communications Development.

Cornell University Law School, Legal Information Institute. *Assault*. Retrieved from https://www.law.cornell.edu/wex/assault (accessed June 26, 2015).

Cornish, D.B. (1994). Crimes as scripts. In D. Zahm and P. Cromwell (Eds.). *Proceedings of the International Seminar on Environmental Criminology and Crime Analysis* (pp. 30–45). Tallahassee, FL: Florida Statistical Analysis Center and Florida Criminal Justice.

Corsaro, N., Hunt, E.D., Hipple, N.K., and McGarrell, E.F. (2012). The impact of drug market pulling levers policing on neighborhood violence: An evaluation of the High Point Drug Market Intervention. *Criminology and Public Policy*, 11(2), 167–99.

Corteen, K., Morley, S., Taylor, P., and Turner, J. (Eds.) (2016). *A Companion to Crime, Harm and Victimisation*. Bristol, UK: Policy Press.

Council of Europe (1950). European treaty series—No. 5, Convention for the protection of human rights and fundamental freedoms as amended by protocols No. 11 and No. 14. Rome, 4.XI.1950.

Council of Europe (2018). Chart of signatures and ratifications of Treaty 005: Convention for the protection of human rights and fundamental freedoms. Status as of 14/02/2018. Retrieved from https://www.coe.int/en/web/conventions/full-list/-/conventions/treaty/210?module=signatures-by-treaty&treatynum=005 (accessed September 2, 2021).

Council of the European Union (2004). EU Drugs Strategy (2005–2012). Retrieved from http://www.emcdda.europa.eu/html.cfm/index6790EN.html (accessed June 25, 2017).

Council of the European Union (2005). EU Drugs Action Plan (2005–2008). OJ 2005/C 168/01.

Council of the European Union (2009a). Council conclusions on model provisions, guiding the council's criminal law deliberations. 2979th Justice and Home Affairs Council Meeting. Retrieved from http://www.consilium.europa.eu/uedocs/cms_data/docs/pressdata/en/jha/111543.pdf (accessed June 25, 2017).

Council of the European Union (2009b). Council Decision 2009/426/JHA of 16 December 2008 on the Strengthening of Eurojust and amending decision 2002/187/JHA setting up Eurojust with a view to reinforcing the fight against serious crime. OJ L138, 14–32.

Council of the European Union (2009c). Council Decision of 6 April 2009 establishing the European Police Office (Europol) (2009/371/JHA), *OJ* L121, 37–66.

Council of the European Union (2010). Council conclusions on the creation and implementation of a EU policy cycle for organised and serious international crime. October 25, 15358/10.

Council of the European Union (2012). Serious and organised crime threat assessment (SOCTA) Methodology. Retrieved from https://data.consilium.europa.eu/doc/document/ST-12159-2012-INIT/en/pdf (accessed June 25, 2016).

Cox, L.A. (2008). What's wrong with risk matrices?, *Risk Analysis*, 28(2), 497–512.

Crawford, A. (2009). Governing through anti-social behaviour: Regulatory challenges to criminal justice. *The British Journal of Criminology*, 49(6), 810–31.

Cullen, F.T. (2013). Rehabilitation: Beyond nothing works. *Crime and Justice*, 42(1), 299–376.

Cullen, F.T. and Agnew, R. (Eds.) (2011). *Criminological Theory Past to Present.* New York, NY: Oxford University Press.

Czabański, J. (2008). *Estimates of Cost of Crime: History, Methodologies and Implications*. Berlin, Germany: Springer.

Dalby S. (2014). Rethinking geopolitics: Climate security in the Anthropocene. *Global Policing*, 5(1), 1–9.

Daly, K. and Proietti-Scifoni, G. (2011). Reparation and restoration. In M. Tonry (Ed.). *Oxford Handbook of Criminology and Criminal Justice* (pp. 207–53). New York, NY: Oxford University Press.

Dávalos-Álvarez, E. (2016). New answers to an old problem: Social investment and coca crops in Colombia. *International Journal of Drug Policy*, 31, 121–30.

Dávalos, L.M. (2001). The San Lucas mountain range in Colombia: How much conservation is owed to the violence? *Biodiversity and Conservation*, 10, 69–78.

Dávalos, L.M., Bejarano, A.C., and Correa, H.L. (2009). Disabusing cocaine: Pervasive myths and enduring realities of a globalised commodity. *International Journal of Drug Policy*, 20(5), 381–6.

Dávalos, L.M., Bejarano, A.C., Hall, M.A., Correa, H.L., Corthals, A., and Espejo, O.J. (2011). Forests and drugs: Coca-driven deforestation in tropical biodiversity hotspots. *Environmental Science and Technology*, 45, 1219–27.

Dávalos, L.M., Holmes, J.S., Rodríguez, N., and Armenteras, D. (2014). Demand for beef is unrelated to pasture expansion in northwestern Amazonia. *Biological Conservation*, 170, 64–73.

Dávalos, L.M., Sanchez, K.M., and Armenteras, D. (2016). Deforestation and coca cultivation rooted in twentieth-century development projects. *BioScience*, 66, 974–82.

Davies, P., Francis, P., and Wyatt, T. (2014). *Invisible Crimes and Social Harms*. Basingstoke, UK: Palgrave Macmillan.

DEA (See US Drug Enforcement Administration)

Decorte, T. (2000). *The Taming of Cocaine*. Brussels, Belgium: VUB Press.

Decorte, T., de Ruyver, B., Ponsaers, P., Bodein, M., Lacroix, A.C., Lauwers, S., and Tuteleers, P. (2004). *Drugs en Overlast: Studie van het Fenomeen, de Beheersing en de Effecten van Druggerelateerde Overlast en dit Vanuit Verschillende Invalshoeken [Drugs and Nuisance. Study of the Phenomenon, the Control and the Effects of Drug-Related Nuisance from Different Perspectives]*. Gent, Belgium: Academia Press.

De Coninck, D. (2014, April 21). Drie lijken en kalasjnikovschoten uit rijdende golfjes: De cokeoorlog in Antwerpen [Three corpses and Kalasjnikov shots from moving VW Golfs: The cocaine war in Antwerp]. *De Morgen*. Retrieved from https://www.demorgen.be/binnenland/drie-lijken-en-kalasjnikovschoten-uit-rijdende-golfjes-de-cokeoorlog-in-antwerpen-bb44238c/ (accessed February 25, 2018).

DeKeseredy, W. and Hinch, R. (1991). *Woman Abuse: Sociological Perspectives*. Toronto, ON: Thompson.

De Middeleer, F., van Nimwegen, S., Ceulen, R., Gerbrands, S., Roevens, E., Spapens, A. (…), and Colman, C. 2018. *Illegale Drugsmarkten In België En Nederland: Communicerende Vaten? [Illegal Drug Markets in Belgium and the Netherlands: Communicating Vessels?]*. Brussels, Belgium: Belspo.

Dernière Heure, Le (2007, June 7). Un policier arrête [A police officer arrested]. Retrieved from www.dhnet.be/infos/faits-divers/article/174647/un-policier-arrete.html (accessed February 25, 2012).

Devlin, P. (1965). *The Enforcement of Morals*. Oxford, UK: Oxford University Press.

Devroe, E., Edwards, A., and Ponsaers, P. (Eds.) (2017). *Policing European Metropolises: The Politics of Security in City-Regions*. London, UK: Routledge.

Dienst mensenhandel, Federale Politie (2008a). *Beeld: Mensenhandel Economische Uitbuiting [Situation Report: Human Trafficking for Economic Exploitation]*. Brussels, Belgium: Dienst mensenhandel.

Dienst mensenhandel, Federale Politie (2008b). *Beeld: Mensenhandel Seksuele Uitbuiting [Situation Report: Human Trafficking for Sexual Exploitation]*. Brussels, Belgium: Dienst mensenhandel.

Dienst voor het Strafrechtelijk Beleid (2008). *Jaarrapport 2007. Georganiseerde Criminaliteit In België 2005–2006 [Yearly Report 2007. Organized Crime in Belgium 2005–2006]*. Brussels, Belgium: Federale Politie.

Dion, M.L. and Russler, C. (2008). Eradication efforts, the state, displacement and poverty: Explaining coca cultivation in Colombia during Plan Colombia. *Journal of Latin American Studies*, 40(3), 399–421.

Dominguez, P. and Raphael, S. (2015). The role of the cost-of-crime literature in bridging the gap between social science research and policy making: Potentials and limitations. *Criminology and Public Policy*,14(4), 589–62.

Dorn, N. (2009). The end of organised crime in the European Union. *Crime, Law and Social Change*, 51, 283–95.

Dorn, N., Levi, M., and King, L. (2005). *Literature Review on Upper Level Drug Trafficking (Home Office Online Report 22/05)*. London, UK: Home Office.

Dorn, N. and van de Bunt, H. (2010). *Bad Thoughts: Towards an Organised Crime Harm Assessment and Prioritisation System*. Rotterdam: Erasmus University.

Douglas, M. (1966). *Purity and Danger: An Analysis of the Concept of Pollution and Taboo*. London, UK: Routledge.

Douglas, M. (1990). Risk as a forensic resource. *Daedalus*. 119(4), 1–16.

Douglas, M. (1992). *Risk And Blame: Essays in Cultural Theory*. London, UK: Routledge.

Douglas, T., Pugh, J., Singh, I., Savulescu, J., and Fazel, S. (2017). Risk assessment tools in criminal justice and forensic psychiatry: The need for better data. *European Psychiatry*, 42 (May), 134–7.

Doyal, L. and Gough, I. (1991). *A Theory of Human Need*. Basingstoke, UK: Macmillan.

Drahos, P. (Ed.) (2017). *Regulatory Theory*. Canberra, AU: Australian University Press.

Dubourg, R. and Prichard, S. (2007). The impact of organised crime in the UK: Revenues and economic and social costs. In R. Dubourg and S. Prichard (Eds.). *Organised Crime: Revenues, Economic and Social Costs, and Criminal Assets Retrieved from Seizure* (pp. 1–53). London, UK: Home Office.

Duff, R.A. (2003). Restoration and retribution. In A. von Hirsch, J.V. Roberts, A.E. Bottoms, K. Roach and M. Schiff (Eds.). *Restorative Justice and Criminal Justice: Competing or Reconcilable Paradigms?* (pp. 43–60). London, UK: Hart Publishing.

Duff, R.A. (2007). *Answering for Crime: Responsibility and Liability in the Criminal Law*. London, UK: Hart.

Duff, R.A. (2010). Perversions and subversions of criminal law. In R.A. Duff, L. Farmer, S.E. Marshall, M. Renzo, and V. Tadros (Eds.). *The Boundaries of the Criminal Law* (pp. 88–112). Oxford, UK: Oxford University Press.

Duff, R.A. (2011). Responsibility, restoration and retribution. In M. Tonry (Ed.). *Retributivism Has a Past: Has It a Future?* (pp. 63–85). New York, NY: Oxford University Press.

Duff, R.A. (2013). Theories of criminal law. In E.N. Zalta (Ed.). *The Stanford Encyclopedia of Philosophy*. Retrieved from https://plato.stanford.edu/archives/sum2013/entries/criminal-law/ (accessed February 25, 2015).

Duff, R.A. (2014). Towards a modest legal moralism. *Criminal Law and Philosophy*, 8, 217–35.
Duff, R.A. and Marshall, S.E. (2014). Remote harms and the two harm principles. In A.P. Simester, A. du Bois-Pedain, and U. Neumann (Eds.). *Liberal Criminal Theory: Essays for Andreas von Hirsch* (pp. 205–24). London, UK: Hart.
Duff, R.A., Farmer, L., Marshall, S.E., Renzo, M., and Tadros, V. (2010). *The Boundaries of the Criminal Law*. Oxford, UK: Oxford University Press.
Dugan, L. (1999). The effect of criminal victimization on a household's moving decision. *Criminology*, 37, 903–28.
Duke, J.A., Aulik, D., and Plowman, T. (1975). Nutritional value of coca. *Botanical Museum Leaflets Harvard University*, 24(6), 113–18.
Dupont, B (2004). Security in the age of networks. *Policing and Society*, 14(1), 76–91.
Dupont, B. and Wood, J. (Eds.) (2006). *Democracy, Society and the Governance of Security*. Cambridge, UK: Cambridge University Press.
Dupont, B., Grabosky, P., and Shearing, C. (2003). The governance of security in weak and failing states. *Criminal Justice*, 3(4), 331–49.
Durkheim, E. ([1893] 1997). *The Division of Labor in Society*. New York, NY: Free Press.
Durkheim, E. ([1900] 1969). Two laws of penal evolution. *University of Cincinnati Law Review*, 38, 32–60.
Dworkin, R. (1977). *Taking Rights Seriously*. Cambridge, MA: Harvard University Press.
Economist, The (2016, September 3). Bobbies on the spreadsheet: A new way to count crimes could reduce the amount of harm they cause. Retrieved from https://www.economist.com/britain/2016/09/01/bobbies-on-the-spreadsheet (accessed February 25, 2018).
Economist, The (2017, March 23). An unwelcome resurgence: Coca-growing in Colombia is at an all-time high. Retrieved from https://www.economist.com/the-americas/2017/03/23/coca-growing-in-colombia-is-at-an-all-time-high (accessed October 25, 2020).
Edwards, A. and Hughes, G. (2009). The preventive turn and the promotion of safer communities in England and Wales. In A. Crawford (Ed.). *Crime Prevention Policies in Comparative Perspective* (pp. 62–85). Cullompton, UK: Willan.
Edwards, A., Hughes, G., and Lord, N. (2013). Urban security in Europe: Translating a concept in public criminology. *The European Journal of Criminology*, 10(3), 260–83.
Eisner, M., Murray, A.L., Ribeaud, D., Averdijk, M., and Gelder, J.L. (2017). From the savannah to the magistrate court: The roots of criminal justice in evolved human psychology. In B. Jann and W. Przepiorka (Eds.). *Social Dilemmas, Institutions, and the Evolution of Cooperation* (pp. 61–84). Berlin: de Gruyter.
Elias, N. ([1939] 2000). *The Civilizing Process: Sociogenetic and Psychogenetic Investigations* (2nd ed). Oxford, UK: Blackwell.
Elmore, B.J. (2016). Coca-cola has always had a connection to the cocaine business. *Huffington Post*. https://www.huffpost.com/entry/coca-cola-has-always-had-a-connection-to-the-cocaine_b_57c8757ae4b07addc4119330 (accessed on April 11, 2021).

EMCDDA (See European Monitoring Centre for Drugs and Drug Addiction)

Ericson, R.V. (2007). *Crime in an Insecure World*. Cambridge, UK: Polity.

Ericson, R.V. and Doyle, A. (2003). *Risk and Morality*. Toronto, ON: University of Toronto Press.

Ericson, R.V. and Haggerty, K.D. (1997). *Policing the Risk Society*. Clarendon Press.

Eser, A. (1966). The principle of harm in the concept of crime: A comparative analysis of criminal protected legal interests. *Duquesne University Law Review*, 4, 345–417.

Etter, A., McAlpine, C., Pullar, D., and Possingham, H. (2006a). Modelling the conversion of Colombian lowland ecosystems since 1940: Drivers, patterns, and rates. *Journal of Environmental Management*, 79, 74–87.

Etter, A., McAlpine, C., Wilson, L., Phinn, S., and Possingham, H. (2006b). Regional patterns of agricultural land use and deforestation in Colombia. *Agriculture, Ecosystems and Environment*, 114, 369–86.

European Commission (2013). Cybersecurity strategy of the European Union: An open, safe and secure cyberspace. Retrieved from http://eeas.europa.eu/archives/docs/policies/eu-cyber-security/cybsec_comm_en.pdf (accessed February 25, 2018).

European Commission (2015). Communication from the Commission to the European Parliament, the Council, the European Economic and Social Committee and the Committee of the Regions: The European agenda on security. Com(2015) 185 Final.

European Commission and High Representative of the European Union for Foreign Affairs and Security Policy (2013). Joint communication to the European Parliament, the Council, the European Economic and Social Committee and the Committee of the Regions: Cybersecurity strategy of the European Union: An Open, Safe and Secure Cyberspace. JOIN (2013) 1 final.

European Council (2003). A secure Europe in a better world: European security strategy. Brussels, 12 December. Retrieved from http://eur-lex.europa.eu/legal-content/IT/TXT/?uri=LEGISSUM%3Ar00004 (accessed February 20, 2016).

European Council (2005). EU drugs action plan (2005–2008). OJ C168, 1–18.

European Council (2010). The Stockholm programme: An open and secure Europe serving and protecting citizens. OJ C115, 1–38.

European Court on Human Rights (n.d.). European convention on human rights. Strasbourg: European Court on Human Rights. Retrieved from http://www.echr.coe.int/Documents/Convention_ENG.pdf (accessed February 25, 2018).

European Monitoring Center for Drugs and Drug Addiction (2007). *Cocaine And Crack Cocaine: A Growing Public Health Issue*. Luxembourg: Office for Official Publications of the European Communities.

European Monitoring Center for Drugs and Drug Addiction (2010). *Harm Reduction: Evidence, Impacts and Challenges*. Lisbon: EMCDDA.

European Monitoring Centre for Drugs and Drug Addiction (2011). *Annual Report on the State of the Drugs Problem in Europe*. Luxembourg: Publication Office of the European Union.

European Monitoring Centre for Drugs and Drug Addiction (2017). *Contribution from the EMCDDA Scientific Committee on Drug-Related Research Priorities for the HDG's Annual Dialogue on Research*. Brussels, November. Unpublished.

European Monitoring Centre for Drugs and Drug Addiction and Europol (2010). *Cocaine: A European Perspective in the Global Context.* EMCDDA–Europol Joint Publications No. 2. Luxembourg: Publications Office of the European Union.

[European Union] (2008). Consolidated Version of the Treaty on the Functioning of the European Union. OJ C115, 47–199.

Europol (2013). *SOCTA 2013: European Union Serious and Organised Crime Threat Assessment. 'S-Gravenzande,* The Netherlands: Deventer.

Europol (2017). *SOCTA 2017: European Union Serious and Organised Crime Threat Assessment: Crime in the Age of Technology.* The Hague, The Netherlands: Europol.

Faiola, A. (2018, June 17). A conservative 'D.C. Colombian' wins his country's presidency. Peace may be the loser. *The Washington Post.* Retrieved from https://www.washingtonpost.com/world/the_americas/dc-colombian-squares-off-against-former-guerrilla-as-colombians-vote/2018/06/17/ab8c213e-6d89-11e8-b4d8-eaf78d4c544c_story.html?utm_term=.2b832adf6dcc (accessed June 19, 2018).

Farmer, L. (2010). Criminal wrongs in historical perspective. In R.A., Duff, L. Farmer, S.E. Marshall, M. Renzo, and V. Tadros (Eds.). *The Boundaries of the Criminal Law* (pp. 214–37). Oxford, UK: Oxford University Press.

Farrington, D. (2000). Explaining and preventing crime: The globalization of knowledge—The American Society of Criminology 1999 Presidential Address, *Criminology*, 38(1), 1–24.

FATF (See Financial Action Task Force)

Fattah, E.A. (Ed.) (1986). *From Crime Policy to Victim Policy: Reorienting the Justice System.* Basingstoke, UK: Macmillan.

Fattah, E.A. (Ed.) (1992). *Towards a Critical Victimology.* New York, NY: St. Martin's Press.

Fattah, E.A. (2010). The evolution of a young and promising discipline: Sixty years of victimology, a retrospective and prospective look. In S.G. Shohan, P. Knepper, and M. Kett (Eds.). *International Handbook of Victimology* (pp. 43–94). Boca Raton, FL: CRC Press.

Fazel, S., Singh, J.P., Doll, H., and Grann, M. (2012). Use of risk assessment instruments to predict violence and antisocial behaviour in 73 samples involving 24,827 people: Systematic review and meta-analysis. *BMJ*, 345, e4692.

Federale Gerechtelijke Politie OA Airport Team Zware Criminaliteit, FGP–Airport (2010). Internationaal rapportering Brussels Airport 2006–2009. Unpublished memo.

Federale Politie België. (2006). *Nationaal Politieel Veiligheidsbeeld 2006 [National Police Safety Plan].* Brussels, Belgium: Dienst Strategische Analyse.

Federale Politie België. (2008, March). Beeld van Cocaïne in België [Situation of Cocaine in Belgium]. Unpublished memo.

Federale Politie België (2010). Database Georganiseerde Criminaliteit [Database Organized Crime].

Feeley, M.M. (2014). *Learning Care Lessons: Literacy, Love, Care and Solidarity.* Basingstoke, UK: Palgrave Macmillan.

Feeley, M.M. and Simon, J. (1992). The new penology: Notes on the emerging strategy of corrections and its implications. *Criminology*, 30, 449–74.

Feeley, M.M. and Simon, J. (1994). Actuarial justice: The emerging new criminal law. In D. Nelken (Ed.). *The Future of Criminology* (pp. 173–201). New York, NY: Sage.

Feinberg, J. (1984). *Harm to Others*. New York, NY: Oxford University Press.

Feinberg, J. (1985). *Offense to Others*. New York, NY: Oxford University Press.

Fergusson, L., Romero, D., and Vargas, J.F. (2014). *The Environmental Impact of Civil Conflict: The Deforestation Effect of Paramilitary Expansion in Colombia.* Bogotá: University of the Andes, Center for Studies on Economic Development (CEDE).

Field, F. (2003). *Neighbours from Hell: The Politics of Behaviour.* London, UK: Politico's.

Fijnaut, C. (2017). *Criminology and the Criminal Justice System: A Historical and Transatlantic Introduction*. Cambridge: Intersentia.

Financial Action Task Force (2010). *Global Money Laundering and Terrorist Financing Threat Assessment*. Paris: FATF.

Fischer, B., and Kendall, P. (2011). Nutt Et Al.'S harm scales for drugs-room for improvement but better policy based on science with limitations than no science at all. *Addiction*, 106 (11), 1891–1892.

Financial Action Task Force (2013). *FAFT Guidance: National Money Laundering and Terrorist Financing Risk Assessment*. Paris: FATF.

Fjeldså, J., Álvarez, M.D., Lazcano, J.M., and León, B. (2005). Illicit crops and armed conflict as constraints on biodiversity conservation in the Andes region. *Ambio*, 34(3), 205–11.

Fortes, M. (1983). *Rules and the Emergence of Society. Royal Anthropological Institute of Great Britain and Ireland.* Occasional Paper No. 39. London, UK: Royal Anthropological Institute.

Foucault, M. (1977). *Discipline and Punish: The Birth of the Prison.* New York, NY: Pantheon.Frankena, W. (1980). *Thinking about Morality.* Ann Arbor, MI: University of Michigan Press.

Frans, B. (2010, September). Statement made at the European Society of Criminology 10th Annual Conference. Liège, Belgium.

Frederix, B. (2018). De schade van georganiseerde btw-fraude in België (The harm of VAT-fraud in Belgium). Leuven: KU Leuven Faculty of Law, unpublished master's thesis.

Freudenberg, N. (2014). *Lethal But Legal: Corporations, Consumption and Protecting Public Health*. Oxford, UK: Oxford University Press.

Friedrichs, D. and Schwartz, M. (2007). On social harm and a twenty-first century criminology. *Crime, Law and Social Change*, 48(1), 1–7.

Furedi, F. (1999). *Courting Mistrust*. London, UK: Centre for Policy Studies.

Galli, F. and Weyembergh, A. (Eds.) (2012). *EU Counterterrorism Offences: What Impact on National Legislation and Case Law*. Bruxelles, Belgium: Editions de l'Université de Bruxelles.

Gallie, W.B. (1956). Essentially contested concepts. *Proceedings of the Aristotelian Society*, 56, 167–98.

Garbett, C. (2013). The truth and the trial: Victim participation, restorative justice, and the International Criminal Court. *Contemporary Justice Review* 16(2), 193–213.

Garbett, C. (2017). The International Criminal Court and restorative justice: Victims, participation and the processes of justice. *Restorative Justice* 5(2), 198–220.
Garland, D. (1990). *Punishment And Modern Society*. Oxford, UK: Clarendon.
Garland, D. (1996). The limits of the sovereign state: Strategies of crime control in contemporary society. *The British Journal of Criminology*, 36(4), 445–71.
Garland, D. (2001a). *The Culture of Control: Crime and Social Order in Contemporary Society*. Chicago IL: University of Chicago Press.
Garland, D. (2001b). The rise of risk. In R. Ericson and A. Doyle (Eds.). *Risk and Morality* (pp. 48–86). Toronto, ON: University of Toronto Press.
Garland, D. (2009). Disciplining criminology? *Sistema Penal and Violência*, 1(1), 114–25.
Garside, R. (2013). Addressing social harm: Better regulation versus social transformation. *Revisita Critica Penal y Poder*, 5, 247–65.
Gert, B. and Gert, J. (2017). The definition of morality. In E.N. Zalta (Ed.). *The Stanford Encyclopedia of Philosophy*. Retrieved from https://plato.stanford.edu/archives/fall2017/entries/morality-definition/ (accessed October 25, 2017).
Giddens, A. (1999). Risk and responsibility. *Modern Law Review*, 62(1), 1–10.
Gledhill, K. (2011). Preventive sentences and orders: The challenges of due process. *Journal of Commonwealth Criminal Law*, 1, 78–104.
Goldstein, H. (1977). *Policing a Free Society*. Cambridge, MA: Ballinger.
Goldstein, H. (1979). Improving policing: A problem-oriented approach. *Crime and Delinquency*, 25(2), 236–58.
Goldstein, H. (1990). *Problem-Oriented Policing*. Philadelphia, PA: Temple University Press.
Gottfredson, M. 2011. Some advantages of a crime-free criminology. In M. Bosworth and C. Hoyle (Eds.). *What Is Criminology?* (pp. 35–48). Oxford, UK: Oxford University Press.
Gough, I. (2014). Lists and thresholds: Comparing the Doyal-Gough theory of human need with Nussbaum's capabilities approach. In F. Comim and M.C. Nussbaum (Eds.). *Capabilities, Gender, Equality: Towards Fundamental Entitlements* (pp. 357–81). Cambridge, UK: Cambridge University Press.
Gouldner, A.W. (1973). *For Sociology: Renewal and Critique in Sociology Today*. New York, NY: Basic Books.
Graham, J., Nosek, B., Haidt, J., Iyer, R., Koleva, S., and Ditto, P.H. (2008). Mapping the moral domain. *Journal of Personality and Social Psychology*, 101(2), 366–85.
Gray, D. (2010). Punishment as suffering. *Vanderbilt Law Review*, 63, 1619–93.
Greenfield, V.A. (2008). Contractors on the Battlefield: When and How?: Using the US Military's Risk Management Framework to Learn from the Balkans Support Contract. *Service Contractor*, Summer, p. 9.
Greenfield, V.A. (1991). *Bolivian Coca: A Perennial Leaf Crop Subject to Supply Reduction Policies*. Doctoral Dissertation, University of California at Berkeley.
Greenfield, V.A. and Camm, F. (2005). *Risk Management and Performance in the Balkans Support Contract*. Santa Monica, CA: RAND Corporation.
Greenfield, V.A. and Paoli, L. (2012). If supply-oriented drug policy is broken, can "harm reduction" help fix it? *International Journal of Drug Policy*, 23, 6–15.

Greenfield, V.A. and Paoli, L. (2013). A framework to assess the harms of crime. *The British Journal of Criminology*, 53(5), 864–85.

Greenfield, V.A. and Paoli, L. (2017). Research as due diligence: What can supply-side interventions accomplish and at what cost? *International Journal of Drug Policy*, 41, 162–163.

Greenfield, V.A., Crane, K., Bond, C.A., Chandler, N., Luoto, J., and Oliker, O. (2015a). *Reducing the Cultivation of Opium Poppies in Southern Afghanistan. Full Document and Appendixes A–E.* Santa Monica, CA: RAND Corporation.

Greenfield, V.A., Shelton, S.R., Balkovich, E., Davis, J.S., II, and Adamson, D.M. (2015b). *The Federal Voting Assistance Program and the Road Ahead: Achieving Institutional Change Through Analysis and Collaboration.* Santa Monica, CA: RAND Corporation.

Greenfield, V.A., Paoli, L., and Zoutendijk, A. (2016). The harms of human trafficking: Demonstrating the applicability and value of a new framework for systematic, empirical analysis. *Global Crime*, 17(2), 152–80.

Greenfield, V.A., Bond, C.A., and Crane, K. (2017). A household model of opium-poppy cultivation in Afghanistan. *Journal of Policy Modeling*, 39, 741–61.

Grosso, C.F., Pelissero, M., and Petrini, D. (2017). *Manuale Di Diritto Penale. Parte Generale [Handbook of Criminal Law. General Part]*. Milan, Italy: Giuffrè.

Haelterman, H. (2016). *Crime Script Analysis: Preventing Crimes against Business.* New York, NY: Palgrave Macmillan.

Hagan, J. (1985). *Modern Criminology: Crime, Criminal Behavior and Its Control.* New York, NY: McGraw-Hill.

Haidt, J. (2012). *The Righteous Mind: Why Good People Are Divided by Politics and Religion.* New York, NY: Vintage.

Haidt, J., Koller, S.K., and Dias, M.G. (1993). Affect, culture, and morality, or is it wrong to eat your dog? *Journal of Personality and Social Psychology*, 65(4), 613–28

Haines, F. (2017). Regulation and risk. In P. Drahos (Ed.). *Regulatory Theory* (pp. 181–96). Canberra, AU: Australian University Press.

Hall, J. (1960). *General Principles of Criminal Law.* Indianapolis, IN: Bobbs-Merill.

Hall, M. (2010). *Victims and Policy Making: A Comparative Perspective.* Oxon, UK: Willan.

Harcourt, B.E. (1999). The collapse of the harm principle. *Journal of Criminal Law and Criminology*, 90, 109–94.

Harden, C.P. (2006). Human impacts on headwater fluvial systems in the northern and central Andes. *Geomorphology*, 79, 249–63.

Hart, H.L.A. (1963). *Law, Liberty and Morality.* Standford, CA: Stanford University Press.

Hart, H.L.A. ([1968] 2008). *Punishment and Responsibility: Essays in the Philosophy of Law.* Oxford, UK: Clarendon.

Hassemer, W. (2004). The harm principle and the protection of 'legal goods' (Rechtsgüterschutz): A German perspective. In A.P. Simester, A. du Bois-Pedain, and U. Neumann (Eds.). *Liberal Criminal Theory: Essays for Andreas von Hirsch* (pp. 187–204). London, UK: Hart.

Healy, K. (1986). The boom within the crisis: Some recent effect of foreign cocaine markets on Bolivian rural society and economy. In D. Pacini and C. Franquemont

(Eds.). *Coca and Cocaine: Effects on People and Policy in Latin America* (pp. 5–33). Cultural Survival Report 23, publication of Cultural Survival Inc. and the Latin American Studies Program, Cornell University. Peterborough, NY: Transcript Printing Company.

Healy, K. (1988). Coca, the state, and the peasantry in Bolivia, 1982–1988. *Journal of Interamerican Studies and World Affairs*, 30(2/3), 105–26.

Heaton, P. (2010). *Hidden in Plain Sight: What Cost-of-Crime Research Can Tell Us about Investing in Police*. Rand Occasional Paper. Santa Monica, CA: RAND Corporation.

Hedley, S. (2013). Tort and personal injuries, 1850 to the present. In T.T. Arvind and J. Steele (Eds.). *Tort Law and the Legislature: Common Law, Statute and the Dynamics of Legal Change* (pp. 235–52). London, UK: Hart.

Hefendehl, R. (2003). Das Rechtsgut als materieller Angelpunkt einer Strafnorm [The legal interest as the material pivot of a criminal norm]. In R. Hefendehl, A. von Hirsch, and W. Wohlers (Eds.). *Die Rechtsgutstheorie: Legitimationsbasis des Strafrechts Oder Dogmatisches Glasperlenspiel? [The Legal Interest Theory: Legitimation Basis of Criminal Law or Dogmatic Glass Bead Game?]* (pp. 119–32). Baden-Baden, Germany: Nomos.

Hefendehl, R., von Hirsch, A, and Wohlers, W. (Eds.) (2003). *Die Rechtsgutstheorie: Legitimationsbasis des Strafrechts Oder Dogmatisches Glasperlenspiel? [The Legal Interest Theory: Legitimation Basis of Criminal Law or Dogmatic Glass Bead Game?]* Baden-Baden, Germany: Nomos.

Henao Muñoz, L.M., Montes Rojas, C.M., and Bernal Bautista, M.H. (2015). Acute toxicity and sublethal effects of the mixture glyphosate (Roundup® Active) and Cosmo-Flux®411F to anuran embryos and tadpoles of four Colombian species. *International Journal of Tropical Biology*, 63(1), 223–33.

Henman, A. and Metaal, P. (2009). *Coca Myths*. Drugs and Conflict Debate Papers No. 17. TNI Briefing Series. Amsterdam, The Netherlands: Transnational Institute

Henry, S. and Milovanovic, D. (1996). *Constitutive Criminology: Beyond Postmodernism*. London, UK: Sage.

Hewitt, A.J., Solomon, K.R., and Marshall, E.P.J. (2009). Spray droplet size, drift potential, and risks to nontarget organisms from aerially applied glyphosate for coca control in Colombia. *Journal of Environmental Toxicology and Environmental Health, Part A*, 72(15–16), 921–9.

Heymans, P. Slegers, S., and De Jaegere, A. (2019, December 03). Granaatexplosie in Antwerpen, deze keer in Wommelgem: vermoedelijk link met aanslag in Deurne [Grenade explosion in Antwerp, this time in Wommelgem: probably link with attack in Deurne]. *Vrt.nieuws*. Retrieved from: https://www.vrt.be/vrtnws/nl/2019/12/03/straat-in-wommelgem-afgesloten-vermoedelijk-opnieuw-een-granaat/ (accessed November 6, 2021).

Hillyard, P. and Tombs, S. (2004). Beyond criminology? In P. Hillyard, C. Pantazis, S. Tombs, and D. Gordon (Eds.). *Beyond Criminology: Taking Harm Seriously* (pp. 10–29). London, UK: Pluto Press.

Hillyard, P. and Tombs, S. (2007). From 'crime' to social harm? *Crime, Law and Social Change*, 48, 9–25.

Hillyard, P. and Tombs, S. (2017). Social harm and zemiology. In A. Liebling, S. Maruna, and L. McAra (Eds.). *The Oxford Handbook of Criminology* (6th ed., pp. 284–303). Oxford, UK: Oxford University Press.

Hillyard, P., Pantazis, C., Tombs, C., and Gordon, D. (Eds.) (2004). *Beyond Criminology: Taking Harm Seriously*. London, UK: Pluto Press.

Hirschi, T. (1969). *Causes of Delinquency*. Berkeley, CA: University of California Press.

Hirschi, T. and Gottfedson, M. (1990). Substantive positivism and the idea of crime. *Rationality and Society*, 2, 412–28.

HLN (2014, May 19). Minder cocaïne in beslag genomen op Brussels Airport [Less cocaine seized at Brussels Airport]. Retrieved from https://www.hln.be/nieuws/binnenland/minder-cocaine-in-beslag-genomen-op-brussels-airport~a3e6efff/ (accessed February 25, 2018).

Hobbes, T. ([1668] 1994). *Leviathan with Selected Variants from the Latin Edition of 1668*. Ed. E. Curley. Indianapolis, IN: Hackett.

Holmes, J.S. and Gutiérrez de Piñeres, S.A. (2006). The illegal drug industry, violence and the Colombian economy: A departmental level analysis. *Bulletin of Latin American Research*, 25(1), 104–18.

Holmes, J.S., Gutiérrez de Piñeres, S.A., and Curtin, K.M. (2006). Drugs, violence, and development in Colombia: A department-level analysis. *Latin American Politics and Society*, 48(3), 157–84.

Hoyle, C. and Sanders, A. (2000). Police response to domestic violence. *British Journal of Criminology*, 40(1), 14–36.

Hudson, J. (2012). *The Oxford History of the Laws of England*, vol. II: *900–1216*. Oxford, UK: Oxford University Press.

Huemer, M. (2017). Sense-data. In E.N. Zalta (Ed.). *The Stanford Encyclopedia of Philosophy (Spring 2017 Edition)* Retrieved from https://plato.stanford.edu/archives/spr2017/entries/sense-data/ (accessed February 25, 2018).

Hughes, G. (2006). Book review—Beyond criminology: Taking harm seriously. *Social and Legal Studies*, 15(1), 157–9.

Huisman, W., Huikeshoven, M., van de Bunt, H.G., van Wijk, J., and Meijer, A.D. (2003). *De Zwakste Schakel: Logistieke Processen van Georganiseerde Criminaliteit [The Weakest Link: Logistical Processes of Organized Crime]*. Amsterdam, The Netherlands: Vrije Universiteit.

Hulsman, L.H. (1986). Critical criminology and the concept of crime. *Contemporary Crises*, 10(3–4), 63–80.

Humo, De (2017, April 17). Hoe de Marokkaanse cocaïnemaffia Antwerpen veroverde: Molotovcocktails, kalasjnikovs, ontvoering en omkoping [How the Moroccan cocaine mafia conquered Antwerp: Molotov cocktails, Kalashnikovs, kidnapping and corruption]. Retrieved from http://www.humo.be/humo-archief/377051/hoe-de-marokkaanse-cocainemaffia-antwerpen-veroverde-molotovcocktails-kalasjnikovs-ontvoering-en-omkoping (accessed February 25, 2018).

Hunt, N., with contributions from Ashton, M., Lenton, S., Mitcheson, L., Nelles, B., and Stimson, G. (2003). Forward thinking on drugs a release initiative: A review of the evidence-base for harm reduction approaches to drug use. Retrieved from http://www.ihra.net/files/2010/05/31/HIVTop50Documents11.pdf (accessed March 23, 2011).

Husak, D. (2008). *Overcriminalization: The Limits of the Criminal Law*. New York, NY: Oxford University Press.

Husak, D. (2013a). Crimes outside the core, *Tulsa Law Review*, 39, 755–80.

Husak, D. (2013b). Preventive detention as punishment? Some possible obstacles. In A. Ashworth, L. Zedner, and P. Tomlin (Eds.). *Prevention and the Limits of the Criminal Law* (pp. 178–93). Oxford, UK: Oxford University Press.

Ibanez, M. and Carlsson, F. (2010). A survey-based choice experiment on coca cultivation. *Journal of Development Economics*, 93(2), 249–63.

Ibanez, M. and Martinsson P. (2013). Curbing coca cultivation in Colombia: A framed field experiment. *Journal of Public Economics*, 105, 1–10.

Ignatans D. and Pease, K. (2016). Taking crime seriously: Playing the weighting game. *Policing*, 10(3), 184–93.

Illuminati, G. (2005). Italy. In P.J. Tak (Ed.). *Tasks and Powers of the Prosecution Services in the EU Member States*, vol. II (pp. 935–54). Nijmegen, The Netherlands: Wolf.

Inciardi, J.A. and Harrison, L.A. (Eds.) (2000). *Harm Reduction: National and International Perspectives*. London, UK: Sage.

Innes, M. (2004). Signal crimes and signal disorders: Notes on deviance as communicative action. *The British Journal of Sociology*, 55, 335–55.

International Criminal Court (2021). 30 Cases. Retrieved from https://www.icc-cpi.int/Pages/cases.aspx (accessed October 14, 2021).

International Women's Human Rights Clinic, City University of New York Law School Trafficking Victims Advocacy Project, and Legal Aid Society of New York (2015). *Criminalization of Trafficking Victims*. Retrieved from http://www.law.cuny.edu/academics/clinics/iwhr/publications/Criminalization–of–Trafficking–Victims.pdf (accessed February 25, 2016).

Jackson, B.A., Dixon, L., and Greenfield, V.A. (2007). *Economically Targeted Terrorism: A Review of the Literature and a Framework for Considering Defensive Approaches*. Santa Monica, CA: RAND Corporation.

Jaén, S. and Dyner, I. (2014). A system dynamics approach to the study of Colombian coca cultivation and the counter-intuitive consequence of law enforcement. *International Journal of Drug Policy*, 25(2), 226–34.

Joffe, H. (1999). *Risk and "the Other."* Cambridge, UK: Cambridge University Press.

Johnston, L. and Shearing, C. (2003). *Governing Security: Explorations in Policing and Justice*. London, UK: Routledge.

Joyce, S. (1999). Spheres of influence. Environmental casualties of the war on drugs. *Environmental Health Perspectives*, 107(2), A74–77.

Judicial College (2017). *Guidelines for the Assessment of General Damages in Personal Injury Cases* (14th ed.). Oxford: Oxford University Press.

Kaakinen M., Keipi T., Räsänen P., and Oksanen A. (2018). Cybercrime victimization and subjective well-being: An examination of the buffering effect hypothesis among adolescents and young adults. *Cyberpsychology, Behavior, and Social Networking*, 21(2), 129–37.

Kahneman, D. (2011). *Thinking, Fast and Slow*. London, UK: Penguin.

Kaizen, J. and Nonneman, W. (2007). Irregular migration in Belgium and organized crime: An overview. *International Migration*, 45(2), 121–46.

Karstedt, S. (2014). State crime: The European experience. In S. Body-Gendrot, M. Hough, K. Kerezsi, and R. Lévy (Eds.). *The Routledge Handbook of European Criminology* (pp. 125–53). Oxford, UK: Routledge.

Kermer, D.A., Driver-Linn, E., Wilson, T.D., and Gilbert, D.T. (2006). Loss aversion is an affective forecasting error. *Psychological Science*, 17, 649–53.

Kersten, L. (2022). Sound and safe: regulatory practices and harm reduction in the Belgian meat sector, unpublished PhD thesis.

Kitcher, P. (2001). *Science, Truth, and Democracy*. Oxford, UK: Oxford University Press.

Kleemans, E.R. and Smit, M. (2014). Human smuggling, human trafficking, and exploitation in the sex industry. In L. Paoli (Ed.). *Handbook of Organized Crime* (pp. 381–400). New York, NY: Oxford University Press.

Kopp, P. and Besson, F. (2009). A methodology to measure the impact of organised crime activities at the EU Level. In E. Savona (Ed.). *Organised Crime in the EU* (pp. 301–20). Rotterdam, The Netherlands: Erasmus University School of Law.

Korps Landelijke Politiediensten (2005). *Criminaliteitsbeeldanalyse Cocaïnehandel [Crime Analysis: Cocaine Trafficking]*. Utrecht, The Netherlands: Dienst Nationale Recherche.

Kraul, C. (2017, November 24). Colombian coca farmers, facing a threat to their livelihood, resist U.S.-backed efforts to eradicate cocaine production. *Los Angeles Times*. Retrieved from http://www.latimes.com/world/mexico-americas/la-fg-colombia-cocaine-2017-htmlstory.html (accessed October 25, 2020).

Lacey, N. (2009). Historicising criminalisation: Conceptual and empirical issues. *Modern Law Review*, 72(6), 936–61.

LaFave, W.R. (2003). *Criminal Law* (4th ed.). St. Paul, MN: West.

Lamont, J. and Favor, C. (2017). Distributive justice. In E.N. Zalta (Ed.), *The Stanford Encyclopedia of Philosophy*. https://plato.stanford.edu/entries/justice-distributive/ (accessed September 2, 2021).

Lappi-Seppälä, T. (2007). Penal policy in Scandinavia. In M. Tonry (Ed.). *Crime, Punishment, and Politics in Comparative Perspective* (pp. 217–95). Chicago, IL: University of Chicago Press.

Lappi-Seppälä, T. (2011). Explaining imprisonment in Europe. *European Journal of Criminology*, 18(4), 303–28.

Lasslett, K. (2010). Crime or social harm? A dialectical perspective. *Crime, Law and Social Change*, 54, 1–19.

Lasswell, H.D. (1950). *National Security and Individual Freedom*. New York, NY: McGraw-Hill.

Laub, J. (2004). The life course of criminology in the United States: The American Society of Criminology 2003 Presidential Address. *Criminology*, 42, 1–26.

Leclerc, B. (2014). Script analysis for crime controllers: Extending the reach of situational crime prevention. In S. Caneppele and F. Calderoni (Eds.). *Organized Crime, Corruption and Crime Prevention* (pp. 13–20). New York, NY: Springer.

Lefelon, P. (2018, January 5). "War on drugs" in Antwerpen anno 2017: Vastgoed in Marokko, recordvangst cocaïne en 135 arrestaties ["War in drugs" in

Antwerp: Real estate in Morocco, record seizure of cocaine and 135 arrests]. *HLN*. Retrieved from https://www.hln.be/binnenland/war-on-drugs-in-antwerpen-anno-2017-vastgoed-in-marokko-recordvangst-cocaine-en-135-arrestaties~a5492ed0/?referrer=https%3A%2F%2Fwww.google.com%2F (accessed February 25, 2018).

Leiss, W. and Hrudey, S.E. (2005). On proof and probability: Introduction to law and risk. In Law Commission of Canada (Ed.). *Law and Risk* (pp. 1–19). Vancouver, BC: University of British Colombia Press.

Letschert, R. and van Dijk, J. (Eds.) (2011). *The New Faces of Victimhood*. Dordrecht, The Netherlands: Springer.

Levi, M. (2017). Emerged from the American shadows? Reflections on the growth of criminology in the UK. *Criminology in Europe*, 16(2), 4–8.

Levi, M. and Burrows, J. (2008). Measuring the impact of fraud in the UK. *The British Journal of Criminology*, 48, 293–318.

Liebling, A. and Maruna, S. (Eds.) (2005). *The Effects of Imprisonment*. Cullompton, UK: Willan.

Lippke, R.L. (2012). Anchoring the sentencing scale: A modest proposal. *Theoretical Criminology*, 16(4), 463–80.

Loader, I. and Percy, S. (Eds.) (2015). *Reordering Security: Crossing the Criminology/IR Divide*. London, UK: Routledge.

Loader, I. and Sparks, R. (2002). Contemporary landscapes of crime, order, and control: governance, risk, and globalization. In M. Maguire, R. Morgan and R. Reiner (Eds.) *The Oxford Handbook of Criminology* (pp. 83–111). Oxford, UK: Oxford University Press.

Loader, I. and Sparks, R. (2011). *Public Criminology?* New York, NY: Routledge.

Loader, I and Walker, N. (2007). *Civilizing Security*. Cambridge, UK: Cambridge University Press.

Lombroso, C. ([1876] 2006). *Criminal Man*. Durham, NC: Duke University Press.

Lucia, E. (2015). *Fragility, Conflict and Violence in the Gulf of Guinea*. Birmingham, UK: University of Birmingham, Governance and Social Development Resource Centre.

Luna R., Rhine E., Myhra M., Sullivan R., and Kruse C.S. (2016). Cyber threats to health information systems: A systematic review. *Technology Health Care*, 24(1), 1–9.

Lynch, J.D. and Arroyo, S.B. (2009). Risks to Colombian amphibian fauna from cultivation of coca (Erythroxylum coca): A geographical analysis. *Journal of Environmental Toxicology and Environmental Health, Part A*, 72(15–16), 974–85.

Lyon, D. (2001). *Surveillance Society: Monitoring Everyday Life*. Buckingham, UK: Open University Press.

Lyon, D. (2015). *Surveillance after Snowden*. Cambridge, UK: Polity Press.

MacCormick, N. (1982). *Legal Rights and Social Democracy: Essays in Legal and Political Philosophy*. Oxford, UK: Clarendon Press.

MacCoun, R.J. (1998). Towards a psychology of harm reduction. *American Psychologist*, 53(11), 1199–208.

MacCoun, R.J. and Reuter, P. (2001). *Drug War Heresies: Learning from Other Vices, Times, and Places*. Cambridge, UK: Cambridge University Press.

MacCoun, R.J., Reuter, P., and Schelling, T. (1996). Assessing alternative drug control regimes. *Journal of Policy Analysis and Management*, 15, 1–23.

MacDonald, Z., Tinsley, L., Collingwood, J., Jamieson, P., and Pudney, S. (2005). *Measuring the Harm from Illegal Drugs Using the Drug Harm Index: Home Office Online Report 24/05*. London, UK: Home Office.

MacKenzie, D.L. (2006). *What Works in Corrections? Reducing the Criminal Activities of Offenders and Delinquents*. Cambridge, UK: Cambridge University Press.

MacKenzie, S. and Hamilton-Smith, N. (2011). Measuring police impact on organized crime. *Policing*, 34, 7–30.

Maltz, M.D. (1990). *Measuring the Effectiveness of Organized Crime Control Efforts*. Chicago, IL: Office of International Criminal Justice.

Management of Risk in Law Enforcement (2017). *Tactical Risk Model: Policy and Guidance Document*. Mimeo.

Manning, M., Johnson, S.D., Tilley, N., Wong, G.T.W., and Vorsina, M. (2016). *Economic Analysis and Efficiency in Policing, Criminal Justice and Crime Reduction*. Basingstoke, UK: Palgrave-Macmillan.

Marshall, T. (1996). Criminal mediation in Great Britain 1980–1996. *The European Journal on Criminal Policy and Research*, 4(4), 21–43.

Maruschak, L.M. and Minton, T.D. (2020). Correctional Populations in the United States, 2017–2018, Bulletin. U.S. Department of Justice, Office of Justice Programs, Bureau of Justice Statistics, August. Retrieved from https://www.bjs.gov/index.cfm/content/acf/index.cfm?ty=pbdetail&iid=7026 (accessed on October 19, 2021).

Matza, D. (1969). *Becoming Deviant*. Englewood Cliffs, NJ: Prentice-Hall.

Mayaud, Y. (Ed.). with Gayet, C. (2016). *Code Penal: Annotations de Jurisprudence et Bibliographie [Penal Code: Annotation of Jurisprudence and Bibliography]*. Paris, France: Dalloz.

Mayhew, P. (2003). *Counting the Costs of Crime in Australia: Trends and Issues in Crime and Criminal Justice*. Griffith, AU: Australian Institute of Criminology.

Mayhew, P., Clarke, R.V., Sturman, A., and Hough, J.M. (1976). *Crime as Opportunity*. London, UK: Home Office Research and Planning Unit.

McAnany, P.D. (1978). Restitution as idea and practice: The retributive process. In B. Galaway and J. Hudson (Eds.). *Offenders Restitution in Theory and Action* (pp. 15–32). Lexington, MA: Lexington Books.

McCollister, K.E., French, M.T., and Fang, H. (2010). The cost of crime to society: New crime-specific estimates for policy and program evaluation. *Drug and Alcohol Dependence*, 108, 98–109.

McFadden, M. (2006). The Australian federal police drug harm index: a new methodology for quantifying success in combating drug use. *Australian Journal of Public Administration*, 65(4): 68–81. https://doi.org/10.1111/j.1467-8500.2006.00505a.x

McGonagle, T (2016). *Freedom of Expression and Defamation: A Study of Case Law of the European Court of Human Rights*. Strasbourg, France: Council of Europe.

Mejía, D. and Posada, C.E. (2008). *Cocaine Production and Trafficking: What Do We Know?* Policy Research Working Paper 4618. Washington, DC: World Bank.

Mejía, D., Restrepo, P., and Rozo, S.V. (2017). On the effects of enforcement on illegal markets: Evidence from a quasi-experiment in Colombia. *The World Bank Economic Review*, 31(2), 570–94.

Merton, R.K. (1938). Social structure and anomie. *American Sociological Review*, 3, 672–82.

Messina, J.P. and Delamater, P.L. (2006). Defoliation and the war on drugs in Putumayo, Colombia. *International Journal of Remote Sensing*, 27(1), 121–8.

Mill, J.S. ([1859], 1978). *On Liberty*. Ed. E. Rappaport. Indianapolis, IN: Hackett.

Miller, T.R., Cohen, M.A., and Wiersema, B. (1996). *Victim Costs and Consequences: A New Look*. Washington, DC: US Department of Justice. Retrieved from https://www.ncjrs.gov/App/Publications/abstract.aspx?ID=155282 (accessed January 28, 2016).

Ministeries van Binnenlandse Zaken en Justitie (2012). *Nationaal Veiligheidsplan 2012–2015. [National Security Plan 2012–2015.]* Brussels, Belgium.

Ministerraad (2016). *Kadernota Integrale Veiligheid, 2016–2019 [Framework Paper Integral Security 2016–2019]*. Brussels, Belgium: FOD Justitie.

Monar, J. (2009). The area of freedom, security and justice. In J. Bast and A. von Bogdandy (Eds.). *Principles of European Constitutional Law* (pp. 551–85). Oxford, UK: Hart.

Moore, M. (1997). *Placing Blame: A Theory of Criminal Law*. Oxford, UK: Clarendon.

Moore, T.M. (2007). Working estimates of the social costs per gram and per user for cannabis, cocaine, opiates and amphetamines. Drug Policy Modelling Project Monograph Series No. 14. Sydney: National Drug and Alcohol Research Centre.

Moreno-Sanchez, R., Kraybill, D.S., and Thompson, S.R. (2003). An econometric analysis of coca eradication policy in Colombia. *World Development*, 31(2), 375–83.

MoRiLE (See Management of Risk in Law Enforcement)

Mos, B. (2010, March 3). Marechaussee gearresteerd in België voor cokehandel [Dutch Marechaussee officer arrested in Belgium for cocaine trafficking]. *De Telegraaf*. Retrieved from http://www.telegraaf.nl/binnenland/6210368/__Marechaussee_opgepakt_voor_coke__.html (accessed June 23, 2013).

Mueller, G.O.W. (1955). Tort, crime and the primitive. *The Journal of Criminal Law, Criminology, and Police Science*, 46, 303–32.

Muñoz-Mora, J.C., Tobón, S., and d'Anjou, J.W. (2018). The role of land property rights in the war on illicit crops: Evidence from Colombia. *World Development*, 103, 268–83.

Mythen, G. (2014). *Understanding the Risk Society: Crime, Security and Justice*. Basingstoke, UK: Macmillan.

Naesen, Y. and Demeyer, P. (2005, June 14). Vlaams jacht vervoert 3 ton drugs [Flemish yacht transported three tons cocaine]. *Het Nieuwsblad*. Retrieved from http://www.nieuwsblad.be/article/detail.aspx?articleid=GNIFK0G2 (accessed June 23, 2013).

Nagin, D.S. (2013). Deterrence in the twenty-first century. *Crime and Justice*, 42(1), 199–263.

National Academies of Sciences, Engineering, and Medicine (2018). *Reducing the Threat of Improvised Explosive Device Attacks by Restricting Access to Explosive Precursor Chemicals*. Washington, DC: The National Academies Press.

National Police of Colombia, Antinarcotics Directorate (2014). *Coca: Deforestation, Pollution, and Poverty*. Bogotá, Colombia: National Printing of Colombia.

Navarro, I.A. (2013). Housing markets on cocaine: Explaining the relationship between cocaine exports and local housing markets in the Andes. *Journal of Housing Research*, 22(1), 59–74.

Newburn, T. (2017). *Criminology* (3rd ed). London, UK: Routledge.

Newcombe, R. (1992). The reduction of drug-related harm: A conceptual framework for theory, practice and research. In P.A. O'Hare, R. Newcombe, A. Matthews, E.C. Buning, and E. Drucker (Eds.). *The Reduction of Drug-Related Harm* (pp. 1–14). London, UK: Routledge.

Nieuwblad, Het (2017, September 8). Politiebaas luidt alarmklok: "Drugsmaffia infiltreert in Antwerpse politie, douane en bedrijven" [Police chief rings alarm bell: "Drugs mafia" infiltrates Antwerp police, customs and businesses]. Retrieved from https://www.nieuwsblad.be/cnt/dmf20170907_03059658 (accessed February 25, 2018).

Nordgren. L. and McDonnell, M.H. (2011). The scope-severity paradox: Why doing more harm is judged to be less harmful. *Social Psychological and Personality Science*, 2(1), 97–102.

Nozick, R. (1972). *Anarchy, State and Utopia*. Oxford, UK: Blackwell.

Nussbaum, M.C. (1997). Capabilities and human rights. *Fordham Law Review*, 66, 273–300.

Nussbaum, M.C. (2003). Capabilities as fundamental entitlements: Sen and social justice. *Feminist Economics*, 9(2–3), 33–59.

Nutt, D. (2011). Let not the best be the enemy of the good. *Addiction*, 106 (11), 1892–1893.

Nutt, D.J., King, L.A., Saulsbury, W., and Blakemore, C. (2007). Development of a rational scale to assess the harm of drugs of potential misuse. *The Lancet*, 369(9566), 1047–53.

Nutt, D.J., King, L.A., and Phillips, L.D. (2010). Drug harms in the UK: A multicriteria decision analysis. *The Lancet*, 376(9752), 1558–65.

O'Connell, M. and Whelan, A. (1996). Taking wrongs seriously. *The British Journal of Criminology*, 36(2), 299–318.

Obot, I.S. (2011). Improved ranking of drugs on harmfulness can bring sense and order to a failed system. *Addiction*, 106(11), 1894–1895.

Office of Management and Budget (2003). *Circular No. A–4: Regulatory Analysis*. Washington, DC, September. Retrieved from https://www.whitehouse.gov/sites/whitehouse.gov/files/omb/circulars/A4/a-4.pdf (accessed October 19, 2021)

Office for National Statistics (2016). Research outputs: Developing a crime severity score for England and Wales using data on crimes recorded by the police. Retrieved from https://www.ons.gov.uk/peoplepopulationandcommunity/crimeandjustice/articles/researchoutputsdevelopingacrimeseverityscoreforenglandandwalesusingdataoncrimesrecordedbythepolice/2016-11-29 (accessed October 20, 2017).

Office for the Victims of Crime (2017). *Overview of Crime Victims' Rights*. Retrieved from https://www.ovc.gov/rights/overview_rights.html (accessed February 25, 2018).

O'Keefe, R. (2017). *International Criminal Law*. Oxford, UK: Oxford University Press.

O'Malley, P. (2006). Criminology and risk. In G. Mythen and S. Walklate (Eds.). *Beyond The Risk Society: Critical Reflections on Risk and Human Security* (pp. 43–59). Maidenhead, UK: Open University Press.

O'Malley, P. (2008). Experiments in risk and criminal justice. *Theoretical Criminology*, 12(4), 451–69.

Openbaar Ministerie (2012, October 12). Recordvangst 8 ton cocaine [Record seizure of 8 tons cocaine]. Retrieved from https://www.om.nl/@30914/recordvangst-8-ton/ (accessed February 25, 2018).

Oram S., Stöckl H., Busza J., Howard L.M., Zimmerman, C. (2012). Prevalence and Risk of Violence and the Physical, Mental, and Sexual Health Problems Associated with Human Trafficking: Systematic Review. PLoS Med 9(5): e1001224. doi:10.1371/journal.pmed.1001224.

Organisation for Economic Co-operation and Development (2008). *OECD Glossaries—Corruption: A Glossary of International Standards in Criminal Law*. Paris, France: OECD.

Osborne, D. and Wernicke, S. (2003). *Introduction to Crime Analysis: Basic Resources for Criminal Justice Practice*. New York, NY: Haworth Press.

Owens, E.G. (2009). More times, less crime? Estimating the incapacitative effects of sentence enhancements. *Journal of Labor Economics* 53, 551–79.

Pacula, R.L., Hoorens, S., Kilmer, B., Reuter, P., Burgdorf, J., and Hunt, P. (2009). Issues in estimating the economic cost of drug abuse in consuming nations. In P. Reuter and F. Trautmann (Eds.). *A Report on Global Illicit Drug Markets, 1998–2007, Subreports and Appendix* (pp. 78–109). Brussels, Belgium: European Communities.

Palacios, P. (2012). Forced displacement: Legal versus illegal crops. *Defence and Peace Economics*, 23(2), 133–60.

Pantazis, C. and S. Pemberton (2009). Nation states and the production of social harm: Resisting the hegemony of "TINA." In R. Coleman, J. Sim, S. Tombs, and D. Whyte (Eds.). *State, Power and Crime* (pp. 214–33). London, UK: Sage.

Paoli, L. (2000). *Pilot Project to Describe and Analyse Local Drug Markets—First Phase Final Report: Illegal Drug Markets in Frankfurt and Milan*. Lisbon, Portugal: EMCDDA.

Paoli, L. (2014). How to tackle (organized) crime in Europe? The EU policy cycle on serious and organized crime and the new emphasis on harm. *The European Journal of Crime, Criminal Law and Criminal Justice*, 22, 1–12.

Paoli, L. (2018, February 28). De zeven mythes in het drugsdebat. *De Morgen*: 26.

Paoli, L. and Donati, A. (2014). *The Sport Doping Market: Understanding Supply and Demand, and the Challenges of Their Control*. New York, NY: Springer.

Paoli, L. and Greenfield, V.A. (2013). Harm: A neglected concept in criminology, a necessary benchmark for crime-control policy. *The European Journal of Crime, Criminal Law and Criminal Justice*, 21(3–4), 359–77.

Paoli, L. and Greenfield, V.A. (2015). Starting from the end: A plea for focusing on the consequences of crime. *The European Journal of Crime, Criminal Law and Criminal Justice*, 23(2), 87–100.

Paoli, L. and Greenfield, V.A. (2018). Harm: A substitute for crime or central to it? In A. Boukli and J. Kotze (Eds.) (2017). *Zemiology: Reconnecting Crime and Social Harm* (pp. 57–84). Cham, UK: Palgrave.

Paoli, L. and Reuter, P. (2008). Ethnic minorities and drug trafficking. *The European Journal of Criminology*, 5, 13–37.

Paoli, L., Kersten, L., and Greenfield V.A. (2015). The harms of cocaine trafficking in the Netherlands and Belgium: Policy insights from comparative assessment. Presentation prepared for the Ninth Annual Conference of the International Society for the Study of Drug Policy (ISSDP), May 20–22, 2015, Ghent, Belgium, unpublished.

Paoli, L., Greenfield, V.A., and Reuter, P. (2009). *The World Heroin Market: Can Supply Be Cut?* New York, NY: Oxford University Press.

Paoli, L., Zoutendijk, A., and Greenfield, V.A. (2012). De schade van georganiseerde criminaliteit (The harm of organised crime). In T. Vander Beken, L. Paoli, A. Zoutendijk, and N. Klima (Eds.). *Het inschatten van de gevaarlijkheid van georganiseerde criminaliteit (Assessing the Danger of Organized Crime)* (pp. 19–84). Gent, Belgium: Academia Press.

Paoli, L., Greenfield, V.A., and Zoutendijk, A. (2013). The harms of cocaine trafficking: Applying a new framework for assessment. *Journal of Drug Issues*, 43(4), 407–36.

Paoli, L., Decorte, T., and Kersten, L. (2015). Assessing the harms of cannabis cultivation in Belgium. *International Journal of Drug Policy*, 26, 277–89.

Paoli, L., Adriaenssen, A., Greenfield, V.A., and Coninckx, M. (2017). Exploring definitions of serious crime in EU policy documents and academic publications: A content analysis and policy implications. *The European Journal on Criminal Policy and Research*, 23(3), 269–85.

Paoli, L., Visschers, J., and Verstraete, C. (2018a). The impact of cybercrime on businesses: A new conceptual framework and its application to Belgium. *Crime, Law and Social Change*, 70(4), 397–420.

Paoli, L., Visschers, J., Verstraete, C., and Van Hellemont, E. (2018b). *The Impact of Cybercrime on Belgian Businesses*. Antwerp: Intersentia.

Paoli, L., Visschers, J., Adriaenssen, A., Karstedt, S. and Greenfield, V.A. (2020). Public Perceptions of the Seriousness of Crime: A Valid Indicator of Actual Crime Seriousness? In T. Daems and S. Pleysier (Eds.) *Criminology and Democratic Politics* (pp. 184–205). Abingdon: Routledge.

Parliament of the United Kingdom (2014). Anti-Social Behaviour, Crime and Policing Act 2014. Annex B: Summary of powers to tackle anti-social behaviour to be replaced by the provisions in parts 1 to 4 of the Act. The anti-social behaviour order. Retrieved from https://www.legislation.gov.uk/ukpga/2014/12/notes/annex/2?view=plain (accessed October 20, 2021).

Parmentier, S., Valiñas, M., and Weitekamp, E. (2009). How to repair the harm after violent conflict in Bosnia: Results of a population-based survey. *Netherlands Quarterly of Human Rights*, 27(1), 27–44.

Passas, N. and Goodwin, N.R. (Eds.) (2004). *It's Legal But It Ain't Right: Harmful Consequences of Legal Industries*. Ann Arbor, MI: University of Michigan Press.

Pearson, G. and Hobbs, D. (2001). *Middle Market Drug Distribution*. London, UK: Home Office Research, Development and Statistics Directorate.

Pemberton, A., Winkel, F.W., and Groenhuijsen, M. (2007). Taking victims seriously in restorative justice. *International Perspectives in Victimology*, 3(1), 4–14.

Pemberton, S. (2007). Social harm future(s): Exploring the potential of the social harm approach. *Crime Law and Social Change*, 48(1), 27–41.

Pemberton, S. (2015). *Harmful Societies: Understanding Social Harm*. Bristol, UK: Policy Press.

Peršak, N. (2007). *Criminalising Harmful Conduct: The Harm Principle, Its Limits and Continental Counterparts*. New York, NY: Springer.

Peters, B.C. (2020). Nigerian piracy: Articulating business models using crime script analysis. *International Journal of Law, Crime and Justice*. https://doi.org/10.1016/j.ijlcj.2020.100410.

Peters, B.C. and Paoli, L. (2020). Nigerian Piracy: A systematic assessment of its harms. *Acta Criminologica: African Journal of Criminology and Victimology*, 33(1), 132–56.

Petersen, M.B., Sell, A., Tooby, J., and Cosmides, L. (2010). Evolutionary psychology and criminal justice: A recalibrational theory of punishment and reconciliation. In H. Høgh-Olesen (Ed.). *Human Morality and Sociality: Evolutionary and Comparative Perspectives* (pp. 72–125). New York, NY: Palgrave.

Phillips, L. and Votey, H.L. (1981). *The Economics of Crime Control*. Beverly Hills, CA: Sage.

Pidoto, R.R., Agliata, A.M., Bertolini, R., Mainini, A., Rossi, G., and Giani, G. (2002). A new method of packaging cocaine for international traffic and implications for the management of cocaine body packers. *Journal of Emergency Medicine*, 23, 149–53.

Plowman, T. (1986). Coca chewing and the botanical origins of coca (Erythroxylum spp.) in South America. In D. Pacini and C. Franquemont (Eds.). *Coca and Cocaine: Effects on People and Policy in Latin America* (pp. 5–33). Cultural Survival Report 23, publication of Cultural Survival Inc. and the Latin American Studies Program, Cornell University. NY. Peterborough, NY: Transcript Printing Company.

Politie (2018). Bijna 7.000 kg cocaïne onderschept in haven Antwerpen [Almost 7,000 Kg of cocaine recovered in the Port of Antwerp]. January 1. Retrieved from https://www.politie.nl/nieuws/2018/januari/3/11-bijna-7.000-kg-cocaine-onderschept-in-haven-antwerpen.html (accessed February 25, 2018).

Port of Antwerp (2010). *Focus on the Port*. Retrieved from http://www.portofantwerp.com/#6 (accessed November 25, 2012). For more recent information about the port, see Port of Antwerp (2021).*A global port.*. Retrieved from https://www.portofantwerp.com/en/international-port(accessed November 25, 2012).

Port of Antwerp (2018a). Port of Antwerp. Retrieved from http://www.portofantwerp.com/en (accessed February 25, 2018).

Port of Antwerp (2018b). Stroomplan voorziet meldpunt voor criminaliteit en verdachte handelingen [Flow plan foresees reporting point for crime and suspicious actions]. Retrieved from https://www.portofantwerp.com/nl/news/str

oomplan-voorziet-meldpunt-voor-criminaliteit-en-verdachte-handelingen (accessed August 8, 2020).

Porteous, S.D. (1998). *Organized Crime Impact Study: Highlights*. Ottawa, ON: Public Works and Government Services of Canada.

Presser, L. (2013). *Why We Harm?* New Brunswick, NJ: Rutgers University Press.

Provost, C. (2017). The industry of inequality: Why the world is obsessed with private security *The Guardian*, May 17. Retrieved from https://www.theguardian.com/inequality/2017/may/12/industry-of-inequality-why-world-is-obsessed-with-private-security (accessed August 26, 2018).

Public Safety Canada (2017). About public safety Canada. Retrieved from https://www.publicsafety.gc.ca/cnt/bt/index–en.aspx (accessed February 25, 2018).

PwC, Pricewaterhouse Coopers (2016). Global Economic Crime Survey 2016: Adjusting the lens on economic crime: Preparation brings opportunity back into focus. Retrieved from https://www.pwc.com/gx/en/economic-crime-survey/pdf/GlobalEconomicCrimeSurvey2016.pdf (accessed February 25, 2018).

Quill, E. and Friel, R.J. (2016). Introduction. In E. Quill and R.J. Friel (Eds.). *Damages and Compensation Culture: Comparative Perspectives* (pp. 1–12). Oxford, UK: Hart.

Quimbayo Ruiz, G.A. (2008). *Crops for Illicit Use and Ecocide. Drug Policy Briefing Nr. 28*. Amsterdam, The Netherlands: Transnational Institute.

Ramsay, P. (2012). Imprisonment under the precautionary principle. In R. Sullivan and I. Dennis (Eds.). *Seeking Security: Pre-empting the Commission of Criminal Harms* (pp. 193–218). Oxford, UK: Hart.

Ratcliffe, J.H. (2014). Towards an index for harm-focused policing. *Policing*, 9(2), 164–82.

Rawls, R. (1971). *A Theory of Justice*. Cambridge, MA: Harvard University Press.

Reese, S. (2013). Defining homeland security: Analysis and congressional considerations. Congressional Research Service 7–5700, January 8. Retrieved from https://fas.org/sgp/crs/homesec/R42462.pdf (accessed February 20, 2018).

Reiman, J. (2006). Book review: 'Beyond criminology: Taking harm seriously'. *The British Journal of Criminology*, 46, 362–4.

Reiner, R. (2016). *Crime: The Mystery of the Common-Sense Concept*. Cambridge, UK: Polity Press.

Reiss, J. (2009). Causation in the social sciences: Evidence, inference, and purpose. *Philosophy of the Social Sciences*, 39(1), 20–40.

Relyea, R.A. (2004). Growth and survival of five amphibian species exposed to combinations of pesticides. *Environmental Toxicology and Chemistry*, 23(7), 1737–42.

Relyea, R.A. (2005a). The lethal impacts of Roundup and predatory stress on six species of North American tadpoles. *Archives of Environmental Contamination and Toxicology*, 48, 351–7.

Relyea, R.A. (2005b). The lethal impact of Roundup on aquatic and terrestrial amphibians. *Ecological Applications*, 15(4), 1118–24.

Relyea, R.A. (2009). A cocktail of contaminants: How mixtures of pesticides at low concentrations affect aquatic communities. *Oecologia*, 159, 363–76.

Relyea, R.A. (2012). New effects of Roundup on amphibians: Predators reduce herbicide mortality; herbicides induce antipredator morphology. *Ecological Applications*, 22(2), 634–47.

Relyea, R.A. and Diecks, N. (2008). An unforeseen chain of events: Lethal effects of pesticides on frogs at sublethal concentrations. *Ecological Applications*, 18(7), 1728–42.

Relyea, R.A. and Jones, D.K. (2009). The toxicity of Roundup Original Max® to 13 species of larval amphibians. *Environmental Toxicology and Chemistry*, 28(9), 2004–8.

Relyea, R.A., Schoeppner, N.M., and Hoverman, J.T. (2005). Pesticides and amphibians: The importance of community context. *Ecological Applications*, 15(4), 1125–34.

Repetto, R. (1992). Accounting for environmental assets. *Scientific American*, 266(6), 94–100.

Resick, P.A. (1990). Victims of sexual assault. In A.J. Lurigio, W.G. Skogan, and R.C. Davis (Eds.). *Victims Of Crime: Problems, Policies and Programs* (pp. 69–86). London, UK: Sage.

Reuter, P. and Haaga, J. (1989). *The Organization of High-Level Drug Markets: An Exploratory Study*. Santa Monica, CA: RAND Corporation.

Reyes, L.C. (2014). Estimating the causal effect of forced eradication on coca cultivation in Colombian municipalities. *World Development*, 61, 70–84.

Riggsby, A. (2016). Public and private criminal law. In P.J. Plessis, C. Ando, and K. Tuori (Eds.). *Oxford Handbook of Roman Law and Society* (pp. 310–21). Oxford, UK: Oxford University Press.

Rijksoverheid (2013). Internationale veiligheidsstrategie: Veilige wereld, veilig Nederland [International security strategy: Safe world, safe Netherlands]. Retrieved from https://www.rijksoverheid.nl/documenten/rapporten/2013/06/21/veilige-wereld-veilig-nederland-internationale-veiligheidsstrategie (accessed February 23, 2018).

Riley, D., Sawka, E., Conley, P., Hewitt, D., Mitic, W., Poulin, C., Room, R., Single, E., and Topp, J. (1999). Harm reduction: Concepts and practice. A policy discussion paper. *Substance Use and Misuse*, 34, 9–22.

Rincón-Ruiz, A. and Kallis, G. (2013). Caught in the middle: Colombia's war on drugs and its effects on forest and people. *Geoforum*, 46, 60–78.

Rincón-Ruiz, A., Pascual, U., and Flantua, S. (2013a). Examining spatially varying relationships between coca crops and associated factors in Colombia, using geographically weight regression. *Applied Geography*, 37, 23–33.

Rincón-Ruiz, A., Pascual, U., and Romero, M. (2013b). An exploratory spatial analysis of illegal coca cultivation in Colombia using local indicators of spatial association and socioecological variables. *Ecological Indicators*, 34, 103–12.

Rincón-Ruiz, A., Correa, H.L., León, D.O., and Williams, S. (2016). Coca cultivation and crop eradication in Colombia: The challenges of integrating rural reality into effective anti-drug policy. *International Journal of Drug Policy*, 33, 56–65.

Ripstein, A. (2006). Beyond the harm principle. *Philosophy and Public Affairs*, 34, 215–45.

Ritter, A. (2009). Methods for comparing drug policies—The utility of composite Drug Harm Indexes. *The International Journal of Drug Policy*, 20(6), 475–479.

Roach, K. (2011). *The 9/11 Effect: Comparative Counter-Terrorism*. Cambridge, UK: Cambridge University Press.

Roberts, J.V. (2011). The future of state punishment: The role of public opinion in sentencing. In M. Tonry (Ed.). *Retributivism Has a Past: Has It a Future?* (pp. 101–29). Oxford, UK: Oxford University Press.

Robinson, E.H. (2013). The distinction between state and government. *Geography Compass*, 7(8), 556–66.

Robinson, P.H. and Kurzban, R. (2007). Concordance and conflict in intuitions of justice *Minnesota Law Review*, 91, 1829–907.

Rodríguez, N., Armenteras, D., Retana, J., and Molowny-Horas, R. (2012). Patterns and trends of forest loss in the Colombian Guyana. *Biotropica*, 44(1), 123–32.

Roman, J. 2011. How do we measure the severity of crime? New estimates of the cost of criminal victimization. In J. MacDonald (Ed.). *Measuring Crime and Criminality: Advances in Criminological Theory* (pp. 37–70). Piscataway, NJ: Rutgers University Press.

Rome Statute of the International Criminal Court (1998). 2187 UNTS 90, UN Doc. A/CONF.183/9 July 17. Retrieved from https://treaties.un.org/doc/Publication/UNTS/Volume%202187/v2187.pdf (accessed November 20, 2018).

Room, R. (2011). Scales and blinkers, motes and beams—whose view is obstructed on drug scheduling? *Addiction*, 106(11), 1895–1896.

Rorty, R.M. (1989). *Contingency, Irony and Solidarity*. Cambridge, UK: Cambridge University Press.

Rorty, R.M. (1990). The priority of democracy to philosophy. In A. Makachowski (Ed.). *Reading Rorty: Critical Responses to 'Philosophy and the Mirror of Nature' (and Beyond)* (pp. 279–302). Oxford, UK: Basil Blackwell.

Rosen, L.W. (2015). *International Drug Control Policy: Background and U.S. Responses*. CRS Report, RL34543. Washington, DC: Congressional Research Service.

Rosenmerkel, S.P. (2001). Wrongfulness and harmfulness as components of seriousness of white-collar offenses. *Journal of Contemporary Criminal Justice*, 17(4), 308–27.

Rossi P.H., Waite, E., Bose, C.E., and Berk, R.E. (1974). The seriousness of crimes: Normative structure and individual differences. *American Sociological Review*, 39(2), 224–37.

Rossow, I. (2011). Can harm ratings be useful? *Addiction*, 106(11), 1893–1894.

Rothe, D. and Kauzlarich, D. (2014). *Towards a Victimology of State Crime*. London, UK: Routledge.

Rouse, S.M. and Arce, M. (2006). The drug-laden balloon: U.S. military assistance and coca production in the Central Andes. *Social Science Quarterly*, 87(3), 540–57.

Roxin, C. (2006). *Strafrecht, Allgemeiner Teil [Criminal Law, General Part]* (4th ed.). Munich, Germany: CH Beck.

Rozell, D.J. (2015). A cautionary note on qualitative risk ranking of homeland security threats. *Homeland Security Affairs* 11: Art. 3.

Rozo, S.V. (2014). On the unintended consequences of anti-drug eradication programs in producer countries. University of California, Los Angeles, California Center for Population Research, Population Working Papers, January revision. Retrieved from http://papers.ccpr.ucla.edu/index.php/pwp/article/view/PWP-CCPR-2013-016 (accessed June 19, 2018).

Rubin, E.L. (1999). Introduction: Minimizing harm as a solution to the crime policy conundrum. In E.L. Rubin (Ed.). *Minimizing Harm: A New Crime Policy for Modern America* (pp. 1–33). Boulder, CO: Westview.

Ryberg, J. (2004). *The Ethics of Proportionate Punishment: A Critical Investigation*. Dordrecht, The Netherlands: Kluwer International.

Sampson, R.J. (2012). *Great American City: Chicago and the Enduring Neighborhood Effect*. Chicago, IL: University of Chicago Press.

Sampson, R.J. and Laub, J.H. (2005). A life-course view of the development of crime. *Annals of the American Academy of Political and Social Science*, 602, 12–45.

Sánchez-Cuervo, A.M. and Aide, T.M. (2013). Consequences of the armed conflict, forced human displacement, and land abandonment on forest cover change in Colombia: A multi-scaled analysis. *Ecosystems*, 16, 1052–70.

Sánchez-Cuervo, A.M., Aide, T.M., Clark, M.L., and Etter, A. (2012). Land cover change in Colombia: Surprising forest recovery trends between 2001 and 2010. *PLoS One*, 7(8), e43943.

Saunders, J., Ober, A.J., Kilmer, B., and Greathouse, S.M. (2016). *A Community-Based, Focused-Deterrence Approach to Closing Overt Drug Markets: A Process and Fidelity Evaluation of Seven Sites*. Santa Monica, CA: RAND Corporation.

Saunders, L.E. and Pezeshki, R. (2015). Glyphosate in runoff waters and in the root-zone: A Review. *Toxics*, 3, 462–80.

Sauviller, R. (2017). *Borgerokko Maffia: Marokkaanse Drugsmisdaad in Antwerpen [Borgerokko Mafia: Moroccan Drug Crime in Antwerp]*. Antwerp, Belgium: Horizon.

Schauer, F. (2013). The ubiquity of prevention. In A. Ashworth, L. Zedner and P. Tomlin (Eds.). *Prevention and the Limits of the Criminal Law*. (pp. 1–22). Oxford, UK: Oxford University Press.

Schuilenburg, M. (2015). *The Securitization of Society. Crime, Risk and Social Order*. New York. NY: New York University Press.

Schuilenburg, M. and van Steden, R. (2014). Positive security: A theoretical framework. In M. Schuilenburg, R. van Steden, and B. Oude Breuil (Eds.). *Positive Criminology* (pp. 19–32). The Hague, The Netherlands: Boom.

Schwendinger, H. and Schwendinger, J. ([1970] 2014). Defenders of order or guardians of human rights? *Social Justice*, 40(1–2), 87–117.

Sellin, T. (1938). *Culture, Conflict and Crime*. New York, NY: Social Science Research Council.

Sellin, T. and Wolfgang, M.E. (1964). *The Measurement of Delinquency*. New York, NY: John Wiley.

Sen, A. (1984). The living standard. *Oxford Economic Papers*, 36 (Supplement: Economic Theory and Hicksian Themes, November), 74–90.

Sen, A. (1987). The standard of living: Lecture I, concepts and critiques; Lecture II, lives and capabilities, in G. Hawthorn (Ed.). *The Standard of Living: The*

Tanner Lectures, Clare Hall, Cambridge, 1985 (pp. 1–19, 20–38). Cambridge, UK: Cambridge University Press.

Sen, A. (1993). Capability and well-being. In M.C. Nussbaum and A. Sen (Eds.). *The Quality of Life* (pp. 30–53). Oxford, UK: Oxford University Press.

Sen, A. (2005). Human rights and capabilities. *Journal of Human Development*, 6(2), 151–66.

Sen, A. (2008). The economics of happiness and capability. In L. Bruni, F. Comim, and M. Pugno (Eds.). *Capabilities and Happiness* (pp. 16–27). Oxford, UK: Oxford University Press.

Sen, A. (2009). *The Idea of Justice*. Cambridge, MA: Harvard University Press.

Sentencing Council (2016). Robbery: Definitive guideline. Retrieved from https://www.sentencingcouncil.org.uk/wp-content/uploads/Robbery-definitive-guideline-Web.pdf (accessed February 25, 2018).

Sentencing Council (2017). Terrorism guidelines: Consultation. Retrieved from https://www.sentencingcouncil.org.uk/wp–content/uploads/Terrorism–guideline–consultation–final.pdf (accessed February 25, 2018).

Serious Organised Crime Agency (2008). *The United Kingdom Threat Assessment of Serious Organized Crime 2008/9*. London, UK: Serious Organised Crime Agency.

Serious Organised Crime Agency (2010). *Annual Plan 2010/2011*. London, UK: Serious Organised Crime Agency.

Shearing, C. (1995). Reinventing policing: Policing as governance. In F. Sack, M. Vob, D. Frehsee, A. Funk, and H. Reinke (Eds.). *Privatisieirung Staatlicher Kontrolle: Befunde, Konzepte, Tendenze* (pp. 70–87). Baden-Baden, Germany: Nomos.

Shearing, C. (2015). Criminology and the anthropocene. *Criminology and Criminal Justice*, 15(3), 255–69.

Shearing, C. and Johnston, L. (2005). Justice in the risk society. *The Australian and New Zealand Journal of Criminology*, 38(1), 25–38.

Shearing, C.D. and Stenning, P. (1984). From the Panopticon to Disney World: The development of discipline. In A.N. Doob, and E.L. Greenspan (Eds.). *Perspectives in Criminal Law: Essays in Honour of John LL. J. Edwards* (pp. 335–49). Toronto, ON: Canada Law Books.

Shepherd, J. (1997). Violence: The relation between seriousness of injury and outcome in the criminal justice system, *Journal of Accident and Emergency Medicine*, 14, 204–8.

Shepherd, S.M. and Lewis-Fernandez, R. (2016). Forensic risk assessment and cultural diversity: Contemporary challenges and future directions. *Psychology, Public Policy and Law*, 22, 427–38.

Sheptycki, J.B., Jaffel, H., and Bigo, D. (2011). International organized crime in the European Union. Note prepared for the European Parliament Directorate General for Internal Policies, Policy Department C: Citizens' rights and constitutional affairs. Retrieved from http://www.europarl.europa.eu/document/activities/cont/201206/20120627ATT47775/20120627ATT47775EN.pdf (accessed March 20, 2015).

Sheremeti, F. (2017, August, 30). It's about time to seriously talk about war crimes and more. Kosovo 2.0. Retrieved from: https://kosovotwopointzero.com/en/time-seriously-talk-war-crimes/ (accessed October 21, 2021).

Sherman, L.W. (2007). The power few: Experimental criminology and the reduction of harm. The 2006 Joan McCord Prize Lecture. *Journal of Experimental Criminology*, 3(4), 299–321.

Sherman, L.W. (2013). The rise of evidence-based policing: Targeting, testing, and tracking. *Crime and Justice*, 42, 377–451.

Sherman, L.W., Gartin, P.R., and Buerger, M.E. (1989). Hot spots of predatory crime: Routine activities and the criminology of place. *Criminology*, 27, 27–55.

Sherman, L.W., Gottfredson, D., MacKenzie, D., Eck, J., Reuter, P., and Bushway, S. (1997). *Preventing Crime: What Works, What Doesn't, What's Promising. A Report to the United States Congress.* Washington, DC: National Institute of Justice.

Sherman, L., Neyroud, P.W., and Neyroud, E. (2016). The Cambridge crime harm index: Measuring total harm from crime based on sentencing guidelines. *Policing*, 10(3), 171–83.

Sherret, L. (2005). Futility in action: Coca fumigation in Colombia. *Journal of Drug Issues*, 35(1), 151–68.

Shoham, S.G., Knepper, P., and Kett, M. (2010). *International Handbook of Victimology.* Boca Raton, FL: CRC Press.

Shue, H. (1996). *Basic Rights* (2nd ed.). Princeton, NJ: Princeton University Press.

Sieber, U. (2012). Risk prevention by means of criminal law: On the legitimacy of anticipatory offenses in Germany's recently enacted counter-terrorism law. In F. Galli and A. Weyembergh (Eds.). *EU Counter-Terrorism Offences: What Impact on National Legislation and Case-Law?* (pp. 251–79). Brussels, Belgium: Editions de l'Université de Bruxelles.

Sieber, U. and Bögel, M. (1993). *Die Logistik Organisierter Kriminalität [The Logistics of Organized Crime]*. Wiesbaden: Bundeskriminalamt.

Simester, A.P. and von Hirsch, A. (2006). Regulating offensive conduct through two-step prohibitions. In A.P. Simester and A. von Hirsch (Eds.). *Incivilities: Regulating Offensive Behavior* (pp. 173–94). Oxford, UK: Hart.

Simester, A.P. and von Hirsch, A. (2011). *Crimes, Harms and Wrongs: On the Principles of Criminalization*. Portland, OR: Hart.

Simester, A.P., Spencer, J.R., Stark, F., Sullivan, G.R., and Virgo, G.J. (2016). *Simester and Sullivan's Criminal Law: Theory and Doctrine* (6th ed). Oxford, UK: Hart.

Singh, J.P., Desmarais, S.L., Hurducas, C., Arbach-Lucioni, K., Condemarin, C., Dean, K., et al. (2014). International perspectives on the practical application of violence risk assessment: A global survey of 44 countries. *International Journal of Forensic Mental Health*, 13, 193–206.

Slack, A., O'Dea, D., Sheerin, I., Norman, D., Wu, J. and Nana, G. (2008). New Zealand drug harm index: Report to the New Zealand police. Wellington, New Zealand: BERL House. Retrieved from: https://fyi.org.nz/request/1213/response/4866/attach/4/BERL%202008%20New%20Zealand%20Drug%20Harm%20Index%20final%20report.pdf (accessed October 11, 2021).

Skilbrei, M.-L. and Tveit, M. (2008). Defining trafficking through empirical work: Blurred boundaries and their consequences. *Gender, Technology, and Development*, 12(1), 9–30.

Smith, A. ([1763] 1896). *Lectures On Justice, Police, Revenue and Arms, Delivered in the University of Glasgow, By Adam Smith. Reported by a Student in 1763 and Edited with an Introduction and Notes by E. Cannan*. Oxford, UK: Clarendon Press.

Smith, A. ([1790] 1976). *The Theory of Moral Sentiments*. Oxford, UK: Clarendon Press.

SOCA (See Serious Organised Crime Agency)

Solomon, K.R., Anadón, A., Carrasquilla, G., Cerdeira, A.L., Marshall, J., and Sanin, L.-H. (2005). *Environmental and Human Health Assessment of the Aerial Spray Program for Coca and Poppy Control in Colombia: A Report Prepared for the Inter-American Drug Abuse Control Commission (CICAD) Section of the Organization of American States*. Washington, DC: Organization of American States.

Solomon, K.R., Anadón, A., Brain, R.A., Cerdeira, A.L., Crossan, A.N., Marshall, J., Sanin, L.-H., and Smith, L. (2007a). Comparative hazard assessment of the substances used for production and control of coca and poppy in Colombia. In I. Kennedy et al. (Eds.). *Rational Environmental Management of Agrochemicals* (pp. 87–99). Washington, DC: American Chemical Society.

Solomon, K.R., Anadón, A., Carrasquilla, G., Cerdeira, A.L., Marshall, J., and Sanin, L.-H. (2007b). Coca and poppy eradication in Colombia: Environmental and human health assessment of aerially applied glyphosate. *Review of Environmental Contamination and Toxicology*, 190, 43–125.

Solomon, K.R., Marshall, E.P.J., and Carrasquilla, G. (2009). Human health and environmental risks from the use of glyphosate formulations to control the production of coca in Colombia: Overview and conclusions. *Journal of Environmental Toxicology and Environmental Health, Part A*, 72, 914–20.

Spalek, B. (2017). *Crime Victims: Theory, Policy and Practice* (2nd ed.). Basingstoke, UK: Macmillan.

Sparrow, M. (2008). *The Character of Harms: Operational Challenges in Control*. Cambridge, UK: Cambridge University Press.

Spierenburg, P. (2013). *Violence and Punishment: Civilizing the Body through Time*. London, UK: Wiley.

Stahn, C. (2015). Reparative justice after the Lubanga appeal judgment: New prospects for expressivism and participatory justice or 'juridified victimhood' by other means? *Journal of International Criminal Justice*, 13, 801–13.

Standaard, De (2007, June 7). Drugshandel Zaventem: 2 verdachten gevlucht, 3 vrij [Drug trafficking Zaventem: 2 suspects fled, 3 free]. Retrieved from http://www.standaard.be/artikel/detail.aspx?artikelid=B17259632070607 (accessed June 20, 2011).

Standaard, De (2020, Februari 5). Stroomplan tegen drugscriminaliteit geëvalueerd: 'Dit gaat niet enkel over Antwerpen' [Flow plan against drug crime evaluated: 'This is not just about Antwerp']. Retrieved from https://www.standaard.be/cnt/dmf20200205_04836142 (accessed August 8, 2020).

Standaard, De (2021, March 17). Sky ECC: Raadkamer bevestigt aanhouding van drugsspeurder [Sky ECC: Judge's Chamber confirms arrest of drug detective]. Retrieved from: https://www.standaard.be/cnt/dmf20210317_93389263 (accessed November 6, 2021).

Stanko, E.A. and Hobdell, K. (1993). Assault on men. *British Journal of Criminology*, 33, 400–40.

Statistics Canada (2009). *Measuring Crime in Canada: Introducing the Crime Severity Index and Improvements to the Uniform Crime Reporting Survey*. Ottawa, ON: Minister of Industry.

Steiker, C.S. (1998). The limits of the preventive state. *Journal of Criminal Law and Criminology*, 88(3), 771–808.

Stephen, J.F. ([1873] 1967). *Liberty, Equality, Fraternity*, Ed. R.J. White. Cambridge, UK: Cambridge University Press.

Stewart, H. (2010). The limits of the harm principle. *Criminal Law and Philosophy*, 4, 17–35.

Stuart, H. and Lanier, M. (2001). *What Is Crime? Controversies over the Nature of Crime and What to Do about It*. Lanham, MD: Rowman and Littlefield.

Stuntz, W. (2011). The pathological politics of criminal law. *Michigan Law Review*, 100(3), 505–608.

Stylianou, S. (2003). Measuring crime seriousness perceptions: What have we learned and what else do we want to know. *Journal of Criminal Justice*, 31, 37–56.

Sullivan, C. and Su-Wuen, O. (2013). Justice Sector Seriousness Score (2012 revision). 13 December. Retrieved from https://www.justice.govt.nz/assets/Documents/Publications/justice-sector-offence-seriousness-score-faq.pdf (accessed February 23, 2018).

Sullivan, G.R. and Dennis, I. (Eds.) (2012). *Seeking Security: Pre-Empting the Commission of Criminal Harms*. Oxford, UK: Hart.

Sunstein, C.R. (2002). Beyond the precautionary principle. *University of Pennsylvania Law Review*, 151, 1003–58.

Sunstein, C.R. (2005). Moral heuristics. *The Behavioral and Brain Sciences*, 28(4), 531–542.

Sunstein, C.R. (2008). Legal implications of the new research on happiness. *Journal of Legal Studies*, 37, 157–94.

Sutherland, E.H. (1945). Is "white collar crime" crime? *American Sociological Review*, 10(2), 132–9.

Tadros, V. (2011). *The Ends of Harm: The Moral Foundations of Criminal Law*. Oxford, UK: Oxford University Press.

Tak, P. (Ed.) (2005). *Tasks and Powers of the Prosecution Services in the EU Member States*. Nijmegen, The Netherlands: Wolf.

Tappan, P. (1947). Who is the criminal? *American Sociological Review*, 12(1), 96–102.

Taylor, I., Walton, P., and Young. J. (1973). *The New Criminology: For a Social Theory of Deviance*. London, UK: Routledge.

Taylor-Powell, E. and Henert E. (2008). *Developing a Logic Model: Teaching and Training Guide*. Madison, WI: University of Wisconsin-Extension, Cooperative Extension.

Thaler, R. (1978). A note on the value of crime control. Evidence from the property market, *Journal of Urban Economics*, 5, 137–45.

Thilagaraj, R. and Liu, J. (2017). *Restorative Justice in India: Traditional Practice and Contemporary Applications*. New York, NY: Springer.

Thoumi, F. (1995) *Political Economy and Illegal Drugs in Colombia*. Lynne Rienner Publishers: London.

Tilley, N. and Sidebottom, A. (Eds.) (2017). *Handbook of Crime Prevention and Community Safety*. London, UK: Routledge.

Tirole, J. (2017). *Economics for the Common Good*. Princeton, NJ: Princeton University Press.

Tonry, M. (Ed.) (2007). *Crime, Punishment, and Politics in Comparative Perspective*. Chicago: University of Chicago Press.

Tonry, M. (2011). Can twenty-first century punishment policies be justified in principle? In M. Tonry (Ed.). *Retributivism Has a Past: Has It a Future?* (pp. 3–29). New York, NY: Oxford University Press.

Tonry, M. (2015). The fog around cost-of-crime studies may finally be clearing. *Criminology and Public Policy*, 14(4), 653–71.

Transnational Institute (2005). *The CICAD Study on the Impacts of Glyphosate and the Crop Figures, Drug Policy Briefing No. 14*. Amsterdam, The Netherlands: Transnational Institute.

Transparency International (2009). *The Anti-Corruption Plain Language Guide*. Berlin, Germany: TI International Secretariat.

Travis, J., Western, B., and Redburn, S. (Eds.) (2014). *The Growth of Incarceration in the United States: Exploring Causes and Consequences*. Washington, DC: National Academies Press.

Triana, T.M., Henao, L.M., and Bernal, M.H. (2017). Acute toxicity of the insecticide cypermethrin (CYPERMON® 20 EC) on four species of Colombian anurans. *Acta Biológica Colombiana*, 22(3), 340–7.

Trumbull, W.N. (1990). Who has standing in cost–benefit analysis? *Journal of Policy Analysis and Management*, 9(2), 201–18.

Tusikov, N. (2012). Measuring organised crime-related harms: Exploring five policing methods. *Crime, Law and Social Change*, 57, 99–115.

Tyler, T.R. (2006). *Why People Obey the Law*. Princeton, NJ: Princeton University Press.

Tyler, T.R. and Jackson, J. (2013). Future challenges in the study of legitimacy and criminal justice. Yale Law School, Public Law Working Paper No. 264.

UK (See United Kingdom)

UN (See United Nations)

UNDP (See United Nations Development Program)

UNGA (See United Nations General Assembly)

United Kingdom Drug Policy Commission (2009). *Refocusing Drug-Related Law Enforcement to Address Harms*. London: UK Drug Policy Commission.

United Kingdom Home Office (2011). *The National Crime Agency: A Plan for the Creation of a National Crime-Fighting Capability*. London: Home Office.

United Nations (1945). Charter of the International Military Tribunal: Annex to the agreement for the prosecution and punishment of the major war criminals of the European Axis ("London Agreement"), August 8. Retrieved from http://www.refworld.org/docid/3ae6b39614.html (accessed October 8, 2017).

United Nations (1961). *Single Convention on Narcotic Drugs, 1961, as Amended by the 1972 Protocol Amending the Single Convention on Narcotic Drugs*. New York: United Nations.

United Nations (1971). *United Nations Convention on Psychotropic Substances.* New York, NY: United Nations.

United Nations (1988). *United Nations Convention against Illicit Traffic in Narcotic Drugs and Psychotropic Substances,* New York, NY: United Nations.

United Nations (2000). *Protocol to Prevent, Suppress and Punish Trafficking in Persons, Especially Women and Children, Supplementing the United Nations Convention against Transnational Organized Crime.* New York, NY, United Nations.

United Nations Development Program (1994). *Human Development Report.* New York, NY: Oxford University Press.

United Nations Development Program (1994). *New Dimensions of Human Security.* New York, NY: Oxford University Press.

United Nations Economic and Social Council (2002a). Ecosoc Resolution 2002/12 Basic Principles on the Use of Restorative Justice Programmes in Criminal Matters.

United Nations Economic and Social Council (2002b). ECOSOC Resolution 2002/13 Action to promote effective crime prevention.

United Nations General Assembly (1948). International Bill of Human Rights: A universal declaration of human rights, General Assembly resolution 217 (III) of 10 December.

United Nations General Assembly (1966a). International Covenant on civil and political rights, General Assembly resolution 2200A (XXI) of 16 December.

United Nations General Assembly (1966b). International Covenant on economic, social and cultural rights, General Assembly resolution 2200A (XXI) of 16 December.

United Nations General Assembly (1985). Declaration of basic principles of justice for victims of crime and abuse of power, A/RES/40/34.

United Nations General Assembly (2000). Resolution adopted by the General Assembly: Keeping the promise: United to achieve the Millennium Development Goals. October 19, sixty-fifth session, RES/65/1.

United Nations General Assembly (2006). Resolution adopted by the General Assembly on 16 December 2005: Basic principles and guidelines on the right to a remedy and reparation for victims of gross violations of international human rights law and serious violations of international humanitarian law. March 21, sixtieth session, RES/60/147.

United Nations General Assembly (2015). Resolution adopted by the General Assembly: Transforming our world: The 2030 agenda for sustainable development. October 21, seventieth session, RES/70/1.

United Nations Office on Drugs and Crime (2005). *World Drug Report 2005.* Vienna: United Nations.

United Nations Office on Drugs and Crime (2006). *Características Agroculturales de los Cultivos de Coca en Colombia [Agricultural Characteristics of Coca Crops in Colombia].* Vienna: United Nations Office on Drugs and Crime.

United Nations Office on Drugs and Crime (2010a). *Guidance on the Preparation and Use of Serious and Organized Crime Threat Assessments: The SOCTA Handbook.* New York: United Nations.

United Nations Office on Drugs and Crime (2010b). Online database. Retrieved from http://www.unodc.org/unodc/en/data-and-analysis/Research-Database.html?ref=menuside (accessed January 20, 2012).

United Nations Office on Drugs and Crime (2010c). *World Drug Report 2010.* Vienna, Austria: United Nations.

United Nations Office on Drugs and Crime (2011). *The Transatlantic Cocaine Market.* Vienna, Austria: United Nations Office on Drugs and Crime.

United Nations Office on Drugs and Crime (2016). *World Drug Report.* Vienna, Austria: United Nations Office on Drugs and Crime.

United Nations Office on Drugs and Crime (2017). *World Drug Report.* Vienna, Austria: United Nations Office on Drugs and Crime.

United Nations Office on Drugs and Crime (2020). *World Drug Report. Booklet 3. Drug Supply.* Vienna, Austria: United Nations Office on Drugs and Crime.

United Nations Office on Drugs and Crime and Governments of Bolivia, Colombia, and Peru (2008). *Coca Cultivation in the Andean Region: A Survey of Bolivia, Colombia, and Peru.* Vienna, Austria: United Nations Office on Drugs and Crime.

United Nations Office on Drugs and Crime and Government of Colombia (2006). *Colombia: Coca Cultivation Survey.* Vienna, Austria: United Nations Office on Drugs and Crime.

United Nations Office on Drugs and Crime and Government of Colombia (2007). *Colombia: Coca Cultivation Survey.* Vienna, Austria: United Nations Office on Drugs and Crime.

United Nations Office on Drugs and Crime and Government of Colombia (2009). *Colombia: Coca Cultivation Survey.* Vienna, Austria: United Nations Office on Drugs and Crime.

United Nations Office on Drugs and Crime and Government of Colombia (2010). *Colombia: Coca Cultivation Survey.* Vienna, Austria: United Nations Office on Drugs and Crime.

United Nations Office on Drugs and Crime and Government of Colombia (2011). *Colombia: Coca Cultivation Survey.* Vienna, Austria: United Nations Office on Drugs and Crime.

United Nations Office on Drugs and Crime and Government of Colombia (2012). *Colombia: Coca Cultivation Survey.* Vienna, Austria: United Nations Office on Drugs and Crime.

United Nations Office on Drugs and Crime and Government of Colombia (2013). *Colombia: Coca Cultivation Survey.* Vienna, Austria: United Nations Office on Drugs and Crime.

United Nations Office on Drugs and Crime and Government of Colombia (2014). *Colombia: Coca Cultivation Survey.* Vienna, Austria: United Nations Office on Drugs and Crime.

United Nations Office on Drugs and Crime and Government of Colombia (2015). *Colombia: Coca Cultivation Survey.* Vienna, Austria: United Nations Office on Drugs and Crime.

United Nations Office on Drugs and Crime and Government of Colombia (2016). *Colombia: Coca Cultivation Survey.* Vienna, Austria: United Nations Office on Drugs and Crime.

United Nations Office on Drugs and Crime and Government of Colombia (2017). *Colombia: Survey of Territories Affected by Illicit Crops—2016.* Vienna, Austria: United Nations Office on Drugs and Crime.

United Nations Office on Drugs and Crime and Ministry of Justice and Law (2010). *Características Agroculturales de los Cultivos de Coca en Colombia 2005–2010 [Agricultural Characteristics of Coca Crops in Colombia 2005–2010]*. Retrieved from http://www.odc.gov.co/Portals/1/publicaciones/pdf/oferta/estudios/OF04012010-caracteristicas-agroculturales-cultivos-coca-colombia-.pdf (accessed October 25, 2020).

United Nations Office on Drugs and Crime and Government of Peru (2017). *Peru Coca Survey For 2016, Fact Sheet and Executive Summary in English*. Vienna, Austria: United Nations Office on Drugs and Crime. Retrieved from https://www.unodc.org/documents/crop-monitoring/Peru/Peru_Coca_survey_2016_engl_Factsheet_ExSum.pdf (accessed October 25, 2020).

United Nations Office on Drugs and Crime and World Bank (2007). *Stolen Asset Recovery (Star) Initiative: Challenges, Opportunities, and Action Plan*. Washington, DC: World Bank.

UNODC (See United Nations Office on Drugs and Crime)

US Department of the Army (1998). *Risk Management (FM 100–14)*. Washington, DC: US Department of the Army.

US Department of the Army (2006). *Composite Risk Management (FM 5–19 [FM 100–14])*. Washington, DC: Headquarters, US Department of the Army.

US Department of the Army (2014). *Risk Management (ATP 5–19)*. Washington, DC: Headquarters, US Department of the Army.

US Department of the Army, Marine Corps, Navy, and Air Force (2001). Risk management: Multiservice tactics, techniques, and procedures for risk management (FM3–100.12, MCRP 5–12.1c, NTTP 5–03.5, and AFTTP[I] 3–2.34), Air Land Sea Application Center.

US Department of Education (2016). State and local expenditures on corrections and education. July. Retrieved from https://www2.ed.gov/rschstat/eval/other/expenditures-corrections-education/brief.pdf (accessed October 25, 2020).

US Department of Justice (2011). *Solicitation: Research and Evaluation on International Organized Crime. OMB No. 1121–0329*. Washington, DC: US Department of Justice, Office of Justice Programs, National Institute of Justice.

US Department of State (2006). *2006 International Narcotics Control Strategy Report*.

US Department of State (2007). *2007 International Narcotics Control Strategy Report*.

US Department of State (2010). *2010 International Narcotics Control Strategy Report*.

US Drug Enforcement Administration (1993). *Coca Cultivation and Cocaine Processing: An Overview*. Washington, DC: US Drug Enforcement Administration, Intelligence Division, Strategic Intelligence Section. Retrieved from https://erowid.org/archive/rhodium/chemistry/coca2cocaine.html (accessed October 25, 2020).

van Bruggen, A.H.C., He, M.M., Shin, K., Mai, V., Jeong, K.C., Finckh, M.R., and Morris, J.G., Jr. (2018). Environmental and health effects of the herbicide glyphosate. *Science of the Total Environment*, 616–17, 255–68.

van Daele, D., Goossens, F., and Mergaerts, L. (2017). *Het Belgische Politiewezen: Wetgeving en Beleid [Belgian Policing: Legislation and Policy]*. Mechelen, Belgium: Wolters Kluwer.

van Dam, C. (2013). *European Tort Law* (2nd ed.). Oxford, UK: Oxford University Press.

van den Berge, Y. (2013). De terbeschikkingstelling van de strafuitvoeringsrechtbank: Alweer een nieuwe straf, alweer een nieuwe uitvoering [The provision of the sentencing court: Yet another new sentence, yet another new execution]. *Tijdschrift voor strafrecht,* 14(4), 222–3.

van der Aa, J. (2009, November 11). "Bende van 700 miljoen" riskeert tot 15 jaar cel [700 million gang risks 15 years of prison]. *Het Nieuwsblad*. Retrieved from http://www.nieuwsblad.be/Article/PrintArticle.aspx?articleId=IJ2I8NPQ (accessed February 20, 2018).

Vander Beken, T., Paoli, L., Zoutendijk, A., and Klima, N. (Eds.) (2012). *Het Inschatten van de Gevaarlijkheid van Georganiseerde Criminaliteit [Assessing the Danger of Organized Crime]*. Gent, Belgium: Academia Press.

Van Der Laan, P. H., Smit, M., Busschers, I., and Aarten, P. (2011). Cross-border trafficking in human beings: Prevention and intervention strategies for reducing sexual exploitation. *Campbell Systematic Reviews*. doi:10.4073/csr.2011.9

van Dijk, J., van Kesteren, J., and P. Smit (2008). *Criminal Victimisation in International Perspective: Key Findings from the 2004–2005 ICVS and EU ICS*. The Hague, The Netherlands: Boom.

van Duyne, P.C. and Levi, M. (2005). *Drugs and Money: Managing the Drug Trade and Crime-Money in Europe*. Oxon, UK: Routledge.

van Duyne, P.C. and Vander Beken, T. (2009). The incantations of the EU organised crime policy making. *Crime, Law and Social Change*, 51(2), 261–81.

van Dyke, C. and Byck, R. (1982). Cocaine. *Scientific American*, 246(3), 128–41.

van Gestel, B. and Verhoeven, M.A. (2017). *Verkennende Voorstudie Liquidaties. [Exploratory Preliminary Study of Liquidations]. Cahier 2017-7.* The Hague, The Netherlands: WODC.

van Horenbeek, J. and van den Broek, A. (2018, January 16). Coke in 't Stad: Antwerpen zit er tot aan de neus in [Coke in the city: Antwerp has it up to its nose]. *De Morgen*. Retrieved from https://www.demorgen.be/binnenland/coke-in-t-stad-antwerpen-zit-er-tot-aan-de-neus-in-b1c0d17f/ (accessed February 25, 2018).

van Ness, D. (1986). *Crime and Its Victims*. Leicester, UK: Inter-Varsity Press.

van Ness, D. (1999). Legal issues of restorative justice. In G. Bazemore and L. Walgrave (Eds.). *Restorative Juvenile Justice: Repairing the Harm of Youth Crime* (pp. 263–83). Monsey, NY: Criminal Justice Press.

van Nuijs, A.L.N., Pecceu, B., Theunis, L., Dubois, N., Charlier, C., Jorens, P.G., and Covaci, A. (2009). Can cocaine use be evaluated through analysis of wastewater? A nation-wide approach conducted in Belgium. *Addiction*, 104, 734–41.

Vermeulen, G., van den Herrewegen, E., and van Puyenbroeck, L. (2007). *Mensenhandel in Beeld: Eerste Kwantitatieve en Kwalitatieve Analyse van Belgische Slachtofferdata [Human Trafficking in Picture: First Quantitative and Qualitative Analysis of Belgian Victim Data]*. Antwerp, Belgium: Appeldoorn.

Viscusi, W.K. (2008). How to value a life. *Journal of Economics and Finance*, 32, 311–23.

Viscusi, W.K. and Aldy, J.E. (2003). The value of a statistical life: A critical review of market estimates throughout the world. *The Journal of Risk and Uncertainty*, 27, 5–76.

Volkskrant, De (2005, September 6). Recordvangst van cocaïne [Record seizure of cocaine]. Retrieved from http://www.volkskrant.nl/vk/nl/2680/Economie/article/detail/675323/2005/09/06/Recordvangstvan-coca-iuml-ne.dhtml (accessed June 20, 2011).

von Hirsch, A. (1986). *Doing Justice: The Choice of Punishments*. Boston, MA: Northeastern University Press.

von Hirsch, A. (1993). *Censure and Sanctions*. Oxford, UK: Oxford University Press.

von Hirsch, A. (1996). Extending the harm principle: "Remote" harms and fair imputation. In A.P. Simester and A.T.H. Smith (Eds.). *Harm And Culpability* (pp. 259–75). Oxford, UK: Oxford University Press.

von Hirsch, A. (2003). Der Rechtsgutsbegriff und das Harm Principle [The concept of legal interest and the harm principle]. In R. Hefendehl, A. von Hirsch, and W. Wohlers (Eds.). *Die Rechtsgutstheorie: Legitimationsbasis des Strafrechts oder Dogmatisches Glasperlenspiel? [The Legal Interest Theor: Legitimation Basis of Criminal Law or Dogmatic Glass Bead Game?]* (pp. 11–25). Baden-Baden, Germany: Nomos.

von Hirsch, A. (2009). Proportionate sentences: A desert perspective. In A. von Hirsch, A. Ashworth, and J. Roberts (Eds.). *Principled Sentencing: Readings on Theory and Policy* (pp. 115–25). Portland, OR: Hart.

von Hirsch, A. (2011). Punishment futures: The desert-model debate and the importance of criminal law context. In M. Tonry (Ed.). *Retributivism Has a Past: Has It a Future?* (pp. 256–73). New York, NY: Oxford University Press.

von Hirsch, A. and Ashworth, A. (2005). *Proportionate Sentencing*. Oxford, UK: Oxford University Press.

von Hirsch, A. and Jareborg, N. (1991). Gauging criminal harm: A living-standard analysis. *Oxford Journal of Legal Studies*, 11(1), 1–38.

von Hirsch, A. and Simester, A.P. (Eds.) (2006). *Incivilities: Regulating Offensive Behaviour*. London, UK: Hart.

von Hirsch, A. Bottoms, A.E., Roberts, J., and Roach, K. (Eds.) (2003). *Restorative Justice and Criminal Justice: Competing or Reconcilable Paradigms?* London, UK: Hart.

von Hirsch, A., Ashworth, A., and Jareborg, N. (2005). Gauging crime seriousness: A 'living standard' conception of criminal harm. In A. von Hirsch and A. Ashworth (Eds.). *Proportionate Sentencing* (Appendix 3, pp. 186–219). Oxford, UK: Oxford University Press.

Wacquant, L. (2001). Deadly symbiosis: When ghetto and prison meet and mesh. *Punishment and Society*, 3(1), 95–133.

Wade, M. (2005). The power to decide: Prosecutorial control, diversion and punishment in European criminal justice systems today. In. J.-M. Jehle and M. Wade. *Coping with Overloaded Criminal Justice Systems: The Rise of Prosecutorial Power across Europe* (pp. 27–115). Berlin, Germany: Springer.

Waelkens, L. (2015). *Amne Adverso: Roman Legal Heritage in European Culture.* Leuven, Belgium: Leuven University Press.

Waldron, J. (2002). Is the rule of law an essentially contested concept (in Florida)? *Law and Philosophy*, 21(2), 137–64.

Walgrave, L. (2003). Imposing restoration instead of inflicting pain. In A. von Hirsch, J.V. Roberts, A.E. Bottoms, K. Roach, and M. Schiff (Eds.). *Restorative Justice and Criminal Justice: Competing or Reconcilable Paradigms?* (pp. 61–78). London, UK: Hart.

Walgrave, L. (2008). *Restorative Justice and the Law*. Cullompton, UK: Wiley.

Walgrave, L. (2011). Investigating the potentials of restorative justice practice. *Journal of Law and Policy*, 36, 91–139.

Walgrave, L. (2013). From civilising punishment to civilising criminal justice: From punishment to restoration. In D. Cornwell, J. Blad, and M. Wright (Eds.). *Civilising Criminal Justice. An International Restorative Agenda for Penal Reform* (pp. 347–77). Hook, UK: Waterside Press.

Walker, N. (1997). Harms, probabilities and precautions. *Oxford Journal of Legal Studies*, 17, 611–20.

Walklate, S. (2007a). *Handbook of Victims and Victimology*. Cullompton, UK: Willan.

Walklate, S. (2007b). *Imagining the Victim of Crime*. Maidenhead, UK: Open University Press.

Wallerstein, S. (2007). Criminalising remote harm and the case of anti-democratic activity. *Cardozo Law Review*, 28, 2697–738.

Warr, M. (1989). What is the perceived seriousness of crimes? *Criminology*, 27(4), 795–822.

Washington Office on Latin America (2008). *Chemical Reactions. Fumigation: Spreading Coca and Threatening Colombia's Ecological and Cultural Diversity*. Washington, DC: Washington Office on Latin America.

Weber, M. (1960). *Rechtssoziologie*. Ed. J. Winckelmann. Neuwied, Germany: Luchterhand.

Weisburd, D., Bruinsma, G.J.N., and Bernasco, W. (Eds.) (2009). *Putting Crime in Its Place: Units of Analysis in Geographic Criminology*. New York, NY: Springer.

Weisburd, D., Farrington, D.P., and Gill, C. (Eds.) (2016). *What Works in Crime Prevention and Rehabilitation: Lessons from Systematic Reviews*. New York, NY: Springer.

Wells, C. and Quick, O. (2010). *Lacey, Wells and Quick: Reconstructing Criminal Law Text and Materials* (4th ed.). Cambridge, UK: Cambridge University Press.

Welsh, B.C. and Farrington, D.P. (2012). *The Oxford Handbook of Crime Prevention*. New York, NY: Oxford University Press.

Wenzel, M., Okimoto, T.G., Feather, N.T., and Platow, M.J. (2008). Retributive and restorative justice. *Law and Human Behavior*, 32(5), 375–89.

W.K. Kellogg Foundation (2004). *Logic Model Development Guide*, Battle Creek, MI.

White, R. (Ed.) (2010). *Global Environmental Harm: Criminological Perspectives*. Oxon, UK: Willan.

White, R. (2013). *Environmental Harm: An Eco-Justice Perspective*. Bristol, UK: Policy Press.

Whittington, D. and MacRae, D., Jr. (1986). The issue of standing in cost–benefit analysis. *Journal of Policy Analysis and Management*, 5(4), 665–82.

Whittington, D. and MacRae, D., Jr. (1990). Comment: Judgments about who has standing in cost-benefit analysis. *Journal of Policy Analysis and Management* 9(4), 536–547.

Whyte, D. (2007). Victims of corporate crime. In S. Walklate (Ed.). *Handbook of Victims and Victimology* (pp. 446–64). Cullompton, UK: Willan.

Wickramasekera, N., Wright, J., Elsey, H., Murray, J., and Tubeuf, S. (2015). Cost of crime: A systematic review. *Journal of Criminal Justice*, 43, 218–28.

Wikstrom, P.O. (2008). In search of causes and explanations of crime. In R.D. King and E. Wincup (Eds.). *Doing Research on Crime and Justice* (2nd ed.; pp. 117–40). Oxford, UK: Oxford University Press.

Wikstrom, P.O., Oberwittler, D., Treiber, K., and Hardie, B. (2012). *Breaking Rules: The Social and Situational Dynamics of Young People's Urban Crime*. Oxford, UK: Oxford University Press:

Williams, B. (1987). The standard ofliving: Interests and capabilities. In G. Hawthorn (Ed.). *The Standard of Living: The Tanner Lectures, Clare Hall, Cambridge, 1985* (pp. 94–102). Cambridge, UK: Cambridge University Press.

Williams, B. (2005). *In the Beginning Was the Deed: Realism and Moralism in Political Argument*. Princeton, NJ: Princeton University Press.

Williams, K. (2005). "State of fear": Britain's "compensation culture" reviewed. *Legal Studies*, 25(3), 499–515.

Williams, L. (2016). *Crime against Businesses: Findings from the 2015 Commercial Victimisation Survey*. London: Home Office.

Wilson, D.P., Donald, B., Shattock, A.J., Wilson, D., and Fraser-Hurt, N. (2015). Commentary: The cost-effectiveness of harm reduction. *International Journal of Drug Policy*, 26 (Supplement 1), 5–11.

Wodak, A. and Saunders, B. (1995). Harm reduction means what I choose it to mean. *Drug and Alcohol Review*, 14(3), 269–71.

Wood, J. and Dupont, B. (Eds.) (2006). *Democracy, Society and the Governance of Security*. Cambridge, UK: Cambridge University Press.

Wortham, C.-L. (2007–8). Methamphetamine and cocaine manufacturing effects on the environment and agriculture. *San Joaquin Agricultural Law Review*, 17, 343–59.

Yar, M. (2012). Critical criminology, critical theory and social harm. In S. Hall and S. Winlow (Eds.). *New Directions in Criminological Theory* (pp. 52–65). Abingdon, UK: Routledge.

Young, J. (2007). *The Vertigo of Late Modernity*. London, UK: Sage.

Yuan, X. (2017). *Restorative Justice in China: Comparing Theory and Practice*. New York, NY: Springer.

Zaitch, D. (2002). *Trafficking Cocaine: Colombian Drug Entrepreneurs in the Netherlands*. The Hague, The Netherlands: Kluwer Law International.

Zedner, L. (2002). Dangers of dystopias in penal theory. *Oxford Journal of Legal Studies*, 22(2), 341–66.

Zedner, L. (2003). Too much security? *International Journal of the Sociology of Law*, 31, 155–84.

Zedner, L. (2007). Pre-crime and post-criminology? *Theoretical Criminology*, 11(2), 261–81.

Zedner, L. (2009). *Security*. Oxon, UK: Routledge.

Zedner, L. (2011). Putting crime back on the criminological agenda. In M. Bosworth and C. Hoyle (Eds.). *What Is Criminology?* (pp. 271–85). Oxford, UK: Oxford University Press.

Zehr, H. (1990). *Changing Lenses: A New Focus on Crime and Justice*. Harrisonburg, PA: Herald Press.

Zimmerman, C., Hossain, M., Yun, K., Gajdadziev, V. Guzun, N. Tchomarova, M., Ciarrocchi, R.A. et al. (2008). The health of trafficked women: A survey of women entering posttrafficking services in Europe. *American Journal of Public Health*, 98: 55–59. doi:10.2105/AJPH.2006.108357.

Zimring, F.E. (2012). *The City that Became Safe: New York's Lessons for Urban Crime and Its Control*. New York, NY: Oxford University Press.

Zimring, F. and Hawkins, G. (1995). *Incapacitation: Penal Confinement and the Restraint of Crime*. New York, NY: Oxford University Press.

Zoutendijk, A. (2010). Organised crime threat assessments: A critical review. *Crime, Law and Social Change*, 54, 63–86.

Name Index

For the benefit of digital users, indexed terms that span two pages (e.g., 52–53) may, on occasion, appear on only one of those pages.

Tables, figures, and boxes are indicated by *t*, *f*, and *b* following the page number.

Subject Index

For the benefit of digital users, indexed terms that span two pages (e.g., 52–53) may, on occasion, appear on only one of those pages.

Tables, figures, boxes, and footnotes are indicated by *t*, *f*, *b*, and n following the page number.